TRADE, FOOD SECURITY, AND HUMAN RIGHTS

This book discusses global food issues from a unique perspective. It builds a link between human rights and international trade. The solutions proposed in this book offer policymakers practical advice to reduce world hunger and malnutrition. This book is a must read for policymakers from India to Indiana!
Scott Bates, Center for National Policy, USA

Ying Chen's book starts with a simple premise—the primacy of food for the survival of humans—and then provides an expansive and thorough coverage of the complexities of the global food system that reminds us that food policies and legal frameworks matter when it comes to food security.
Michael T. Roberts, Resnick Program for Food Law and Policy,
UCLA School of Law, USA

This exposé documents how hunger in poor nations is made worse by rich nations. Protectionist trade rules, and subsidies to agribusiness, put steak on affluent tables, but leave many of the world's poor bereft of beans. To end hunger we need, not so much another green revolution, as a policy revolution.
Douglass Cassel, University of Notre Dame, USA

T0362196

This book is dedicated to my parents and grandparents who have always believed and supported me in all my endeavors.

Trade, Food Security, and Human Rights

The Rules for International Trade in Agricultural
Products and the Evolving World Food Crisis

YING CHEN

Independent Research Consultant, USA

Routledge
Taylor & Francis Group

LONDON AND NEW YORK

First published 2014 by Ashgate Publishing

2 Park Square, Milton Park, Abingdon, Oxfordshire OX14 4RN
52 Vanderbilt Avenue, New York, NY 10017

Routledge is an imprint of the Taylor & Francis Group, an informa business

First issued in paperback 2020

British Library Cataloguing in Publication Data
A catalogue record for this book is available from the British Library

The Library of Congress has cataloged the printed edition as follows:
Chen, Ying (Legal researcher)
 Trade, food security, and human rights : the rules for international trade in agricultural products and the evolving world food crisis / by Ying Chen.
    pages cm
 Based on author's dissertation (S.J.D. -- Indiana University Robert H. McKinney School of Law), 2013.
 Includes bibliographical references and index.
 ISBN 978-1-4724-3742-6 (hardback)
1. Right to food. 2. Foreign trade regulation.
3. Agricultural laws and legislation 4. Food supply--Law and legislation. 5. Food security. I. Title.

 K3260.C44 2014
 363.8--dc23
                                                                                2014005361
ISBN 978-1-4724-3742-6 (hbk)
ISBN 978-0-367-60037-2 (pbk)

Contents

List of Figures and Tables

Figures

Tables

Preface

Food crises have frequently occurred throughout history and are said to be as old as history itself. The phenomenon of hunger, as well as concerns with crop failures, have been recorded by ancient Chinese, Greek, and many medieval scholars. Along with the development of society generally, new agricultural technologies have been widely introduced and effectively applied to agricultural cultivation. Under these circumstances, agricultural productive capacity has greatly improved, and one would think that the problem of food insecurity should now be solved, or at least mitigated. Yet it continues to be a critical issue in the modern world.

This book explains a few factors that contribute to the current world food crisis—poverty, human overpopulation, a lack of farmland, and the expansion of biofuel programs. Several enforceable solutions to reduce world hunger and malnutrition are proposed, including national capacity building, the improvement of governance, population control, farmland preservation, and the strategic development of biofuel programs. However, another significant factor that causes world hunger has been overlooked. This book examines EU and US agricultural policies and WTO negotiations in agriculture and how they affect international agricultural trade; it suggests that current food insecurity is not caused by an absolute food shortage but rather the result of inequitable food distribution and trade practices. The international trade regime is advised to reconcile trade rules with the consideration of food security issues.

This book may be of interest to agricultural trade professionals, consultants, and policy makers, not only in the US and the EU, but also in developing countries. Students and researchers with a concentration on international trade, agricultural economics, global governance, and international law may also find this book helpful in understanding the world food crisis and agricultural trade.

Dr. Ying Chen
Indianapolis, January 2014

Acknowledgements

I would like to thank Prof. Frank Emmert for his constant encouragement, guidance, and valuable comments at every step of this book. I would also like to thank Prof. James P. Nehf and Prof. Timothy Webster for their continued support and invaluable advice. Without them, I would have not been able to bring my book to successful completion.

Above all I want to thank my parents and grandparents, who have always believed and supported me in all my endeavors.

Ms. Alison Kirk, Ms. Gemma Hayman, Ms. Amanda Buxton, and Ms. Alex Papworth are the best editors and publishers an author could ever wish for. Needless to say, the responsibility for any oversights or mistakes remain mine alone. Readers are invited to direct comments and suggestions for the improvement of subsequent editions directly to me at ychen36@gmail.com.

Dr. Ying Chen
Indianapolis, January 2014

List of Abbreviations

AAA	Agricultural Adjustment Act (US, 1933)
AMS	Aggregate Measurement of Support
AOA	Agreement on Agriculture (Uruguay Round)
BASF	Badische Anilin- und Soda-Fabrik
CAP	Common Agricultural Policy
CESR	Center for Economic and Social Rights
CRP	Conservation Reserve Program (US)
EC	European Community
EEC	European Economic Community
EEP	Export Enhancement Program (US, 1990)
EU	European Union
FAIR	Federal Agriculture Improvement and Reform Act (US)
FAO	Food and Agriculture Organization of the United Nations
FDA	Food and Drug Administration (US)
GAEC	Good Agricultural and Environmental Conditions
GATT	General Agreement on Tariffs and Trade
GDP	Gross Domestic Product
GHO	Global Health Observatory
GMO	Genetically Modified Organism
ICCPR	International Covenant on Civil and Political Rights
ICESCR	International Covenant on Economic, Social and Cultural Rights
IFPRI	International Food Policy Research Institute
IMF	International Monetary Fund
IMR	Infant Mortality Rate
ITO	International Trade Organization
MDGs	Millennium Development Goals
NDRC	National Development and Reform Commission (China)
NGO	Non-governmental Organization
NIFA	National Institute of Food and Agriculture
NMK	Njaa Marufuku Kenya
NRC	National Research Council
NRDC	Natural Resources Defense Council
PFC	Production Flexibility Contract
PL480	Public Law 480 (US)
RDA	Rural Development Administration (US)
RFS	Renewable Fuel Standard
SANE	Sustainable Agriculture Network and Extension

SCM	Agreement on Subsidies and Countervailing Measures
SPS	Agreement on Sanitary and Phytosanitary Measures
TEC	Treaty Establishing the European Community
TRQ	Tariff-rate Quota
UDHR	Universal Declaration of Human Rights
UK	United Kingdom
UN	United Nations
UNDESA	United Nations Department of Economic and Social Affairs
UNDP	United Nations Development Program
UNESCAP	United Nations Economic and Social Commission for Asia and the Pacific
UNICEF	United Nations Children's Fund
US	United States
USDA	United States Department of Agriculture
WFP	World Food Program (UN)
WHO	World Health Organization
WIC	Women, Infants, and Children Program
WTO	World Trade Organization

Chapter 1

Introduction

The 2008 Food Crisis: Food Shortage or Uneven Distribution?

Food crises have frequently occurred throughout history and are said to be as old as history itself. The phenomenon of hunger and concerns with crop failures have been recorded by ancient Chinese, Greek, and many medieval scholars.[1] Along with the development of society generally, new agricultural technologies have been widely introduced and effectively applied to agricultural cultivation.[2] Under these circumstances, agricultural productive capacity has greatly improved, and one would think that the problem of food insecurity should now be solved or at least mitigated.[3] Yet it continues to be a critical issue in the modern world.

Based on a recent report by the United Nations (UN), there are 1.2 billion vulnerable people in the world—about one fifth of the total population—who continue to live on less than one dollar per day.[4] The estimates of the Food and Agriculture Organization of the United Nations (FAO) also show that more than 923 million people are suffering from chronic hunger, malnutrition, or related diseases, and this number grows with continually rising food prices.[5]

Table 1.1 demonstrates international price changes of different food commodities (food, meat, diary, cereals, oils, and sugar) from 1990 to 2012, weighted with the average export share of each of the groups for 2002–2004. In 2008, the price of food commodities surged to record high levels, causing the world to experience a severe food crisis, which constitutes an unprecedented threat to the livelihood of millions of poor people on the planet. Although the price of food commodities on global markets has dropped since 2009, the overall trend is upwards, as we can see from the table:

---

1 Dinah Shelton, *The Duty to Assist Famine Victims*, 70 Iowa L. Rev. 1309 (1985).

2 The Green Revolution in the 1960s and the 1970s is an example of such technology. Green Revolutions refer to a series of technological transformations which include improved seeds, farm technology, better irrigation, and chemical fertilizers. Food & Agric. Org. of the UN, Women and Green Revolution, *available at* http://www.fao.org/focus/e/women/green-e.htm (last visited Feb. 22, 2009).

3 John Madeley, Food for All: The Need for a New Agriculture 34 (2002).

4 See World Food Program, Reducing Poverty and Hunger: The Critical Role of Financing for Food, Agriculture and Rural Development (2002), *available at* http://www.wfp.org/policies/introduction/background/documents/JointPaper.pdf.

5 Food & Agric. Org. of the UN, Briefing paper: Hunger on the Rise—Soaring Prices Add 75 Million People to Global Hunger Rolls (Sept. 17, 2008), *available at* http://www.fao.org/newsroom/common/ecg/1000923/en/hungerfigs.pdf.

Table 1.1   Annual real food price indices (2002–2004=100)[6]

Date	Food Price Index	Meat Price Index	Dairy Price Index	Cereals Price Index	Oils Price Index	Sugar Price Index
1990	103.2	121.3	73.2	95.6	72.4	174.3
1991	102.4	123.9	78.6	95.9	78.2	125.7
1992	105.4	121.6	92.7	99.5	81.9	124.8
1993	101.4	114.5	82.0	96.5	83.3	137.9
1994	107.5	111.8	80.0	101.6	110.2	167.0
1995	109.6	105.4	97.6	106.2	111.3	167.8
1996	118.5	117.9	100.4	129.3	102.1	155.8
1997	116.3	120.9	103.2	110.3	110.5	158.4
1998	111.8	107.8	103.5	104.3	135.6	132.2
1999	94.8	100.4	88.6	93.0	94.0	91.3
2000	92.9	98.5	98.1	87.6	69.7	119.3
2001	101.4	104.8	116.3	94.0	73.4	133.1
2002	97.8	97.5	89.5	102.8	94.7	106.4
2003	98.0	97.0	95.4	98.4	101.1	100.8
2004	103.7	104.9	113.1	99.1	103.5	93.8
2005	103.3	105.8	119.2	91.2	91.3	123.6
2006	108.2	101.2	109.3	103.9	96.0	179.0
2007	127.7	100.7	170.9	134.3	136.8	115.1
2008	147.6	113.2	162.2	175.6	167.8	134.2
2009	123.9	105.0	111.8	137.2	119.2	203.2
2010	139.4	114.6	150.8	137.4	146.1	227.3
2011	154.0	119.5	149.2	167.0	170.7	249.7
2012	141.4	116.8	126.1	161.0	150.6	204.3

Source: Food & Agric. Org. of the UN (FAO Food Price Index).

---

6   Data are from Food & Agric. Org. of the UN, FAO Food Price Index (Jan. 10, 2013), http://www.fao.org/worldfoodsituation/wfs-home/foodpricesindex/en/.

Food insecurity generates economic instability, social unrest, political tensions, and even armed conflict in some developing countries.[7] Food riots from Haiti to Bangladesh and, in all, in nearly 50 countries in 2008 brought the food crisis to boiling point.[8] The food security issue captured the whole world's attention. It is time to bring it back onto the global agenda.

In ancient times, hunger and malnutrition were primarily caused by food shortage because the success of a crop heavily depended on the weather and other natural factors. For example, the Great Famine in the early fourteenth century caused millions of deaths in Europe. This famine started with bad weather in 1315, which resulted in universal crop failures in the following years.[9] Europe did not fully recover from the Great Famine until 1322. From the fifteenth century to the eighteenth century, famines in Europe were more frequent than they had been during previous centuries due to undesirable weather and other natural disasters. Natural risks "historically made the practice of farming an uncertain pursuit."[10] Drought, flooding, pestilence, and other natural disasters harmfully impacted vulnerable agriculture at that time. These adverse conditions caused famine to be at its worst.

Hunger and malnutrition continue to be critical issues today. Most scholars attribute systemic causes of food insecurity to poverty, human overpopulation, and a lack of farmland. However, another significant factor has been overlooked. This book argues that current food insecurity cannot be blamed on a general food shortage. The world's food producers manage to provide more food than ever before. Despite natural or man-made disasters, global food production still exceeds the need of the entire world population, which is currently about seven billion.[11] According to the FAO, the planet could produce sufficient food to feed 12 billion people.[12] Current food insecurity is not down to absolute food shortage, but a problem of how to secure access to resources. Food supplies are not appropriately distributed to the hungry.[13] Distorted agricultural trade undermines world food distribution and uneven distribution impedes people's access to food, particularly people in poor developing countries.

---

7   Ruosi Zhang, *Food Security: Food Trade Regime and Food Aid Regime*, 7 J. INT'L ECON. L. 566 (2004) (describing that under some circumstances, food insecurity may result in international and regional conflicts threatening peace and security).

8   *Riots, Instability Spread as Food Prices Skyrocket*, CNN NEWS (APR. 14, 2008), http://www.cnn.com/2008/WORLD/americas/04/14/world.food.crisis/.

9   WILLIAM CHESTER JORDAN, THE GREAT FAMINE: NORTHERN EUROPE IN THE EARLY FOURTEENTH CENTURY 2 (1996).

10   Kelvin Goertzen, *Leveling the Playing Field*, 3 ASPER REV. INT'L BUS. & TRADE L. 81, 81 (2003).

11   World population is estimated by the World Bank. World Bank, *Population, Total*, WORLD BANK, http://data.worldbank.org/indicator/SP.POP.TOTL (last visited Jan. 14, 2013).

12   Human Rights Council Res. 7/14, The Right to Food, ¶ 3 (Mar. 27, 2008).

13   Anthony Paul Kearns, III, *The Right to Food Exists via Customary International Law*, 22 SUFFOLK TRANSNAT'L L. REV. 223 (1998).

Nevertheless, some scholars believe that the global demand for food is increasing. We may experience absolute food shortage in the future no matter how much agricultural output grows. This may be true. Absolute food shortage may happen if we do not take food issues seriously from now on.

First, there has been a tendency to blame food shortage on the rising consumption of meat and dairy products. Traditionally, people in developed countries consume more meat than vegetables compared to the consumption of meat by people in developing countries. Nevertheless, the trend of consuming more meat and dairy products is expanding to the well-off in many fast-growing developing countries. For example, economic growth is very dramatic in many developing countries, such as China and India. The income level of people in these fast-growing developing countries is increasing rapidly as well. As a result, people's diet in these countries is gradually shifting towards greater milk, meat, and dairy consumption. This change of diet indirectly leads to more absorption of food grains for animal feed. Greater milk, meat, and dairy consumption may be a factor in contributing to future absolute food shortage.

Second, food waste also contributes to future absolute food shortage. Far too much food is not consumed. A large portion of food is wasted at the processing and distribution stages. Considerable quantitative perishable food, such as fruits, vegetables, meat, and dairy products are wasted in grocery stores. Consumers and restaurants are also to blame for wasting food. Consumers sometimes do not shop wisely. They buy more food than they need. Restaurants prepare large portions of food, which often causes leftovers to go uneaten. A study conducted by the FAO shows that about one third of all food produced for human consumption, which is about 1.3 billion tons, gets lost or goes to waste annually.[14] Food waste is a problem not only in developed countries but also in developing countries. According to a report released by the Natural Resources Defense Council in August 2012, 40 percent of food in the United States is wasted at the processing, distribution, retail, and consumption stages every year.[15] The European Commission also estimates that about 90 million tons of food is wasted in Europe annually, excluding agricultural food waste and fish discards.[16] Similarly, in developing countries, over 40 percent of food is lost after harvest and during production.[17]

Third, current global food reserves are dangerously low. We are now facing very tight margins between food reserves and demand. Food reserves are an effective alternative to correct crop or market failures; they protects people from

---

14   Food & Agric. Org. of the UN, *Cutting Food Waste to Feed the World*, Food & Agric. Org. of the UN (May 21, 2011), http://www.fao.org/news/story/en/item/74192/icode/.

15   Dana Gunders, Natural Res. Def. Council, Wasted: How America Is Losing Up to 40 Percent of Its Food from Farm to Fork to Landfill (Aug. 2012), *available at* http://www.nrdc.org/food/files/wasted-food-IP.pdf.

16   European Comm'n, *Stop Food Waste*, http://ec.europa.eu/food/food/sustainability/index_en.htm (last visited Jan. 10, 2013).

17   *Id.*

hunger and malnutrition caused by food shortage or volatile food prices. Ideally, food reserves should include enough for about a year to address any failures that may happen. However, according to the United States Department of Agriculture (USDA), the current global grain supply stocks would plunge to less than two months equivalent which is possibly the lowest level in over a century.[18]

Consequently, absolute food shortage may come true if not enough attention is paid to the situation. However, considering absolute food shortage is a potential issue that may or may not happen in the future, this research will only focus on the current food insecurity issues that are severely threatening the health and lives of millions of vulnerable people in the world.

The Structure and Purpose of this Book

This book addresses food issues and explains why the right to food is vital to human beings. It examines the factors that have resulted in the current food insecurity. It also proposes some feasible solutions regarding how to reduce world hunger and malnutrition.

Starting with the question "why should we care?" the work emphasizes the importance of food in human life, which is that it is one of the most basic human needs. Without sufficient food and nutrition, human survival and development are at risk.

Globalization and the expansion of international trade have made food security an international issue rather than a regional or local issue. A theoretical problem that is further addressed in Chapter 2 asks if there is any legal obligation for the State to protect vulnerable people from hunger and malnutrition. Stated differently, is there a human right to food? Many international treaty instruments explicitly uphold the protection and promotion of the right to food.[19] Likewise, many States explicitly endorse a right to food or similar rights to protect their people from hunger and malnutrition. A brief examination of the international treaties and instruments that explicitly proclaim the protection of the right to food, such as the Universal Declaration of Human Rights (UDHR), and the International Covenant on Economic, Social and Cultural Rights (ICESCR) is therefore provided. Given the fact that the right to food is not universally accepted and many scholars still doubt its existence, its legal basis from the perspective of customary international law is further explored. The work discusses whether the right to food can be seen as "a general and consistent practice of States," and whether it is accepted

---

18   NAT'L FAMILY FARM COALITION, THE URGENT NEED FOR STRATEGIC RESERVES, *available at* http://www.nffc.net/Learn/Fact%20Sheets/Reserves%20Q%20&%20A.pdf (last visited July 25, 2010). USDA released predictions estimating that global grain supply "will plunge to a 53-day equivalent—the lowest level ever recorded since USDA began publishing this data 47 years ago and possibly the lowest level in over a century." *Id.*

19   *See* discussion *infra* Chapter 2, "International Treaty Instruments".

with legally binding effects (*"opinio juris"*).[20] The book continues to discuss the implementation of the right to food at the national level. Considering that the constitution is the supreme law for a sovereign State and most States reserve fundamental rights to their citizens in constitutions, the justiciability of the right to food under constitutions is examined. States are encouraged here to create explicit legal obligations at the national level in order to better protect people's right to food. The work also includes a complete list of constitutional provisions of the countries of the world that proclaim the right to food and life.[21]

Reducing world hunger requires an understanding of the forces that fuel this issue. Therefore, in Chapters 3–5, the following important factors that contribute to current world food insecurity are examined: poverty, overpopulation, lack of farmland, and the expansion of biofuel programs. This section also proposes some enforceable solutions to reduce poverty, control population, protect limited farmland, and develop biofuel programs in a more responsible way.

As already noted, an important factor that contributes to current world food insecurity has often been overlooked—uneven global food distribution and distorted international agricultural trade. Chapter 6 primarily examines the international trade regime's actions in regards to agricultural trade, with the main focus on the World Trade Organization (WTO) and its trade rules in agriculture. It first introduces what subsidy is, why countries provide subsidies to protect their farmers and agricultural production, and why countries set a variety of tariffs and non-tariff barriers to restrict the import of agricultural commodities from other countries.

Chapter 6 proceeds to examine the General Agreement on Tariffs and Trade (known as original GATT), which excluded agriculture from most of the coverage of the negotiations and only focused on trade in industrial goods. It further discusses the breakthrough step in the process of liberalizing international agricultural trade—the Uruguay Round negotiations and the Agreement on Agriculture. The most important three pillars—market access, domestic support, and export subsidies—are examined in depth. The Peace Clause in Article 13 of the Agreement on Agriculture, which set out reduction commitments in trade barriers, is also examined here. In addition to the Agreement on Agriculture, the Agreement on Subsidies and Countervailing Measures which was adopted during the Uruguay Round negotiations to impose significant restrictions on agricultural subsidies are also explored.

The Uruguay Round negotiations were not the end point of the negotiations on agricultural subsidies and tariff reduction. Instead, the negotiations set up future negotiations with the long-term goal of achieving greater trade liberalization. The

---

20   Michelle M. Kundmueller, *The Application of Customary International Law in US Courts: Custom, Convention, or Pseudo-Legislation?* 28 J. Legis. 359, 361 (2002).

21   *See infra* Appendix 1.

book goes on to discuss a new round of multilateral trade negotiations, the Doha Round negotiations, which were launched in Doha, Qatar in November 2001.[22]

However, both the Agreement on Agriculture and the Doha Round negotiations did little to substantially reduce trade distortion. A radical change in the current agricultural trade system is urgently needed. Chapter 7 presents the prospects for further agricultural trade reform, primarily examining three major areas that the WTO members should focus on—substantial reduction in tariffs, domestic support, and export subsidies. It also discusses different agricultural models, including industrial farms, small farms, and organic farms. Furthermore, it gives a general idea of what governments can do to select appropriate agricultural models in order to reduce world hunger, and in the meantime, to promote sustainable agriculture.

In addition to the three major areas, the study also explores other factors that may affect international agricultural trade—sanitary and phytosanitary measures (SPS measures), genetically modified organisms, and food aid programs.

The book explains what SPS measures are and what issues the SPS measures may create when protecting people's health and lives in trade. It then relates SPS measures with genetically modified organisms, one of the most debatable issues. The US consistently upholds research into and the consumption of genetically modified foods, believing these improve agricultural outputs within minimum inputs.[23]

The EU, however, considers this path suspect; it worries about the environmental, health, ethical, legal, and other undesirable consequences of genetically modified foods.[24] Here, the advantages and disadvantages of genetically modified foods are compared, and the reasons why these foods should be considered a short-term alternative to alleviate immediate food insecurity are presented.

In any situation where there is a food shortage caused by natural disasters, economic instability, social unrest, armed conflicts, or any other man-made disasters, or combinations of some of these factors, and a State lacks the resources to provide sufficient food to feed its people, the immediate response is to offer food aid. This book reaffirms the importance of food aid in mitigating emergency food shortage. However, it also emphasizes that food aid is not reliable. Instead, it is detrimental to food deficit countries if not well managed. Thus, food aid is still needed, but reforms are required. A few reforms that the international trade regime may consider focusing on in order to increase the effectiveness of food aid are suggested.

---

22 World Trade Organization, Ministerial Declaration of 14 November 2001, 13–14, WT/MIN(01)/DEC/1, 41 I.L.M. 746 (2002) [hereinafter WTO Ministerial Declaration].

23 Kim JoDene Donat, *Engineering Akerlof Lemons: Information Asymmetry, Externalities, and Market Intervention in the Genetically Modified Food Market*, 12 MINN. J. GLOBAL TRADE 417, 421–23 (2003).

24 Ruth MacKenzie & Silvia Francescon, *The Regulation of Genetically Modified Foods in the European Union: An Overview*, 8 N.Y.U. ENVTL. L.J. 530, 531 (2000).

Developed countries affect agricultural trade not only through trade policies, but also through domestic agriculture policies.[25] To establish a more liberal trading system for agricultural products, and thereby to reduce world hunger, it is important to understand what domestic agriculture policies have been implemented in the major developed countries, what impacts these policies have had on domestic agriculture, and how they have distorted international agricultural trade. The EU and the US are the two major dominants in international trade. Chapter 8 examines how international agricultural trade is distorted through a comparative study of EU and US agricultural policies. It also explains the reasons behind the continuing government support for agriculture: traditional protectionism and the absence of political will to correct the distorted agricultural trade system.

As for agricultural policies in Europe, Chapter 8 focuses on the Common Agricultural Policy (CAP) and its several reforms in the form of a summary of the history, objectives, and effects of the CAP. It reaffirms the success of the CAP in achieving its goals to guarantee food supply and assure farmers' income. It also stresses the CAP's significant role in reviving the European Community's agricultural economy. Despite these great achievements, the European Community (later the European Union) has fallen victim to its own success.[26] The European Community/European Union has gradually realized the negative impacts brought about by the CAP and the necessity to adjust to newly emerging challenges and opportunities. In an attempt to maintain the competitiveness of European agricultural commodities in the world market, coupled with pressure from the public and its trade partners,[27] the European Community/European Union has made several major improvements in its agricultural policies, moving away from a policy of direct price and production support to a more comprehensive regime to promote sustainable agriculture and rural development.[28] These reforms include the MacSharry Reforms (1992), Agenda 2000 (2000), the 2003 Reforms (2003), the Sugar Policy Reform (2006), the 2008 "Heath Check" of the Common Agricultural Policy, and the Common Agricultural Policy post-2013.

The book also explores agricultural policies in the United States and their impacts on international agricultural trade, including the Great Depression and the Agricultural Adjustment Act of 1933, farm policies in the 1950s, 1960s, 1970s,

---

25   Liane L. Heggy, *Free Trade Meets US Farm Policy: Life after the Uruguay Round*, 25 Law & Pol'y Int'l Bus. 1367, 1367 (1994).

26   Robert P. Cooper, II, *The European Community's Prodigal Son—The Common Agricultural Policy—Undergoes Reform: Will Multilateral Trading Schemes Fostered by the GATT Blossom or Wither and Die?* 1 Colum. J. Eur. L. 233, 234 (1995).

27   Alan Greer, Agricultural Policy in Europe 78 (2005) (explaining the role of public opinions).

28   European Comm'n, The CAP Reform, Accomplishing a Sustainable Agricultural Model for Europe Through the Reformed CAP—The Tobacco, Olive Oil, Cotton and Sugar Sectors, *available at* http://ec.europa.eu/agriculture/capreform/com554/index_ en.htm (last visited Dec. 31, 2010).

and 1980s, the Federal Agriculture Improvement and Reform Act of 1996, the Farm Security and Rural Investment Act of 2002, and the Food Conservation and Energy Act of 2008.

In conclusion, this work reaffirms the indispensable role of food in human life and survival. It believes that food is a unique commodity that deserves special attention and that the right to food must be fully respected, protected, and fulfilled in practice. Actions to free humankind from hunger and malnutrition require a coordinated mix of poverty reduction, population control, farmland protection, the strategic development of biofuel programs, food aids, international cooperation, and much more. Nevertheless, given the fact that global agricultural outputs exceed the need of the entire global population and current food issues are primarily caused by uneven food distribution, the international trade regimes are advised to reconcile trade rules with the consideration of world hunger issues. More efforts are needed from national governments in order to progressively reduce world hunger and malnutrition.

Chapter 2
Why Should We Care?[*]

A Basic Human Need

Food is the most basic human need. Without sufficient food and nutrition, human survival and development are at risk. Food insecurity impairs all levels of social, economic, cultural, and political life.[1] At the national level, food insecurity may cause economic instability, social unrest, political tension, high crime rates, and even armed conflicts. At the household level, hunger and malnutrition adversely affect the more vulnerable members of the family, mostly children and women. It is crucial to ensure each individual's sustainable access to nutritionally adequate food.

Global Issue or Regional Issue?

In the past, the food issue was an internal affair of one country. It had very little influence on other countries. Today, globalization makes countries more dependent on each other. If one country suffers from economic or political disruption, all other dependent countries will also be adversely affected. The food insecurity issue in the modern world is no longer a regional or a national problem but becomes a global issue.

Hunger results in poor health and low levels of energy. It leads to greater poverty by reducing people's ability to work. Hunger and poverty, in a vicious circle, impede a country's ability to promote economic and social development. Even worse, chronic hunger can drive people to extremes, and, as discussed previously, it may cause economic instability, social unrest, political tensions, high crime rates, and even armed conflicts. These undesirable social, economic, and political consequences caused by hunger may adversely impact a country's foreign policies and trade policies.[2] The shift of a country's foreign policies and trade policies may largely impact other dependent countries. While it is true that States should feed their own people, as a global issue, food insecurity should be addressed

---

* This chapter is based on an original article published in the *European Journal of Law Reform.*

1 D. Moyo, *The Future of Food: Elements of Integrated Food Security Strategy for South Africa and Food Security Status in Africa,* 101 Am. Soc'y Int'l L. Proc. 103, 104 (2007).

2 Jacobo Schatan & Joan Gussow, Food as Human Right 22, 24 (Asbjorn Eide et al. eds., 1984).

without national boundaries. This does not necessarily mean that rich developed countries should provide more charitable contributions of food to hungry people in poor developing countries. Instead, they are advised to consider global hunger issues when they form their own agricultural policies and trade policies that could possibly affect the food availability in poor developing countries. They are also encouraged to provide development assistance, such as technical assistance and financial contributions to promote rural development, so that poor developing countries can gradually build their national capacity.

Is there a Right to Food?

Before discussing the current food crisis, a theoretical issue must be addressed: is there any legal basis for both the international community and national governments to protect people from hunger and malnutrition? Stated differently, is there a human right to food?

This issue has long been debated. Many international treaty instruments and international organizations explicitly uphold the protection and promotion of the right to food; many countries proclaim the right to food in their constitutions. Most countries have addressed some aspects of the same or similar protection of the right to food through legislative efforts, such as social security guarantees and food security regulations. The US, however, differs from these countries. The US government has consistently opposed the recognition of the right to food, labeling it as "overly burdensome and inconsistent with constitutional law."[3] The US Constitution does not address a right to food; the word "food" does not appear anywhere in the text of the US Constitution or its amendments. The US Constitution protects more civil and political rights than social and economic rights because the US constitutional tradition sees most social and economic rights as "negative" rights on which government is not obliged to take action.[4] If these social and economic rights are interpreted as constitutional, it could empower courts against the government—the executive—in ways perceived as undemocratic and against the basic constitutional principle of maintaining the separate powers of the three branches of the federal government.[5] Although human rights to health, education, and social security are protected to a certain extent through legislation, they still are suspected as unconstitutional.

---

3 Ellen Messer and Marc J. Cohen, The Human Right to Food as a US Nutrition Concern, 1976–2006, at 2 (2007), *available at* http://purl.umn.edu/42368 (stating that although the US government has consistently "expanded food and nutrition assistance," it has continually "opposed formal right to food legislation").

4 Kathleen S. Swendiman, Cong. Research Serv., R40846, Health Care: Constitutional Rights and Legislative Powers (2012).

5 Cass R. Sunstein, *Social and Economic Rights? Lessons from South Africa* (Univ. of Chicago, Public Law Working Paper No. 12, 2001).

Is the right to food justiciable? The justiciability of the right to food would create an appropriate framework to end global hunger and malnutrition. States would be obligated to guarantee the right, and to ensure that sufficient supply of nutritious food is provided to their people. A transparent and predictable regulatory environment would also be established to help promote the design of a national strategy for the realization of the right to food. This research will thoroughly examine this right's justiciability.

Definition

The right to food is defined by the International Covenant on Economic, Social and Cultural Rights (ICESCR) as "the right of everyone to be free from hunger."[6] General Comment No. 12 also defines the right to food as "[t]he right of every man, woman and child alone and in community with others to have physical and economic access at all times to adequate food or means for its procurement in ways consistent with human dignity."[7]

Similarly, the FAO defines the right as every individual's basic human right to have sustainable access to adequate food, not only for mitigating hunger, but also for ensuring livelihood and the well-being of every human being. The FAO further interprets the right to food stating that (1) government itself must not deprive or abuse its people's right to food; (2) government must protect every individual from being deprived or in violation of this right in any way; (3) when anyone lacks adequate food, government is obligated to provide sufficient support within its resources ability in order to ensure its people's full enjoyment of this right.[8]

The Center for Economic and Social Rights (CESR) defines the right to food as a right that "guarantees all people the ability to feed themselves."[9] People have the basic right to the amount of food necessary for survival; they also have the right to food of "high enough quality and quantity to live in adequate dignity."[10]

The United Nations Special Rapporteur on the Right to Food describes the right to food as

---

6 International Covenant on Economic, Social and Cultural Rights. art. 11, Dec. 16, 1966, G.A. Res. 2200 (XXI), 21 UNGAOR Supp. (No. 16) at 50–51, UN Doc. A/6316 (1967).

7 UN Econ. & Soc. Council, UN Comm. on Econ., Soc., & Cultural Rights, General Comment No. 12, The Right to Adequate Food, 20th Sess., Apr. 26–May 14, 1999, para. 14, UN Doc. E/C. 12/1999/5 (May 12, 1999) [hereinafter CESCR General Comment No. 12].

8 FOOD & AGRIC. ORG. OF THE UN, WHAT IS RIGHT TO FOOD? (2007), *available at* http://www.fao.org/righttofood/wfd/pdf2007/what_is_rtf_en.pdf [hereinafter FAO, What Is Right to Food].

9 Ctr. for Econ. & Soc. Rights, *The Right to Food*, CTR. FOR ECON. & SOC. RIGHTS, http://www.cesr.org/article.php?id=111 (last visited Feb. 28, 2013).

10 *Id.*

[t]he right to have regular, permanent and free access, either directly or by means of financial purchases, to quantitatively and qualitatively adequate and sufficient food corresponding to the cultural traditions of the people to which the consumer belongs, and which ensures a physical and mental, individual and collective, fulfilling and dignified life free of fear.[11]

In addition to these definitions in international treaty instruments, some countries have their own interpretations regarding the right to food—particularly South Africa. The right to food is a right explicitly proclaimed under the South African Constitution. Therefore, in order to "meet the dietary and food preferences for an active and healthy life,"[12] South Africans define food security as "physical, social and economic access to sufficient, safe, and nutritious food."[13] This obligates the South African government to provide sufficient, nutritious, and safe food to all its citizens at both the national and the household level, while also guaranteeing the purchasing power of its citizens to ensure that they have the economic ability to buy this food.[14] Most importantly, realizing food must be able to be distributed to the vulnerable people in need at the right time and place, the South African definition addresses the food distribution issue, which is ignored in most others.[15]

Right to food is well defined in both international treaty instruments and national constitutions. Although the statements are slightly different, these definitions explain the same core element of the right to food—every individual in the world should have sustainable access to adequately nutritious food. Then how exactly is the right to food recognized in international treaty instruments?

International Treaty Instruments

Many international treaty instruments expressly recognize the human right to food. Most notably, the Universal Declaration of Human Rights (UDHR) pronounces

---

11   UN Office of High Comm'r for Human Rights, *Special Rapporteur on the Right to Food*, http://www.ohchr.org/EN/Issues/Food/Pages/FoodIndex.aspx (last visited Jan. 12, 2013).

12   Moyo, *supra* note 1, at 103.

13   Article 27 of the Constitution of South Africa ensures "everyone has the right to have access to a. health care services, including reproductive health care; b. sufficient food and water; c. social security, including, if they are unable to support themselves and their dependents, appropriate social assistance." S. Afr. Const., 1996. This Constitution was first adopted by the Constitutional Assembly on May 8, 1996. In terms of a judgment of the Constitutional Court, delivered on September 6, 1996, the text was referred back to the Constitutional Assembly for reconsideration. The text was accordingly amended to comply with the Constitutional Principles contained in Schedule 4 of the interim Constitution. It was signed into law on December 10, 1996. South African Government Information, http://www.info.gov.za/documents/constitution/1996/96cons2.htm (last visited Feb. 28, 2013).

14   Moyo, *supra* note 1, at 103.

15   *Id.* at 104.

everyone's human right to a standard of living, which includes food, clothing, and housing.[16] As an elaboration of the UDHR, the International Covenant on Economic, Social and Cultural Rights not only recognizes the right of everyone to be free from hunger, but also imposes legal obligations on its Member States to "take, individually and through international cooperation, the measures … to ensure an equitable distribution of world food supplies in relation to need."[17] Similar proclamations are found in the Convention on the Rights of the Child (1989),[18] the Universal Declaration on the Eradication of Food, Hunger and Malnutrition,[19] the Rome Declaration on World Food Security,[20] General Comment No. 12,[21] the Millennium Development Goals (MDGs),[22] and the Voluntary Guidelines.[23]

The Universal Declaration of Human Rights (UDHR)
The UDHR is the direct expansion of the United Nations Charter and is universally recognized.[24] It defines individuals' fundamental rights, and exhorts all

---

16   A.H. Robertson & J. G. Merrills, Human Rights in the World: An Introduction to the Study of the International Protection of Human Rights 29 (4th ed. 1998).

17   *See* International Covenant on Economic, Social and Cultural Rights, *supra* note 6, art. 11.

18   Article 6 of the Convention on the Rights of the Child promulgates the right to life as following: "States Parties recognize that every child has the inherent right to life. States Parties shall ensure to the maximum extent possible the survival and development of the child." Convention on the Rights of the Child, Nov. 20, 1989, UN Doc. A/44/49.

19   The Universal Declaration on the Eradication of Food, Hunger and Malnutrition was adopted by the World Food Conference in 1974.

20   *See* Food & Agric. Org. of the UN, *World Food Summit*, Food & Agric. Org. of the UN (1996), http://www.fao.org/WFS/index_en.htm [hereinafter FAO, World Food Summit] (explaining that the Rome Declaration on World Food Security was adopted in 1996 and reaffirms "the right of everyone to have access to safe and nutritious food, consistent with the right to adequate food and the fundamental right of everyone to be free from hunger").

21   General Comment 12 reaffirms the right to food as a fundamental human right that is "indivisibly linked to the inherent dignity of the human person and is indispensable for the fulfillment of other human rights enshrined in the International Bill of Human Rights." *See* CESCR General Comment No. 12, *supra* note 7, para. 15.

22   It was declared by the United Nations in 2000. The first goal is to "Eradicate extreme poverty and hunger." *See The Millennium*, UN Dev. Prog., http://www.undp.org/mdg/goal1.shtml (last visited Feb. 28, 2013) [hereinafter Millennium Development Goals].

23   The Voluntary Guidelines provide guidance to States on how to progressively achieve the right to adequate food. *See* UN Food & Agric. Org., Voluntary Guidelines to Support the Progressive Realization of the Right to Adequate Food in the Context of National Food Security, Annex 1, 16, FAO Doc. No. CL 127/10-Sup.1 (Sep. 23, 2004) [hereinafter FAO Voluntary Guidelines].

24   Louis B. Sohn, *The New International Law: Protection of the Rights of Individuals Rather than States*, 32 Am. U. L. Rev. 1, 17–18 (1982).

governments to protect these rights. The human rights pronounced in the UDHR are considered the legal basis for all other international human rights instruments.[25]

The expression of the right to food is first found in the UDHR. Under Article 25(1), it promulgates

> Everyone has the right to a standard of living adequate for the health and well-being of himself and of his family, including food, clothing, housing, and medical care and necessary social services, and the right to security in the event of unemployment, sickness, disability, widowhood, old age or other lack of livelihood in circumstances beyond his control.[26]

Article 25 of the UDHR declares a standard of living for every individual. Section I lists the primary needs for human beings as food, clothing, housing, medical care, and necessary social services; and secondary needs as the right to security in the event of unemployment, sickness, disability, widowhood, old age, and other lacks of livelihood.[27] Because ratification of the UDHR was not a compulsory requirement when it was proclaimed, it was accepted with no binding effects.[28] However, some rights pronounced under the UDHR create legal obligations because they are considered rules of customary international law. The question here is whether the right to food has the status of customary international law. If the answer is yes, it imposes binding effects on its Member States; otherwise, the right to food has no binding nature. This question will be discussed below as a separate issue.

The International Covenant on Economic, Social and Cultural Rights (ICESCR)
As an elaboration of the UDHR, the ICESR ensures and protects rights that are "derived from the inherent dignity of the human person."[29] The ICESCR generally restates the relevant economic, social, and cultural rights enumerated in the UDHR, but it is relatively more specific and stronger than the UDHR in its mandate to its signatories.[30] According to the ICESCR, the right to adequate food derives from

---

25   William A. Schabas, *Canada and the Adoption of the Universal Declaration of Human Rights*, 43 McGill L.J. 403, 405 (1998).

26   Universal Declaration of Human Rights, G.A. Res. 217 (III) A, UN Doc. A/Res/217(III) (Dec. 10, 1948).

27   Adam Rehof et al., The Universal Declaration of Human Rights: A Commentary 389 (1993).

28   Hannah A. Saona, *The Protection of Reproductive Rights under International Law: The Bush Administration's Policy Shift and China's Family Planning Practices*, 13 Pac. Rim L. & Pol'y J. 229 (2004).

29   *See* International Covenant on Economic, Social and Cultural Rights, *supra* note 6, pmbl.

30   Joy A. Weber, *Famine Aid to Africa: An International Legal Obligation*, 15 Brook. J. Int'l L. 369, 380 (1989).

the right to an adequate standard of living and is one of the key components for all economic, social, and cultural rights.

Article 11 of the ICESCR not only recognizes the right to adequate food, but establishes its State Parties' enforcement obligations as follows:

> Firstly, the States Parties to the present Covenant recognize the right of everyone to an adequate standard of living for himself and his family, including adequate food, clothing, and housing, and to the continuous improvement of living conditions. The States Parties will take appropriate steps to ensure the realization of this right, recognizing to this effect the essential importance of international cooperation based on free consent. Secondly, the States Parties to the present Covenant, recognizing the fundamental right of everyone to be free from hunger, shall take, individually and through international cooperation, the measures, including specific programs, which are needed: (a) To improve methods of production, conservation and distribution of food by making full use of technical and scientific knowledge, by disseminating knowledge of the principles of nutrition and by developing or reforming agrarian systems in such a way as to achieve the most efficient development and utilization of natural resources; (b) Taking into account the problems of both food-importing and food-exporting countries, to ensure an equitable distribution of world food supplies in relation to need.[31]

Some scholars interpret Article 11 as providing two separate rights: (1) the right to adequate food, and (2) the right to be free from hunger, and they argue about the priority of each.[32] However, this separation makes no sense. Under Article 11, the core obligation imposed on the State Parties is to mitigate hunger and further ensure each individual's right to have sustainable access to nutritiously adequate food. The term—the right to food—is a multi-leveled concept, covering both "the right to be free from hunger" and "the right to adequate food."[33] In other words, Article 11 only proclaims one right—the right to food. Ensuring that people are free from hunger is the minimum obligation of the right to food. The ICESCR further requires that States Parties take effective measures to progressively ensure the availability of nutritiously adequate food to satisfy everyone's dietary and

---

31   *See* International Covenant on Economic, Social and Cultural Rights, *supra* note 6, art. 11.

32   Laura Niada, *Hunger and International Law: The Far-reaching Scope of the Human Right*, 22 Conn. J. Int'l L. 136, 151 (2006).

33   D.E. Buckingham, *A Recipe for Change: Towards an Integrated Approach to Food Under International Law*, 6 Pace Int'l L. Rev. 285, 293 (1994). (The right to food contains two separate standards. The right to be free from hunger is the minimum standard and the right to adequate food is a relative standard that is more difficult to spell out as an international minimum standard.) *Id.*

cultural needs as expeditiously as possible.[34] The right to be free from hunger is the initial step on the way towards the full realization of the right to adequate food. Together, they both constitute the right to food and share the common goal of reducing world hunger.

Moreover, Article 11 of the ICESCR dedicates particular attention to the enforcement of the right to food. The Member States are required to recognize the right of everyone to be free from hunger and to have sustainable access to food in a quantity and quality sufficient to satisfy their dietary and cultural needs.[35] They are obligated to take workable measures, such as promoting methods of food production, conservation, and distribution in order to implement the ICESCR and to ensure every individual's full enjoyment of the right to food. Article 11 advocates that both State and non-State-actors cooperate to fight again food insecurity. Member States are also obligated to submit regular reports to the Committee on Economic Social and Cultural Rights, explaining the measures they have taken and the progress they have made towards fulfilling their obligations under the ICESCR.[36]

Unlike the UDHR, the ICESCR was created with explicit binding effect. All Member States that have ratified this Covenant are bound by it. The ICESCR is an essential step towards granting the right to food to every individual on the planet.[37] Why, then, do we still have hunger issues?

Although the ICESCR obligates its Member States to submit implementation reports regularly, a monitoring system is still not functional.[38] States Parties are free to indicate in their reports any factors, difficulties, challenges affecting the degree of fulfillment of their obligations under the Covenant.[39] The ICESCR Committee is only able to supervise the reporting procedure. It has no power to force its Member States to comply or to accept any improvements the Committee suggests.[40]

Other international treaty instruments proclaiming a right to food
The right of a child to access adequate food is encompassed in Article 27 of the Convention on the Rights of the Child (1989). States Parties of this convention

---

34   Smita Narula, *The Right to Food: Holding Global Actors Accountable Under International Law*, 44 COLUM. J. TRANSNAT'L L. 691, 694 (2006).

35   *Id.*

36   Kitty Arambulo, *Drafting an Optional Protocol to the International Covenant on Economic, Social and Cultural Rights: Can an Ideal Become Reality*, 2 U.C. DAVIS J. INT'L L. & POL'Y 111, 122 (1996).

37   FAO, What Is Right to Food, *supra* note 8.

38   Aaron N. Lehl, *China's Trade Union System Under the International Covenant on Economic, Social and Cultural Rights: Is China in Compliance with Article 8?*, 21 U. HAW. L. REV. 203, 235 (1999).

39   International Covenant on Economic, Social and Cultural Rights, *supra* note 6, art. 17.2.

40   Audrey Chapman, *A "Violations Approach" for Monitoring the International Covenant on Economic, Social and Cultural Rights*, 18 HUM. RTS. Q. 23, 26–27 (1996).

are required to recognize "the right of every child to a standard of living adequate for the child's physical, mental, spiritual, moral, and social development."[41] It proclaims that parents and other responsible guardians of a child are obligated to "secure the conditions of living necessary for the child's development."[42] It also specifies States Parties' obligations to take all appropriate and workable measures to guarantee children's basic needs.[43]

The Convention on the Rights of the Child was adopted by the UN General Assembly with legal binding effect. The Convention specifically protects the rights of people under the age of 18. By ratifying this Convention, States Parties have agreed to commit themselves to protecting and ensuring children's civil, political, social, economic, and cultural rights. The United Nations Children's Fund (UNICEF),[44] guided by the Convention, has made significant progress in protecting and promoting children's rights in the past 20 years. However, the rights of millions of children in the world are still left unprotected.[45] Children's sustainable access to food is one of the biggest unsolved issues. The World Health Organization estimates one out of six children, roughly 100 million, is underweight.[46] At a United Nations Summit on World Food Security in 2009, Secretary-General Ban Ki-moon warned that six million children die of hunger

---

41 Convention on the Rights of the Child, *supra* note 18, art. 6.

42 *Id.*

43 Article 27 states "1. States Parties recognize the right of every child to a standard of living adequate for the child's physical, mental, spiritual, moral, and social development. 2. The parent(s) or others responsible for the child have the primary responsibility to secure, within their abilities and financial capacities, the conditions of living necessary for the child's development. 3. States Parties, in accordance with national conditions and within their means, shall take appropriate measures to assist parents and others responsible for the child to implement this right and in case of need provide material assistance and support programs, particularly with regard to nutrition, clothing and housing. 4. States Parties shall take all appropriate measures to secure the recovery of maintenance for the child from the parents or other persons having financial responsibility for the child, both within the State Party and from abroad. In particular, where the person having financial responsibility for the child lives in a State different from that of the child, States Parties shall promote the accession to international agreements or the conclusion of such agreements, as well as the making of other appropriate arrangements." Convention on the Rights of the Child, *supra* note 18, art. 27.

44 UNICEF's primary mission is "to advocate for the protection of children's rights, to help meet their basic needs and to expand their opportunities to reach their full potential." *See* UNICEF, *Convention on the Rights of the Child*, http://www.unicef.org/crc/ (last visited Jan. 12, 2013).

45 UNICEF, A BETTER LIFE FOR EVERY CHILD: A SUMMARY OF THE UNITED NATIONS CONVENTION ON THE RIGHTS OF THE CHILD, *available at* http://childrenandyouthprogramme. info/pdfs/pdfs_uncrc/uncrc_summary_version.pdf (last visited Jan. 12, 2013).

46 Global Health Observatory (GHO), *Underweight in Children*, WORLD HEALTH ORG., http://www.who.int/gho/mdg/poverty_hunger/underweight_text/en/index.html (last visited: January 12, 2013).

every year, which is about 17,000 every day.[47] There remains much to be done to better protect and promote children's rights.

The Universal Declaration on the Eradication of Food, Hunger and Malnutrition declares that every individual has "the inalienable right to be free from hunger and malnutrition in order to develop fully and maintain their physical and mental faculties."[48] It emphasizes the importance of tackling the grave food crisis, advocating that the participating States of the World Food Conference make full use of the United Nations' system to eliminate hunger and malnutrition, internationally, nationally, and regionally. The Universal Declaration on the Eradication of Food, Hunger and Malnutrition is convened by the General Assembly of the United Nations. However, since the General Assembly Resolutions are not binding in nature, Member States are not bound by this Declaration.[49]

After the Universal Declaration on the Eradication of Food, Hunger and Malnutrition was adopted in 1974, little progress was made until 1996, when the World Food Summit was held with the aim of reviewing world leaders' commitments to "the eradication of hunger and malnutrition and the achievement of food security for all."[50] In accordance with the purpose of the World Food Summit, the Rome Declaration on World Food Security and the World Food Summit Plan of Action were adopted by the Heads, Deputy Heads, and high-level representatives of the States.[51] The Rome Declaration reaffirms "the right of everyone to have access to safe and nutritious food, consistent with the right to adequate food and the fundamental right of everyone to be free from hunger,"[52] while the Plan of Action provides practical guidelines for the States to implement

---

47   United Nations, *At UN Food Summit, Ban Lays out Steps to Save Billions from Hunger*, UN NEWS CTR. (Nov. 16, 2009), http://www.un.org/apps/news/story. asp?NewsID=32959#.UPInxyeRSSo.

48   Adopted on 16 November 1974 by the World Food Conference convened under General Assembly resolution 3180 (XXVIII) of 17 December 1973; and endorsed by General Assembly resolution 3348 (XXIX) of 17 December 1974. Universal Declaration on the Eradication of Food, Hunger and Malnutrition, G.A. Res. 3348 (XXIX) (Dec. 17, 1974).

49   United Nations, *Background Information, Functions and Powers of the General Assembly*, UNITED NATIONS, http://www.un.org/ga/61/background/background.shtml (last visited Dec. 3, 2008).

50   FAO, World Food Summit, *supra* note 20.

51   *See id.* The Rome Declaration on World Food Security and the World Food Summit Plan of Action were adopted by 112 Heads or Deputy Heads of State and Government, and by over 70 high-level representatives from other countries at a meeting which saw the active involvement of representatives of inter-governmental and non-governmental organizations. The adoption of the Rome Declaration and the Plan of Action widespread influenced public opinion. It provided a framework for bringing about significant changes in policies and actions needed to achieve food security for all people. *Id.*

52   Food & Agric. Org. of the UN, *The Rome Declaration on World Food Security*, FOOD & AGRIC. ORG. OF THE UN (1996), http://www.fao.org/docrep/003/w3613e/w3613e00. HTM.

the commitments set forth in the Declaration.[53] The Rome Declaration and the Plan of Action share a common objective of food security which exists only when all people on this planet have sustainable access at all time to nutritiously adequate food to satisfy their dietary and cultural needs.

The 1996 World Food Summit was a great opportunity for heads of States to make binding commitments to reduce world hunger. However, as is the case with most UN conferences and meetings, the Rome Declaration on World Food Security and the World Food Summit Plan of Action were reached with no binding effects, which makes it difficult to implement the commitment and to improve global food security.

General Comment No. 12, adopted in May 1999 by the Committee on Economic, Social and Cultural Rights, reaffirms the right to food as a fundamental human right that is "indivisibly linked to the inherent dignity of the human person and is indispensable for the fulfillment of other human rights enshrined in the International Bill of Human Rights."[54] It elaborates the right to food as "the right of every man, woman, and child alone and in community with others to have physical and economic access at all times to adequate food or means for its procurement in ways consistent with human dignity."[55]

General Comment No. 12 requires that States Parties ensure "the availability of food in a quantity and quality sufficient"[56] to meet the dietary and cultural needs of all the individuals in order to live a healthy life. It also requires that States Parties guarantee the accessibility of such food in sustainable ways that "do not interfere with the enjoyment of other human rights."[57] It explicitly imposes legal obligations on States Parties to respect, protect, and fulfill the right to food. States Parties should refrain from any actions that might impair an individual's access to food, take effective measures to ensure that nobody suffers from hunger, proactively participate in relevant activities, and work closely with other States to reduce food insecurity globally.[58] The Committee also emphasizes the necessity of a monitoring system, advising States to develop and maintain effective mechanisms to "monitor progress towards the realization of the right to adequate food for all."[59] With respect to violations of the right to food, victims should be entitled to the right to have access to appropriate monetary and legal remedies at both the international and national level.[60] Furthermore, General Comment No. 12 addresses the issue of international cooperation. Governments, international organizations, and financial institutions are encouraged to work together more closely to promote

---

53 FAO, World Food Summit, *supra* note 20.
54 CESCR General Comment No. 12, *supra* note 7, para. 15.
55 *Id.*
56 *Id.*
57 *Id.*
58 MESSER & COHEN, *supra* note 3.
59 CESCR General Comment No. 12, *supra* note 7.
60 *Id.*

the preservation of everyone's human dignity. It encourages the international community to provide timely and sufficient assistance to the States for the realization of the right to food. It also makes efforts to attract more attention from the international financial institutions, encouraging them to adjust their lending policies and credit agreements in order to mitigate world hunger and malnutrition.[61]

General Comments function as the interpretation of the content of human rights provisions within the UN human rights system.[62] As such, they enjoy a particular authority. However, they are not legally binding and, therefore, do not create any obligations on the States Parties.

The MDGs declared by the UN in 2000 also present the right to be free from hunger as a universally accepted human right. They identify eradicating extreme poverty and hunger as the first overarching goal for development policy to be achieved by 2015.[63] The three main targets set forth in the first goal of the MDGs are (1) reducing by half the proportion of people living on less than one dollar a day, (2) achieving full and productive employment for all, and (3) reducing by half the proportion of people who suffer from hunger.[64]

The MDGs are political commitments with no binding effect. However, they create a blueprint for poverty reduction and world development by 2015. The goals were agreed to by all the countries and world leading development institutions.[65] Unexpectedly, most countries and development institutions have so far proven to comply with the MDGs. They have made an unprecedented effort to meet the needs of the world's poorest.

In 2004, based on the goals of the World Food Summit Plan of Action, the FAO proclaimed the Voluntary Guidelines, which provide guidance to the States regarding how to progressively realize the right to adequate food at the national level.[66] These Guidelines establish the four pillars of food security as "availability, stability of supply, access, and utilization."[67] Food security exists when all people have sustainable physical and economic access to nutritiously sufficient food to meet their dietary and cultural needs. States are encouraged to provide food

---

61   *Id.*

62   Office of the UN High Comm'r for Human Rights, *Human Rights Bodies—General Comments*, http://www2.ohchr.org/english/bodies/treaty/comments.htm (last visited Jan. 13, 2013).

63   *See* Millennium Development Goals, *supra* note 22. (In response to the world's major development challenges, the Millennium Development Goals (MDGs) are eight proposed goals to be achieved by 2015. The eight Millennium Development Goals cover areas of income, health, education, gender, environmental sustainability, and governance.) *Id.*

64   *Id.*

65   United Nations, *Millennium Goals: Background*, UNITED NATIONS, http://www. un.org/millenniumgoals/bkgd.shtml (last visited Jan. 13, 2013).

66   Food & Agric. Org. of the UN, The Right to Food Guidelines, Information Papers and Case Studies 72 (2006), *available at* http://www.fao.org/docs/eims/upload/214344/ RtFG_Eng_draft_03.pdf [hereinafter FAO, Right to Food Guidelines].

67   *Id.*

assistance to those in need. They can also request assistance if their own resources are not enough to feed their people.[68]

The Voluntary Guidelines provide practical guidance on how to achieve progressive realization of the right to adequate food in the context of national food security.[69] They represent the attempts of the States Parties to work together in order to reduce world hunger. They also improve the current world development framework, helping accelerate attainment of the MDGs. However, as merely guidelines, they lack a legally binding quality.[70] Member States' actions are voluntary.

In summary, increasing numbers of international treaties and instruments are signed and ratified by States. The international community and national governments show their strong attempts to solve the world hunger issue. However, most of the treaties and instruments do not have binding effects, creating additional difficulty for implementation.

Many scholars still doubt the existence of the right to food. They may also inquire about the States that have not signed or ratified those international treaty instruments regarding the protection of the right to food. Are these States obligated to protect their people from hunger?

First of all, to be fair, no countries in the world would really want to see their people suffer from hunger and malnutrition, unless there are some political factors involved that prevent the government from feeding its own people, such as a power struggle. In most cases, hunger happens when governments do care but they are unable to provide sufficient food to their people for a variety of reasons, such as food shortage, poverty, and poor governance. Creating an obligation will assure a more transparent and predictable regulatory environment for governments to design and implement a national strategy for the progressive realization of the right to food.

Secondly, it is undeniable that the right to food is still not universally accepted by all the States in the world, if compared to the right to liberty, the right to freedom of thought, conscience and religion, and other civil and political rights. However, this research asserts that the problems of non-recognition and the incompatibility of multiple legal regimes can be alleviated by locating the right to food in customary international law. Norms that have achieved the status of customary international law are binding upon all States.

---

68 *Id.*

69 Olivier De Schutter, United Nations Special Rapporteur on the Right to Food, *The Right to Food as a Human Right*, http://www.srfood.org/index.php/en/right-to-food (last visited Jan. 13, 2013).

70 P. MALANCZUK, AKEBURST'S MODERN INTRODUCTION TO INTERNATIONAL LAW 54 (1997).

Locate the Right to Food in Customary International Law

Customary international law is considered one of the principal sources of international law. It is formally accepted by both the international legal community and national courts.[71] If the right to food were proven to be a rule of customary international law, there would be a much wider and stronger legal basis for the right's global protection. However, the right to food as a rule of customary international law remains debatable; it has not been adequately analyzed. Some scholars state that providing humanitarian assistance in the form of food aid to the prisoners of war is protected under international law.[72] However, in peacetime, there is no customary international legal obligation imposed on States to provide assistance to people in need of food.[73] On the contrary, other scholars believe that the right to food does exist as a rule of customary international law and that it should enjoy the status of international law. This research agrees with the latter approach, asserting the existence of the right to food as a rule of customary international law. Therefore, the right to food should formerly be recognized, respected, and fulfilled by all States.

A large number of international rules and principles are generated by means other than the explicit consent of States expressed in treaties and agreements.[74] Customary international law is not promulgated as statutory law or treaty instrument, but derived from a general and consistent practice of States and accepted by them as legally binding.[75] Therefore, to evaluate whether a norm or a

---

71   The International Court of Justice and the United Nations accept customary international law as one of the major sources of international law. Article 38 (1) (b) of the Statute of the International Court of Justice affirms the existence of customary international law by pronouncing "The Court, whose function is to decide in accordance with international law such disputes as are submitted to it, shall apply ... international custom, as evidence of a general practice accepted as law." *See* Statute of the International Court of Justice, art. 38, 59 Stat. 1055, 1060, T.S. No. 993, at 30, 3 Bevans 1153, 1187 (1945), *available at* http://www.icj-cij.org/documents/index.php?p1=4&p2=2&p3=0#CHAPTER_II (last visited Feb. 28, 2013).

72   JEAN DEPREUX, COMMENTARY: GENEVA CONVENTION III, at 173 (1960). Article 20 states that "the Detaining Power shall supply prisoners of war who are being evacuated with sufficient food and potable water ..." Art. 26 states that "the basic daily food rations shall be sufficient in quantity, quality and variety to keep prisoners of war in good health and to prevent loss of weight or the development of nutritional deficiencies ... collective disciplinary measures affecting food are prohibited." Geneva Convention Relative to the Treatment of Prisoners of War art. 20, 26, Aug. 12, 1949, 6 UST. 3316, 75 U.N.T.S. 135.

73   *See* Buckingham, *supra* note 33, at 301 (claiming that there is no customary international legal obligation to provide food assistance in peacetime, and many States only provide food aid during peacetime based on bilateral or multilateral agreements). *Id.*

74   MARK WESTON JANIS, INTERNATIONAL LAW 43 (5th ed. 2008).

75   Statute of the International Court of Justice, ch. II, art. 38 (1)(b), 59 Stat. 1055, 1060, T.S. No. 993, at 30, 3 Bevans 1153, 1187 (1945).

principle is a rule of customary international law, two elements must be analyzed. First, the practice must have a general, constant, and uniform usage by States. Second, it must be proven that it is established with binding effects in practice (that is, accepted as law—*opinio juris*).[76]

A general and consistent practice of States
Although there is no solid requirement that States ensure their people's sustainable and adequate access to food, States have made it their general practice, naturally, because this particular pattern of behavior can affect its economic, social, and political interests.

Historically, functional governments have always prioritized food issues in their public policies.[77] In times of famine or food shortage, the ancient Egyptian government lowered its national taxes on food. Local officials delivered food from areas of plenty to nearby areas where people were starving.[78] Ensuring an adequate food supply was equally important to European governments. In pre-industrial times, European governments employed food price controls, timely food distribution, and other measures to ensure food security. Similarly, in ancient China, people's access to sufficient food was regarded as a significant indicator of which dynasty or government was more functional.[79] In 221 B.C., the Qin Dynasty[80] established a performance evaluation system, in which food supply was one of the most significant indicators. This tradition has been adopted by succeeding Chinese governments, lasting more than 2000 years.[81] Public grain policies have also been enforced in China for about 4000 years as a response to natural and man-made disasters.[82] Undoubtedly, food security is not an issue limited to the contemporary world but one with long historical recognition. Although protecting people's access to adequate food was not labeled as "the right to food" at that time, it still was one of the most important public policies implemented by governments.

Today, protecting people from hunger and malnutrition continues to be a general and consistent practice of all States. This practice is reflected by States' adoption of many international treaty instruments that repeatedly emphasize the importance of implementing the right to food and the actions that States have taken to ensure their people's access to adequate food. Every country, developed

---

76   VAUGHAN LOWE, INTERNATIONAL LAW 37 (1st ed. 2007).

77   ROBERT ROBERTSON, HUMAN RIGHTS IN THE TWENTY-FIRST CENTURY A GLOBAL CHALLENGE 451 (Kathleen E. Mahoney & Paul Mahoney eds., 1993).

78   BRUCE G. TRIGGER, UNDERSTANDING EARLY CIVILIZATIONS: A COMPARATIVE STUDY 387 (2003).

79   Hong Bo, *History of Kang Yong Qiang Dynasty*, GUANGMING NEWS (Sept. 14, 2004), http://news.blcu.edu.cn/detail.asp?id=6466.

80   221 B.C. to 206 B.C.

81   *Performance Evaluation System in Ancient China* (Dec. 12, 2005), http://www.cnicw.gov.cn/info_disp.php?id=5948.

82   Dinah Shelton, *The Duty to Assist Famine Victims*, 70 IOWA L. REV. 1309 (1985).

or developing, has its own food or nutrition programs or other social security programs to reduce national hunger and malnutrition. Both rich developed countries and poor developing countries make the best efforts to feed their people. For instance, in the US, a large portion of the US Department of Agriculture's budget goes to the food stamp program, the school meal program, and the Women, Infants, and Children (WIC) program.[83] In China, the government provides food subsidies to poor people who cannot afford food. In Kenya, the Agriculture Sector Ministries developed the Njaa Marufuku Kenya Program (NMK) to improve national food security.[84]

Consequently, from a historical perspective, protecting people from hunger and malnutrition (the right to food) is a general and consistent practice of states. Therefore, the next issue to be examined is if the second element to being a rule of customary international law is met. In other words, is the right to food accepted as law?

Acceptance of a general practice as law—opinio juris

There are varieties of general practices in international relations, but not all of them are considered rules of customary international law. To be a rule of customary international law, the general practice must be accepted as law by States. The acceptance of a general practice as law is known as *"opinio juris."*[85] Determining whether *opinio juris* exists, in Vaughan Lowe's view, is a process of characterizing the practice of the State.[86] State action is presumed to have intent and, therefore, if that action is in compliance with international law, *opinio juris* exists. The protection of the right to food can be traced back to the establishment of the UN.

Beginning in 1945, when the United Nations was established, the international community realized the necessity to codify human rights. The codification process started with the promulgation of the UN Charter, which is the constitutional treaty

---

83　US Dep't of Agric., *Food and Nutrition*, US Dep't of Agric. http://www.usda. gov/wps/portal/usda/usdahome?navid=FOOD_NUTRITION&navtype=SU (last visited Jan. 13, 2013).

84　United Nations, *2008 AAPAM Award for Innovative Management*, http:// unpan1.un.org/intradoc/groups/public/documents/aapam/unpan032707.pdf (last visited Jan. 13, 2013).

85　Lowe, *supra* note 76, at 38.

86　Alan Vaughan Lowe QC (born 1952) is a leading barrister and academic specialist in the field of international law. He has been Chichele Professor of Public International Law in the University of Oxford, and a Fellow of All Souls College, Oxford, since 1999. He was called to the Bar of England and Wales at Gray's Inn in 1993 and appointed Queen's Counsel on March 28, 2008. Associé de l'Institut de droit international since 2005. Lowe, *supra* note 76, at 51.

for the UN,[87] and prevails over all other treaties and laws throughout the world.[88] All the Member States of the UN are bound by this Charter. Even though the Charter does not explicitly specify what kinds of rights should be afforded to each individual, in accordance with its purpose of "promoting and encouraging respect for human rights and for fundamental freedoms for all without distinction as to race, sex, language, or religion,"[89] the Charter expressly emphasizes the importance of the protection and promotion of human rights.[90] In observance of this purpose, a series of codifications were made subsequently to the Charter's promulgation, including the UDHR, which encompasses the most fundamental human rights, the ICCPR, and ICESCR, which elaborate the fundamental human rights listed in the UDHR. Therefore, the UDHR can be seen as a direct expansion of the UN Charter.

Whether the UDHR has binding effect is arguable. Some scholars see it as a non-binding treaty because it was accepted initially with no binding nature. However, other scholars see it as a set of rules of customary international law because it presents an authoritative expansion and interpretation of the UN Charter provisions.[91] Regardless of the discussion and ambiguities of the UDHR's binding effect, it is undisputed that the Declaration has been affirmed and cited by both the international institutions and States.[92] In particular, State governments constantly invoke the UDHR in support of their arguments before the UN General Assembly.[93] Therefore, the UDHR should be considered as having binding effect. Since the UN Charter is legally binding on all the States, the UDHR, as its direct expansion and authoritative interpretation, should enjoy a primary status in international law and bind all the Member States. As the UDHR explicitly proclaims the legal right to food, all States Parties should recognize and respect this right, and fulfill their

---

87   BARDO FASSBENDER, UN SECURITY COUNCIL REFORM AND THE RIGHT OF VETO: A CONSTITUTIONAL PERSPECTIVE 90 (1998).

88   The UN Charter prevails hierarchically over all other treaties and laws throughout the world. *See* SCHATAN & GUSSOW, *supra* note 2, at 13–14.

89   UN Charter art. 1, para. 3. Article 1.3 specifies that "the purposes of the United Nations are ... 3. to achieve international cooperation in solving international problems of an economic, social, cultural, or humanitarian character, and in promoting and encouraging respect for human rights and for fundamental freedoms for all without distinction as to race, sex, language, or religion."

90   Article 1, para. 3. emphasizes the importance of human rights issues. *See id.* Also, in the preamble, the UN Charter stresses the necessity of the protection and promotion of human rights. "We the people of the United Nations determined to reaffirm faith in fundamental human rights, in the dignity and worth of the human person, in the equal rights of men and women and of nations large and small ..." UN Charter pmbl.

91   Philip Alston, *International Law and the Human Right to Food, in* The RIGHT TO FOOD 9, 22 (Philip Alston & Katarina Tomasevski eds., 1984).

92   J.P. Humphrey, *The Universal Declaration of Human Rights: Its History, Impact and Juridical Character, in* HUMAN RIGHTS: THIRTY YEARS AFTER THE UNIVERSAL DECLARATION at 21 (B.G. Ramcharan ed., 1979).

93   Sohn, *supra* note 24, at 16–17.

obligation of protecting their people from hunger and malnutrition. Consequently, *opinio juris* for the right to food exists, attributing to the general acceptance of the UDHR and the State's intent to act in conformity with it.

In addition to Vaughan Lowe's interpretation regarding *opinio juris*, the International Law Commission presents a clear guideline on *Ways and Means for Making the Evidence of Customary International Law More Readily Available.*[94] A variety of available means are listed by the International Law Commission: 1) mandate,[95] 2) studies undertaken by the Secretariat and reports of the Secretary-General, 3) reports of the working group or sub-committee, 4) reports of the special rapporteur,[96] 5) reports of the drafting Committee, 6) comments by governments, 7) reports of the International Law Commission, 8) General Assembly actions.

According to this guideline, General Comment No. 12, the Millennium Development Goals, and the World Food Summit Plan of Action, as the UN actions agreed by its Member States, can be cited as the best evidence for *opinio juris*. The appointment of a UN Special Rapporteur on the Right to Food in April 2000 also indicates the existence of the right to food as a rule of customary international law.[97] Moreover, the UN General Assembly resolutions reaffirm the right to food. The Right to Food Resolution 57/226 recognizes the problems of food insecurity; it encourages all the States to "take steps with a view to achieving progressively the full realization of the right to food."[98] Similar statements are found in the Right to Food Resolution 58/186, adopted by the General Assembly, and the Resolution 2003/25, adopted by the United Nations Commission on Human Rights.[99] The UN General Assembly resolutions impose obligations upon

---

94   The International Law Commission provides a guide to make the evidence of customary international law more available. For a collection of UN documents that are relevant to this issue, *see* Ways and Means for Making the Evidence of Customary International Law More Readily Available, G.A. Res. 487 (V) (Dec. 12, 1950), *available at* http://untreaty.un.org/ilc/guide/1_4.htm.

95   Statute of the International Law Commission, art. 24, G.A. Res. 174 (II) (Nov. 21, 1947).

96   Manley O. Hudson, *Article 24 of the Statute of the International Law Commission*, UN Doc. A/CN.4/16 and Add.1 (Working Paper 1950), *available at* http://untreaty.un.org/ilc/documentation/english/a_cn4_16.pdf.

97   Office of the UN High Comm'r for Human Rights, *Special Rapporteur on the Right to Food*, www2.ohchr.org/English/issues/food/index.htm (last visited Feb. 28, 2013). The Special Rapporteur on the right to food was initially appointed by the UN Commission on Human Rights in April 2000, and was extended subsequently by the Human Rights Council through its resolution 6/2 of September 27, 2007.

98   *See* The Right to Food Resolution, A/RES/57/226 (2003), *available at* http://www.fao.org/righttofood/KC/downloads/vl/docs/AH361_en.pdf.

99   *See* UN Commission on Human Rights Resolution 2003/25, The Right to Food, E/CN.4/RES/2003/25 (Apr. 22, 2003), *available at* http://www.unhchr.ch/Huridocda/Huridoca.nsf/(Symbol)/E.CN.4.RES.2003.25.En?Opendocument.

States to reduce worldwide food insecurity. It reflects a general agreement among the States.

To summarize, the right to food is a general and consistent practice of States. It is accepted as legally binding (*"opinio juris"*). Therefore, the right to food is established as a norm of customary international law. As such, all States must respect, protect, and fulfill the right to food. They are obligated to make efforts to ensure sufficient food is supplied to their own people within their resources.

National Implementation

Constitutions of Different Countries in the World

Having proven the right to food as a recognized human right under international law, the right's protection at the national level must be examined. A constitution is the supreme law for a sovereign State; it establishes the framework and principles of the State as a political entity. Moreover, most States reserve their citizens' most fundamental rights under their constitutions.

Whether a State has a legal basis for the right to food, the level of commitment it devotes to assuring food access can be directly determined by examining the provisions of its constitution. However, only 28 out of 198 Constitutions in the world explicitly establish the right to food.[100] Other countries affirm the right to food in connection with the right to life,[101] which implicitly includes the right to food, or in connection with some other provision of their constitutions, such as social security or social welfare.[102] In contrast, some countries only make practical efforts to guarantee sufficient food for its people, but they do not have a relevant constitutional provision.[103]

The right to food is explicitly proclaimed under the Constitution of the Republic of South Africa (1996). It was formulated consistent with Article 11 of the ICESCR.[104] The South African Constitution entitles all citizens the right to have access to sufficient food and water; it provides a framework to enforce this human right practically. Within its available resources, the South African government is obligated to take effective legislative, administrative, and other supporting measures to progressively reduce hunger and achieve national food security. Moreover, the South African government promises to provide appropriate social security and sufficient assistance to people who are financially unable to provide themselves and their dependents with enough food.

---

100   *See infra* Appendix 1.

101   Japan and Canada are examples of such countries.

102   China and Italy are examples of such countries.

103   The United States is an example of such a country.

104   Food & Agric. Org. of the UN, Recognition of the Right to Food at the National Level, IGWG/2/INF/1 (Feb. 2004).

Similarly, the right to food is enshrined in the Constitution of Brazil. In the Chapter of Individual and Collective Rights and Duties, the Brazilian Constitution establishes a nationally unified minimum wage to satisfy its people's basic living demands, such as "housing, food, education, health, leisure, clothing, hygiene, transportation, and social security."[105] Other countries whose constitutions explicitly recognize the right to food include Belarus, Bolivia, Colombia, Congo, Cuba, Czech Republic, Ecuador, Guatemala, Guyana, Haiti, Honduras, Iran, Italy, The Democratic People's Republic of Korea (North Korea), Mexico, Moldova, Nepal, Nigeria, Panama, Paraguay, Seychelles, Sierra Leone, South Africa, Suriname, Switzerland, Uganda, and Ukraine.

Unlike South Africa and Brazil, some countries only recognize the right to life in their constitutions. The right to life, in a biological sense, includes the right to food, water, clothing, housing, medical care, and anything else that is essential for people to live.[106] In this regard, these constitutions provide the right to food, but not explicitly. Article 13 of the Constitution of Japan affirms every individual's right to life, liberty, and the pursuit of happiness, provided that the enjoyment of these rights does not interfere with public welfare.[107] The Japanese Constitution also promulgates other provisions that are connected with the right to food. Article 25 requires the Japanese government to "use its endeavors for the promotion and extension of social welfare and security, and of public health."[108] Similarly, the Canada Act of 1982 proclaims that "everyone has the right to life, liberty, and security of the person, and the right not to be deprived thereof except in accordance with the principles of fundamental justice."[109] The Constitutions

---

105   Article 7 of the Brazil Constitution states that "nationally unified minimum wage, established by law, capable of satisfying their basic living needs and those of their families with housing, food, education, health, leisure, clothing, hygiene, transportation and social security, with periodical adjustments to maintain its purchasing power, it being forbidden to use it as an index for any purpose," CONSTITUIÇÃO FEDERAL [C.F.] [CONSTITUTION] art. 7 (Braz.).

106   BERTRAND G. RAMCHARAN, HUMAN RIGHTS AND HUMAN SECURITY 9 (2002).

107   NIHONKOKU KENPŌ [KENPŌ] [CONSTITUTION], art. 9, para. 2 (Japan).

108   *Id.*

109   Canada Act, 1982, c. 11 (U.K.), art. 7, *reprinted in* R.S.C. 1985, app. II, no. 44 (Can.).

of the Russian Federation,[110] Spain,[111] Finland,[112] and South Korea[113] also assure people's right to food in this indirect manner.

Some States do not mention the right to food or the right to life in their constitutions. These inalienable human rights can be affirmed in connection with other constitutional provisions. The Constitution of the People's Republic of China does not have an explicit provision regarding the right to food, however, Article 45 proclaims people's right to "material assistance from the state and the society when they are old, ill or disabled."[114] The Chinese Constitution focuses more on social welfare to ensure adequate food, water, housing, health care, and other social services.[115] Similarly, the Italian Constitution ensures every individual access to adequate food by providing people a right to social welfare.[116]

Unlike the countries stated above, the United States ensures its people's right to continuous access to nutritiously adequate food without a relevant constitutional provision. Even though the US government has consistently carried out food assistance policies at home, such as the Food Stamp Program,[117] and abroad, such as the US Food Aid Programs,[118] it opposes a legal right to food as inconsistent with the US Constitution, as previously explained.

---

110 KONSTITUTSIIA ROSSIISKOI FEDERATSII [KONST. RF] [CONSTITUTION] art. 20.1 (Russ.).

111 Constitution of Spain, Article 15 pronounces the right to life by stating "Everyone has the right to life and physical and moral integrity and in no case may be subjected to torture or inhuman or degrading punishment or treatment. The death penalty is abolished except in those cases which may be established by military penal law in times of war." CONSTITUTION ESPANOLA, B.O.E. n. 311, Dec. 29, 1978, art. 15 (Spain).

112 Section 7.1 of the Constitution of Finland entitles its people the right to life, personal liberty and integrity. "Everyone has the right to life, personal liberty, integrity and security." FIN. CONST. June 11, 1999, art. 7.1.

113 Article 34.1 of the Constitution of South Korea entitles all citizens a life worthy of human beings. DAEHANMINKUK HUNBEOB [HUNBEOB] [CONSTITUTION] art. 34.1 (S. Kor.).

114 XIANFA [CONSTITUTION] art. 45 (1982) (China).

115 *Id.*

116 Constitution of Italy, Article 38 reads "All citizens unable to work and lacking the resources necessary for their existence are entitled to private and social assistance." Art. 38 COSTITUZIONE [COST.] (It.).

117 In order to reduce hunger and malnutrition, the US Congress initiated the Food Stamp Program in 1964. This program was created to increase the food-buying power of low-income households in the US. The federal government of the United States pays 100 percent of the cost of food stamps. It also covers half of the administrative costs. *See* DEBORAH HARRIS ET AL., FOOD STAMP ADVOCACY GUIDE 1 (2007).

118 The US food aid program was created in the early 1950s. Its objectives include international humanitarian assistance and economic development support in recipient countries. In the late 1980s, the US provided about 60 percent of global food aid donations, but US donations fell considerably from the late 1980s. However, the US consistently is the major food aid donor. *See* US Dep't of Agric., *Fifty Years of US Food Aid and Its Role in Reducing World Hunger*, http://www.ers.usda.gov/AmberWaves/September04/Features/usfoodaid.htm (last visited Feb. 13, 2009).

To be fair, we should not evaluate a State's commitment by merely looking at its constitutions. However, the fact that only 28 countries out of 198 have constitutional provisions regarding food security is a warning to the international community. The incorporation of the right to food into constitutions deserves more international and national attention. It will highlight the need for States to fulfill their obligations of ensuring sustainable access to adequate food for their citizens. It will also help create a transparent and predictable regulatory environment for governments to design and implement a comprehensive strategic plan for progressive realization of the right to food.

Establish a National Legal Basis for Ensuring the Right to Food

Incorporating the right to food into the domestic legal system is imperative for national implementation. States see the interaction between international and national law in different ways. Some States assume that the international and national legal systems are unified and that international treaty instruments are immediately incorporated by and binding on the State through the act of ratification. These States are called "monist" States and include the US. The domestic courts of a monist State can cite the relevant international rules and principles immediately upon ratification of an international treaty instrument.[119] By contrast, other States distinguish international law from their national law, and are called "dualist" States. They require additional transformation before international agreements can be implemented as enforceable law by domestic courts. Put simply, no binding effects are imposed on national courts of a dualist State until the State's legislative body makes additional acts of translation. The majority of countries in the world, including all EU Member States, follow the "dualist" mode.[120]

Domestic implementation of the right to food, however, remains a problem. Some monist States are not making adequate efforts to implement their international obligations, particularly their obligations to provide international food aid. Not many dualist States transform the right to food into enforceable national law. Incorporating the right to food into a national legal system gives the national courts a standard with which to measure government actions.[121] In order to tackle the global food crisis and assure that every individual has access to adequate food, all States should incorporate the right to food into their national legal system, whether by direct application or by transformation. Dualist States should pay special attention in the process of transformation. The legislative body

---

119   This kind of incorporation of international treaties into national law is called "monism." *See* John H. Jackson, *Status of Treaties in Domestic Legal Systems: A Policy Analysis*, 86 Am. J. Int'l L. 310, 314 (1992).

120   This form of translating international law into national law is referred to as "dualism." M. Akehurst, Modern Introduction to International Law 45 (1970).

121   Food & Agric. Org. of the UN, Legislate for the Right to Food (2007), *available at* http://www.fao.org/righttofood/wfd/pdf2007/how_legislate_eng.pdf.

needs first to review whether existing national legislation adequately covers the content of the right to food and accompanied implementation procedures, and to check whether effective remedies are available for every individual whose right is deprived, abused, or neglected.[122]

---

122 INT'L FOOD POLICY RESEARCH INST., FOOD AS A HUMAN RIGHT (2001), *available at* http://www.ifpri.org/2020/NEWSLET/nv_0401/nv_0401_Interview.htm.

Chapter 3

Causes of the Current Food Insecurity and Potential Solutions: Poverty

Poverty Results in Hunger

Not every poor person is hungry; however, almost all hungry people are poor. In most cases, hungry people are hungry simply because they do not have money to purchase enough food from the market or they cannot afford the farming supplies they need to grow enough food for themselves and their families. Therefore, they are caught in a poverty trap.[1] Poverty directly causes hunger and malnutrition.

In turn, hunger results in poor health and low levels of energy. It reduces people's ability to work, making them even poorer and hungrier. Hunger perpetuates the vicious cycle of poverty. It is difficult for poor people to get out of the vicious cycle of poverty and hunger. Reducing poverty helps alleviate world hunger issues. A meaningful long-term strategy for hunger eradication must include continuous efforts to alleviate poverty.

Although the world has been making progress to reduce global poverty, it remains a problem, and has not yet been eradicated. Economic growth is the foundation for national income increase; it helps poverty reduction.

Figure 3.1,[2] by Dr Xavier Sala-i-Martin and Dr Maxim Pinkovskiy, shows the changes of the economic growth rate and the number of people living on less than a dollar a day in Sub-Saharan Africa from 1970 to 2006. It demonstrates that poverty decreases while the economy grows.

Similarly, China is also seen as an example of how a high economic growth rate can reduce poverty and hunger. China has made great achievements in promoting economic growth since the far-reaching economic reforms of the late 1970s. The average rate of per capita GDP has been up to 8.1 percent since then.[3] In the meantime, China's rural poverty population (at a poverty line of $1.25 per

1   Justin Stole, *The Energy Policy Act of 2005: The Path to Energy Autonomy?*, 33 J. Legis. 121, 122 (2006).

2   Xavier Sala-i-Martin & Maxim Pinkovskiy, *African Poverty is Falling ... Much Faster than You Think*, Vox (Dec. 6, 2010), http://www.voxeu.org/article/african-poverty-falling-faster-you-think.

3   Hu Angang et al., China's economic growth and poverty reduction (1978–2002), *available at* http://www.imf.org/external/np/apd/seminars/2003/newdelhi/angang.pdf (last visited Jan. 15, 2013).

Figure 3.1 $1/day poverty and growth in Sub-Saharan Africa, 1970–2006
Source: Dr Xavier Sala-i-Martin & Dr Maxim Pinkovskiy 2010.

day) has dropped from 250 million in 1978 to 28.2 million in 2002, decreasing by 88.7 percent.[4]

Consequently, economic growth reduces poverty; poverty reduction enables people to afford to produce or purchase sufficient food to meet their dietary needs. The economic health of a country substantially impacts the realization of people's food security.[5]

Economic growth is largely determined by a country's national capacity.[6] In other words, improving national capacity will significantly stimulate economic development. Generally, government efforts are essential for the improvement of national capacity.[7] Many public works and programs that are critical for economic

---

4   *Id.*

5   Frank Tenente, *Feeding the World One Seed at a Time: A Practical Alternative for Solving World Hunger*, 5 Nw. U. J. Int'l Hum. Rts. 298, 298 (2007).

6   UN Dept. of Econ. and Soc. Affairs, Strengthening Efforts to Eradicate Poverty and Hunger 98 (2007), *available at* http://www.un.org/en/ecosoc/docs/pdfs/07-49285-ecosoc-book-2007.pdf [hereinafter UN, Strengthening Efforts].

7   *Id.* at 275 (stating that national efforts are very important to economic development and can have direct effects on eradicating poverty).

growth can only be provided by governments.[8] Therefore, governments are strongly encouraged to commit to national capacity building. A combination of investments in basic infrastructure, professional training, and improved public services is necessary for a country's national capacity building.

National Capacity Building and Poverty Reduction Strategies

Appropriate Government Interventions and Good Governance

Hunger is the result of a series of economic and social problems that the government plays a critical role in shaping. The reduction of poverty and hunger is an achievable goal only if government makes the right policy decisions.[9] Development strategies and national food policies, in essence, are a set of direct and indirect government interventions.

Appropriate government interventions require good governance. Governance refers to government policies and the relevant enforcement mechanisms. It is defined as "the process of decision-making and the process by which decisions are implemented (not implemented)."[10] Good governance generates effective policies and, therefore, it helps promote national capacity and economic development, and vice versa. In addition, good governance is indispensable for governments to make right decisions on poverty and hunger reduction and sustainable development as well. Conversely, poor governance largely impedes a government's ability to promote economic growth. It is one of the main reasons why many developing countries are poor.

Bureaucracy has been a big issue in many developing countries. Bureaucratic inefficiency generally undermines every aspect of national development. Unfortunately, this is not something new. Using food aid distribution as an example, in time of emergency, bureaucratic inefficiency may weaken the function of emergency food aid. It delays food aid distribution by placing undesirable barriers to quick, effective, and appropriate food distribution. Foreign food aid may be delayed in customs, or later in the process of distribution because of cumbersome and slow administrative procedures. For example, on December 26, 2004, many Southeast Asian countries were hit by a destructive tsunami triggered by

---

8   Andy Gutierrez, *Codifying the Past, Erasing the Future*, 4 Hastings W.-N.W.J. Envtl. L. & Pol'y 161, 162 (1998).

9   US Dept. of State & Bureau of Int'l Info. Programs, *US Food Aid: Reducing World Hunger*, 12 eJournal USA 1 (September 2007), [hereinafter *Reducing World Hunger*] ("Ending hunger and malnutrition is an achievable goal, but only if governments in both developed and developing countries make the right policy decisions").

10   UN Econ. & Soc. Comm'n for Asia & Pacific, What Is Good Governance, *available at* http://www.unescap.org/pdd/prs/ProjectActivities/Ongoing/gg/governance.pdf (last visited Feb. 28, 2013) [hereinafter What is Good Governance].

an undersea megathrust off the coast of Sumatra. Governments, humanitarian organizations, and individuals around the world offered immediate help in response to this disaster. However, due to bureaucracy, over 400 containers of relief goods were still held in Indonesian customs a year after the tsunami.[11] As of April 2006, a backlog of 1,154 containers of emergency goods was awaiting clearance in Sri Lanka's customs.[12] Bureaucracies are inefficient and wasteful. Coordination between different government departments and the improvement of accountability with a clear allocation of responsibilities help enhance government performance and reduce waste.[13] Reducing bureaucracy is critical for effective food distribution.

Many countries do not have comprehensive laws or policies regarding how to deal with sudden-impact disasters, such as how to mitigate a food emergency caused by crop or market failures.[14] They only find it necessary to create such laws when the disaster really happens. At this point, regulatory problems pose extra obstacles to hunger reduction. It is urgent for governments to adopt emergency laws ensuring that the right to food is justiciable before national courts and other forms of redress are available.

Corruption is an issue that exists in almost every single country in the world, more or less. It by no means is the product of modern times. The causes and effects of corruption have been studied by many scholars and policy makers. This research will not repeat these studies. Despite the differences in these studies, it is all agreed that corruption impedes democracy and undermines social and economic development.[15] Therefore, corruption inevitably impairs a government's efforts to reduce hunger. When a country's resources are stolen or diverted through corruption, people are left without social security, especially those poor people that are barely able to put food on the table. Corruption prevents food aid from reaching its designated beneficiaries; it tragically intensifies hunger and malnutrition.[16] The

---

11   *See* David Fisher, *From Hand to Mouth, via the Lab and the Legislature: International and Domestic Regulations to Secure the Food Supply*, 40 VAND. J. TRANSNAT'L L. 1127, 1140 (2007).

12   *Id.*

13   OLIVIER DE SCHUTTER, MANDATE OF THE SPECIAL RAPPORTEUR ON THE RIGHT TO FOOD, BACKGROUND NOTE: ANALYSIS OF THE WORLD FOOD CRISIS BY THE UN SPECIAL RAPPORTEUR ON THE RIGHT TO FOOD 5 (May 2, 2008) *available at* http://www.srfood.org/images/stories/ pdf/otherdocuments/1-srrtfnoteglobalfoodcrisis-2-5-08.pdf (stressing the importance of improving accountability, with a clear allocation of responsibilities).

14   Fisher, *supra* note 11, at 1139 ("[V]ery few states have comprehensive laws for policies concerning the receipt of international disaster relief").

15   United Nations, *Global Issues—Governance*, http://www.un.org/en/globalissues/ governance/ (last visited Jan. 16, 2013). The other two threats are violence and poverty.

16   Gregory W. MacKenzie, *ICSID Arbitration as a Strategy for Leveling the Playing Field between International Non-Governmental Organizations and Host States*, 19 SYRACUSE J. INT'L L. & COM. 197 (1993).

fight against corruption is critical to eradicate poverty and hunger. It requires transparency in the financial and monetary systems.[17]

The failure of international assistance to North Korea explains how poor governance prevents people from getting enough food and, therefore, how it intensifies hunger and poverty. In the early 1990s, the economy of North Korea was severely depressed because of the termination of the historic trading relationships with the Soviet Union and a series of natural disasters.[18] People in North Korea had suffered from hunger and malnutrition for years. Although the international community provided food assistance to help North Korea lower their hunger level, the food shortage problem was not solved due to North Korea's poor governance.

North Korea has long been notorious for its dictatorship. Dictatorial governments have had a history of poor governance, troubles with democracy and the rule of law, and a total disregard for fundamental human rights. North Korea's dictatorial government controlled the transportation, storage, and distribution of food aid, but it refused to provide mandatory reports on food use and food distribution.[19] Food aid provided to North Korea could not be adequately monitored or tracked. International donors did not know if their contributions reached the designated beneficiaries. Given these obstacles set by North Korea's government, donor countries and individual groups were reluctant to make further contributions. The United States even planned to terminate their aid if they were continually unable to monitor or track down their contributions.[20] Similar action by other countries further exacerbated hunger and malnutrition in North Korea.

Poor governance has negative effects on all aspects of social, economic, and political developments; it intensifies hunger and poverty. Conversely, good governance is one of the key ingredients of any successful strategy for sustainable development. This is hardly new. However, why does poor governance still exist and why can the world not stop it from being a challenging issue to address?

It is unfortunate that poverty causes poor governance, and poor governance causes poverty. Similar to the relationship between hunger and poverty, this is another trap, the governance trap. When a government has limited resources, it is difficult to implement a national development strategy and, therefore, it is difficult to make a positive contribution to improve people's standard of living. Poverty impedes a government's ability to work functionally.

On the other hand, poverty is a failure of governance. Bureaucracy, mismanagement, and corruption imperil a country's economic, social, and political development. They are among the biggest barriers to ending poverty.

---

17   United Nations Millennium Declaration, G.A. Res. 55.2, UN Doc. A/RES/55/2 (Sept. 18, 2000).

18   Jongeun Lee, *Study of the International Food Security Regime: Food Aid to North Korea During the Famine of 1995–2000*, 11 CARDOZO J. INT'L & COMP. L. 1037, 1042 (2004).

19   GEN. ACCOUNTING OFFICE, FOREIGN ASSISTANCE: NORTH KOREA RESTRICTS FOOD AID MONITORING, GAO/ NSIAD-00–35 (Oct. 1999).

20   Lee, *supra* note 18, at 1053.

Poor governance stops funds from reaching healthcare, education, and other essential public services; it prevents development aid from working effectively in the poorest regions; it also limits individuals' access to social welfare.[21] Poor governance impedes poverty alleviation.

As former UN Secretary-General Kofi Annan has said, "good governance is perhaps the single most important factor in eradicating poverty and promoting development."[22] Improving the capacity for good governance is critical for sustainable human development. The United Nations Economic and Social Commission for Asia and the Pacific (UNESCAP) interprets good governance as having eight distinct characters: participation, transparency, rule of law, responsiveness, consensus orientation, equity and inclusiveness, effectiveness and efficiency, and accountability.[23] With regard to these eight distinct characters, there are a few things governments can do in order to improve governance.

People's right to substantially participate in the decision-making process, either directly or through legitimate intermediate institutions that represent their interests, should be protected. Most importantly, the voices of the most vulnerable people must be heard. A government's policies and activities in all aspects should make its people feel included in the mainstream of society and able to enjoy equal rights.[24] In regards to food or agricultural issues, governments should consult with their people, particularly farmers and groups that represent farmers' interests, before they decide to adopt any new agricultural policies.[25] However, this is not easy to achieve. Although most States protect their people's rights to participate in the decision-making process, in the real world, implementation is different from the law as it is on paper. This is especially true in many poor developing countries where democracy remains an issue. People's right to participate in decision-making processes is not well protected in practice.

Transparency is a core principle of good governance. It means decisions and enforcement are made in a manner that follows laws and regulations, and should be transparent to the public.[26] Information concerning how government conducts public affairs and manages public resources should be provided to the

---

21 The Global Poverty Project, *Global Poverty Info Bank*, http://www. globalpovertyproject.com/infobank/corruption (last visited Jan. 17, 2013).

22 KOFI ANNAN, PARTNERSHIPS FOR GLOBAL COMMUNITY: ANNUAL REPORT ON THE WORK OF THE ORGANIZATION (1998).

23 UN ECON. & SOC. COMM'N FOR ASIA & PACIFIC, WHAT IS GOOD GOVERNANCE, *supra* note 10.

24 *Id.*

25 OXFAM INT'L, THE TIME IS NOW: HOW WORLD LEADERS SHOULD RESPOND TO THE FOOD PRICE CRISIS (June 3, 2008), *available at* http://oxfam.qc.ca/sites/oxfam.qc.ca/files/2008–06–03_the%20Time%20is%20Now.pdf. (advocating that "[a]gricultural policy should be decided as part of a negotiation by a country's government, in consultation with its citizens, including farmers' groups").

26 UN ECON. & SOC. COMM'N FOR ASIA & PACIFIC, WHAT IS GOOD GOVERNANCE, *supra* note 10.

public in a timely and accurately manner, and should also be in a form that is easily understandable. By informing the public of updates about new policies and actions, government shows its strong interest in listening to the views of the public and in responding to its people's concerns. This in turn strengthens the legitimacy of the decision-making process.

Well-functioning governments are bound by the rule of law. Good governance requires a fair legal framework with effective enforcement mechanisms.[27] As for solving the hunger issues, States are encouraged to clearly allocate the government's responsibility, and to regulate how food should be effectively distributed and what remedies are available if the right to food is infringed upon. Most importantly, as previously stated, emergency law is critical in responding to a sudden food shortage when natural or man-made disasters happen.[28]

To be fair, good governance is an ideal that is difficult to achieve in full, even in liberal democratic States. Good governance needs well-intentioned policymakers who would like to bring their experiences and ideas to policymaking. It can only be considered a good start when all of the considerations are included in ensuring that stakeholder interests are carefully addressed and reflected in policy initiatives. Furthermore, a corresponding enforcement and monitoring system must be fully functional so that the policies can be practically implemented. Consequently, government efforts are required to fully achieve good governance. Regardless of the difficulties, good governance is one of the most important forces to remove the roots that cause poverty and hunger, therefore, governments must make efforts to progressively promote transparency, responsiveness, effectiveness, efficiency, accountability, and the implementation of the rule of law.[29]

Increase Government Spending on Rural Infrastructure and Adaptive Agricultural Research

Rural infrastructure
In Asia, rapid progress in poverty and hunger reduction has been associated with increased government spending on agriculture and rural development.[30] In the many food deficit countries, such as African countries, however, agriculture has

---

27   *Id.*

28   World Food Summit, Nov. 13–17, 1996, *Technical Background Documents for the World Food Summit*, ch. 13, ¶ 3.14 ("[T]the import displacement time for international food aid has usually been long because of the time it takes governments to assess the disaster situation and food aid needs and to find or request from donors the finances or commodities required").

29   UN, STRENGTHENING EFFORTS, *supra* note 6, at 172 (stating the importance of good governance in poverty eradication and employment creation and stating that "freedom, peace and security, domestic stability, respect for human rights, including the right to development, the rule of law, gender equality, market-oriented policies and an overall commitment to just and democratic societies, are also essential and mutually reinforcing").

30   *Id.* at 246.

been neglected for a very long period. In contrast with 8–15 percent agricultural expenditure in Asian countries, many African countries only spend 4–5 percent of their total national budget on agriculture.[31] Lack of investment in agriculture has exacerbated hunger and malnutrition. It leaves vulnerable people exposed to negative consequences caused by global food price increases.

Poverty and hunger reduction is closely correlated with government spending on agriculture and rural development. Increased agricultural investment is crucial to help reduce hunger and to promote sustainable development. First, 75 percent of economically disadvantaged people in the world depend mainly on agriculture or agriculture-based industries. To reduce poverty and hunger, governments should improve the income of these poor people by supporting the areas in which they work to earn their livelihoods and by expanding market demand for the items they produce or possess.[32] Second, farmers need to have sufficient access to land, agricultural inputs, new agricultural technologies and equipment, extension services, and communications.[33] Without the government's support to create a favorable farming environment, farmers will face more challenges in maintaining and increasing agricultural production. Third, the improvement of agriculture productivity also requires the reconstruction of institutions in education, technology, research, and other services. Government plays a significant role in improving these public services.

Government support for rural infrastructure development is advised to focus on the following areas: water and irrigation systems, transportation, rural communication, and agriculture-related services.

First, successful agriculture largely depends on farmers' sustainable access to water. Adverse weather is often cited to be the major source of crop failure. An efficient irrigation system minimizes the damages caused by drought, ensuring sustainable agricultural production. Moreover, globally, 70 percent of fresh water consumption is used for producing food and other agricultural products.[34] Water shortage has become one of the world's major problems in the last few decades. It threatens the health of billions of people globally, and is already a serious constraint to farming in many countries in the world. To shore up the problem of excessive water use in farming, it is important to build efficient irrigation systems.

---

31 SHENGGEN FAN ET AL., INVESTING IN AFRICAN AGRICULTURE TO HALVE POVERTY BY 2015 (Feb. 2008), *available at* http://www.ifpri.org/pubs/dp/ifpridp00751.pdf.

32 JOACHIM VON BRAUN & EUGENIO DIAZ-BONILLA, GLOBALIZATION OF FOOD AND AGRICULTURE AND THE POOR (SEPT. 2008), *available at* http://www.ifpri.org/pubs/ib/ib52.pdf.

33 Press Release, UN Special Rapporteur on the Right to Food, Political Will Needed to Tackle Food Crisis and Restructure Agriculture, Warns UN Right to Food Expert (Sept. 18, 2009), *available at* http://www.srfood.org/images/stories/pdf/otherdocuments/srrtf_pressrelease_hrc_18sept09_web.pdf [hereinafter Press Release, UN Special Rapporteur].

34 WATER FOR FOOD, WATER FOR LIFE: A COMPREHENSIVE ASSESSMENT OF WATER MANAGEMENT IN AGRICULTURE 2 (David Molden ed., 2007).

If water and irrigation systems are not available or not working appropriately, a serious crop failure would wipe out the income of poor farmers. Thus, increasing government spending on water and irrigation projects helps reduce the likelihood of crop failures, making agricultural activities more productive.

Irrigation investment is important; effective project management is equally important. Many developing countries have largely increased funding to improve their irrigation systems. However, there are many irrigation systems that do not work as expected because of bad design or poor management, particularly in many African countries.[35] In Zimbabwe, for example, Osborne Dam on the Odzi River was built to irrigate many places down to Nyanyadzi in Chimanimani. However, due to its poor design, a very insignificant percentage of water is actually used for agricultural production.[36] Lower parts of the Nyando basin of Kenya have the greatest potential for irrigation, but poor management of irrigation systems in the upper reaches of the basin results in the block of irrigation supply channels and, therefore, makes farming in the Nyando flood plain more difficult.[37] Consequently, in addition to irrigation investment, governments should also pay attention to the design and management of irrigation projects, and all other potential problems that may prevent the efficient use of water resources.

Second, many rural communities are isolated; they have limited connections outside of their communities. The improvement of roads, bridges, railways, and other public transportation systems is vital to facilitate the movement of agricultural inputs; it makes services more accessible. Improved transportation also enables farmers to have access to markets in urban centers so they can sell their agricultural produce before it spoils.[38]

Third, a favorable environment enables farmers to access agricultural markets. Farmers, including those in remote areas, should be connected to domestic,

---

35   Many developing countries, particularly in Africa, have numerous water supply networks that do not work because of wrong design, poor management, failure to collect water charges from water users and the government's lack of resources to compensate for the shortfall in the networks' revenue. Under those circumstances, development designers must address whether the central government should finance the tubewells included in a community plan, or refuse to do it because the district envisages serving the area differently in the future. *See* INT'L FUND FOR AGRIC. DEV., COMMUNITY-DRIVEN DEVELOPMENT DECISION TOOLS FOR RURAL DEVELOPMENT PROGRAMS 41 (2009), *available at* http://www.ifad.org/english/cdd/pub/decisiontools.pdf /.

36   Isidore Guvamombe, *Zimbabwe: Irrigation—the Answer to Climate Change*, HERALD, Dec. 30, 2011, *available at* http://allafrica.com/stories/201201030203.html.

37   BRENT SWALLOW ET AL., IRRIGATION MANAGEMENT AND POVERTY DYNAMICS: CASE STUDY OF THE NYANDO BASIN IN WESTERN KENYA (2007), *available at* http://www.iwmi.cgiar.org/publications/CABI_Publications/CA_CABI_Series/Community_Law/protected/Ch%2012.pdf.

38   UN, STRENGTHENING EFFORTS, *supra* note 6, at 47. Crops become rotten because of poor roads and the improvement of transportation enables farmers to have access to markets in the urban centers in a timely manner. *Id.*

regional, and world markets. Governments need to improve distribution systems to facilitate diversified agricultural trade. Particular policies are necessary to make agriculture-related information available to the farmers in a timely manner, for example, an information system that can update farmers on market demand, supply, and price changes.

Fourth, farmers face a number of risks in agricultural operations. Inclement weather, as an unanticipated force, is one of the major sources of risk. It can lead to a dramatic decrease in agricultural production. Thus accurate and timely weather predictions are important for farmers to plan for the planting and harvesting of their crops, and to make their best efforts to prepare for adverse weather conditions and, therefore, reduce potential risks.[39]

Weather forecasting has its limitations; it is not always accurate, especially long-range forecasting. However, with the use of various modern forecasting technology, observation, and the knowledge of trends and patterns, reasonably accurate weather predications can be made a few days in advance. Coupled with efficient warning systems, this will help mitigate the damages caused by adverse weather conditions.

The improvement of weather forecasting and warning systems needs government effort, including the improvement of weather forecasting technology, and the establishment and maintenance of a comprehensive weather prediction and emergency warning system that is easily accessible to farmers. Moreover, governments should train local leaders on how to interpret weather data and take action if adverse weather is likely, so that local leaders will be able to advise farmers to prepare as best they can.

It is true that many poor developing countries have small budgets; many policy makers may think improving weather forecasting and warning systems is not a priority. Nevertheless, the investment in building such a system is worth every penny it costs. In 2007 and 2008, Bangladesh experienced three major floods. Each flood was successfully predicted, and mitigation steps were taken. According to a World Bank report, for the three Bangladesh floods, about $40 was saved for each dollar the government invested in the regional weather forecasting and warning system.[40]

Fifth, technical services from agricultural experts also help farmers cope with problems in farming. Governments may consider establishing local technical assistance centers to teach farmers proper agro-forestry techniques, and answer their questions when they encounter problems in farming. Agricultural experts are also welcome to hold workshops on a regular basis to introduce new agricultural technology and equipment.

---

39   C.W. Fraisse et al., *AgClimate: A Climate Forecast Information System for Agricultural Risk Management in the Southeastern USA*, 53 COMPUTERS & ELECTRONICS IN AGRIC. 13 (2006).

40   Peter Webster, *Meteorology: Improve Weather Forecasts for the Developing World*, 493 NATURE 17 (2013).

China's agricultural development is largely promoted by the technical services provided by the Chinese government. Rural and agricultural development has been the top priority in the Chinese development agenda. The Chinese government has been significantly investing in agriculture for decades. It has built a fairly comprehensive system to provide local farmers with timely technical services. Today, China has the world's largest agricultural economy, and it is the largest global producer of pork, wheat, rice, tea, cotton, and fish.[41] Additionally, China has been active in providing agricultural assistance to African countries for the last half century. Since the 1960s, China has implemented about 200 agricultural cooperation programs in more than 40 African countries.[42] To help reduce hunger and malnutrition, China has also been transferring agricultural technology to Africa. By 2012, China had built 20 agricultural demonstration centers across Africa. It had also sent more than 10,000 agricultural experts and technicians to train local African farmers, and advise them on how to increase agricultural productivity.[43] China has made significant contributions to agricultural development in many African countries by providing agriculture-related technical services.

Adaptive agricultural research
Agriculture in most food deficient countries is based on human labor, simple hand tools, and little fertilizer.[44] Agricultural research has been overlooked, mostly because these countries are not able to afford it. However, limited amounts of farmland and other natural resources restrict the possibility that food supplies will increase through expanding land use. In the meantime, continuing population growth further decreases the availability of farmland. Under this circumstance, land-saving technologies that increase the crop yield per unit have become the dominant source for maintaining and promoting the food-population balance. Moreover, pressure from the world market has also pushed farmers to increasingly adopt advanced agricultural technologies to increase their productivity and remain competitive.[45] A lack of government attention to agricultural research denies farmers' access to necessary knowledge, undermining agricultural development.

---

41   COLIN A. CARTER, CHINA'S AGRICULTURE: ACHIEVEMENTS AND CHALLENGES (2011), *available at* http://giannini.ucop.edu/media/are-update/files/articles/V14N5_2.pdf (noting that China now "produces 18 percent of the world's cereal grains, 29 percent of the world's meat, and 50 percent of the world's vegetables").

42   HANNAH EDINGER, NETWORK FOR POLICY RESEARCH, REVIEW AND ADVICE ON EDUCATION AND TRAINING COMING TO THE TABLE: CHINA'S AGRICULTURAL COOPERATION IN AFRICA (September 2010), *available at* http://www.norrag.org/issues/article/1334/en/coming-to-the-table-china_s-agricultural-cooperation-in-africa.html?PHPSESSID=34227 322ff4f8994954c5e1376e9018c.

43   *Id.*

44   Cheryl Christensen & Charles Hanrahan, *African Food Crises: Short-, Medium-, and Long-Term Responses*, 70 IOWA L. REV. 1293, 1295 (1985).

45   Christopher D. Merrett & Cynthia Struthers, *Globalization and the Future of Rural Communities in the American Midwest*, 12 TRANSNAT'L L. & CONTEMP. PROBS. 34, 58 (2002).

Increasing investment in agricultural research, however, produces structural changes that will improve productivity and, therefore, increase agricultural output.

Within a knowledge-driven society, the improvement of agricultural productivity heavily depends on the enhancement of agricultural technology, while advanced technology requires further commitment being put into agricultural research. It is of great importance that the food deficit countries' governments strengthen and expand agricultural research. International, national, and regional research centers focusing on adaptive agriculture research must be established. Research has to be environmentally, economically, socially, and culturally adapted to local agricultural conditions and, in particular, environmental sustainability has to be prioritized. The core objective of these research centers is to acquire and generate knowledge, and then put it into practice.[46] Knowledge transfer from research institutions to practice enables farmers to apply innovative technologies to actual farming activities. Building networks, partnerships, or cooperative programs between universities, research institutions, and local communities accelerates the process of knowledge transfer.

Increased investment in agricultural research has positive impacts on the improvement of agricultural productivity, and it has been proven to be cost-effective in the long run. In the 1960s, the Cuban government developed an extensive network of agriculture-related research institutions. Many people challenged its feasibility and value costs. However, as a consequence of many years of research and experimentation, green manure crops have been promoted, and many chemical and nonchemical fertilization techniques have been developed. Agricultural productivity has thus greatly increased and the Cuban people's access to food has, therefore, been substantially enhanced.[47]

Food Reserve Programs

A food reserve program is one of the essential components of a successful food security scheme; it keeps government in good shape to respond to food emergencies caused by natural or man-made disasters.[48] As previously mentioned, current global food reserves are dangerously low, and we now face very tight margins between food reserves and demand. Therefore, the establishment of food reserve programs is urgent so that full insurance will be provided against domestic crop or market failures.

In their attempts to alleviate future tragedies caused by food shortage, governments should increase spending on building and reconstituting food reserve

---

46   Ogundeji Abiodun Akintunde, Education and Knowledge Transfer: A Priority for the Future (2007), *available at* http://purl.umn.edu/44904.

47   Carmen G. Gonzalez, *Seasons of Resistance: Sustainable Agriculture and Food Security in Cuba*, 16 Tul. Envtl. L.J. 685, 722 (2003).

48   Mark Ritchie & Kristin Dawkins, *WTO Food and Agricultural Rules: Sustainable Agriculture and the Human Right to Food*, 9 Minn. J. Global Trade 9, 30 (2000).

programs at national and regional levels. Food surplus in good-harvest years should be stored to prepare for an emergency. Also, food reserve centers should be established near centers of population to ensure sufficient food supplies can be distributed to hungry people in a timely manner when food emergency occurs.[49]

Investment in Education and Other Essential Public Services

Education has multi-faceted effects which make it an indispensable means of fighting poverty.[50] More funds should be allocated to education. Investment in education not only includes agriculture-related education, but extends to education in general. However, many people may ask how general education is connected with agriculture. The answer is that agricultural development requires the improvement of productivity, and the improvement of productivity can only be achieved through scientific research and the transfer of research into practice. Education is the foundation for any scientific research. Without education, no technological innovations can be achieved. Education determines the current and future development of a country and, therefore, it deserves special attention.

Knowledge is power. It enables people to take greater control of their destinies.[51] In a narrow sense, the promotion of agriculture-related education stimulates technological innovations, and it also increases agricultural productivity, which helps maintain and improve a country's competitiveness in the global agricultural market. In a broader sense, education in general directly and indirectly affects people's incomes and their standards of living. It determines a country's national capacity. A survey that covers almost all the countries in the world indicates that per capita income is in direct proportion with education level.[52] Countries with higher education levels have relatively higher incomes and standards of living, such as the US and many European countries. On the contrary, less developed and least developed countries, such as many African countries, have lower incomes and lower education levels. Education is one of the determinant factors that affects national capacity building and human development. Government plays a critical role in promoting education. In general, a comprehensive education system has to be built, including primary, secondary, and higher education, and skills training at all age levels.

There have been impressive achievements in promoting access to schooling globally. Following the Millennium Development Goals, many developing

---

49   *Id.* ("Stocks of food held near centers of population in virtually every country are one of the most important components of any successful food security scheme").

50   UN, STRENGTHENING EFFORTS, *supra* note 6, at 221–22.

51   Joseph P.G. Chimombo, *Issues in Basic Education in Developing Countries: An Exploration of Policy Options for Improved Delivery*, 8 J. INT'L COOPERATION EDUC. 129 (2005).

52   J. Carroll Bottum, *Education-Treatment for Poverty, available at* http://ageconsearch.umn.edu/bitstream/17393/1/ar650123.pdf (last visited Feb. 28, 2013).

countries—47 out of 163—have achieved universal free primary education. They have tried to provide equal education opportunities for both boys and girls.[53] An additional 20 countries are expected to achieve this goal by 2015. However, huge challenges remain in 44 developing countries, 23 of which are in Sub-Saharan Africa. It is unlikely that these countries will meet the goal of universal primary education anytime soon. According to the World Bank, there are about 77 million children of school age, including 44 million girls, who have no opportunity to go to school due to financial, social, or physical challenges.[54] Education remains a big issue in many poor developing countries. In order to reduce world poverty and to promote human development, free and compulsory primary education must be accessible to all, in law as well as fact, regardless of one's gender, ethnicity, religion, disability, social and economic status.[55]

Special attention must be paid to gender equity in educational enrollment. Currently, girls continue to face discrimination in receiving education in many developing countries, particularly in countries where people have a strong preference for boys, such as countries in Sub-Saharan Africa and the Middle East, and India and Pakistan.[56] However, it is important to ensure girls' right to access to education.[57] Education enables women to have positive opportunities and, thereby, it helps them earn a living, and lifts them out of poverty. It also makes women aware of their basic human rights in the economic, social, and political arenas. Moreover, girls' access to education is also important for the next generation. Girls are the mothers of the future. Mothers generally play a significant role in raising and educating their children because the mother is usually the first person a child is with after he/she is born, and a child spends a lot of time with his/her mother during childhood. Hence, a mother's morals and character can largely influence

---

53   Burundi made education free in 2005 and has seen half a million more children in school. Bangladesh has managed to reduce the numbers of girls not in school to just 60,000. *See* Oxfam Int'l, Credibility Crunch, Food, Poverty, and Climate Change: An Agenda for Rich Country Leaders (2008), *available at* http://www.oxfam.org.uk/resources/policy/debt_aid/downloads/bp113_credibility_crunch.pdf.

54   The World Bank, *Education for All (EFA)*, http://web.worldbank.org/WBSITE/EXTERNAL/TOPICS/EXTEDUCATION/0,contentMDK:20374062~menuPK:540090~pagePK:148956~piPK:216618~theSitePK:282386,00.html (last visited Jan. 18, 2013).

55   UN, Strengthening Efforts, *supra* note 6, at 46 (recommending that States should develop some projects to improve education. Projects includes "building school blocks, providing free tuition at the primary level, provision of meals to children at the basic level (school feeding program) and other efforts aimed at encouraging teachers to stay in rural communities").

56   UNESCO, *Primary Education*, http://portal.unesco.org/education/en/ev.php-URL_ID=30870&URL_DO=DO_TOPIC&URL_SECTION=201.html (last visited Jan. 18, 2013).

57   United Nations Millennium Declaration, *supra* note 17 (noting that both boys and girls will have to complete a full course of primary schooling to have equal access to all levels of education).

her children's morals and character. Well-educated women are more likely to have virtuous morals and character which will influence their children in a more positive way.

Secondary and higher education is one of the key driving forces for modernization and national development. Thus governments should also support and strengthen their secondary and higher education. However, building an education system, especially a higher education system, is not easy. Developing countries face many challenges. First, most developed countries have been building and promoting their higher education systems for decades or even centuries. Now, developing nations are catching up, and they have to do so within a very short period of time.[58] Second, higher education is extremely expensive. It includes the cost of buildings, libraries, network systems, faculty and staff, everyday utilities, and many more expenses. Many developing countries are already financially disabled. To find more money to support higher education is extraordinarily difficult.

Practical skills training is another significant component of modernization strategies. It ensures people, particularly less-educated young populations, acquire necessary skills within a short period of time so that they have more opportunities when entering the labor market. Developing countries should prioritize skills training, making it available to people who want to master a new skill or improve their current skill levels.

To summarize, education is a powerful tool in ending poverty. Governments should increase their budget level in financing education at all levels. Building more schools and improving teaching facilities are necessary for education improvement. However, spending all the money on infrastructure development alone will not radically increase student achievement. The improvement of educational quality and learning outcomes is equally important. A World Bank report shows that close to half of the students in school have not reached the grade of schooling they are supposed to; many teachers in developing countries lack the qualifications to teach.[59] Therefore, in addition to investment in "hardware improvement,"[60] more emphasis should be put on training qualified teachers that can effectively deliver knowledge to the students, which is "software improvement."[61]

To build and further improve national capacity, other essential public services must be provided as well. Substantial amounts of capital must be expended on health care systems, making medical treatment affordable to all people, regardless of whether they are rich or poor. More health facilities, and, in particular, health

---

58 Steve Maharey, Higher Education: Challenges for Developing Countries (2011), *available at* http://www.cedol.org/wp-content/uploads/2012/02/Steve-Maharey-article.pdf (last visited Jan. 18, 2013).

59 The World Bank, *supra* note 54.

60 Hardware improvement refers to education-related infrastructure development, such as school buildings, computers, and lab equipment.

61 Software improvement refers to human-based knowledge improvement, for instance, teacher training.

facilities in rural communities need to be built. National immunization and disease control systems need to be established and improved. More qualified doctors and nurses need to be trained.[62] Governments are able to do many beneficial things like initiate public works and programs that are hard for individuals to do. In addition to affordable health care, governments should also promote social security programs, create more job opportunities for local people, and provide loans for local people to start small businesses, and so on.

Issues?

Capacity building strategies vary from country to country. All in all, the strategies must meet the country's actual development needs. There are various capacity building strategies that can make positive changes. However, the issue for most poor developing countries is not whether they want to develop, but how to develop with limited resources. What can they do if they are on a tight budget and have little to spend?

A government needs to spend money wisely. Strategic planning is always important as it provides the framework for informed decision making. An effective development plan requires government to consider all aspects of its development needs, categorize these needs, and then prioritize the ones that are critical to promote social security and sustainable development. Undeniably, development plans are expensive. Substantial amounts of money are needed to implement these plans. International aid and foreign investment play an important role in assisting developing countries to achieve development goals. In an effort to receive more foreign capital, developing countries must improve their governance, creating a favorable business environment.

---

62 USAID, *Capacity   Building   and   Health   Systems   Strengthening*, http://www.healthsystems2020.org/section/where_we_work/senegal/capacitybuilding (last visited Feb. 28, 2013).

Chapter 4

Causes of the Current Food Insecurity and Potential Solutions: Human Overpopulation

Current and Future Population Situations and their Impact on Food Security

Overpopulation is a term that refers to "the condition of having a population so dense as to cause environmental deterioration, an impaired quality of life, or a population crash."[1] Current human population has exceeded the carrying capacity that the earth can sustain. Rising carbon dioxide levels, global warming, pollution, and fresh water shortage are severe environmental problems aggravated by overpopulation. Resources on the earth are finite while human population continues growing. The levels of consumption of natural resources are much faster than the rate of regeneration. World population has increased from one billion in 1800[2] to seven billion as of October 31, 2011.[3] It will continue to grow in the next few decades. The earth used to feed one billion people but now has to feed seven billion, and will have to feed even more in the future. The US Census Bureau estimates that the world population will be over nine billion by 2050.[4] Overpopulation contributes to world hunger, especially in many poor developing countries that have more population than they can feed.[5]

Although the current and future population growth rate is not as high as it was during the 1960s and the 2000s, the UN predicts that population growth will not turn to a negative rate until 2040–2045.[6] Population growth rates are especially high

---

1 *Overpopulation Definition*, MERRIAM-WEBSTER DICTIONARY, http://www.merriam-webster.com/dictionary/overpopulation (last visited Feb. 28, 2013).

2 John Bongaarts, *Population Policy Options in the Developing World*, SCIENCE, Feb. 11, 1994, at 771.

3 UN, *As World Passes 7 Billion Milestone, UN Urges Action to Meet Key Challenges*, UN NEWS CENTER (October 31, 2011), http://www.un.org/apps/news/story.asp?NewsID=40257&Cr=population&Cr1=.

4 US Census Bureau, *International Data Base*, http://www.census.gov/population/international/data/idb/worldpopgraph.php (last updated June 2011).

5 Even in 1986, William L. Church saw the population growth trend. He states that "[f]uture worldwide population increases may be substantial. Current growth rates are high, especially in the Less Developed Countries. Few demographers expect growth rates to decrease dramatically in the near future." *See* William L. Church, *Farmland Conversion: The View from 1986*, 1986 U. ILL. L. REV. 521, 524 (1986).

6 *See infra* Appendix 2.

in developing countries. Figure 4.1 shows the population growth in developing countries and developed countries, respectively. It is obvious that in the next 40 years, population growth is mainly concentrated in developing countries.[7]

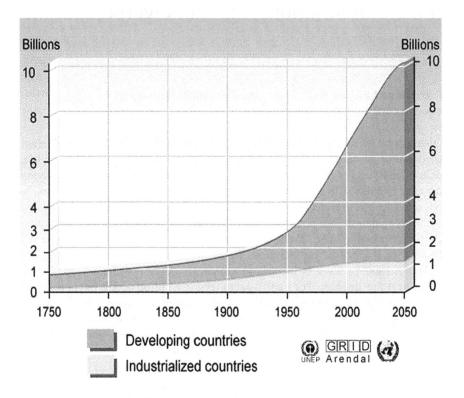

Figure 4.1 World population development
Source: Philippe Rekacewicz, UNEP/GRID-Arendal 2005.[8]

---

7   *See infra* Appendix 2.
8   Philippe Rekacewicz, UNEP/GRID-Arendal, *World Population Development* (2005), http://www.grida.no/graphicslib/detail/world-population-development_29db#.

Research shows that the sustainable level of global population is 2.1 births per woman.[9] The current world fertility rate is about 3.1.[10] Thus, the world has no problem in meeting the sustainable level of global population. However, the rates vary from region to region. Appendix 4 shows that most developed countries' fertility rates range from 1.5 to 2, which is far below the sustainable rate of 2.1. For instance, the US rate is about 1.9–2; the UK rate is about 1.7–1.8. On the contrary, most developing countries have much higher fertility rates than developed countries. In particular, the fertility rates of African countries are higher, ranging from 4 to 7.[11] Some Asian countries' rates are even as high as 8, such as Afghanistan.[12]

Appendix 2 "World Population Growth Rate" and Appendix 4 "Fertility Rates" together illustrate the fact that millions of people per year are added to the world's population base but that birth rates are generally decreasing. As a result, the total population is expected to decrease eventually. However, due to the large base of world population, the decrease will not occur any time soon, but may happen in decades or half of a century.

Current and future growth in the world's population primarily occurs in the less and least developed countries in Africa, Asia, and Latin America. The world's less and least developed countries have already been economically disabled, and associated with overpopulation, it will be more difficult for these countries to feed their people if no meaningful population control methods are implemented. The increasing population in many developing countries puts a strain on the food supply to its people. In particular, in Sub-Saharan Africa, populations are growing so rapidly that food production is unable to keep pace with the expanding local population growth rate.[13] To reduce hunger and malnutrition in these overpopulated developing countries, enforceable population control methods are advised. However, these population control methods must not violate human rights, such as women's reproductive rights.

What Can Governments do to Control Population?

Governments are able to keep population under control if they have good policies associated with effective enforcement mechanisms. Therefore, the overpopulated

---

9 David Crank, *The Population Bust*, 5 Unless the Lord Mag. 3 (Sept. 4, 2008), *available at* http://www.unlessthelordmagazine.com/articles/Population%20Bust.htm.

10 Terrence J. Sorg, *Global Hunger, A Doubling Population, and Environmental Degradation: Justifying Radical Changes in US Farm Policy*, 6 Ind. Int'l & Comp. L. Rev. 680, 686 (1996).

11 *See infra* Appendix 4.

12 *See infra* Appendix 4, Afghanistan.

13 Sorg, *supra* note 10, at 690.

developing countries' governments are encouraged to adopt appropriate methods to control population, but without violating basic human rights.

First, what governments should *not* do to control population must be emphasized. Coercive population control methods, such as forced sterilization and forced abortion, must be prohibited because of the violations of human rights, including women's reproductive rights and children's rights.[14] Even though coercive population control methods can effectively slow down rapid population growth in a very short time, it is against people's will, causing human rights abuses. China provides an example of these human rights violations. The One Child Policy[15] keeps China's booming population under control. It stimulated China's economic growth within a very short time period. However, involuntary contraception, forced sterilization, and abortion frequently occur in some regions of China, which seriously violate women's basic dignity and reproductive rights. Thus, governments that implement coercive population control must abolish such inhumane methods. They should seek other feasible alternatives that will keep population under control without violating people's human rights.

Second, governments are advised to focus on the advocacy of birth control. They should work with mass media, stressing the importance of population control and its relationship with poverty and hunger reduction. Dedicated funding should be available for education programs.[16] These programs should inform people about current population situations, and why birth control is necessary for sustainable economic, social, and cultural development. They should also educate people on contraception measures, and help people to understand their personal sexuality so that they can make informed decisions on whether they want a pregnancy. Special education must be provided to children, juveniles, and people living in rural areas. For children and juveniles, they must be taught with knowledge regarding the risks associated with irresponsible sexual behavior, and, in order to

---

14   Reproductive rights are a well-recognized human right. *See* Ying Chen, *China's One Child Policy and Its Violations of Women's and Children's Rights*, 22 N.Y. INT'L L. REV. 1 (2009) (discussing the One Child Policy implemented in China with the attempt to control rapid population growth and its violations of women's and children's rights).

15   In order to promote economic development and eliminate poverty, the Chinese government is devoted to removing the burden of overpopulation and, therefore, the One Child Policy was developed. The One Child Policy limits Ethnic Han Chinese couples living in urban places to having only one child. However, citizens living in rural areas and 55 ethnic minorities are not subject to the policy. In most rural areas, if the first child is female or disabled, upon application and approval by the relevant family planning departments, couples are allowed to have another child. The second child is subject to a birth spacing requirement, which is usually three or four years. Even though there is no law on paper allowing forced abortions, sterilization and some other forced methods to carry out this policy, in practice, many abuses of human rights cases occurred in China. *See Id.*, at 407.

16   Examples of education programs include Population Education program and Sexuality Education program. *See* EDMUND H. KELLOGG & JAN STEPAN, THE WORLD'S LAWS AND PRACTICES ON POPULATION AND SEXUALITY EDUCATION 7 (1975).

prevent unwanted pregnancies, they must also be taught birth control methods. With respect to the people living in rural areas, they generally lack knowledge on birth control. Therefore, it is important that governments pay special attention to rural populations, and promote appropriate education programs that are acceptable on the basis of their knowledge levels.

Third, men's responsibility in birth control has been ignored in most instances. It must be addressed. In general, due to traditional, religious, or other factors, birth control is regarded as women's "exclusive" duty. However, the use of contraception is not a female's personal affair. Men have the same rights and duties as women in determining the size and spacing of their family. Thus, it is necessary to encourage men to undertake reproductive responsibility. Mass media plays an important role in changing people's ideas on specific issues. Governments may use mass media as tools to make such change.

However, in many poor developing countries, although overpopulation has already been a big challenge to economic growth and human development, people still believe they need more children because of a high infant mortality rate and lack of social insurance to take care of parents in old age.

The infant mortality rate (IMR) refers to the number of deaths of infants under one year of age per thousand live births.[17] Table 4.1[18] shows the infant mortality rates from 1950 to 2010 in developed, less developed, and least developed countries, respectively.

The overall trend in IMR is decreasing globally. However, developing countries, especially least developed countries, have a much higher infant mortality rate than developed countries. It is understandable that people in poor developing countries may want more children because there is a higher possibility than in developed countries that their children may die at an early age. Infant mortality rate is often seen as an indicator of a population's health status because it is associated with the availability of health services in a country.[19] The availability of health services is largely determined by the economic situation in a country. Thus, this returns to the issues of national capacity building and essential public services as previously discussed.

When people grow older, they will gradually lose the ability to work and earn a living. They will need financial support and proper health care. In developed countries, governments usually have fairly comprehensive social welfare systems ensuring that older members of the population can maintain a basic quality of life. However, in many developing countries, poor governments lack the ability to do so. Thus, the elderly in poor developing countries have to take care of themselves. As they cannot rely on the government and have to deal the situation

---

17   D.D. Reidpath & P. Allotey, *Theory and Methods, Infant Mortality Rate as an Indicator of Population Health*, 57 J. EPIDEMIOLOGY & COMMUNITY HEALTH 344 (2003).

18   UN Depart. of Econ. & Social Affairs, World Population Prospects: The 2010—Infant Mortality Rate, UN Doc. POP/DB/WPP/Rev.2010/01/F06–1 (2011).

19   Reidpath & Allotey, *supra* note 17.

Table 4.1 World population prospects (2010 revision)—infant mortality rate

Major area, region and country	Infant mortality rate for both sexes combined (infant deaths per 1,000 live births)											
	1950–1955	1955–1960	1960–1965	1965–1970	1970–1975	1975–1980	1980–1985	1985–1990	1990–1995	1995–2000	2000–2005	2005–2010
WORLD	133	122	114	94	86	80	71	64	60	56	51	46
More developed regions	60	43	33	26	22	18	15	13	11	9	7	6
Less developed regions	151	140	130	105	96	89	79	71	66	62	56	50
Least developed countries	192	176	164	152	150	136	125	116	109	100	89	80
Less developed regions, excluding least developed countries	145	134	125	98	86	80	70	62	56	52	46	41
Major area, region and country	1950–1955	1955–1960	1960–1965	1965–1970	1970–1975	1975–1980	1980–1985	1985–1990	1990–1995	1995–2000	2000–2005	2005–2010
Less developed regions, excluding China	165	149	135	123	113	101	90	81	74	69	61	55

Source: The United Nations is the author of the original materials (UN Depart. of Econ. & Social Affairs 2011).

by themselves, the majority depend on their children. Children are the main source of support for parents in old age. Not surprisingly, then, it is very common that in many developing countries people believe, the more children, the more guarantee of support.

The idea that more children are needed in order to take care of parents in old age can only be changed by improving public health care and social welfare. As discussed previously, social welfare is another significant component of national capacity building. Governments should make affordable health care accessible to all people. Social security should also be provided so that people will not worry about everyday life in old age. Such government efforts will help remove one of the significant root causes of overpopulation.

Chapter 5

Causes of the Current Food Insecurity and Potential Solutions: Lack of Farmland and Expansion of the Biofuel Industry

What Causes Cropland Depletion?

Sustainable access to farmland is important for the millions of people in rural areas who live on agriculture. It enables farmers to produce food they need for self-consumption and for trade. In the meantime, it improves sustainable farming, as farmers will be more responsible in the use of soils and water resources if they have sustainable access to farmland.

However, continuing population growth and urbanization lead to the conversion of agricultural land for other uses. While the population is growing, the amount of available farmland per capita is decreasing dramatically. According to a report by the Badische Anilin- und Soda-Fabrik (BASF), farmland shrank from more than 4,000m² per capita in 1960 to 2,200m² per capita in 2005. It is estimated to drop to about 1,800m² per capita by 2030.[1]

Large amounts of farmland have been or are being lost to the residential, commercial, industrial, and transportation pressure that attend metropolitan expansion.[2] Pollution, drought, desertification, soil erosion, and energy production also result in the loss of cropland.[3] The loss of farmland substantially decreases global food production, intensifying world hunger and malnutrition.

In the past few decades, the desire to reduce the consumption of fossil fuels and to promote energy independence, as well as growing concerns in regards to global environmental protection, has triggered the world's great interest in developing

---

1 BASF, CROP PROTECTION, THAT'S FOR SURE, *available at* http://www.agro.basf. com/agr/AP-Internet/en/function/conversions:/publish/upload/competences/1_BASF_jg_ innen_24s_engl_new_V2.pdf (last visited Jan. 24, 2013).

2 William L. Church, *Farmland Conversion: The View from 1986*, 1986 U. ILL. L. REV. 521, 536 (1986).

3 *Id.* at 535. It is believed that several factors may deplete cropland. Major problems include the use of cropland for energy production, losses due to pollution and soil erosion, and losses due to pollution and past irrigation practices and water supply reductions. *Id.*

and expanding renewable energy programs.[4] With the hope of promoting secure supplies of environmentally friendly energy, biofuel has become one of the fastest growing industries in many countries, not only in developed countries, such as the US and many European countries, but also in developing countries that are striving to power their growing economies. The expansion of the biofuel industry leads to the shift of planted acreages. Large amounts of farmland are converted for biofuel purposes. Biofuels compete with food for farmland, and push up food prices and, therefore, impose a severe threat to global food security.

Protect Limited Farmland

Discipline Large-scale Land Acquisitions or Lease for Non-agricultural Uses

To slow down farmland conversion and to protect agricultural activities, governments must take the lead. Relevant laws and effective implementation methods should be available to regulate land use and protect diminishing farmland. In particular, large-scale land acquisition or lease for non-agricultural uses should be closely monitored. Unless necessary, they should be strictly prohibited. Many people may think large-scale land acquisition or lease is often seen in developed countries but not an issue in poor developing countries. However, this has happened in developing countries, and has become a widely discussed topic.

Over the past few years, large amounts of farmland that were traditionally used by local farmers were leased or sold to foreign governments and private investors, and this is becoming increasingly common in many developing countries. A recent report by Dr Olivier De Schutter, UN Special Rapporteur on the Right to Food, shows that "between 15 and 20 million hectares of farmland in developing countries, have been subject to transactions or negotiations involving foreign investors since 2006."[5] It is difficult to obtain the data on how exactly these farmlands are used. However, according to De Schutter, some farmlands are used to build factories; some are left idle, as cash-rich governments and private investors wait for future rises in farmland prices; a considerable amount of farmland is used by developed countries to grow biofuels.[6] Large-scale land acquisition or lease for non-agricultural uses has disturbed agricultural production in developing

---

4 Kaylan Lytle, *Driving the Market: The Effects on the United States Ethanol Industry if the Foreign Ethanol Tariff is Lifted*, 28 ENERGY L.J. 693, 697 (2007). ("The rising awareness of climate change and the growing concern about reliance on Middle Eastern oil supplies have triggered renewed interest in the development of ethanol as a fuel source").

5 OLIVIER DE SCHUTTER, LARGE-SCALE LAND ACQUISITIONS AND LEASES: A SET OF CORE PRINCIPLES AND MEASURES TO ADDRESS THE HUMAN RIGHTS CHALLENGE (June 11, 2009), *available at* http://www.oecd.org/site/swacmali2010/44031283.pdf.

6 *Id.*

countries and, therefore, governments must take it seriously. They should make strategic land use plans to avoid falling into the trap of selling farmland for money.

Farmland Preservation Programs

Governments should also preserve farmland to promote sustainable farming practices. By purchasing the development rights, preserved farmland will be protected from development or improvement for any purpose other than agricultural production. Preservation programs help maintain a regulatory environment that enables farmers to conduct agricultural activities in a more sustainable way.

Farmland preservation programs can be carried out in different forms. They can be carried out in the form of political orders. They can also be carried out in the form of financial incentives, such as providing preferential tax incentives, and implementing special purchase programs.[7] For example, US programs are voluntary. Farmers are paid in per-acre amounts that represent the difference between the appraised fair market value of their land, and the value of that land for agriculture. In most cases, governments preserve farmland through financial incentives rather than political orders to avoid potential conflicts.

Regardless of the form, preserved farmland must be distributed in different regions all over the country so that food supply will be substantially localized. The US has well-managed farmland preservation programs that date back to the 1980s. Till now, 1.4 million acres of farmland across the US has been preserved by top state programs.[8] Although a large amount of farmland is in the hands of small groups of rich farmers, the benefits of US farmland preservation programs are still incredibly impressive, if compared to other countries. Farmland is well protected. Fresh and healthy local food is provided to local people at a reasonable price.

Pollution Control

Pollution poses serious threats to agricultural activities. It reduces the soil's productive capacity leading to depressed yields in the longer term. Environmental protection laws and policies associated with efficient enforcement and monitor mechanisms must be available in order to control existing pollution, and to prevent further pollution. Farmers should be encouraged to make changes in farming management for sustainable agriculture. Furthermore, local environments that may contaminate farmland needs to be closely monitored. Relevant government departments must take immediate action to stop and control pollution that may result in farmland loss.

---

7   Church, *supra* note 2, at 544.

8   Deborah Bowers, *Survey Shows 1.4 million Acres Preserved by Top State Programs*, FARMLAND PRESERVATION RPT. (November 2012), http://www.farmlandpreservationreport. com/.

Biofuel and its Impact on Food Security

The world has been debating biofuel issues—the pros and cons—from different perspectives. On the one hand, more farmland is used for biofuel purposes, which severely impairs global food security. On the other hand, biofuel satisfies energy needs and reduces carbon emissions. It also has many other positive effects.

What is Biofuel?

Biofuel is a renewable substitute for fossil fuel, and is produced from organic matter instead of fossil fuels.[9] The sources of biofuels are forest and agricultural products and wastes, such as sugarcane, corn, oilseeds and wheat; animal waste, such as animal fats; and municipal solid waste; and other renewable resources.[10]

Biodiesel and ethanol fuel are two of the principal biofuels. Biodiesel refers to a diesel fuel replacement made from agricultural fats and oils. It must meet a specific commercial fuel definition and specification. Ethanol fuel is a clean burning renewable fuel manufactured from feedstocks. Most ethanol is produced from corn and sugarcane, but any crop that contains abundant sugars can be used to produce ethanol. Grain-based ethanol and cellulosic ethanol are two different types of fuel ethanol.

Ethanol and biodiesel contain no petroleum, but they can be blended at a certain percentage with gasoline and petroleum diesel respectively for use in unmodified internal combustion engines or fuel diesel vehicles.[11] Biofuel is easy to use, and is biodegradable, nontoxic, and essentially sulfur free.[12]

Why the Biofuel Industry Has Developed So Quickly

Increasing global demand has contributed to rising oil prices. The economy of a country that heavily relies on imported oil can be seriously undermined by any oil price spikes. Most problematically, such price spikes will become more frequent due to the fact that the whole world is competing for the remaining oil supply.

The dependence on foreign oil can weaken a country's national security because an oil importer basically ties itself to oil exporters. Unfortunately, many oil exporting countries are politically unstable or undemocratic, such as many countries in the Middle East and North African region. Any chaos in oil exporting

---

9   Kelsey Jae Nunez, *Gridlock on the Road to Renewable Energy Development: A Discussion About the Opportunities and Risks Presented by the Modernization Requirements of the Electricity Transmission Network*, 1 J. Bus. Entrepreneurship & L. 137, 149 (2007).

10   *Id.*

11   John Herbig, *Technical and Legal Considerations for Bio-fuel*, 2 Envt'l & Energy L. & Pol'y J. 343 (2008).

12   Nat'l Biodiesel Bd., *Biodiesel Basics*, Biodiesel.org, http:// www.biodiesel.org/ resources/biodiesel_basics/ (last visited Feb. 28, 2013).

countries could result in economic and social instability in oil importing countries. Oil also increases the risk of armed conflicts in political hotspots in the world.

Many countries have started to worry about their national security and how to achieve energy independence. One of the best alternatives is to produce their own energy and achieve self-sufficiency. Considering that petroleum and coal are exhaustible resources, and many countries do not have enough deposits within their territory, the only option left for them is to develop renewable energy. Promoting renewable energy can significantly reduce the need for imported foreign oil and, therefore, strengthen national security. Moreover, given the fact that trade deficits are primarily caused by oil imports in many oil importing countries, energy independence will decrease the deficit and stimulate economic development in all aspects.[13]

The earth is getting warmer due to greenhouse gases emitted when oil burns. The direct result of global warming is increasing temperatures and the melting of the polar ice caps. Series of global catastrophes, such as floods, droughts, extreme weather, and other various climate crises, occur more frequently. It is believed that a biofuel program, as a solution to the current oil crisis, will also help solve the problems of global warming and climate change.[14]

Biofuel presents significant environmental benefits over traditional fossil fuel. First, biofuels are produced from a renewable source, such as corn, sugarcane, and animal waste, rather than exhaustible energy. The use of renewable sources to produce energy largely reduces the consumption of exhaustible fossil fuel. Second, scientific research has proven that biofuel can reduce carbon emissions.[15] In the US, biodiesel has passed the Clean Air Act testing requirements. A recent study by the US Department of Energy and USDA shows that carbon dioxide emissions from biodiesel are 78 percent lower than emissions from regular diesel.[16] Scientific reports also reveal that the exhaust emitted by biodiesel is less harmful to humans than those given off by traditional diesel.[17]

---

13 Raci Oriona Spaulding, *Fuel from Vegetables? A Modern Approach to Global Climate Change*, 13 Transnat'l L. & Contemp. Probs. 277, 293–94 (2003) (stating that about half of the US trade deficit is caused by oil imports, energy independence would decrease the trade deficit, and thereby stimulate development of the US economy).

14 Oxfam, Another Inconvenient Truth: How Biofuel Policies are Deepening Poverty and Accelerating Climate Change (June 2008), *available at* http://www.oxfam.org.uk/resources/policy/climate_change/downloads/bp114_inconvenient_truth.pdf. ("Ethanol and biodiesel will allow us to continue our love affair with the internal combustion engine, while simultaneously reducing our greenhouse gas (GHG) emissions"). *Id.*

15 Spaulding, *supra* note 13, at 292 (stating that both ethanol and biodiesel have been shown to reduce carbon emissions).

16 *Id.*

17 *Id.*

The Potential Negative Effects of Biofuel

Food vs. fuel

The expansion of biofuel programs decreases the dependence on imported oil. It also presents economic, national security, and environmental benefits. However, biofuel competes with food for farmland, and it pushes up food prices, hurting the world's poor worst of all. The expansion of the biofuel industry imposes a severe threat to global food security, and is creating a new issue—food crisis.

Corn and soybean are the most important feedstocks to produce biofuels. As more countries pass laws and regulations mandating the greater use of non-fossil fuels, the demand for biofuel increases. This leads to a higher consumption of corn and soybean that traditionally used in the food and livestock sectors. Large amounts of maize, sugarcane, and vegetable oil seeds are also used to make biofuels.[18] According to a report by the US Department of Agriculture Food and Agricultural Policy Research Institute, globally, grain for biofuel uses increased from 1 percent of total grain consumption in 2000 to 6 percent in 2010. This number is still growing with the increasing demand for biofuel.[19]

The percentage of food crops used for biofuel purposes is much higher in developed countries. For example, in the US, about half of the increase in food crop consumption is not consumed by human beings or livestock but is attributable to the rapid increase in the use of US corn for biofuels, according to the International Monetary Fund (IMF).[20]

Using food crops as the major source for biofuel leads to a rapid increase in food prices and, therefore, it intensifies world hunger and malnutrition. Figure 5.1 shows biofuel production from 1990 to 2011. If compared to the data in Table 1.1 (Annual real food price indices), it is obvious that food prices rose almost at the same pace as the increasing demand for global biofuel production in the past decade. Although food prices are also influenced by other factors, the changing trends of both are not a coincidence. According to a recent study conducted by the

---

　　18　Jayati Ghosh, *The Global Food Crisis*, Int'l Dev. Econ. Assocs., http://www.networkideas.org/feathm/may2008/ft22_Food_Crisis.htm (last visited June 22, 2010) (explaining that the increasing demand for biofuel has resulted in significant shifts of agricultural output to fuel production, and noting that "[i]n 2006 the US diverted more than 20 percent of its maize production to the production of ethanol; Brazil used half of its sugar cane production to make biofuel, and the EU used the greater part of its vegetable oil seeds production to make biofuel").

　　19　US Dept. of Agric., Food and Agricultural Policy Research Institute. Elisabeth Rosenthal, *Rush to Use Crops as Fuel Raises Food Prices and Hunger Fears*, N.Y. Times, Apr. 6, 2011, at A1, *available at* http://www.nytimes.com/2011/04/07/science/earth/07cassava.html?_r=0.

　　20　James A. Duffield et al., *Ethanol Policy: Past, Present, and Future*, 53 S.D. L. Rev. 425, 451 (2008).

International Food Policy Research Institute (IFPRI), biofuel is estimated to count for 30 percent of the recent increase in global food prices.[21]

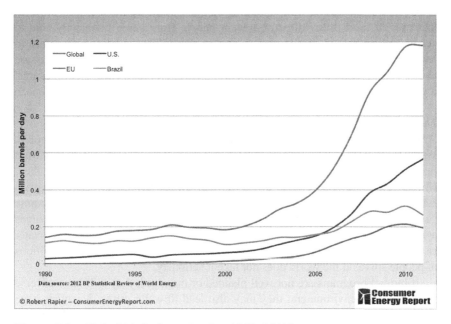

Figure 5.1   Global biofuel production 1990–2011[22]
Source: 2012 BP Statistical Review of World Energy.

The rapid expansion of the biofuel industry has also resulted in many changes in the agricultural economy. One of the significant changes is the shift of planted acreages in response to higher biofuel market prices.[23] This change reduces the plantation of non-biofuel crops, which also contributes to higher prices of competing crops. In the Philippines, the government has designated an area to be planted with biofuel crops that is equivalent to fully half of the area planted with rice, the mainstay of the Filipino's diet.[24] Biofuel crops compete for planting area

---

21   *Id.*

22   Robert Rapier, 2012 BP Statistical Review of World Energy, *available at* http://www.consumerenergyreport.com (last visited Jan, 20, 2013).

23   Duffield et al., *supra* note 20, at 443 ("Farmers have been responding to higher corn prices by increasing corn acreage, however, it has been at the expense of soybeans and other crops. High corn prices relative to soybeans caused soybean planted area to drop by 16 percent in 2007").

24   Peter Rosset, *Food Sovereignty and the Contemporary Food Crisis*, INT'L DEV. ECON. ASSOCS. (Jan. 2009), *available at* http://www.networkideas.org/news/jan2009/Peter_

with food crops. They reduce the available farmland for food production purposes. Furthermore, the rising crop price inevitably increases the feed cost for livestock, affecting the prices of meat and dairy products.

In sum, the expansion of biofuel programs drives up food prices. In turn, increases in food prices directly prevent people from being financially able to access sufficient food. While most people in developed countries may afford to pay slightly higher prices for food, or the governments of developed countries are able to provide adequate food aid for their people by implementing food programs, low-income, developing countries may find it more difficult to feed their people.

The water issue

Water, as another critical issue that affects everyone's life, has long been ignored. Water is an exhaustible resource like fossil fuel. However, it is different from fossil fuel. People can survive without fuel but not without water. So, then, why does the world care more about oil than water? Economic benefits explain everything. Governments see economic development as the priority, and economic development cannot go further if there are no or only limited energy resources available. However, many regions in the world have already suffered serious water issues, and the problem is spreading. Water shortage is a potential threat to billions of people's lives if the world does not take it seriously.

If biofuel programs are not well planned or managed, they will have adverse impacts on the environment; they may also lead to water crises. Scientists have done research on the possibility of catastrophic plant diseases that may be caused by biofuel monocultures. Their analysis is based on the Great Famine that happened in Ireland (also known as the "Irish Potato Famine") between 1845 and 1852 when nearly a quarter of the Irish population starved to death.[25] This famine was the result of eight years of ravaged potato crops. Scientists are worried that so many acres being used for growing corn—the main raw material for ethanol—may result in a famine like the one in Ireland. They further argue that even if famine does not happen in the contemporary world like it did in the nineteenth century, crop monoculture can also cause a series of environmental problems, such as the loss of soil fertility, extensive soil erosion, overuse of pesticides, and depletion of nutrient reserves.

The reliance on corn for both a food and an energy source may lead to drought because corn production requires large amounts of water, according to the National Research Council (NRC).[26] Food crops for biofuel production require

---

Rosset.pdf.

25   Mark Murphey Henry et al., *A Call to Farms: Diversify the Fuel Supply*, 53 S.D. L. Rev. 515, 522 (2008).

26   *Id.* The National Research Council (NRC) report indicates that corn ethanol may adversely affect water supply. It states that "[w]ith the increase in corn prices and subsidies, there is a continued westward trend of corn production into drier climates that may impact water availability." *Id.*

more herbicides, insecticides, and fertilizers. These chemical inputs become residue in well water, polluting water supplies and creating soil erosion. Ethanol itself also leaks into ground water, causing harm to our drinking supply.[27] Thus, the opponents of biofuel programs question if biofuel is truly a renewable fuel when water, as a non-renewable natural resource, is being lost to produce biofuel crops.

Other concerns regarding biofuel development
In addition to food security and environmental concerns, biofuel is criticized for undesirable social consequences. It presents human rights challenges. Under international law, indigenous people are granted the right to access their land, and any shift in land use may only take place with "the free, prior and informed consent of the indigenous peoples concerned and after agreement on just and fair compensation and, where possible, with the option of return."[28]

Expanding the biofuel industry encourages governments and private investors to go to developing countries to buy or lease farmland and grow biofuel crops. This shift in land use may threaten an indigenous people's rights if land acquisition is implemented without an indigenous community's consent. For example, in Indonesia, many cases show that indigenous people's land rights were violated. The increasing demand for palm oil as a source for biofuel doubled the land being converted to palm oil plantation in the last decade.[29] Millions of hectares of forests were bought by foreign investors and converted for growing palm trees. These shifts in land use were mostly implemented without considering indigenous people's interests or even against their will. In Indonesia, the large expansion of

---

27 Tad W. Patzek, *Ethanol from Corn: Clean Renewable Fuel for the Future, or Drain on Our Resources and Pockets*, 7 ENV'T. DEV. & SUSTAINABILITY 319, 320–21 (2005) (describing that there has been over 400,000 reports of ethanol leaks in the last few decades). *Id.*

28 Article 8 para. 2 (b) of the United Nations Declaration on the Rights of Indigenous Peoples states that, "States shall provide effective mechanisms for prevention of, and redress for, any action which has the aim of effect of dispossessing indigenous peoples of their lands, territories or resources." Under Article 10, indigenous people "are guaranteed the right to not be forcibly removed from their lands or territories, and no relocation shall take place without their free, prior and informed consent and after agreement on just and fair compensation and, where possible, with the option of return." Articles 25 and 26 recognize that indigenous people "have the right to own, use, develop and control these lands." "States must therefore give legal recognition and protection to these lands, territories and resources, with due respect to the customs, traditions and land tenure systems of the indigenous peoples concerned." The United Nations Declaration on the Rights of Indigenous Peoples, G.A. Res. 61/295 (Sept. 13, 2007).

29 Elizabeth Rosenthal, *Once a Dream Fuel, Palm Oil May Be an Eco-Nightmare*, N.Y. TIMES, Jan. 31, 2007, *available at* http:// www.nytimes.com/2007/01/31/business/ worldbusiness/31biofuel.html? pagewanted=2&sq=nyt.

biofuel plantations threatens the well-being and livelihoods of 60 to 90 million indigenous people.[30]

The Strategic Development of Biofuel Programs: Diversification of Biofuel Sources

As previously mentioned, well-planned and managed biofuel programs can enhance a country's ability to achieve energy independence. They also protect a country's national security and economy from being affected by unstable foreign oil prices. However, when making a biofuel development plan, policymakers must ensure that biofuel programs do not impair people's sustainable access to adequate food. They should be fully integrated with other relevant policies on food security and poverty reduction. Governments with serious food issues are suggested to scale back their aggressive biofuel plans, and stop taking food out of their people's mouths.

Nevertheless, there is an alternative that enables governments to develop biofuel programs without worrying much about food security issues. Governments may consider, and in fact many countries have already been promoting, the option of diversification of biofuel sources.

Biofuel competes with food. Currently, the output of biofuels made from corns and soybeans is limited. They cannot take the place of gasoline and diesel. In order to achieve a larger percentage of fossil fuel replacement, other feedstocks are needed. Ethanol is primarily made from corn. However, not only corn but any crops that contain abundant sugars can serve as raw materials for ethanol production.[31] Similarly, biodiesel is primarily produced from soybeans and soybean oil, but it can also be made from renewable resources such as vegetable oil, canola oil, sunflower oil, cottonseed oil, animal fats, and recycled restaurant grease.[32]

Making biofuels from various renewable sources can substantially reduce the reliance on a single crop, and release the tension between food and fuel. A long-term sustainable renewable energy plan requires the shift from exclusive feedstocks, such as corn, soybean, and other food crops, to a broader base of raw materials.

The localization of raw materials for biofuel
To make it widely adaptable in different regions, biofuel production is encouraged to use local raw materials because this has more advantages over producing biofuel

---

30　David Adam, *To Bio or Not to Bio: Are "Green" Fuels Really Good for the Earth?*, GUARDIAN, Jan. 26, 2008, *available at* http:// www.guardian.co.uk/environment/2008/feb/11/biofuels.energy (noting that the shift in land use threatens the well-being and livelihoods of 60 to 90 million indigenous people in Indonesia).

31　Lytle, *supra* note 4, at 693.

32　Margaret J. Jennings, *Bioenergy: Fueling the Future*, 12 DRAKE J. AGRIC. L. 205, 220 (2007).

exclusively from corn and soybeans. Scientific research has proven that using native species that vary from region to region lowers the risks that crop disease or adverse weather affecting a single crop will destroy an entire year's production of biofuel. It causes less soil erosion than converting large acres of farmland into corn, soybean, or other biofuel crop plantations. The use of chemical inputs will also be reduced because local plants are more readily adapted to local environmental conditions.[33] From an economic perspective, the local production of raw materials for biofuels also reduces transportation, storage, and other relevant costs.

Consequently, identifying potential biofuel sources individualized to each region is of great importance to promote the diversification of biofuel sources. Different countries have different situations. Land availability, climate conditions, and agricultural history vary from region to region. The biofuel programs in the US and China are examined below to learn what local feedstocks they can use, and what problems they encounter in producing biofuels. This examination, in turn, may inspire interested countries to think about how they can take advantage of their local raw materials for biofuel production.

While the United States has taken the lead in developing and expanding the biofuel industry, it is also criticized for burning food to satisfy its domestic energy needs. Considering the severe global food situation, coupled with its great ambition to further expand biofuel programs, the United States has been looking for alternative raw materials for its biofuel production.

One of the possible alternatives that have been identified in the US is switch grass. Switch grass is extraordinarily drought resistant, and requires fewer chemical inputs.[34] It is high in the structural components cellulose and hemicellulose.[35] Most importantly, it is highly productive compared to corn.[36] The Great Plains area is primarily covered by prairie regions, and switch grass is keenly adapted to the prairie.[37] Switch grass seems an ideal raw material for ethanol as it produces large amounts of cellulose. However, to make cellulosic ethanol, more steps are required to break down the sugar. Scientists are making efforts to make it more cost-effective, hoping that ethanol deriving from switch grass will be commercialized in the near future.

---

33 Henry et al., *supra* note 25, at 523 ("The production of biofuel using native plant species already well adapted to a given region reduces the need for fertilizer and reduces reliance upon a single crop").

34 *Id.* Noting that switch grass "requires very low water and fertilizer inputs yet it is capable of producing 150 percent more biomass per acre of ground than corn."

35 *Id.* at 525–26.

36 *Id.* at 523. It is also true that "[s]witchgrass is a perennial plant, meaning that it will grow for several years once established rather than having to be replanted each year." Switch grass "has the added benefit of being a dual-purpose crop, as cattle can graze switchgrass prior to harvest as did buffalo at one time." *Id.*

37 John Gartner, *Biomass Adds to Ethanol Debate*, WIRED (June 2, 2005), http://www. wired.com/science/planetearth/news/2005/06/67691.

Jatropha is an extremely hardy plant that can grow in arid areas where most plants would die. Some scientific research suggests that Jatropha is a potential feedstock for biodiesel production in southern states such as Arizona, Texas, New Mexico, Florida, Mississippi, and Louisiana.[38] This feature of Jatropha enables farmers to make full use of the land that is not suitable for traditional grain crops. However, using Jatropha as a biofuel source has its limitations.

Jatropha seeds, which can be used to produce biodiesel, are small. Each one is about twice the size of a coffee bean. There are only a few seeds in one fruit pod. Scientists are now selecting Jatropha plants that can produce more seeds, and they are trying to breed high-yielding varieties. However, to date, it still is not practical to use Jatropha as a main source for biofuel production, but perhaps in the future, when high-yielding varieties are available, Jatropha can be as productive as corn or soybean.

As one of the biggest biofuel producers and consumers in the world, China supports renewable energy development with the premise that biofuel programs must not impair Chinese people's sustainable access to sufficient food. How does China promote its biofuel programs and diversify its biofuel sources? China's National Development and Reform Commission (NDRC) functions as a department to "formulate and implement strategies of national economic and social development, annual plans, medium and long-term development plans."[39] In accordance with research conducted by the NDRC, northern China, southeastern China, and the middle region of China are recommended to use sweet sorghum, cassavas, and sweet potatoes as the raw materials for biofuel production.

However, the use of sweet sorghum, cassavas, and sweet potatoes in China has been very slow to develop because there is little commercial-scale infrastructure available compared to that for corn and soybean. To produce these crops on a large scale, several issues need to be resolved. First, farmers may not want to switch from a known crop to one that they are not familiar with. Second, new technology and new equipment are needed to produce these non-traditional biofuel crops. This requires large amounts of capital investment. And, third, a good harvest of sweet sorghum, cassavas, and sweet potatoes needs nutrients, fertile soil, and sufficient water, so it still may be an issue that biofuel feedstocks compete with food crops for farmland.

---

38 Feedstock Fact Sheet, BIODIESL.ORG, http://www.biodiesel.org/resources/ sustainability/pdfs/feedstockfactsheet.pdf (last visited Sept. 1, 2010). "Jatropha can grow in arid areas that are not suitable for traditional grain crops" and "there could be a potential market for growing Jatropha in portions of the United States." Dry southern states like Arizona, Texas, New Mexico, Florida, California, Alabama, Mississippi, and Louisiana can grow Jatropha and use it as raw material for biodiesel productions. *Id.*

39 National Development and Reform Commission of People's Republic of China, Main Functions of the NDRC, http://en.ndrc.gov.cn/mfndrc/default.htm (last visited Feb. 28, 2013).

Cellulosic biofuels

Almost all plant matter—such as agricultural forestry residues, industrial waste, municipal solid waste, trees, and grasses—produce cellulose, and can serve as raw material for biofuels.[40] Scientists believe that the desirable sources for biofuels in the future are these cellulosic feedstocks. However, this plan has obstacles.

Currently, the biggest obstacle to large-scale cellulosic biofuels development is technology, as previously mentioned in the US switch grass plan. Ethanol is mainly produced from corn because the distillation of ethanol from high-sugar grain is relatively inexpensive and straightforward. Cellulose's structural components contain hardly digestible structural polysaccharides which make them difficult to transform into simple sugars. Additional steps are required to break down complex molecules into smaller components.[41] Research sponsored by the US Department of Energy has developed advanced technologies that can "biochemically treat cellulosic biomass from forest residues, agricultural residues, and energy crops to break them down to their component sugars, which are then fermented to produce biofuels like ethanol."[42] However, these processes consume large amounts of energy and money. To date, cellulosic ethanol is not cost-effective, and has not yet been commercially produced. Research continues to be the key factor that drives cellulosic biofuel production towards becoming an economic reality.

Summary

There are various reasons why we should develop biofuel programs. But there is only one reason that stops us from doing so, or at least, makes us rethink our ambitious biofuel plans. This reason is the impacts biofuel programs may have on food production.

There are various potential substitutes for corn, soybean, and other food crops as the raw materials for biofuels, as scientific research indicates, but most of them are not practical. Cellulosic feedstocks, as the desirable sources for biofuels, are too expensive to be converted to biofuels due to technical obstacles. Other newly identified biofuel materials, such as sweet sorghum, cassavas, and sweet potatoes, still lack commercial-scale infrastructure, and are difficult to plant commercially. Some feedstocks are hardy plants that are extraordinarily drought resistant, and require fewer chemical inputs. But they are still plants, like any other plants. Even

---

40   Marie E. Walsh et al., *Agricultural Impacts of Biofuels Production*, 39 J. Agric. & Applied Econ. 365 (2007), available at http://purl.umn.edu/6514 ("[T]he vision of a future biobased industry includes the simultaneous production of biofuels, bioelectricity, and bioproducts that uses not only corn grain and soybean oil but also a host of cellulose feedstocks"). *Id.*

41   *See* Gartner, *supra* note 37 (noting that biofuel production requires enzymatic processes and "[c]ellulose is a more structurally complex substrate." To distill ethanol from cellulose needs additional steps due to its molecular composition).

42   Nunez, *supra* note 9, at 150.

if they can survive bad weather, droughts, or poor soil, they still need fertile soil and sufficient water to produce a good harvest. In other words, in the long term, they still compete for the same productive farmland as food crops. More farmland used for biofuels only means less food for human beings.

It is true that biofuels should be produced from crops do not compete with food. It is also important to diversify and localize raw materials for biofuel production. However, technical obstacles that prevent the use of non-food crops as the main sources for biofuels must be overcome first, though this does not seem like a goal that can be achieved within the next few years. More scientific research needs to be done in order to make biofuel a viable long-term alternative to conventional fossil fuels.

Chapter 6
Uneven Food Distribution and Distorted Agricultural Trade: An Overlooked Factor

Inadequate and Uneven Global Food Distribution: Distorted Agricultural Trade

As previously discussed, fast-developing agricultural technology improves productivity, making global agricultural outputs substantially exceed the need of the world's population. However, the world fails to reduce hunger. Current food insecurity is not caused by absolute food scarcity, but the consequences of ineffective global food distribution, which is the result of distorted international trade.

Great inequities exist between developed countries that have a surplus of food and many poor developing countries that do not have enough food. Developed countries extensively use trade-distorting measures to support their farmers, ensuring their domestic food supply. These support measures inevitably produce plenty of food surpluses. Developed countries need to find a market to dispose of their overproduction. Therefore, developing countries become their target. In recent years, developed countries have been significantly promoting biofuel programs so that they burn a large amount of food to fuel their economy. In the meantime, the rest of the food surpluses are sold or provided as aid to other countries. All the while, many poor developing countries do not have enough food. They struggle with hunger, malnutrition, and related economic, social, and political problems.

Developing countries' agricultural export is substantially disturbed by developed countries' subsidies and other trade barriers. There are two significant obstacles for developing countries' agricultural exports. First, food dumping by developed countries in the past few decades has substantially reduced agricultural productivity in developing countries. Cheaper imported food has forced farmers in developing countries to leave this industry or switch to grow other economic plants rather than food crops. Second, in recent years, the increasing use of food crops for other purposes has significantly reduced the availability of food being distributed to hungry people. Thus, the former factor is the consequence of the long history of distorted agricultural trade, and the latter contributes to the change of international agricultural trade rules.

If dumping is supposed to lower global food prices, which should be good for poor people, why are global food prices increasing and more poor people suffering from hunger and malnutrition? This is a result of the combination of the consequences of dumping in the past and new challenges posed by the increasing use of food for other purposes.

To start with, it is important to understand why developed countries spend lots of money to support agriculture but dump the surpluses on the global market at a lower price. This dumping is all about the importance of agriculture in ensuring a country's economic, social, and political stability. Agriculture has been the most sensitive topic and the most protected sector in international trade.[1] First, agriculture is fundamentally important for human survival, and the task of feeding their people has been the priority of governments throughout history. Second, agriculture plays a vital role in providing job opportunities to people in most countries of the world. Small farmers live on agriculture, and large farms hire workers to cultivate crops and take care of farm animals. Agriculture is the basis of the economic, social, and political stability of a nation. Therefore, governments, regardless of their financial ability, support their agriculture so that they can protect their country from being threatened by food insecurity. Rich countries are economically advantaged so they provide more support to their farmers. Poor countries are less capable, so they provide less support but as much as they can. However, in most cases, the support given to farmers by a poor country is minimal or close to nothing when compared to the significant support provided in rich developed countries.

Developed countries extensively use subsidies, tariffs, and other trade barriers to protect their farmers. Such government support encourages overproduction, resulting in large amounts of food surpluses in excess of domestic consumption.

In the past, in order to dispose of these food surpluses, developed countries had to look for an export market in developing countries. For a very long time, rich developed countries dumped their agricultural products at prices that were below the real market prices, and sometimes, even below the costs of the product itself.[2] Oxfam reported that "the US and EU account for about half of all wheat exports at prices 46 and 34 percent respectively below costs of production."[3] These subsidized agricultural commodities from rich developed countries were much more competitive in the global food market. The dumping of food surplus benefited farmers in developed countries as they received subsidies from their government regardless. It also made cheap affordable food available to many poor people in developing countries, even if only temporarily. In the long term, dumping temporarily depressed food prices, sending wrong signals to the world

---

1   Alan Charles Raul & Kevin J. Brosch, *Global Trade in Agricultural Products*, 510 PLI/COMM 229, 263 (1989). *See also* Cody A. Thacker, *Agricultural Trade Liberalization in the Doha Round: The Search for a Modalities Draft*, 33 GA. J. INT'L & COM. L. 721, 723 (2005).

2   David Fazzino, *The Meaning and Relevance of Food Security in the Context of Current Globalization Trends*, 19 J. LAND USE & ENVTL. L. 435, 440 (2004).

3   William K. Tabb, *The Global Food Crisis and What Has Capitalism to Do With It?*, INT'L DEV. ECON. ASSOCS. (2008), http://www.networkideas.org/feathm/jul2008/Global_Food_Crisis.pdf.

market.[4] Farmers in poor countries were unable to compete with these below-cost subsidized products from rich developed countries.[5] They were forced to leave their farmland or they had to grow economic plants instead of highly competitive food crops. Consequently, it is not a surprise that many developing countries' agricultural productivity has been substantially undermined since then. Lack of rules to discipline agriculture subsidies, tariffs, and other barriers that prevent trade liberalization are to blame for this result. Developed countries have been the dominant force in international trade. Due to the importance of agriculture, they are not willing to regulate international trade rules in agriculture so that they can protect their agriculture without even thinking about any international obligations.

In recent years, developed countries gradually shifted their agricultural policies. More food surpluses are now used to make biofuels to meet domestic energy needs or they are sold or provided as aid to targeted countries which may help seller/donor governments achieve certain political or economic goals. For example, in 1994, the US agreed to provide food aid to North Korea on the condition that North Korea give up its nuclear tests. Food has become the bargaining chip on many occasions. Available food surpluses that can be distributed to developing countries are significantly reduced, and global food prices rise dramatically.

When food prices go up, developing countries realize the importance of growing their own food. Unfortunately, this becomes more difficult because their agricultural productivity has already been severely damaged by the cheap food dumped by developed countries for decades.

It is unlikely that purchasing food from the global market is an ideal option. People in poor developing countries are economically disadvantaged, and they do not have enough foreign currency to purchase food from the global market. Many developing countries depend on, or at least used to depend on, agricultural commodities as their main export earnings. Now, however, many of them have lost their comparative advantage in agricultural export because of the dumping by developed countries.

Distorted agricultural trade has also resulted in single agricultural commodity export in developing countries. As mentioned above, cheap subsidized food from developed countries has made farmers in developing countries leave the industry or switch to grow economic plants. Some of the countries, particularly tropical developing countries, have fallen into the trap of single agricultural commodity export. As an FAO report states, "[a] prominent feature of agricultural commodity exports in many developing countries is that relatively few commodities

---

4   Stacey Willemsen Person, *International Trade: Pushing United States Agriculture toward a Greener Future?*, 17 Geo. Int'l Envtl. L. Rev. 307 (2005).

5   For example, Mexican farmers are unable to compete with corn that is imported from the US at 30 percent below the cost of production. Kristin Dawkins, World Trade Org. Cancun Series Paper No. 5: The TRIPS Agreement: Who owns and controls knowledge and resources? (2003), *available at* http://www.iatp.org.

account for a large share of total export earnings."[6] High dependence on a single agricultural commodity makes developing countries' exports very vulnerable. Any crop or market failure would result in a substantial decrease in export revenues. Even worse, subsidies, tariffs, and other trade barriers adopted by developed countries also restrict developing countries' access to the global market. Under the circumstances when a single agricultural commodity can determine a country's export revenues or even a country's economy, it is unfortunate that poverty remains an unsolved issue, and people still cannot afford to purchase food.

Distorted Agricultural Trade: Subsidies

Agricultural subsidy is government support to "private agricultural industries, businesses, or individuals in order to supplement their income."[7] Generally, agricultural subsidy includes domestic subsidy and export subsidy.

Domestic subsidy is government support to agriculture and local farmers. Support includes many specific types of subsidies, which come in all sizes and forms. They can be a direct payment to farmers, or government services to support agricultural production, such as government investment in agricultural research and rural infrastructure development.

Export subsidy can take the form of services and cash. It includes government support of transportation, marketing, and export facilitation services, and direct government financial support to export sales. Government provides payments to its farmers for export sales and in the meantime, it allows foreign buyers to purchase agricultural commodities at prices lower than the world market prices.[8] Subsidized agricultural commodities are more competitive, but they do not reflect real market prices. The prices of subsidized agricultural commodities are lower than the real market prices or even lower than the actual costs of the production itself. Most developing countries are not financially able to provide such support. Their commodities are not as competitive as subsidized products. Export subsidies substantially undermine developing countries' agricultural export.

Agricultural subsidies have reached out across the world. They have touched every aspect of agriculture. Subsidies substantially affect the production, selling,

---

6   FOOD & AGRIC. ORG. OF THE UN, FAO PAPERS ON SELECTED ISSUES RELATING TO THE WTO NEGOTIATIONS ON AGRICULTURE, *available at* ftp://ftp.fao.org/docrep/fao/004/Y3733E/Y3733E00.pdf (last visited Jan. 24, 2013).

7   William Petit, *The Free Trade Area of the Americas: Is It Setting the Stage for Significant Change in US Agricultural Subsidy Use?*, 37 TEX. TECH L. REV. 127, 128 (2004).

8   Liane L. Heggy, *Free Trade Meets US Farm Policy: Life after the Uruguay Round*, 25 LAW & POL'Y INT'L BUS. 1367, 1375 (1994). In the United States, farm policy "allows US farmers to receive higher payment for export sales than is available to other traders on the global market, while at the same time allowing foreign buyers to purchase agricultural commodities at prices lower than the going market price, with the US." *Id.*

purchasing, and consumption of agricultural commodities.[9] A United Nations Development Program (UNDP) report states that, "[w]hen it comes to world agricultural trade, market success is determined not by comparative advantage, but by comparative access to subsidies—an area in which producers in poor countries are unable to compete."[10] Many developed countries, like the US and many European countries, heavily subsidize their agricultural products to protect their farmers.[11] The UNDP report estimates that developed countries have spent over $350 billion a year to subsidize their agriculture. Due to these trade-distorting agricultural subsidies, developing countries are estimated to lose about $34 billion per year.[12] Subsidies cause inestimable harm to local farmers in other parts of the world, in particular, those in poor developing countries.

Distorted Agricultural Trade: Market Access and Trade Barriers

The most traditional market access barrier is the tariff. A tariff is "a direct tax on the importation of goods which make them less price competitive than domestic products."[13] Government imposes tariffs to control trade between nations for the benefit of its domestic producers. Other barriers that limit the import of foreign products include quotas, import bans, discretionary import licenses, health and safety regulations, technical and quality standards, and other non-tariff restrictions on market access.[14]

Rich developed countries encourage "free trade" in agriculture. They demand developing countries eliminate trade barriers and open their markets. However, on the other hand, these rich countries set various trade barriers to restrict agricultural imports from other countries and protect their domestic market.[15] The liberalization of developing countries' markets and the restriction of access to their domestic

---

9   Kelvin Goertzen, *Leveling the Playing Field*, 3 ASPER REV. INT'L BUS. & TRADE L. 81, 81 (2003) (claiming that agricultural subsidies affect every aspect of agriculture).

10   UN DEV. PROG., HUMAN DEVELOPMENT REPORT 2005: INTERNATIONAL COOPERATION AT A CROSSROADS: AID, TRADE AND SECURITY IN AN UNEQUAL WORLD, 130 (2005).

11   Goertzen, *supra* note 9, at 94 (explaining that the US government prefers the use of direct payments to farmers not tied to production levels, while Europe has relied heavily on export subsidies to support their farmers).

12   OLIVIER DE SCHUTTER, MANDATE OF THE SPECIAL RAPPORTEUR ON THE RIGHT TO FOOD, BACKGROUND NOTE: ANALYSIS OF THE WORLD FOOD CRISIS BY THE UN SPECIAL RAPPORTEUR ON THE RIGHT TO FOOD 13 (May 2, 2008) *available at* http://www.srfood.org/images/stories/pdf/otherdocuments/1-srrtfnoteglobalfoodcrisis-2–5-08.pdf.

13   D. CRANE, A DICTIONARY OF CANADIAN ECONOMICS 328 (1980).

14   David R. Purnell, *International Trade Update: The GATT and NAFTA*, 73 NEB. L. REV. 211, 217 (1994) ("Some representative barriers are health and safety regulations, technical and quality standards, and quotas").

15   Thomas J. Schoenbaum, *Agricultural Trade Wars: A Threat to the GATT and Global Free Trade*, 24 ST. MARY'S L. J. 1165, 1181 (1993).

markets are, in essence, protectionist measures taken by developed countries.[16] Many developing countries depend on agriculture as an important source of export earnings, although most of their agricultural exports are economic plant (non-food) products and some of them may heavily depend on a single commodity.[17] When farmers in developing countries seek access to rich markets in developed countries, they face significant obstacles, and they are harmed by these trade barriers that exclude their agricultural exports from markets in developed countries. For example, the EU, as one of the top three sugar exporters in the world, has a complicated system of tariffs, quotas, and other trade barriers to protect EU sugar producers. Many developing countries' farmers have been severely hurt by these market access restrictions. Similarly, unfair subsidies and trade barriers the US government set to protect its cotton producers restricted Brazilian cotton export. The Brazilian government had to request the establishment of a dispute settlement panel before the WTO when consultations with the US failed.[18] Although Brazil won eventually, this was rare, and most developing countries suffer developed countries' unfair subsidies and trade-restrictive measures without being able to fight back.

Why a Freer and Fairer Environment is Important for International Agricultural Trade

Trade distortions have had significant impacts on both countries that provide support, and on other countries that suffer from subsidies and restricted market access. There is more than one reason to support the promotion of a freer and fairer international trading system for agriculture.

A freer and fairer trade environment is important for developing countries. More than 80 percent of the population in developing countries directly rely on agriculture for their food and livelihood, and many developing countries' governments depend on agriculture as an important source of export earnings. The success of agriculture is essential for developing countries to stimulate economic development, and to reduce poverty and hunger. Disciplining agricultural trade promotes the integration of developing countries into the global market. Export

---

16   Purnell, *supra* note 14, at 212 (noting that market access, in essence, is protectionism and it involves the erection of trade barriers by importing nations).

17   Carmen G. Gonzalez, *Institutionalizing Inequality: The WTO Agreement on Agriculture, Food Security, and Developing Countries*, 27 COLUM. J. ENVTL. L. 433, 447–48 (2002). *See also* Michael R. Taylor, *The Emerging Merger of Agricultural and Environmental Policy: Building a New Vision for the Future of American Agriculture*, 20 VA. ENVTL. L.J. 169, 184 (2001). ("In developing countries, where as many as 80–90 percent of the population are directly dependent on agriculture for their food and livelihood, the success of agriculture is essential to the success of the economy and to food security.") *Id.*

18   William A. Gillon, *The Panel Report in the US—Brazil Cotton Dispute: WTO Subsidy Rules Confront US Agriculture*, 10 DRAKE J. AGRIC. L. 7, 8, (2005).

earnings financially enable developing countries to invest in infrastructure development, which helps poor people break the cycle of poverty-hunger.[19]

A freer and fairer trade environment is also meaningful for developed countries. Admittedly, for developed countries, removal of agricultural subsidies and trade barriers will result in an immediate decrease in the number of agricultural producers and an increase in food prices. However, in the long run, trade liberalization will eventually benefit developed countries. It will ultimately lead to world trade efficiency and balance. Government budgets on agricultural subsidies will be substantially reduced, and resources will be reallocated for better uses, such as education, research, improvement of employment, and more.

A Radical Change in the Global Trading System

To reduce and eventually end world hunger, producing more food will not suffice. A radical change in the global trading system is urgently needed. The establishment of a freer and fairer trading environment is not a goal that any state can achieve in isolation, but requires massive efforts made by the international community. Both developed and developing countries must be committed to promoting an open, equitable, rule-based, predictable, and non-discriminatory multilateral trading system.[20] To make meaningful reforms, we need to first understand the slow progress of agricultural trade liberalization in the past few decades.

Slow Progress towards a Freer and Less-distorted International Agricultural Trade System: From GATT to WTO

Original GATT: Not Much about Trade in Agriculture

In the 1940s, the United States and its allies sought to create institutions that would maintain international peace and security, and eliminate possible causes of wars. The United Nations was created as the peacekeeping institution; the Bretton Woods system was established to ensure monetary stability.[21] In addition to the

---

19   Raj Bhala, *Resurrecting the Doha Round: Devilish Details, Grand Themes, and China Too*, 45 TEX. INT'L L. J. 1, 1 (2009).

20   United Nations Millennium Declaration, G.A. Res. 55.2, UN Doc. A/RES/55/2 (Sept. 18, 2000).

21   UN, *UN at a Glance*, http://www.un.org/en/aboutun/index.shtml (last visited Feb. 6, 2011). The international community created the United Nations as a peacekeeping institution. "The United Nations is an international organization founded in 1945 after the Second World War by 51 countries committed to maintaining international peace and security, developing friendly relations among nations and promoting social progress, better living standards and human rights." *Id. See* Richard Myrus, *From Bretton Woods to Brussels: A Legal Analysis of the Exchange-rate Arrangements of the International Monetary Fund and the European Community*, 62 FORDHAM L. REV. 2095, 2096–97 (1994).

peacekeeping and monetary institutions, it was widely agreed that there was an urgent need to establish an organization to regulate international trade activities.[22] In December 1945, the US invited its war-time allies to enter into negotiations on a couple of issues concerning international trade, including negotiations on a multilateral agreement for tariff reductions, negotiations on the establishment of the International Trade Organization (ITO), and negotiations on the adoption of the General Agreement on Tariffs and Trade (GATT).

In 1948, negotiations on the creation of the ITO were successfully completed and, as a consequence, the Havana Charter was adopted.[23] The Havana Charter established the basic rules and restrictions for international trade and other economic matters. However, the ITO was jeopardized and never came into existence due to disapproval from the US Congress.[24]

Despite the failure of the ITO, negotiations on the GATT in Geneva advanced. In October 1947, participating countries signed the *Protocol of Provisional Application of the General Agreement on Tariffs and Trade.*[25] The 1947 GATT was a multilateral agreement establishing international trading rules and disciplines.[26] It provided an organization to administer these rules, and a forum for its Member States to discuss and resolve trading issues. The purpose of the 1947 GATT was

---

The international monetary system, "the Bretton Woods system," was established to stabilize international currency, to ensure monetary stability and to provide infrastructure loans to war-ravaged nations and help them rebuild after World War I. *Id.*

22   Jon G. Filapek, *Agriculture in a World of Comparative Advantage: The Prospects for Farm Trade Liberalization in the Uruguay Round of GATT Negotiations*, 30 HARV. INT'L L.J. 123, 137 (1989).

23   Havana Charter, United Nations Conference on Trade and Employment, Mar. 24, 1958, *available at* http://www.worldtradelaw.net/misc/havana.pdf.

24   Henricus A. Strating, *The GATT Agriculture Dispute: A European Perspective*, 18 N.C.J. INT'L L. & COM. REG. 305, 307, 311 (1993) (explaining that the US was afraid that such an institution "could undermine agricultural support programs").

25   General Agreement on Tariffs and Trade, Oct. 30, 1947, 61 Stat. A-11, 55 U.N.T.S. 194, *available at* http://www.wto.org/english/docs_e/legal_e/gatt47_01_e.htm. The Governments of the Commonwealth of Australia, the Kingdom of Belgium, the United States of Brazil, Burma, Canada, Ceylon, the Republic of Chile, the Republic of China, the Republic of Cuba, the Czechoslovak Republic, the French Republic, India, Lebanon, the Grand-Duchy of Luxemburg, the Kingdom of the Netherlands, New Zealand, the Kingdom of Norway, Pakistan, Southern Rhodesia, Syria, the Union of South Africa, the United Kingdom of Great Britain and Northern Ireland, and the United States of America signed the GATT in 1947.

26   Kathryn Cameron Atkinson, *United States—Latin American Trade Laws*, 21 N. C. J. INT'L L. & COM. REG. 111, 113 (1995). ("[The GATT] provided a Code of Conduct for government behavior in regulating international trade in goods, by establishing disciplines on assessment of antidumping and countervailing duties, customs valuation of goods, marks of origin and other areas.") *Id.*

to "promote a free and orderly international trading system."[27] It was devoted to substantially reducing subsidies, tariffs, trade barriers, and other discriminatory treatment in international trade.

The 1947 GATT focused on trade in industrial goods. Several rounds of GATT negotiations since its establishment resulted in substantial reduction in industrial tariffs.[28] Nevertheless, agriculture has traditionally been protected by most countries.[29] Especially in developed countries, agricultural policy is characterized by high levels of protectionism. Thus agriculture was excluded from most of the coverage of the GATT negotiations.

The 1947 GATT did apply to agricultural trade, but it contained loopholes. First, the 1947 GATT rules governing subsidies were weakened to accommodate agricultural trade. In trade negotiations, agriculture was treated differently from manufactured goods with regard to subsidies.[30] Second, the 1947 GATT allowed its Member States to use a wide range of non-tariff barriers, such as import quotas and export subsidies, to support agriculture in favor of developed countries like the EC and the US, which inevitably distorted international agricultural trade.[31] In fact, seven out of eight rounds of the GATT negotiations focused on manufacturing goods, and only one round, the Uruguay Round, which was the last one (the WTO later replaced the GATT), started to involve agricultural issues in negotiations.[32] Furthermore, in practice, there were no set rules for agricultural trade under the 1947 GATT. No restrictions were placed on its Member States regarding domestic agriculture support. A variety of "lawful" non-tariff barriers were also allowed.[33]

The 1947 GATT rules for agricultural trade have three special distinctions. They allow exceptions for the use of tariffs and other market access restrictions on agricultural trade; they impose very little restraint on the use of domestic subsidies; they demand limited restrictions on the use of export subsidies.

Under the Pre-Uruguay GATT, tariff is the exclusive means of protection for all domestic industries except agriculture. All other non-tariff barriers, such as

---

27   Lyn MacNabb & Robert Weaver, *The General Agreement on Tariffs and Trade (GATT): Has Agriculture Doomed the Uruguay Round?*, 26 LAND & WATER L. REV. 761, 761 (1991).

28   Jimmye S. Hillman, *Agriculture in the Uruguay Round: A United States Perspective*, 28 TULSA L. J. 761, 765 (1993).

29   Miguel Montana-Mora, *International Law and International Relations Cheek to Cheek: An International Law/International Relations Perspective on the US/EC Agricultural Export Subsidies Dispute*, 19 N.C. J. INT'L L. & COM. REG. 1, 11 (1993).

30   Peggy A. Clarke, *The Future of Food Subsidies*, 101 AM. SOC'Y INT'L L. PROC. 109, 109 (2007).

31   Kevin C. Kennedy, *International Trade in Agriculture: Where We've Been, Where We Are, and Where We're Headed*, 10 MSU-DCL J. INT'L L. 1, 1 (2001).

32   Jeffrey J. Steinle, *The Problem Child of World Trade: Reform School for Agriculture*, 4 MINN. J. GLOBAL TRADE 333, 342 (1995).

33   Heggy, *supra* note 8, at 1391–92.

licenses and quotas, are not permitted unless under certain exemptions.[34] However, the GATT rules allow its Member States to be more protective of their agricultural products. Article XI of the 1947 GATT specifies the general elimination of quantitative restrictions on imports and exports, but it allows exceptions applicable to agricultural trade. Article XI provides for "[e]xport prohibitions or restrictions temporarily applied to prevent or relieve critical shortages of foodstuffs or other products essential to the exporting contracting party."[35] It allows "[i]mport restrictions on any agricultural or fisheries product, imported in any form, necessary to the enforcement of governmental measures which operate" to reduce production and relieve surpluses.[36] Noticeably, the 1947 GATT excludes agriculture from its market access liberalization agenda.

Pre-Uruguay Round disciplines in the area of domestic subsidies were generally weak, not limited to agricultural subsidies. Article XVI.1 of the 1947 GATT simply requires notification in writing with regard to the extent and nature of subsidization and its estimated effects.[37] Only when it is determined that the subsidy may cause serious prejudice to the interests of any other contracting party, "the contracting party granting the subsidy shall, upon request, discuss with the other contracting party or parties concerned, or with the contracting parties, the possibility of limiting the subsidization."[38] Although the Tokyo Round Subsidies Code tried to improve the rules on agricultural subsidies, it did not make a big difference due to the few subscriptions of GATT signatories to the Code.[39]

Pre-Uruguay Round GATT disciplines in the area of agricultural export subsidies are far weaker than those that governed international trade in manufactured goods. For all industries except agriculture, 1947 GATT provisions prohibit the use of export subsidies as a method to support and promote domestic industrial development. Different from industrial products, the 1947 GATT grants special treatment to primary agricultural products, allowing the use of export subsidies under certain conditions. Article XVI provides that,

> as from January 1, 1958 or the earliest practicable date thereafter, contracting
> parties shall cease to grant either directly or indirectly any form of subsidy on

---

34   Dale E. Hathaway, *Reforming World Agricultural Policies in Multilateral Negotiations*, 1 TRANSNAT'L L. & CONTEMP. PROBS. 393, 398–99 (1991).

35   General Agreement on Tariffs and Trade, *supra* note 25. art. XI ("No prohibitions or restrictions other than duties, taxes or other charges, whether made effective through quotas, import or export licenses or other measures, shall be instituted or maintained by any contracting party on the importation of any product of the territory of any other contracting party or on the exportation or sale for export of any product destined for the territory of any other contracting party"). *Id.*

36   *Id.* Article XI.2 (c).

37   *Id.* art. XVI.1.

38   *Id.*

39   Kevin J. Brosch, *The GATT, the WTO and the Uruguay Round Agreements Act, The Uruguay Round Agreement on Agriculture*, 722 PLI/COMM 863, 870 (1995).

the export of any product other than a primary product which subsidy results in the sale of such product for export at a price lower than the comparable price charged for the like product to buyers in the domestic market.[40]

Primary product is defined under Annex I (Notes and Supplementary Provisions) of the 1947 GATT, "to be any product of farm, forest or fishery, or any mineral, in its natural form or which has undergone such processing as is customarily required to prepare it for marketing in substantial volume in international trade."[41] As a consequence, most agricultural products fall into this "primary products" category and are therefore excluded from the GATT disciplines limiting export subsidies. In addition,

> if a contracting party grants directly or indirectly any form of subsidy which operates to increase the export of any primary product from its territory, such subsidy shall not be applied in a manner which results in that contracting party having more than an equitable share of world export trade in that product.[42]

In practice, GATT dispute panels found it difficult to apply the "more than an equitable share" standard due to its elusiveness.[43] Overall, pre-Uruguay Round GATT rules imposed very little restraint on the use of export subsidies in agricultural trade.

Uruguay Round Negotiations:[44] *A Breakthrough, but with Half Success and Half Failure*

Prior to the Uruguay Round, agriculture was substantially exempted from the GATT rules, an exemption which resulted in a large number of trade disputes. In the 1950s, 23 percent of GATT cases involved agriculture,[45] and from the early 1960s to the late 1980s, over 50 percent of GATT cases resulted from agricultural trade

---

40   General Agreement on Tariffs and Trade, *supra* note 25, art. XVI.3.

41   *Id.* Annex I.

42   *Id.* art. XVI, § B.3.

43   Brosch, *supra* note 39, at 866.

44   Uruguay Round Final Act (Final Act) on December 15, 1993 was signed by 124 governments and the European Communities on April 15, 1994 in Marrakesh, Morocco, and it entered into force on January 1, 1995. As of July 1, 1995, 100 countries had ratified the Final Act and become WTO members, 28 GATT members were not yet WTO members, and 28 other countries had made GATT-WTO accession requests. The United States and Mexico are signatories, as are Argentina, Brazil, Colombia, Peru, Venezuela and all other Central and South American countries except Ecuador and Panama. These latter two have made accession requests.

45   Robert Hudec et al., *A Statistical Profile of GATT Dispute Settlement Cases: 1948–1989*, 2 Minn. J. Global Trade 1, 67 (1993).

disputes.[46] Additionally, the great costs of government intervention in agriculture made it an urgent issue to be discussed. It was hoped that agricultural trade issues would be solved during the Uruguay Round negotiations.

GATT Contracting Parties tried to bring agricultural trade into the GATT framework, but no substantial achievements were made until the Uruguay Round.[47] The Uruguay Round negotiations were launched in 1986.[48] One of the most important objectives of the Uruguay Round negotiations was "to achieve greater liberalization of trade in agriculture and bring all measures affecting import access and export competition under strengthened and more operationally effective GATT rules and disciplines,"[49] and thereby, "reduce the uncertainty, imbalances and instability in world agricultural markets."[50] During the Uruguay Round, the GATT Contracting Parties negotiated agricultural trade issues and possible reforms on how to achieve substantial trade liberalization in agriculture. The issues addressed were primarily in three areas—domestic support, market access, and export competition.

Agriculture was the greatest obstacle for the Contracting Parties to reach a final agreement during the Uruguay Round negotiations. Throughout the negotiations, discussions on agricultural trade liberalization were mainly dominated by two key players—the United States and the European Community. The negotiating strategies of both the US and the EC were conditioned by their supposed comparative advantages in agriculture. They both hoped that the reduction of agricultural protectionism would produce an increase in their exports.

During the Uruguay Round negotiations, despite the strong protection for its own farmers, the US led the struggle for the removal of trade-distorting agricultural support, at least on paper.[51] The US proposed the boldest reforms

---

46   *Id.*

47   Montana-Mora, *supra* note 29, at 35. (The Contracting Parties regulated agriculture during the Tokyo Round, but no substantive issues were dealt with.)

48   Dale E. McNiel, *Furthering the Reforms of Agricultural Policies in the Millennium Round,* 9 MINN. J. GLOBAL TRADE 41, 52 (2000).

49   *GATT Ministerial Declaration on the Uruguay Round of Multilateral Trade Negotiations,* Sept. 20, 1986, 25 I.L.M. 1623, 1626 (1986).

50   Raj Bhala, *World Agricultural Trade in Purgatory: The Uruguay Round Agriculture Agreement and Its Implications for the Doha Round,* 79 N.D.L. REV. 691, 714 (2003).

51   Heggy, *supra* note 8, at 1392. ("In July 1987, the United States proposed a phase-out of all agriculture production subsidies affecting international trade by the year 2000. ... In 1989, the United States further proposed converting all agricultural trade barriers, such as import quotas, into tariffs, with the tariffs included as part of the long-term phase-out. ... [However,] facing continued opposition, the United States retreated and offered a revised plan in 1990 that called for a worldwide 90 percent reduction in export subsidies, a 75 percent reduction in internal support measures and a 75 percent reduction in import quotas. The European Community opposed the plan but offered a counter-proposal that included only a 30 percent reduction in domestic price supports and no commitment to cutting export subsidies or border restrictions.") *Id.*

to liberalize agricultural trade, including reducing and progressively eradicating trade-distorting domestic subsidies, and converting all non-tariff barriers into tariffs within 10 years.[52] Meanwhile, to maximize its comparative advantage in agricultural trade, the US placed its primary emphasis on the complete abolition of agricultural export subsidies. The US emphasis on export subsidies is explained by the fact that during the last few decades, the US had supported its agriculture by using a variety of domestic subsidies to farmers while its competitor, the EC, supported its agriculture by the use of export subsidies. In other words, the target of the US proposals was mainly the EC's export subsidies. The primary goal of the US in the Uruguay Round negotiations was to remove export subsidies mainly granted by the EC and, thereby to increase the competitiveness of US agricultural commodities on the global market.[53]

The agricultural trade reforms proposed by the US were backed by the Cairns Group.[54] The Cairns Group consists of 14 farm-exporting countries that collectively produce about 25 percent of total world agriculture exports. These countries include Argentina, Australia, Brazil, Canada, Chile, Colombia, Fiji, Hungary, Indonesia, Malaysia, the Philippines, New Zealand, Thailand, and Uruguay. This Group was created with the intent to increase its members' bargaining power in agricultural trade negotiations. During the Uruguay Round negotiations, the Cairns Group supported dramatic agricultural trade liberalization that they modeled after the US proposals. Similar to US proposals, the basic objective of the Cairns Group's proposals was to eradicate all import and export restrictions and all trade-distorting subsidies.[55] Only measures for rural infrastructure improvement and disaster relief would be allowed. The Cairns Group advocated substantial reduction (elimination if possible) in domestic support, export subsidies, and market access restrictions. It also demanded increased enforcement mechanisms to regulate international agricultural trade.[56]

In the face of attacks from the US and other agricultural exporting countries, the EC sharply opposed the proposals. The EC made it clear that the negotiations should include all measures affecting agricultural trade, not only export subsidies. They should also consider the special factors that may affect agricultural production, such as food security concerns and the dependence of agricultural production on weather conditions.[57] Noticeably, the EC's proposals placed prime concern on maintaining its agricultural support and sought to reduce agricultural support in a modest way.

---

52 Montana-Mora, *supra* note 29, at 39.

53 *Id.* (stating, with regard to the US's negotiation strategies, that the US's major interest "has not been global negotiation, but the export refunds granted by the Community").

54 Thacker, *supra* note 1, at 727.

55 Carlisle F. Runge, *The Assault on Agricultural Protectionism*, 67 FOREIGN AFF. 133, 145 (1988).

56 Heggy, *supra* note 8, at 1395.

57 *Id.*

The Japanese model is very close to the proposal submitted by the EC. Japan, as a net food-importing country, showed its deep concerns for food security. It emphasized the non-economic objectives of farm policies, especially the need to maintain protectionist agricultural policies in order to protect food security.[58] Japan's proposal also addressed sustainability issues such as rural development and environmental protection.[59]

Special and differential treatment was granted to developing countries, including longer timeframes to phase out import restrictions and special allowances to subsidize certain agricultural products. However, the Uruguay Round negotiations were essentially dominated by the two key players, the US and the EC. The voices of developing countries were still ignored in the Uruguay Round.[60]

During the Uruguay Round, it was extremely difficult to smooth over the differences between the US and the EC as they both were trying to maximize their comparative advantages in agriculture and curb the other's trading opportunities. Debates on agriculture issues prolonged the Uruguay negotiations.[61] In 1990, the EC's and Japan's refusal of the proposals presented by the US brought the negotiations to a grinding halt. In December 1991, the Director General of GATT, Arthur Dunkel, produced the *Draft Final Act Embodying the Results of the Uruguay Round of Multilateral Trade Negotiations* (the Dunkel Draft),[62] in an effort to push the negotiations out of the impasse. In November 1992, the US and the EC finally reached the Blair House Agreement. They agreed on domestic support and export subsidy reduction commitments as well as some other issues with regard to agricultural trade.

After more than seven years of negotiations, on December 15, 1993, the Uruguay Round negotiations were concluded with a series of agreements.[63] On the basis of the Dunkel Draft and the Blair House Agreement, the Agreement on Agriculture (AoA), as one of the most notable agreements of the Uruguay Round negotiations, was finally reached. The AoA came into effect in January, 1995.

In addition to the AoA, the Agreement on Subsidies and Countervailing Measures (SCM Agreement) was adopted to impose significant restrictions

---

58   THE GATT URUGUAY ROUND: A NEGOTIATING HISTORY (1986–1992) 131, 186–90 (Terence P. Stewart ed., 1993).

59   Runge, *supra* note 55, at 146.

60   Thacker, *supra* note 1, at 727.

61   Heggy, *supra* note 8, at 1393 ("[P]rogress on the Uruguay Round came to a grinding halt in December 1990, when the European Community, supported by Japan and South Korea, refused to agree to demands made by the United States even though most other members supported the US proposal").

62   Draft Final Act Embodying the Results of the Uruguay Round of Multilateral Trade Negotiations, GATT Doc. MTN.TNC/W/FA (Dec. 20, 1991).

63   GATT Trade Negotiations Comm., Final Act Embodying the Results of the Uruguay Round of Multilateral Trade Negotiations, MTN/FA (Dec. 15, 1993) (restricted); *President Clinton's Submission to Congress of Documents Concerning Uruguay Round Agreement Dec. 15, 1993*, DAILY REP. FOR EXECUTIVES (BNA) (Dec. 17, 1993).

on agricultural subsidies. The SCM rules generally forbid all trade-distorting subsidies, both domestic subsidies and export subsidies, with certain exemptions.[64] It fills in the gaps of the AoA. Sanitary and phytosanitary (SPS) measures were also included in the Uruguay Round negotiations. Considering the negotiation on SPS measures required specialized technical expertise, a separate sub-group was established, and an agreement that is apart from the main text of the AoA was concluded separately— the Agreement on the Application of Sanitary and Phytosanitary Measures (SPS Agreement).

Uruguay Round Agreement on Agriculture (AoA)
The long-term objective of the AoA is to "establish a fair and market-oriented agricultural trading system" through "substantial progressive reductions in agricultural support and protection sustained over an agreed period of time."[65] The AoA imposes three specific binding obligations on its members, dubbed "the three pillars": market access (tariffs)—Article 4; domestic support (domestic subsidies)—Article 6; export competition (export subsidies)—Article 9. The AoA sought to increase market access for agricultural products through the reduction of import barriers. All non-tariff measures except those justified by health and safety reasons are required to be replaced by their tariff equivalents. This process is known as "tariffication." The members are subsequently bound to reduce their trade restrictions confronting imports.[66] The AoA also restricts the use of trade-distorting domestic subsidies and export subsidies on agricultural products. Member States are required to make certain reduction commitments.

Nevertheless, the AoA allows its member countries to support their rural economies through government programs that are decoupled from production and prices, which cause less distortion to international agricultural trade. It also allows some flexibility for developing countries to implement reduction commitments. Under the AoA, developing countries are not required to lower their tariffs or cut their subsidies as much as what is required by developed countries, and developing countries are given extra time to complete their commitments.[67] In addition, considering their economic situation, least-developed countries are not obligated

---

64   Matthew C. Porterfield, *US Farm Subsidies and The Expiration of the WTO's Peace Clause*, 27 U. Pa. J. Int'l Econ. L. 999, 1005 (2006).

65   Agreement on Agriculture, Apr. 15, 1994, 1867 U.N.T.S. 410. pmbl.

66   Human Rights Council, Rep. of Special Rapporteur on the Right to Food, Olivier De Schutter, Promotion and Protection of All Human Rights, Civil, Political, Economic, Social and Cultural Rights, Including the Right to Development, UN Doc. A/HRC/12/31 (July 21, 2009), *available at* http://www.srfood.org/images/stories/pdf/officialreports/srrtf_second%20global%20food%20crisis%20report_a-hrc-12–31.pdf. [hereinafter Report of Special Rapporteur on the Right to Food].

67   Agreement on Agriculture, *supra* note 65, art. 15.2. ("Developing country Members shall have the flexibility to implement reduction commitments over a period of up to 10 years.")

to undertake any reduction commitment.[68] Furthermore, the AoA includes special provisions regarding the interests of net food-importing developing countries.[69]

To understand the importance of the Agreement on Agriculture in regulating world agricultural trade, the "the three pillars"—market access, domestic support, and export subsidies—are examined in depth.

Market access   Before the Uruguay Round negotiations, in addition to tariffs, many non-tariff measures, such as quantitative import restrictions, minimum import prices, and discretionary import licensing, largely restricted agricultural trade. One of the most significant objectives of the AoA is to achieve greater market access. In pursuit of this objective, the AoA eliminates non-tariff barriers through a tariffication process. It also imposes substantive tariff concession obligations on its Member States, with legal binding effect within the WTO trade system. Market access commitments are threefold.

First, pursuant to Article 4.2 of the AoA, Member States are required to convert their non-tariff barriers into their tariff equivalents, which is known as "tariffication." "Members shall not maintain, resort to, or revert to any measures of the kind which have been required to be converted into ordinary customs duties, except as otherwise provided for in Article 5 and Annex 5."[70] After tariffication, domestic producers can only receive protection from governments in the form of tariffs. The goal of tariffication is to make trade restrictions and barriers more transparent.

Second, once tariffication is completed, tariff levels are to be reduced. Developed countries commit to cut their agricultural tariffs for all agricultural products by an average of 36 percent, with a minimum cut per product of 15 percent, over a six-year period beginning in 1995. Developing countries are granted special treatment. They are expected to cut their average agricultural tariffs by two-thirds that of developed countries, and are given double the amount of time to fulfill their reduction obligations. Thus, developing countries are required to reduce their tariffs by an average of 24 percent over a 10-year period, from 1995 to 2004. For developing countries, the minimum cut per product is 10 percent. As for least-developed countries, considering their economic situation, they are not obligated to make any reduction commitments.[71]

The AoA requires guaranteed minimum access import opportunities for all agricultural products if imports have been less than 5 percent of domestic consumption during the 1986 to 1988 base period.[72] For imports that are more than 5 percent of domestic consumption during the base period, Member States

---

68   *Id.*
69   *Id.* art. 16.
70   *Id.* art. 4.2.
71   *Id.* art. 15.2.
72   *Id.* art. 5.

are required to maintain current (existing) market access opportunity.[73] This guaranteed market access is intended to provide some immediate liberalization in agricultural trade in case the conversion of a non-tariff barrier still results in a high tariff equivalent.

Third, Member States are expected to establish a system of minimum market access quotas, also called "tariff-rate quotas" (TRQs), rising from 3 percent to 5 percent of domestic consumption for almost all agricultural products during the implementation period, to ensure that market access commitments are honored. The TRQs ensure lower tariff rates for specified quantities and allow higher (sometimes much higher) rates for quantities that exceed the pre-set quota.[74]

Tariffication, the reduction of tariffs, and the TRQs are related to one another. They operate jointly to improve market access for agriculture trade. Tariffication converts non-tariff barriers into tariff equivalents. This process prevents tariff reduction from being undermined by increased non-tariff barriers. Tariff reduction comes subsequent to tariffication, and helps achieve the ultimate goal of tariffication—the reduction of duty rates. In the meantime, the implementation of TRQs ensures a certain degree of market access while tariff reduction is phased in.

Recognizing that tariffication is not an exact mathematic calculation, the AoA introduces special safeguard measures in Article 5.[75] The safeguard provisions are created to provide importing countries with proper safety measures in response to undue import surges or price drops during the implementation period. Special safeguard measures can only be applied to agricultural products that have undergone tariffication.[76] For agricultural products that were not the subject of tariffication under the AoA, governments are not allowed to take special measures to protect their agricultural producers from swift import surges or price drops. This condition directly excludes many agricultural products from the less- and least-developed countries because their products were not obligated to undergo the process of tariffication.[77]

The AoA also includes the protection of sensitive products. For example, Japan, the Republic of Korea, and the Philippines are allowed to use special treatment provisions to restrict imports of rice. Israel is allowed to provide special

---

73 Randy Green, *Part II: Review of Key Substantive Agreements, Panel II C: Agreement on Agriculture, The Uruguay Round Agreement on Agriculture*, 31 Law & Pol'y Int'l Bus. 819, 821 (2000).

74 World Trade Org., *Understanding the WTO-Agriculture: Fairer Markets for Farmers*, http://www.wto.org/english/thewto_e/whatis_e/tif_e/agrm3_e.htm (last visited Sept. 18, 2010). ("The newly committed tariffs and tariff quotas, covering all agricultural products, took effect in 1995.")

75 Agreement on Agriculture, *supra* note 65, art. 5.

76 World Trade Org., *supra* note 74 ("For products whose non-tariff restrictions have been converted to tariffs, governments are allowed to take special emergency actions ('special safeguards') in order to prevent swiftly falling prices or surges in imports from hurting their farmers").

77 Agreement on Agriculture, *supra* note 65, art. 15.2.

protection for its sheep meat, whole milk powder, and certain cheese products.[78] The protection of sensitive products is subject to strictly defined conditions.[79]

To summarize, the AoA converted non-tariff barriers into tariff equivalents. It also saw the imposition of a schedule for the reduction of these tariffs and tariff equivalents. However, the process of tariffication and subsequent tariff reduction brought minimal substantive benefits to developing countries.

Developed countries that used to have high tariffs and non-tariff barriers agreed to reduce their import restrictions, but they still were allowed to maintain certain levels of protection. Tariffs remain an immense impediment to access by the developing countries to the developed countries' market. Furthermore, the process of tariffication has been criticized for its flaws. Tariffication was expected to promote transparency in border measures so that it allowed Member States to address trade issues more easily. However, the Agreement did not spell out how such conversion must occur. The actual tariffication was left to the Member States themselves.[80] Many members adopted complicated tariff systems that lack transparency. The majority of the members exaggerated prior protection levels so that they could justify higher equivalent protection going forward.[81] As a result, the operative base rate of tariffs was often higher than the genuine equivalents (this is also known as "dirty tariffication"). Unfortunately, tariffication did not really help achieve greater market access.

Furthermore, as already noted, special safeguards essentially excluded agricultural products of developing countries from protection in confronting swift import surges or price drops.[82] The AoA's sensitive products provision also gave its members excuses to provide greater protection. Base tariffs for certain sensitive commodities continued to be very high. As a result, special safeguard provisions and sensitive products provisions could be repeatedly and excessively invoked, which would distort the normal flow of agricultural trade. Consequently, AoA's market access improvement made little practical difference for developing countries. Import restrictions remained one of the biggest barriers for trade liberalization in agriculture.

---

78 World Trade Org., *supra* note 74 (explaining that the protection of sensitive products was effective during the implementation period (to 2000 for developed countries, to 2004 for developing countries)).

79 *Id.* ("Japan and Israel have now given up this right, but Rep. of Korea and the Philippines have extended their special treatment for rice. A new member, Chinese Taipei, gave special treatment to rice in its first year of membership, 2002").

80 Melaku Geboye Desta, *The Bumpy Ride towards the Establishment of "A Fair and Market-oriented Agricultural Trading System" at the WTO: Reflections Following the Cancun Setback*, 8 Drake J. Agric. L. 489, 501 (2003).

81 Gonzalez, *supra* note 17, at 461 (noting that a survey concluded that the majority of developed countries had engaged in dirty tariffication).

82 Agreement on Agriculture, *supra* note 65, art. 15.2.

Domestic support   Domestic support is not directly linked to exports. It generally refers to subsidies, benefits, and any other support provided to agricultural producers by governments.[83] The Agreement on Agriculture contains provisions regarding domestic support for agriculture. Member States agreed to classify, measure, and reduce their domestic agricultural subsidies. Under the AoA, most domestic support programs are subject to certain reduction commitments, but not all. The support measures that meet the criteria prescribed in Annex 2 of the AoA, basically the measures that are decoupled from prices and production, are exempted from reduction commitments.

The Agreement categorizes domestic support programs into three groups—Amber Box measures, Blue Box measures, and Green Box measures. The measures that have direct effects on agricultural production and trade are classified as "Amber Box." Amber Box measures are capped at the 1986 to 1988 level. They are subject to a reduction of 20 percent over the six-year implementation period.[84] The requirements for developing countries are less strict under the AoA. Amber Box measures are permissible but countervailable if they cause injury.[85] In addition, certain direct payments and subsidies to farmers for the purpose of production-control are permitted through the "Blue Box." As for the measures that have minimal impact on agricultural trade, they are exempted from reductions and belong to the "Green Box." They can be used without restrictions. Blue Box measures are permissible, and countervailable if they cause injury, but not subject to reduction. Green Box measures are permissible and non-countervailable.

Amber Box   Amber Box measures include those domestic support programs that are directly tied to production and price. These measures are considered to be highly trade-distortive. Therefore, they are subject to reduction under the AoA. Most domestic subsidies take the form of price support.[86] Market price support is the quintessential Amber Box measure. Governments provide minimum price support for certain agricultural products and these guaranteed minimum prices are normally higher than world market prices.[87] When the real market prices fall below the guaranteed prices, government will make payments to farmers to maintain the guaranteed minimum prices. "The greater the level of production, the greater the aggregate subsidy provided by the sponsoring government."[88] These government subsidies ensure domestic farmers' income. Nevertheless,

---

83   Green, *supra* note 73, at 821.

84   *Id.*

85   Kennedy, *supra* note 31, at 3.

86   Stefan Tangermann, *Cutting Support Can Help Farmers to Prosper*, FIN. TIMES, Aug. 22, 2003, at 11.

87   Bhala, *supra* note 50, at 797 ("Farmers in OECD countries receive prices for their output that, on average, are thirty-one percent above the equivalent international trade prices").

88   Goertzen, *supra* note 9, at 88.

market price support encourages overproduction, and it creates the need for high-volume exportation at prices lower than the world market price and usually much lower than the domestic price of the product.[89] Other subsidies, such as certain government credit subsidies, also fall into the Amber Box. Together with market price support, these Amber Box subsidies are considered the most trade-distorting form of domestic support.

The Agreement on Agriculture requires most of its Member States to reduce their Amber Box subsidies and keep them below a capped amount. It grants special and differential treatment to developing countries, such as a longer implementation period and a smaller reduction commitment. Under the AoA, Member States calculated how much Amber Box subsidies they were providing per year for agriculture in a base calculation period of 1986 to 1988.[90] This calculation is known as the "Total Aggregate Measurement of Support" or "Total AMS." The reduction commitment of the Amber Box subsidies in each country is established on the basis of the "Total AMS."[91] Developed countries agreed to make 20 percent cuts over the six-year implementation period starting in 1995. Developing countries agreed to reduce their domestic subsidies by 13 percent over a 10-year period.[92] Considering their economic situation, least-developed countries were not required to make any cuts under the AoA. To make it clear, the reduction level of the Amber Box subsidies is based on aggregate support instead of a product-by-product basis.[93] Requiring significant reduction in domestic support, this total aggregate AMS approach also allows countries to maintain stronger support for some agricultural products over others. It gives countries greater flexibility in shaping their respective farm support policies. However, the lack of reporting and verification procedures may result in inaccuracy in the Total AMS calculation and the reduction level as well.

Blue Box   Blue Box subsidies are direct payments to farmers made in exchange for restricting production.[94] These subsidies would normally be categorized as Amber box measures. However, they limit rather than encourage agricultural production, and they are less likely to artificially depress market prices. Therefore,

---

89   *Id.*

90   *See* Bhala, *supra* note 50, at 770 ("Article 1(h) of the Agreement on Agriculture articulates these items: 'Total AMS' mean[s] the sum of all domestic support provided in favor of agricultural producers, calculated as the sum of all aggregate measurements of support for basic agricultural products, all non-product-specific aggregate measurements of support and all equivalent measurements of support for agricultural products").

91   Agreement on Agriculture, *supra* note 65, art. 6.1.

92   Goertzen, *supra* note 9, at 88–89.

93   Brosch, *supra* note 39, at 871 ("Initially, there had been proposals to take limitation commitments on a commodity-specific basis, but those proposals were ultimately rejected in favor of the Total Aggregate AMS approach").

94   Agreement on Agriculture, *supra* note 65, art. 6.5.

Blue Box measures are considered to be less trade-distorting, and are exempted from reduction commitment under the AoA.[95]

Pursuant to Article 6.2 of the AoA, certain government assistance programs, offering either direct or indirect support to encourage rural development in developing countries, are permitted under the AoA.[96] Article 6.4 continues to specify other support measures that are not required to be included in the calculation of Current Total AMS, and are exempt from reduction commitments. This is known as "de minimis."[97] For Member States that are developed countries, the following payments are exempted: first, product-specific domestic support that does not exceed 5 percent of that member's total value of production of a basic agricultural product during the relevant year;[98] second, non-product-specific domestic support that does not exceed 5 percent of the value of that member's total agricultural production.[99] The AoA grants special treatment to developing countries. The de minimis percentage for developing countries is expanded to 10 percent.[100]

Moreover, government payments restricting agricultural production are not required to be removed. Article 6.5(a) of the Agreement on Agriculture explains that,

> [d]irect payments under production-limiting programs shall not be subject to the commitment to reduce domestic support if: (i) such payments are based on fixed area and yields, or (ii) such payments are made on 85 percent or less of the base level of production, or (iii) livestock payments are made on a fixed number of head.[101]

---

95 *Id.*

96 *Id.* art. 6.2. ("In accordance with the Mid-Term Review Agreement that government measures of assistance, whether direct or indirect, to encourage agricultural and rural development are an integral part of the development programs of developing countries, investment subsidies which are generally available to agriculture in developing country Members and agricultural input subsidies generally available to low-income or resource-poor producers in developing country Members shall be exempt from domestic support reduction commitments that would otherwise be applicable to such measures, as shall domestic support to producers in developing country Members to encourage diversification from growing illicit narcotic crops. Domestic support meeting the criteria of this paragraph shall not be required to be included in a Member's calculation of its Current Total AMS.")

97 *Id.* art. 6.4.

98 *Id.* ("[P]roduct-specific domestic support which would otherwise be required to be included in a Member's calculation of its Current AMS where such support does not exceed 5 percent of that Member's total value of production of a basic agricultural product during the relevant year").

99 *Id.* ("[N]on-product-specific domestic support which would otherwise be required to be included in a Member's calculation of its Current AMS where such support does not exceed 5 percent of the value of that Member's total agricultural production").

100 *Id.*

101 *Id.* art. 6.5(a).

Article 6.5(b) continues with exclusions of Blue Box subsidies from the calculation of Current Total AMS.[102]

Arguing that Blue Box measures are less trade-distorting, member countries essentially maintain traditionally valued government support without being subject to reduction commitments. The problem with Blue Box subsidies is the lack of a clear spending limits regulated in the AoA. Although Blue Box subsidies are considered to be less distorting, and only a few members provide Blue Box support (mainly the EU and Japan), they still distort agricultural trade to some extent. After all, Blue Box subsidies are an impediment to agricultural trade, and must be reduced or kept within defined minimal (de minimis) levels.

Green Box　　Green Box subsidies are those government support programs that are decoupled from production and price, and are considered non- or minimally trade-distorting. Therefore, Green Box subsidies are not subject to any restrictions or reduction commitment under the AoA. Green Box payments include both general provisions of government services and certain direct payments to farmers.[103] Annex 2 lists a wide range of domestic subsidies members are allowed to provide without any restrictions, including generalized government service programs in the areas of research,[104] pest and disease control,[105] training services,[106] extension and advisory services,[107] inspection services,[108] marketing and promoting services,[109]

102　*Id.* art. 6.5(b) ("The exemption from the reduction commitment for direct payments meeting the above criteria shall be reflected by the exclusion of the value of those direct payments in a Member's calculation of its Current Total AMS").

103　*Id.* annex 2.

104　*Id.* annex 2.2(a) (general research, research in connection with environmental programs, and research programs relating to particular products").

105　*Id.* annex 2.2(b) ("pest and disease control, including general and product-specific pest and disease control measures, such as early-warning systems, quarantine and eradication").

106　*Id.* annex 2.2(c) ("training services, including both general and specialist training facilities").

107　*Id.* annex 2.2(d) ("extension and advisory services, including the provision of means to facilitate the transfer of information and the results of research to producers and consumers").

108　*Id.* annex 2.2(e) ("inspection services, including general inspection services and the inspection of particular products for health, safety, grading or standardization purposes").

109　*Id.* annex 2.2(f) ("marketing and promotion services, including market information, advice and promotion relating to particular products but excluding expenditure for unspecified purposes that could be used by sellers to reduce their selling price or confer a direct economic benefit to purchasers").

infrastructural services,[110] public stockholding for food security[111] and domestic aid purposes.[112] Annex 2 also specifies other government support programs that are exempted from reduction commitment, including government payments made directly to farmers that do not stimulate production,[113] decoupled income support,[114] government financial participation in income insurance and income safety-net programs,[115] payments for relief from natural disasters,[116] structural adjustment assistance provided through producer retirement programs,[117] structural adjustment assistance provided through resource retirement programs,[118] structural adjustment assistance provided through investment aids,[119] payments under environmental programs,[120] and payments under regional assistance programs.[121]

Under the AoA, Green Box subsidies are not subject to reduction disciplines or to a cap counted in a member's AMS. In other words, this exemption allows member countries to provide Green Box payments to its farmers with no spending limits, and the increase in Green Box subsidies will bring no effect on the member's overall domestic support reduction commitment.[122] As such, many Member States have been expanding Green Box support measures that are not subject to reduction schedules.

As WTO members gradually shift towards Green Box measures, it is of great importance to look closely at the long-term effects these subsidies may have on agricultural production and trade, and whether the widespread use of Green Box measures may be trade-distorting in the future. Although critics do not consider the stated non- or minimal effect of Green Box subsidies an accurate reflection of their real market impact, not much attention has yet been paid to this issue. New

---

110   *Id.* annex 2.2(g) ("Infrastructural services, including: electricity reticulation, roads and other means of transport, market and port facilities, water supply facilities, dams and drainage schemes, and infrastructural works associated with environmental programs. In all cases the expenditure shall be directed to the provision or construction of capital works only, and shall exclude the subsidized provision of on-farm facilities other than for the reticulation of generally available public utilities. It shall not include subsidies to inputs or operating costs, or preferential user charges").

111   *Id.* annex 2.3.

112   *Id.* annex 2.4.

113   *Id.* annex 2.5.

114   *Id.* annex 2.6.

115   *Id.* annex 2.7.

116   *Id.* annex 2.8.

117   *Id.* annex 2.9.

118   *Id.* annex 2.10.

119   *Id.* annex 2.11.

120   *Id.* annex 2.12.

121   *Id.* annex 2.13.

122   Stephen J. Powell & Andrew Schmitz, *The Cotton and Sugar Subsidies Decisions: WTO's Dispute Settlement System Rebalances the Agreement on Agriculture*, 10 DRAKE J. AGRIC. L. 287, 291 (2005).

enforcement mechanisms within the WTO system may be needed to regulate the use of Green Box measures, preventing damages it may cause in the long term.

Export subsidies   Under the Agreement on Agriculture, export subsidies are defined as government support measures contingent on export performance. Export subsidies are listed in detail in Article 9 of the Agreement, including:

> (a) the provision by governments or their agencies of direct subsidies, including payments-in-kind, to a firm, to an industry, to producers of an agricultural product, to a cooperative or other association of such producers, or to a marketing board, contingent on export performance;

> (b) the sale or disposal for export by governments or their agencies of non-commercial stocks of agricultural products at a price lower than the comparable price charged for the like product to buyers in the domestic market;

> (c) payments on the export of an agricultural product that are financed by virtue of governmental action, whether or not a charge on the public account is involved, including payments that are financed from the proceeds of a levy imposed on the agricultural product concerned or on an agricultural product from which the exported product is derived;

> (d) the provision of subsidies to reduce the costs of marketing exports of agricultural products (other than widely available export promotion and advisory services) including handling, upgrading and other processing costs, and the costs of international transport and freight;

> (e) internal transport and freight charges on export shipments, provided or mandated by governments, on terms more favorable than for domestic shipments;

> (f) subsidies on agricultural products contingent on their incorporation in exported products.[123]

Export subsidies significantly distort international agricultural trade, and are considered the most harmful agricultural subsidies in the world trading system. They are subject to reduction under the AoA.

Member countries are required to compile a list of all their export subsidies for agricultural products. Countries that did not provide export subsidies during the base period of 1986–1990 are precluded from providing any export subsidies in the future. However, countries that did provide export subsidies during the base period are permitted to continue their support but with increasing reduction

---

123   Agreement on Agriculture, *supra* note 65, art. 9.1.

commitments through the implementation period.[124] Member countries are not allowed to introduce new export subsidies on currently subsidized agricultural products if they were not already in use during the base period of 1986–1990.[125]

To be fair, the AoA deals with export subsidies in a very modest and practical manner. The AoA does not require an entire elimination of export subsidies. Instead, it requires its Member States to make two different reductions. First, Member States are required to reduce the amount/value of agricultural export subsidies ("budgetary outlays") given to specific agricultural products and, second, they are required to reduce the quantities of agricultural products ("export volume") they subsidized.[126]

Using the average annual level of support for 1986–1990 as the base, developed countries agreed to reduce expenditures on export subsidies by 36 percent; they also made a reduction commitment in the quantities of subsidized exports by 21 percent, over a six-year implementation period between 1995 and 2000.[127] Requirements are less stringent for developing countries. The reduction commitments made by developing countries are 24 percent in terms of budgetary support, and 14 percent in terms of export volume over a 10-year implementation period starting in 1995.[128] The least-developed countries do not need to make any reduction commitments, although these countries typically are not financially capable of providing significant export subsidies.[129] Nevertheless, the least-developed countries agreed to "a standstill by binding their export subsidies."[130]

Further, Article 10.1 of the AoA forbids the use of other forms of subsidies or non-commercial transactions which might be used to circumvent export subsidy commitments.[131] Article 10.2 and Article 10.4 stipulate disciplines in the areas of credit, credit guarantees, insurance programs, and food aid. Under Article 10.2, the Agreement requires its members to "work toward the development of internationally agreed disciplines to govern the provision of export credits, export credit guarantees or insurance programs and, after agreement on such

---

124   Brosch, *supra* note 39, at 868–69.

125   Report of Special Rapporteur on the Right to Food, *supra* note 66, at 7 ("[T]he members cannot introduce new export subsidies that were not already in operation in the 1986 1990 base period").

126   Petit, *supra* note 7, at 150 ("The first calculation was based on the amount, or value, of export subsidies given to specific agricultural products for each year of the base period. The second calculation was based on the quantity of agricultural exports that benefitted from those same subsidies in each year of the base period").

127   World Trade Org., *supra* note 74.

128   *Id.*

129   *Id.*

130   Kennedy, *supra* note 31, at 4.

131   Agreement on Agriculture, *supra* note 65, art. 10.1 ("Export subsidies not listed in paragraph 1 of Article 9 shall not be applied in a manner which results in, or which threatens to lead to, circumvention of export subsidy commitments; nor shall non-commercial transactions be used to circumvent such commitments").

disciplines, to provide export credits, export credit guarantees or insurance programs only in conformity therewith."[132] Pursuant to Article 10.4, members donors of international food aid shall ensure:

> (a) that the provision of international food aid is not tied directly or indirectly to commercial exports of agricultural products to recipient countries;

> (b) that international food aid transactions, including bilateral food aid which is monetized, shall be carried out in accordance with the *FAO Principles of Surplus Disposal and Consultative Obligations*, including, where appropriate, the system of Usual Marketing Requirements (UMRs); and

> (c) that such aid shall be provided to the extent possible in fully grant form or on terms no less concessional than those provided for in Article IV of the Food Aid Convention 1986.[133]

Substantial reduction in export subsidies was a big move in the Uruguay Round negotiations. However, some critics have noted that since the AoA prohibits the introduction of any new export subsidies, the whole export subsidies reduction system has essentially been advantageous to the developed countries that had been providing significant export subsidies for their agricultural products prior to the entry into force of the AoA.

Peace clause   Article 13 of the AoA was a compromise. The article set out a reduction commitment in trade barriers, and in the meantime, it exempted the majority of them from challenge for a limited number of years ("during the implementation period") under the Agreement on Subsidies and Countervailing Measures, as long as Member States complied with their obligations under the Agreement on Agriculture.[134] This is commonly referred to as the "Peace Clause." The Peace Clause is an important element of the AoA with regard to subsidies.

The Peace Clause in Article 13 temporarily severely constrained litigation of claims on subsidies.[135] Specifically, it barred imposition of the duty to countervail Green Box payments,[136] and also disallowed countervailing duty actions against an Amber Box (whether or not it was de minimis) and Blue Box subsidy unless these subsidies caused injury or threat of injury under Article VI of the GATT

---

132   *Id.* art. 10.2.

133   *Id.* art. 10.4.

134   *Id.* art. 13.

135   Bhala, *supra* note 50, at 823.

136   Agreement on Agriculture, *supra* note 65, art. 13(b) (declaring domestic support measures conforming to Article 6, Amber Box payments, and direct payments conforming to Article 6.5, Blue Box payments, exempt from countervailing duties, unless injury (or threat) is proven).

and the Subsidy Countervailing Measure Agreement. Likewise, The Peace Clause deferred WTO members' accountability on export subsidies if these subsidies met certain criteria set in the Agreement. Under the Peace Clause, certain qualified export subsidies were only subject to countervailing duty actions when they resulted in injury or threat of injury on the basis of volume, price, or consequent impact.[137] Evidently, the Amber Box subsidy, Blue Box subsidy, and certain export subsidies under the Peace Clause are not granted unconditional immunity. If they cause injury or threat of injury, they are still subject to countervailing duty action.[138]

The Peace Clause expired as of January 1, 2004.[139] All agricultural subsidies, including the subsidies that were exempted from action prior to this expiration date, are now open to challenges under the provisions of the Subsidy Countervailing Measure Agreement.[140] This does not mean that all farm programs are prohibited under the SCM Agreement. Instead, subsidies that are proven to be non-trade-distorting are found to be legal. However, export subsidies are prohibited under Article 3.1(a) of the SCM Agreement without any need to demonstrate their trade-distorting effects.[141]

For those countries that heavily relied on subsidies to support their agriculture, such as the US and those in Europe, the expiration of the Peace Clause is a significant loss. It exposes government subsidies to challenges through the WTO dispute resolution process. However, from a free trade perspective, since large numbers of subsidies are subject to scrutiny and cleansing via WTO litigation after the expiration of the Peace Clause, barriers that distort international agricultural trade are substantially removed. Poor developing countries that are financially unable to provide subsidies and the countries that are dedicated to the reduction of agricultural subsidies can challenge trade-distorting agricultural subsidies through the WTO system. They can use it as a powerful bargaining tool in advancing their trade positions in the world market.

The Subsidy Countervailing Measure Agreement (SCM Agreement)
The AoA includes the SCM Agreement in Article 13, and considers it a basic set of rules that Member States are obligated to respect. As previously stated, the Peace Clause protected certain agricultural subsidies from being challenged during the implementation period. Following the expiration of the Peace Clause on January 1, 2004, the protection no longer applies. All agricultural subsidies

---

137   Bhala, *supra* note 50, at 824.

138   *Id.*

139   Agreement on Agriculture, *supra* note 65, art. 13.

140   Richard H. Steinberg & Timothy E. Josling, *When the Peace Ends: The Vulnerability of EC and US Agricultural Subsidies to WTO Legal Challenge*, 6 J. Int'l Econ L. 369, 388 (2003).

141   Agreement on Subsidies and Countervailing Measures, Apr. 15, 1994, 1867 U.N.T.S. 14, *reprinted in* The Legal Texts: The Results of the Uruguay Round of Multilateral Trade Negotiations 275 (1999). Art. 3.1(a).

are subject to challenge under the SCM Agreement. However, this does not mean all subsidies are illegal under the SCM Agreement. Rather, it means subsidies are actionable if they fall into certain criteria specified in Article 6 of the SCM Agreement.[142]

To be sure, the AoA is still the primary source of authority with regard to agricultural support programs. The SCM Agreement is "intended to further clarify and expand subsidy provisions included in earlier agreements negotiated within the context of the GATT."[143] The SCM Agreement provides general disciplines and rules for all subsidies; it fills the loopholes within the provisions of the AoA in agricultural subsidies.[144] It is important to read and interpret the provisions of the AoA and the SCM Agreement together in the context of agricultural subsidies.

The SCM Agreement establishes a detailed definition of subsidy for the first time, specifying it as "a financial contribution by a government or any public body within the territory of a Member"[145] involving a direct transfer of funds or potential direct transfers of funds or liabilities (such as loan guarantees), foregone government revenue (such as tax credits), or the provision of other goods or services.[146] By clarifying what a subsidy is, the SCM Agreement "eliminates deficiencies of previous trade agreements."[147] Further, it recognizes and distinguishes different subsidies, including: 1) prohibited subsidies, 2) actionable subsidies, and 3) non-actionable subsidies.[148] In an innovative "traffic light" approach, these subsidies are generally referred to as red light subsidies, yellow light subsidies, and green light subsidies, respectively. Breach of the red and yellow light subsidies exposes the offending members to a dispute settlement process or countervailing duty measures. However, the use of green light subsidies is acceptable.

Red light subsidies   Export subsidies and import substitution subsidies are listed as prohibited subsidies (red light subsidies). In accordance with Article 3 of the SCM Agreement, Member States agreed not to grant or maintain subsidies that

---

142   *Id.* art. 6 (specifying what shall be deemed as serious prejudice).

143   *See also* Gillon, *supra* note 18, at 16–17.

144   Petit, *supra* note 7, at 1348 ("This ... means that loopholes within the subsidies provisions of the [AoA] are filled primarily by resorting to relevant provisions of the SCM Agreement").

145   Agreement on Subsidies and Countervailing Measures, *supra* note 141, art. 1.

146   *Id.*

147   William Hett, *US Corn and Soybean Subsidies: WTO Litigation and Sustainable Protections*, 17 Transnat'l L. & Contemp. Probs. 775, 782 (2008).

148   Agreement on Subsidies and Countervailing Measures, *supra* note 141, Article 3 and Article 4 are about prohibited subsidies; Article 5, Article 6, and Article 7 are about actionable (yellow) subsidies; Article 8 and Article 9 are about non-actionable (green) subsidies.

are contingent, whether solely or as one of several other conditions, upon export performance or on the use of domestic goods over imported goods.[149]

Export subsidies refer to those support programs provided by a government to its domestic producers on the condition that these subsidized agricultural products are for export. They are not in conformity with Articles 8, 9, and 10 of the AoA, and fall into this prohibited category.[150]

Import substitution subsidies are those government payments to domestic farmers that purchase domestic goods rather than imported goods for use in domestic manufacturing. Import substitution subsidies lower the cost of domestic content and make market prices artificially low. This suppresses competition from foreign imports.[151]

Both export subsidies and import substitution subsidies have direct and serious trade-distorting effects. They are not permitted under the SCM Agreement. If a subsidy program falls into this prohibited category, it must be removed without delay. Furthermore, the complaining party does not need to demonstrate actual adverse effect or serious prejudice in order to have this subsidy eliminated.[152]

Yellow light subsidies Member States agreed not to provide agricultural subsidies that may result in adverse effects to other members' interests. All other agricultural subsidies except export subsidies and import substitution subsidies are actionable. They fall into the yellow light category. Actionable subsidies are not strictly prohibited, but they are subject to challenges and restrictions if they are shown to be trade-distorting to the interest of another Member State. Article 5 of the SCM Agreement provides a non-exhaustive list of different situations for a complaining party to prove the adverse effects of a subsidy.[153] In practice, a

---

149   *Id.* art. 3.

150   Hett, *supra* note 147 (explaining "[a]rticle 8 prohibits any export subsidy that exceeds a member's total AMS. In addition, export subsidies for non-scheduled commodities are prohibited for members that are bound by reduction commitments. Article 9 delineates what types of export subsidies must be counted toward the total AMS. Article 10 prohibits the use of other export subsidies in a manner that circumvents reduction commitments").

151   Phoenix X.F. Cai, *Think Big and Ignore the Law: US Corn and Ethanol Subsidies and WTO Law*, 40 GEO. J. INT'L L. 865, 870–71 (2009).

152   Gillon, *supra* note 18, at 16–17 ("If a Member is found to be providing a prohibited subsidy, the Member must withdraw it. The complaining Member does not have to prove that the prohibited subsidy caused it any injury"). *Id.*

153   Agreement on Subsidies and Countervailing Measures, *supra* note 141, art. 5 ("No Member should cause, through the use of any subsidy referred to in paragraphs 1 and 2 of Article 1, adverse effects to the interests of other Members, i.e.: (a) injury to the domestic industry of another Member; (b) nullification or impairment of benefits accruing directly or indirectly to other Members under GATT 1994 in particular the benefits of concessions bound under Article II of GATT 1994; (c) serious prejudice to the interests of another Member. This Article does not apply to subsidies maintained on agricultural products as provided in Article 13 of the Agreement on Agriculture").

complaining member is required to demonstrate that the subsidy results in serious prejudice listed in Article 6.3 of the SCM Agreement.[154] Serious prejudice can be proven by demonstrating that the subsidy results in market share loss or causes significant price suppression.[155] Therefore, if a subsidy significantly lowers the price of the subsidized commodity in an applicable market, or if a subsidy enables a country to take a portion of the aggrieved party's market share for that commodity, this subsidy is actionable. Upon determining that a subsidiary is actionable, "the Member granting or maintaining such subsidy shall take appropriate steps to remove the adverse effects or shall withdraw the subsidy."[156]

Green light subsidies   Member States agreed to permit four types of subsidies ("Green light category") under Article 8 of the SCM Agreement. These subsidies include non-specific subsidies (subsidies that are not limited to a particular enterprise, industry or group),[157] certain types of research and development,[158] assistance to disadvantaged regions,[159] and one-time assistance to promote adaptation of existing facilities to new environmental requirements.[160] Green light subsidies are generally used by members without worrying about the risk of being subject to countervailing measures.

Issues   Article 21 (Final Provisions) of the AoA specifies that other multilateral WTO agreements, including the SCM Agreement, shall apply subject to the provisions of the Agreement on Agriculture if they conflict.[161] To be fair, Article

---

154   *See* Porterfield, *supra* note 64, at 1011 ("Although there are a variety of ways in which a WTO Member country can demonstrate that another country's subsidies are illegally trade-distorting, the most important standard is whether the subsidies cause serious prejudice").

155   Agreement on Subsidies and Countervailing Measures, *supra* note 141, art. 6.3 ("(a) the effect of the subsidy is to displace or impede the imports of a like product of another Member into the market of the subsidizing Member; (b) the effect of the subsidy is to displace or impede the exports of a like product of another Member from a third country market; (c) the effect of the subsidy is a significant price undercutting by the subsidized product as compared with the price of a like product of another Member in the same market or significant price suppression, price depression or lost sales in the same market; (d) the effect of the subsidy is an increase in the world market share of the subsidizing Member in a particular subsidized primary product or commodity as compared to the average share it had during the previous period of three years and this increase follows a consistent trend over a period when subsidies have been granted").

156   *Id.* art. 7.8.

157   *Id.* art. 8.1.

158   *Id.* art 8.2(a).

159   *Id.* art. 8.2(b).

160   *Id.* art. 8.2(c).

161   Agreement on Agriculture, *supra* note 65, art. 21.1 ("The provisions of GATT 1994 and of other Multilateral Trade Agreements in Annex 1A to the WTO Agreement shall apply

21 only indicates the prevalence of the AoA "in the event of conflict"; it does not specify that subsidies are still protected from challenges. However, the loopholes it contains allow Member States to misinterpret it in the event of conflict. Despite the expiration of the Peace Clause in 2004, trade-distorting agricultural subsidies could still continue to be protected from challenges under the SCM Agreement. The WTO may consider further interpretation of this provision so as to avoid the implication of unfair agricultural subsidies.

The Agreement on the Application of Sanitary and Phytosanitary Measures (SPS Agreement)
In addition to the SCM Agreement, the AoA also mentions the application of sanitary and phytosanitary measures. According to Article 14 of the AoA, "Members agree to give effect to the Agreement on the Application of Sanitary and Phytosanitary Measures."[162] Considering the negotiation on SPS measures required specialized technical expertise, a separate sub-group was established on the SPS measures. An agreement that is apart from the main text of the AoA was concluded separately—the Agreement on the Application of Sanitary and Phytosanitary Measures (SPS Agreement). The Sanitary and Phytosanitary Agreement addresses government standards on health and disease risks.

Rather than only regulate SPS measures in agricultural trade, the Sanitary and Phytosanitary Agreement "applies to all sanitary and phytosanitary measures which may, directly or indirectly, affect international trade."[163] According to the Sanitary and Phytosanitary Agreement,

> [n]o Member should be prevented from adopting or enforcing measures necessary to protect human, animal or plant life or health, subject to the requirement that these measures are not applied in a manner which would constitute a means of arbitrary or unjustifiable discrimination between Members where the same conditions prevail or a disguised restriction on international trade.[164]

---

subject to the provisions of this Agreement"). *See also* Porterfield, *supra* note 64, at 1009 (noting that the opponents of this argument believe that there is no specific treaty or provision under the WTO system governing conflicts between the AoA and the SCM Agreement. Article 21 of the AoA should not be explained as protecting agricultural subsidies from challenges under the SCM Agreement. Instead, the opponents merely indicate that the AoA prevails in the event of any conflict with the SCM Agreement. Therefore, Porterfield raises relevant questions, such as "which provisions of the Agreement on Agriculture purport to protect agricultural subsidies from challenge under the SCM Agreement, and what is the scope and (more importantly) duration of that protection?").

162   Agreement on Agriculture, *supra* note 65, art. 14.

163   WTO Agreement on the Application of Sanitary and Phytosanitary Measures (SPS Agreement), Apr. 15, 1994, 1867 U.N.T.S. 493, art. 1.1.

164   *Id.*

The SPS Agreement sets the criteria for distinguishing justified protection methods from unjustified trade barriers,[165] and it also sets out the rules to ensure that each WTO members' laws, regulations, and measures regarding human, animal or plant life or health are transparent, scientifically defensible, and non-discriminatory.[166] WTO members "have the right to take sanitary and phytosanitary measures necessary for the protection of human, animal or plant life or health,"[167] but they are obligated to harmonize their sanitary and phytosanitary measures "on the basis of international standards, guidelines and recommendations developed by the relevant international organizations."[168] They also should accept the measures of another member as equivalent if the member objectively demonstrates that "its measures achieve the importing Member's appropriate level of sanitary or phytosanitary protection."[169]

Further, considering that "developing country Members may encounter special difficulties in complying with the sanitary or phytosanitary measures of importing Members,"[170] the Sanitary and Phytosanitary Agreement allows longer timeframes for developing countries to comply when new SPS measures are introduced.[171] Upon request, it also grants developing countries "specified, time-limited exceptions in whole or in part from obligations under this Agreement."[172]

In the event of disputes, SPS measures are subject to WTO dispute settlement procedures and therefore "the provisions of Articles XXII and XXIII of GATT 1994 as elaborated and applied by the Dispute Settlement Understanding shall apply to consultations and the settlement of disputes under this Agreement, except as otherwise specifically provided herein."[173]

Issues   SPS measures are implemented to protect Member States' domestic food safety, animal, and plant health when necessary.[174] They serve legitimate goals. However, what measures are considered to be appropriate? How can governments

---

165   *Id.* arts. 3–6.

166   *Id.* art. 7 ("Members shall notify changes in their sanitary or phytosanitary measures and shall provide information on their sanitary or phytosanitary measures in accordance with the provisions of Annex B").

167   *Id.* art. 2. These measures have to be "based on scientific principles and [a]re not maintained without sufficient scientific evidence, except as provided for in paragraph 7 of Article 5"; and they have to be ensured not to be "arbitrarily or unjustifiably discriminate between Members where identical or similar conditions prevail" or "applied in a manner which would constitute a disguised restriction on international trade."

168   *Id.* art. 3.1.

169   *Id.* art. 4.1.

170   *Id.* pmbl.

171   *Id.* art. 10.2.

172   *Id.* art. 10.3.

173   *Id.* art. 11.1.

174   Eric Gillman, *Making WTO SPS Dispute Settlement Work: Challenges and Practical Solutions*, 31 Nw. J. Int'l L. & Bus. 439, 441 (2011).

ensure that the health and safety standards implemented are not an excuse for protecting domestic producers?

To be fair, as previously discussed, the Sanitary and Phytosanitary Agreement sets out general criteria for distinguishing justified protection methods from unjustified trade barriers. The SPS measures must be based on science.[175] However, there still is a risk that SPS measures may be misused as protectionist devices to keep foreign competitors out of domestic markets. In practice, SPS measures are often used as one of the most pernicious trade barriers. Member States are allowed to set their own standards, and it is difficult to find the right equilibrium between safeguarding each member's interest in protecting its domestic market from products that may threaten the life or health of humans, animals, or plants and ensuring that these threats are not abusively invoked by individual members in order to restrict market access.[176] Although the goal of the Sanitary and Phytosanitary Agreement is to prevent government measures from being abused to protect domestic producers, WTO members may still cite a non-existent risk under the name of protecting the life or health of humans, animals, or plants.

Furthermore, developed countries have the financial, human, and technical resources to use SPS measures. They generally set higher standards of protection, while developing countries lack all these resources to do so, and face many difficulties when using the measures. Many markets in developed countries are still overprotected or even closed behind the protection of scientifically questionable SPS standards.[177] The Sanitary and Phytosanitary Agreement does not practically improve developing countries' access to the world market. Therefore, it is necessary for the WTO to include a comprehensive system into its framework in order to monitor the use of SPS measures, making sure these measures are only applied to the extent necessary to meet the member's chosen level of protection.[178] Such a system will help prevent SPS measures from promoting unfair discrimination, or serving as disguised restrictions on international agricultural trade.[179] Additionally, if the SPS measures are abused for protectionist purposes, immediate remedies must be available to correct the inappropriate application of SPS measures.

---

175   World Trade Org., *Sanitary and Phytosanitary Measures: Introduction—Understanding the WTO Agreement on Sanitary and Phytosanitary Measures* (May 1998), http://www.wto.org/english/tratop_e/sps_e/spsund_e.htm.

176   Andrew T. Guzman, *Dispute Resolution in SPS Cases*, in Ten Years of WTO Dispute Settlement, 215–33 (Horovitz ed., 2007), *available at* http://works.bepress.com/andrew_guzman/4.

177   David S. Johanson & William L. Bryant, *Eliminating Phytosanitary Trade Barriers: The Effects of the Uruguay Round Agreements on California Agricultural Exports*, 6 San Joaquin Agric. L. Rev. 1, 2 (1996).

178   Kent S. Foster & Dean C. Alexander, *The North American Free Trade Agreement and the Agricultural Sector*, 27 Creighton L. Rev. 985, 997 (1993–1994).

179   *Id.* at 997–98.

Summary of the Uruguay Round of multilateral trade negotiations
For the first time, the AoA officially brings agriculture issues into trade negotiations at the international level.[180] It reverses the long-term tendency of governments interfering in agricultural production and trade, and it establishes comprehensive disciplines and rules on agricultural trade which had been ignored for decades. It is the Uruguay Round's greatest accomplishment. Although the AoA far from resembles earlier US proposals to the GATT, it marks a significant beginning in subjecting agricultural trade to the same disciplines and rules that govern trade in other goods.

The AoA establishes specific binding commitment for its members, and it makes significant strides in subsidy and trade barrier reductions. First, the AoA promotes transparency in border measures. Although tariffication was not a success, it introduces the idea of greater market access in agricultural trade. Second, it makes attempts to set reduction commitments for domestic support measures. Third, it enshrines the principle that export subsidies are very trade-distorting, and must be subject to upper bounds. The AoA takes into account the special needs of developing countries. It allows flexibility through its special and differential treatment programs to permit developing countries to make less or no reduction commitments. Additionally, a Committee on Agriculture is established as part of the institutional structure.[181] The Committee supervises the implementation of the AoA. It also provides members a forum to consult related issues.

A fairer and more stable trading environment was expected to be established after the successful conclusion of the Uruguay Round negotiations. Nevertheless, the AoA did not have an immediate impact on agricultural trade liberalization.[182] It was flawed, and did not make dramatic changes in the real world. The implementation of the AoA is full of problems.

The tariffication was expected to promote transparency and, thereby, achieve the goal of allowing Member States to address trade issues more easily. However, as noted previously, when members converted non-tariff barriers into their tariff equivalents, they overstated their tariffs. The resulting tariffs after the tariffication process were often higher than the genuine equivalents ("dirty tariffication"). Dirty tariffication is an immense impediment to greater market access.

Not all trade-distorting support programs were included in the category that is subject to reduction. For the subsidies that are subject to reduction, they were actually set at levels that the US and the EC could easily make without extensively reforming their existing agricultural support programs.[183] As a consequence, the Agreement is still systematically favors developed countries. Furthermore, Member

---

180   Petit, *supra* note 7, at 155–56.

181   Agreement on Agriculture, *supra* note 65, art. 17.

182   Steinle, *supra* note 32, note 334 ("The primary benefit of the Agreement lies not in its immediate impact on liberalizing trade of agricultural products, but rather in the framework it establishes for future trade liberalization").

183   Petit, *supra* note 7, at 155–56.

States, especially rich Member States, have also repeatedly and excessively violated and ignored their obligations concerning agricultural subsidies reduction. They continue paying their farmers massive subsidies, which most developing countries are not able to afford. One of the most debatable programs that showed the ignorance of AoA obligations is the 2002 US Farm Bill. Rather than reduce government support, the 2002 Farm Bill increased subsidies, and authorized a $248.6 billion budget for farm support over a period of six years, which is far beyond its permitted government support under the AoA.[184]

To summarize, the Uruguay Round negotiations are a breakthrough, but they have only resulted in "half success, half failure." The objective of establishing a fair and market-oriented trading system remains unfulfilled, and it has a long way to go. Continuing efforts should be intensified to achieve the long-term objective of substantial progressive reductions in support and protection.

Doha Round Negotiations: Hard to Achieve a Compromise, More Work Needs to Be Done

The AoA was not the end point of the negotiations on subsidy and tariff reductions. Instead, it set up future negotiations with the long-term goal of eventually achieving trade liberalization in agriculture. Pursuant to Article 20 of the AoA, negotiations with regard to further liberalization shall initiate one year before the end of the implementation period.[185]

A new round of multilateral trade negotiations (the Doha Round) was launched in Doha, Qatar in November 2001. The Doha Round negotiations are aimed at establishing an enhanced set of agreed rules for a more transparent, freer, and fairer international trading system. The Doha Round takes into account non-trade concerns and the special development needs of developing countries.[186] In compliance with Article 20 of the AoA, WTO members agreed to include previous agricultural issues in Doha Round negotiations, with the hope that substantial reductions in trade-distorting support measures will be achieved.

The Doha Declaration was signed in 2001. It reaffirms the long-term objective of WTO negotiations as "[e]stablishing a fair and market-oriented trading system through a program of fundamental reform encompassing strengthened rules and specific commitments on support and protection in order to correct and prevent restrictions and distortions in world agricultural markets."[187]

---

184   Porterfield, *supra* note 64, at 1004.

185   Agreement on Agriculture, *supra* note 65, art. 20.

186   UN, HIGH-LEVEL TASK FORCE ON THE GLOBAL FOOD SECURITY CRISIS, OUTCOMES AND ACTIONS FOR GLOBAL FOOD SECURITY, EXCERPTS FROM "COMPREHENSIVE FRAMEWORK FOR ACTION" 3 (July 2008), *available at* http://www.un.org/issues/food/taskforce/pdf/OutcomesAndActionsBooklet_v9.pdf [hereinafter HIGH-LEVEL TASK FORCE].

187   World Trade Organization, Ministerial Declaration of November 14, 2001, 13–14, WT/MIN(01)/DEC/1, 41 I.L.M. 746 (2002) [hereinafter WTO Ministerial Declaration].

WTO members realized the importance of reducing trade-distorting domestic support measures in general rather than just cut Amber Box measures. They also understood the necessity of phasing out all export subsidies rather than just remove those listed in the AoA. During the Doha Round negotiations, WTO members agreed to commit to comprehensive negotiations aimed at "substantial improvements in market access; reductions of, with a view to phasing out, all forms of export subsidies; and substantial reductions in trade-distorting domestic support."[188] They also reaffirmed the commitment to special and differential treatments for developing countries. The special development needs of developing countries, for example, food security and rural development, were considered in Doha negotiations. Other non-trade concerns were also addressed in the Declaration.[189]

However, the Doha Round of negotiations did not develop into a meaningful and successful round. Rather, developed countries failed to deliver the most critical promise—substantial reduction in agricultural protection.[190] The $248.6 billion budget for farm support in the 2002 US Farm Bill, as well as the EU's failure to reform its CAP,[191] made it a joke that the Doha Round was to be a development round. These protectionist policies directly hurt many developing countries that rely on agricultural export as one of their major income sources.

Although timeframes for the reduction of agricultural subsidies and trade barriers were established, it was hard for WTO members to reconcile differences in their positions on many basic issues, let alone make substantial reforms.

Unlike in its proposals during the Uruguay Round negotiations, the US was a major obstacle to further trade liberalization in agriculture during the Doha Round negotiations. Under significant pressure from Congress, the US government "has been attempting to make limited concessions regarding the permissible levels and classifications of subsidies under the AoA."[192] The US has also tried pushing for a new Peace Clause that would protect its farm subsidies from being challenged under the SCM Agreement after the expiration of the previous Peace Clause in 2004.[193] However, the US proposal of minimizing subsidy reduction does not seem to get much support from the EU and other WTO members. US farm subsidies are likely to remain challengeable under the SCM Agreement.

Developing countries have been irritated by the WTO rules that allow trade-distorting subsidies and high tariffs in favor of developed countries. They have

---

188   *Id.*

189   *Id.*

190   Sungjoon Cho, *Doha's Development*, 25 BERKELEY J. INT'L L. 165, 170 (2007).

191   Vance E. Hendrix, *The Farm Bill of 2002, The WTO, and Poor African Farmers: Can They Co-exist?*, 12 TULSA J. COMP. & INT'L L. 227, 243 (2004). ("European countries were unable to decide on the most appropriate reform measures to be taken concerning the Common Agriculture Policy (CAP).")

192   Porterfield, *supra* note 64, at 1023–24.

193   *Id.* at 999–1001.

also been frustrated by the developed countries' inadequate implementation of their commitments in subsidy reduction. Developing countries began to form large coalitions and started to raise their voices at WTO negotiations. With the hope of progress, the Doha Round negotiations were continued with midpoint meetings in Cancun, Mexico in September 2003. During the Cancun meetings, a new alliance of developing countries, the Group of 21, was established. The Group of 21 was led by a few developing countries that are comparatively strong economically, such as Brazil, India, South Africa, and China.[194] They argued that the US and EU proposals failed to make substantial reductions in trade-distorting subsidies, and failed to increase market access.[195] The Group of 21 urged developed countries, primarily the US and the EU, to substantially reduce government interventions in agriculture. In addition to the Group of 21, other developing countries also made demands on developed countries—for example, a group of West African countries that produce cotton challenged the US over its trade-distorting subsidies in cotton.[196] Developing countries have gradually become important negotiators since the Doha Round. The participation of developing countries in trade negotiations is a positive sign for the WTO; it promotes an international trade environment that is less discriminatory.

Unfortunately, the Cancun meetings did not achieve the expected goals. Many countries, both developed and developing, are unwilling to make significant concessions. Developing countries demanded a substantial reduction in trade-distorting subsidies that adversely impact their agricultural exports, but they were reluctant to forego their own subsidies.[197] When the results of the negotiations seemed to move away from the pre-set objectives, many developing countries walked out.[198] Furthermore, in response to the West African cotton-producing countries' demand on developed countries, the US refused to make cotton the only target for subsidy reform.[199] The breakdown in negotiations set back the timetable for meeting deadline requirements.

To summarize, the developed countries' inadequate implementation of their commitment in subsidy and tariff reductions, the frustrations of developing countries in WTO negotiations, and most importantly, WTO members' sharp divide over many key issues, make reaching a consensus in agricultural trade

---

194   Petit, *supra* note 7, at 157.

195   *Id.* at 158 (explaining that the US and EU proposals "[do] not reflect the level of ambition of the Doha mandate, for [they fail] to deliver substantial cuts on trade-distorting domestic support, substantial increases in market access and elimination of export subsidies").

196   *Id.* A group of West African countries challenged the US "to make cotton a test case of the [WTO's] commitment to a level playing field for trade in agricultural goods." *Id.*

197   Hendrix, *supra* note 191, at 244.

198   Elizabeth Becker, *Poorer Countries Pull Out of Talks over World Trade*, N.Y. TIMES, Sept. 15, 2003, at A1.

199   Hendrix, *supra* note 191, at 245.

liberalization difficult. The deadlines set by the Doha Declaration were not met. Furthermore, the Doha Round negotiations were indefinitely suspended on July 28, 2006 by the General Council of the WTO. Many critical issues remained to be resolved. When negotiations were resumed in 2007, WTO members still were not able to come to a compromise. Intense negotiations have been on and off since July 2008. As of February 2013 the issue of agricultural trade liberalization remains uncertain.[200] The US insists that the EU should substantially reduce tariffs, improve market access, and also limit the number of sensitive products that would be exempt from reduction commitment. The EU, backed by many developing countries, insists that the US should make a significant cut in its domestic support for agriculture. The Doha Round remained in deadlock after years of negotiations. It failed to deliver any significant progress.

It has been more than 10 years since the Doha Round negotiations were first launched in 2001. It would be a big loss if members throw away 10 years of solid multilateral work.[201] WTO Director-General Pascal Lamy asked Member States to "think hard about the consequences"; he encouraged Member States to take "small steps, gradually moving forward the parts of the Doha Round which were mature, and re-thinking those where greater differences remained."[202] A new round of comprehensive and wide-ranging agricultural trade negotiations is critical in order to bring more disciplines and predictability to international agricultural trade. Moreover, reform programs need to seek a balance between agricultural trade liberalization and governments' desire to pursue legitimate agricultural protectionist policies.[203]

---

200   WTO General Council, Lamy: Members Continue to Explore Opportunities for Doha Progress (May 2, 2012), http://www.wto.org/english/news_e/news12_e/gc_rpt_01may12_e.htm.

201   World Trade Org., DOHA Development Agenda: Negotiations, Documents from the Negotiating Chairs (April 21, 2011), *available at* http://www.wto.org/english/tratop_e/dda_e/chair_texts11_e/chair_texts11_e.htm.

202   WTO General Council, *supra* note 200.

203   Marc Kleiner, *United States vs. European Union: Transatlantic Debate on Issues Close to Home VI. Export Subsidies*, 10 U. MIAMI INT'L & COMP. L. REV. 129, 140–41 (2002).

Chapter 7
Prospects for Further Agricultural Trade Reform

As previously discussed, the WTO's long term objective in agriculture is greater trade liberalization through substantial reductions in tariffs, subsidies, and other trade-distorting government interventions. Basically, there are three major areas that WTO members can address. The first area is market access, which can only be enhanced through substantial tariff reductions. The second area is domestic subsidies. Trade-distorting domestic subsidies need to be removed eventually, but the complete elimination of subsidies in the next few years will not be easy; substantial reduction is the most urgent mission, and that should be tackled as soon as possible. WTO members may consider progressively converting Blue Box measures into Amber Box measures and subject both to reduction. As for Green Box measures, WTO members may take advantage of it as they are allowed to preserve criteria-based Green Box policies, and to support non-specific rural development programs and environmental programs that are disconnected with production or price. The third area is export competition. The complete elimination of multilateral export subsidies is the ultimate goal. WTO members may continue to provide special and differential treatment to developing countries due to their special development and food security needs.

In addition to the three major areas that the WTO members should focus on, this research explores other factors that may affect international agricultural trade and world hunger—sanitary and phytosanitary measures and genetically modified organisms, food aid programs, and the role of international organizations in world hunger reduction. This research further proposes some feasible reforms concerning these factors with the goal to reduce world hunger.

Enhance Market Access through Substantial Tariff Reduction

As previously discussed, one of the great innovations of the Agreement on Agriculture was the conversion of non-tariff barriers into their tariff equivalents. However, the resulting tariffs after the process of tariffication were often higher than the protection afforded by the equivalent non-tariff barriers for the 1986–1988 base period. Tariffication thus resulted in higher levels of protection than under the old system of quotas, import bans, and variable import levies.[1] By engaging in dirty tariffication, WTO member(s) successfully avoided liberalizing trade on certain products without violating the tariff reduction requirements set by the Agreement on Agriculture, declaring the failure of the AoA's tariff reduction plan. The international trade regime therefore did little to expand market opportunities during the Uruguay Round negotiations.

Despite the failure, improving market access is still on the agenda of the WTO agricultural trade negotiations. WTO members are still hoping they can make a compromise in further trade liberalization. To be fair, greater market access can only be achieved through substantial tariff reductions. Negotiation parties need to compromise the desire to protect their agriculture with the requirements of international trade liberalization. The international trade regime must establish a comprehensive framework for the implementation of a substantial reduction of tariffs in agricultural commodities. This research addresses a few key issues in tariff reduction.

First, rich developed countries dominate world trade. They protect their domestic agricultural markets by imposing high tariffs on foreign agricultural imports. Developing countries' agricultural products thus have restricted access to developed countries' markets. To improve global market access, tariff reductions should primarily be targeted to the achievement of greater access by developing country agricultural producers to developed country markets. However, considering the vulnerability of many poor developing countries, new tariff reductions should not impair developing countries' ability to utilize appropriate tariffs to ensure their food security and to promote rural development.[2] Developing countries should not be required to make additional tariff reductions unless developed countries have made significant concessions. Otherwise, if developing countries cut their tariffs while developed countries still provide extensive support, agricultural trade continues to be severely displaced. Tariff reduction in developed countries would increasingly integrate developing countries into the global trading system.

Second, current tariff reductions in agricultural commodities are not made on a product-by-product basis but on an industry-wide average. On the one hand, selective tariff reductions give governments the flexibility to decide on which product(s) they would like to reduce more tariffs and on which product(s) they

---

1   Raj Bhala, World Agricultural Trade in Purgatory: The Uruguay Round Agriculture Agreement and Its Implications for the Doha Round, 79 N.D.L. Rev. 691, 731 (2003). ("[P]ost-Uruguay Round tariffs resulting from tariffication are 'very high' on many agricultural products because of the 'excessively high tariff equivalents' used by many countries. Such products include staple items like cereals, dairy products, meat, milk, and sugar, where tariffication of quantitative restrictions has resulted in duty rates above 100 percent.")

2   Carmen G. Gonzalez, Institutionalizing Inequality: The WTO Agreement on Agriculture, Food Security, and Developing Countries, 27 Colum. J. Envtl. L. 433, 485 (2002).

would like to maintain high tariffs. On the other hand, this may result in the overprotection of certain agricultural product(s), which may severely disturb the free flow of foreign imports in the global market. Thus, a clear product-by-product tariff reduction method is desirable. Or at least, a general cap on individual agricultural products is necessary so that governments will not overwhelmingly go over the limit.

Third, tariff escalation occurs when "the tariff applied to a product category rises as the level of processing increases, from raw material to manufactured product."[3] Tariff escalation results in "a higher level of protection of the more processed products in the importing country and smaller imports of the more processed products."[4] When importing countries, mostly developed countries, apply higher tariffs for more processed agricultural products, they hold back exporting countries' production of value-added products for export. Tariff escalation essentially reduces market opportunities for agricultural exporting countries, and it also obstructs their export diversification.[5] Furthermore, tariff escalation potentially causes environmental damage to exporting countries because an excessive reliance on certain primary product exports can result in the depletion of natural resources and affect sustainable development. Therefore, it is strongly recommended that the WTO makes a change in trade measures that would allow tariff escalation to be substantially reduced and eventually eliminated. The reduction of tariff escalation on products of export interest to developing countries would produce significant improvements in market access.

Reduce/Eliminate Subsidies Progressively

Governments provide, either individually or in combination, different types of subsidies to protect their domestic production of certain agricultural products. Subsidy covers almost all areas of international agricultural trade, and is one of the most important elements while also one of the most difficult and debatable issues addressed in recent trade negotiations. WTO members have been discussing the substantial reduction of trade-distorting agricultural subsidies since the Uruguay Round negotiations (1986–1994). However, there has not been much success. To promote greater trade liberalization, it is essential to have a better understanding of the advantages and disadvantages of agricultural subsidies so that WTO members

---

3   World Trade Org., The WTO and Developing Countries, Tariff Escalation, available at http://www.inquit.com/iqebooks/WTODC/Webversion/uruguay/four.htm (last visited June 23, 2011).

4   Id.

5   NASREDIN ELAMIN & HANSDEEP KHAIRA, TARIFF ESCALATION IN AGRICULTURAL COMMODITY MARKETS, available at http://www.fao.org/DOCREP/006/Y5117E/y5117e0e.htm (last visited June 23, 2011).

can build bridges, and make feasible reforms on subsidy reduction, rather than going to a deadlock again as in the Doha Round negotiations.

Weigh the Pros and Cons of Agricultural Subsidies

Agricultural subsidies come in different forms and sizes.[6] They are grouped into three "boxes"—Amber Box, Blue Box, and Green Box—in accordance with the degree to which they potentially distort international agricultural trade. Developed countries employ significant subsidies to support their agriculture. By offering an above-market price, subsidies ensure farmers' income, encourage agricultural production, and protect food security and national security. However, these agricultural subsidies inevitably promote overproduction and the unnecessary use of agricultural inputs. The overuse of agrochemicals, such as fertilizers and pesticides, inevitably results in undesirable environmental consequences.[7] Internationally, these subsidies distort agricultural trade, undercutting market opportunities for developing world farmers. Thus farmers in developing countries are hurt by the continuous price support in developed countries and are forced to leave the industry or move into a less trade-distorted form of agriculture.

Weighing the pros and cons of agricultural subsidies, in the long-term, the substantial reduction and eventual elimination of agricultural subsidies is vital to accelerate progress on the broader free trade agenda.[8] Nevertheless, many opponents argue that it is still too early to conclude that trade-distorting agricultural subsidies must be eliminated. Understanding who pays for and who receives the agricultural subsidies may make it clearer whether agricultural subsidies should be kept or not.

Who Pays for Agricultural Subsidies?

Agricultural subsidy measures are basically employed by governments rather than individuals. Where do governments get the revenues to provide such support? The truth is that agricultural protectionism is costly to domestic consumers and taxpayers.[9]

---

6   Thomas Richard Poole, Silly Rabbit, Farm Subsidies Don't Help America, 31 WM. & MARY ENVTL. L. & POL'Y REV. 183, 183 (2006). (Agricultural subsidies include "payments made directly to farmers without respect to the amount they produce, loans guaranteed by the government, payments for leaving land unproductive, and price guarantees for particular commodities paid to farmers by the government.") Id.

7   DANIEL IMHOFF, FOOD FIGHT: THE CITIZEN'S GUIDE TO A FOOD AND FARM BILL 19 (2007).

8   UN, HIGH-LEVEL TASK FORCE ON THE GLOBAL FOOD SECURITY CRISIS, OUTCOMES AND ACTIONS FOR GLOBAL FOOD SECURITY, EXCERPTS FROM "COMPREHENSIVE FRAMEWORK FOR ACTION" 14 (July 2008), available at http://www.un.org/issues/food/taskforce/pdf/OutcomesAndActionsBooklet_v9.pdf [hereinafter HIGH-LEVEL TASK FORCE].

9   Miguel Antonio Figueroa, The GATT and Agriculture: Past, Present, and Future, 5 KAN. J. L. & PUB. POL'Y 93, 99 (Fall 1995).

Consumers in countries where agriculture is largely subsidized spend extra money on food because they are the ones who pay the bills for agricultural subsidies or export support.[10] At the grocery store checkout, they pay more than they should due to the pre-set minimum prices for agricultural commodities. In addition to the extra money they pay at the checkout counter, consumers and taxpayers together bear the cost when their governments provide agricultural subsidies to eligible farmers. Taxes are predominantly lined with the generous subsidization of overproduction and storage of surplus agricultural products.[11] Billions of tax dollars also finance environmental clean-up and environmental damage caused by the overproduction and overuse of fertilizers and pesticides.[12]

One reason that the majority of consumers and taxpayers do not realize how much they actually pay for agricultural subsidies is that they are disconnected from the price-policy-making process and the programs supported by taxes. They do not understand the true costs of subsidized agriculture and they do not recognize the necessity to reform the current over-subsidized agricultural system. Thus, the public needs to understand existing agricultural subsidy programs and their impacts on domestic markets and international trade.

Who Receives Government Support?

Unfortunately, agricultural subsidies typically do not benefit all farmers as most people believe. Current support programs provide little assistance for the majority of farmers. Small farmers only receive minimal government support. Ironically, large and relatively wealthy farmers, in particular large industrial farmers, are the major beneficiaries of agricultural subsidies.[13] Agricultural protectionism policies simply benefit small groups of rich farmers at the expense of the interest of the majority.

As already noted, the US has been overwhelmingly employing subsidies to support its agriculture. Studying the US case helps understand where the massive government funds flow to, and how current agricultural policies prevent small farmers from receiving government subsidies.

---

10   Id. ("Consumers bear the costs by paying higher than world market price for products they buy at home"). Id.

11   Jodi Soyars Windham, Putting Your Money Where Your Mouth Is: Preserve Food Subsidies, Social Responsibility & America's 2007 Farm Bill, 31 ENVIRONS ENVTL. L. & POL'Y J. 1, 6 (Fall 2007).

12   Frank A. Seminerio, A Tale of Two Subsidies: How Federal Support Programs for Ethanol and Biodiesel Can Be Created in Order to Circumvent Fair Trade Challenges Under World Trade Organization Rulings, 26 PENN. ST. INT'L L. REV. 963, 974 (2008) ("Overuse of fertilizers and pesticides adds to runoff that pollutes rivers, lakes and oceans"). Id.

13   Hilary K. Josephs, Learning from the Developing World, 14 KAN. J. L. & PUB. POL'Y 231, 233 (Winter 2005). ("[M]ost of subsidies go to a handful of relatively wealthy farmers. At present, subsidies benefit those who need it least, the largest and richest farmers.") Id.

Many Americans may believe that the government has been providing support to all American farmers. However, the fact is that US agricultural payments have primarily been given to producers of a few commodity crops, which are corn, cotton, wheat, rice, and soybeans.[14] This concentration of government subsidies on certain crops excludes many American farmers from government financial assistance.[15] Even worse, the payments are heavily concentrated in terms of recipients.[16] Research shows that the richest 10 percent of agricultural subsidy recipients, mainly large farm enterprises, receive approximately two-thirds of all subsidy payments under the US's Farm Bills.[17] Agribusiness is the biggest beneficiary of government subsidies. Ironically, the remaining American farmers receive little or even no subsidy payments. Data show that 60 percent of American farmers receive no financial assistance at all.[18] Although the US government has done a great job of preserving farmland compared to other countries, US Farm Bills are not successful in preserving small family farms; they disproportionately favor industrial agriculture.

Small farmers alone, without government support, have little financial and political power to protect and increase their profits. Not surprisingly, the most direct consequence of the US's agricultural subsidy programs is the utter destruction of the small family farm and the continued exodus of independent family farmers from their farmland. The percentage of small family farms is shrinking rapidly as the percentage of large industrial farms swells.

Most of the public, including the majority of farmers, assume government payments are divided up equally among the farmers. They do not know who the real beneficiary of subsidy programs actually is. Thus, it is necessary for the American public to recognize that despite the initial objective of US Farm Bills, to protect small farmers, subsidy programs have essentially failed to meet their original goals.

---

14 William S. Eubanks II, A Rotten System: Subsidizing Environmental Degradation and Poor Public Health with Our Nation's Tax Dollars, 28 Stan. Envtl. L.J. 213, 227 (2009). ("Despite the fact that thousands of plant and animal species [are] cultivated for human use, more than 84 percent of the $172 billion spent to subsidize our nation's agriculture during that period went solely to these five crops.") Id.

15 Windham, supra note 11, at 14 ("Fruit and vegetable producers, as well as most organic farmers, are not eligible for commodity subsidies under the 2002 Farm Bill"). Id.

16 J.B. Ruhl, Three Questions for Agriculture about the Environment, 17 J. Land Use & Envtl. L. 395, 407 (2002).

17 See Windham, supra note 11, at 14 (noting that farm subsidies are "heavily concentrated into the hands of only ten percent of the farm subsidy recipients"). Id. Some other data shows "the top 20 percent of subsidy recipients receive eighty seven percent of all the available money." See Amanda Stokes, Selling Out the Farm? The Impact of the Farm Security and Rural Investment Act of 2002 on Lending Institutions and the Small Farmer, 9 N.C. Banking Inst. 243, 246 (2005).

18 Windham, supra note 11.

Is It Worth It? Calculate the Costs of Subsidies

The pros and cons of agricultural subsidies have already been briefly discussed. However, the next question to address is whether it is worth it for governments to offer such generous support for agriculture. With fewer pros, subsidies essentially have more cons. The substantial reduction of subsidies will be a remarkable step forward for agricultural trade liberalization.

Developed countries provide generous support to protect their agriculture, but the cost of government subsidies is significant. According to a UNDP report, developed countries have spent $350 billion a year to support their agriculture.[19] Other data show $400 billion a year.[20] Regardless, in addition to this estimable amount of government budget allocated to agricultural support programs, the actual cost of agricultural subsidies is inestimably exacerbated because of the inefficient allocation of resources and other economic distortions.

Overwhelming amounts of financial resources are used to support agriculture and farmers. Natural resources, labor, land, and other resources are shifted from other sectors of the economy to agricultural production. Government revenues are also needed to finance environmental clean-up and environmental damages caused by overproduction and the overuse of fertilizers and pesticides. Furthermore, considering large industrial farmers receive the most of the government subsidies and small family farms are shrinking, the farm population is gradually declining. Farmers that left the agricultural industry may find it difficult to find a job in other areas because they may not have other technical skills. They remain unemployed, looking for new jobs, and need social security provided by the government. Nevertheless, the items listed above are not all the potential costs. Agricultural support programs widely affect the allocation of government budgets in every aspect of the economy. Massive resources are wasted on unnecessary agricultural production, and they are costly and inestimable.

Governments of developed countries, farmers themselves, and many other interested groups are concerned that the phase-out of agricultural subsidies will bring disaster to their agricultural industry. However, scientific research estimates that the elimination of trade-distorting agricultural subsidies will benefit the subsidy hosts—the developed countries themselves—in the long term. Using the US, the world's biggest exporter of agricultural products, as an example, economists predict that the US will see an increase in the real value of its agricultural exports

---

19   Olivier De Schutter, Mandate of the Special Rapporteur on the Right to Food, Background Note: Analysis of the World Food Crisis by the UN Special Rapporteur on the Right to Food 13 (May 2, 2008), available at http://www.srfood.org/images/stories/pdf/otherdocuments/1-srrtfnoteglobalfoodcrisis-2-5-08.pdf.

20   Mehadi Shafaeddin, Knocked-Down Agriculture after De-Industrialization; Another Destructive Influence of Neo-Liberalism (2008), available at http://www.ideaswebsite.org/feathm/jul2008/Neo_Liberalism.pdf (stating that "[d]eveloped countries spent nearly $400 billion a year on support for their agricultural products"). Id.

by 19 percent each year.[21] They continue to predict that "[t]he overall US economy will gain an estimated $13.3 billion in annual total welfare from agricultural trade liberalization, and 381 additional imports will provide variety and lower prices."[22] As for developing countries, artificially low market prices result in detrimental effects to poor farmers in developing countries and the health of the world agricultural economy, as mentioned previously. A UNDP report estimates a $34 billion loss in developing countries due to the significant subsidies provided by developed countries.[23] Moreover, a study by the USDA found that if agricultural subsidies were removed, developing countries would see annual gains of up to $21 billion.[24]

Many people may be concerned that in the absence of government subsidies, prices of agricultural commodities will go up because farming activities will be exposed to weather and unpredictable market risks. However, this is only a short-term effect of trade liberalization. In the long run, resources will be shifted back to their optimal use. Agricultural production will be more efficient when the prices are driven by the market.

After doing the math, it is very clear that governments, especially governments of rich developed countries, have been paying way more than they need to to support agriculture. It is true that governments should ensure food supply and protect farmers' income. However, such protection should be within an appropriate limit. The elimination, or at least the substantial reduction, of trade-distorting agricultural subsidies is critical for agricultural trade liberalization and world economic development as a whole. To clarify the situation, New Zealand's experience of subsidy reduction is examined.

Case Study: New Zealand's Experience of Subsidy Cutting

New Zealand is a country that heavily depends on agricultural exports. It is no surprise then that the New Zealand government significantly subsidized its agricultural economy. Before 1984, New Zealand farmers substantially relied on government subsidies.[25] Notwithstanding farmers' dependence, in 1984, New Zealand deregulated its agricultural economy by phasing out farm subsidies over a three-year period. Undoubtedly, farmers were resistant to this farm policy, and New Zealand agriculture failed at the beginning of the implementation period.[26]

---

21   Erin Morrow, Agri-Environmentalism: A Farm Bill for 2007, 38 Tex. Tech L. Rev. 345, 381 (2006).

22   Id.

23   De Schutter, supra note 19.

24   William Petit, The Free Trade Area of the Americas: Is It Setting the Stage for Significant Change in US Agricultural Subsidy Use?, 37 Tex. Tech L. Rev. 127, 129 (2004).

25   Morrow, supra note 21, at 381.

26   Id.

Without agricultural subsidies, New Zealand farmers gradually got used to producing agricultural commodities according to market demand.[27] They moved from growing traditional agricultural products into new areas of production, such as wine, venison, and dairy.[28] Data show that "[t]he New Zealand farm sector before 1984 had a productivity increase of one percent a year."[29] However, since the elimination of agricultural subsidies, productivity has increased to almost 4 percent a year.[30] New Zealand's reform on farm policy was a great success. In addition to economic benefit, the elimination of agricultural subsidies brought New Zealand significant environmental benefits, resulting from the more efficient use of farmland, water, fertilizer, pesticide, and other agricultural chemicals.

In summary, when agricultural subsidies are phased out, farmers are exposed to weather and other unpredictable changes in market conditions. This brings short-term failure in agriculture. Food prices initially increase. In the long-term, however, the elimination of trade-distorting agricultural subsidies will eventually lead to a thriving agricultural economy. It will also bring benefits to other sectors of society. The success of New Zealand's agricultural policy reform further proves the necessity of the elimination, or at least substantial reduction, of trade-distorting agricultural subsidies.

Completely Eliminating All Trade-distorting Subsidies in the Immediate Future May Not Be Easy

The elimination of trade-distorting agricultural subsidies is inevitable in order to achieve the goal of trade liberalization. However, is it feasible to completely cut all trade-distorting subsidies in the immediate future? The answer, unfortunately, is "no." The complete elimination of subsidies within a few years is politically and practically unlikely.

Political reasons
The slow progress of agricultural trade liberalization may be explained by the absence of political will.[31] As one *Financial Times* columnist observes: "[f]arms are no longer mere farms. They are monuments to the political power of a tiny group that holds the rest of us hostage."[32] In the US and the EU, farm lobbies wield tremendous power. They have significant influence on making or reforming

---

27   New Zealand Farmers Thrive after Agony of Pruning, THE TIMES, Aug. 28, 2002, at 13.
28   Morrow, supra note 21, at 381.
29   Windham, supra note 11, at 29.
30   Id.
31   Jonathan Carlson, Hunger, Agricultural Trade Liberalization, and Soft International Law: Addressing the Legal Dimensions of a Political Problem, 70 IOWA L. REV. 1187, 1193–94 (1985).
32   Bhala, supra note 1, at 768.

agricultural policies. Agricultural subsidy programs under the support of farm lobbies have made massive government subsidies end up in the hands of the wealthy agribusiness industry. The same wealthy agribusiness industry is behind these farm lobbies supporting them. This greatly influences Congress. Considering the interests of the wealthy agribusiness industry, farm lobbies refuse the deregulation of agricultural subsidy policies.

Although many politicians and policy-makers have realized the necessity to phase out agricultural subsidies, they also know there is "a separation between what is seen as desirable from a policy perspective and what is politically expedient."[33] Strong political pressure from farm lobbies has made any substantial reforms on agricultural subsidies difficult.

In the US, political realities make the US government get involved in agriculture. Political considerations contribute to the US's dedication to assisting its farmers, especially the owners of large industrial farms.

First, farm states have a disproportionate voice in US Congress.[34] When US independence was declared in 1776, 90 percent of Americans lived on agriculture. Due to this situation, when the founders created the structure of the US government, they gave farm states a disproportionately high representation in Congress. Despite the decline of the farm population in the modern world, Senate districts in the US are still drawn in accordance with land mass instead of population, and as a consequence, more than half of US Senators are from rural states in which agriculture is a key element of the economy.[35] For instance, North Dakota and Nebraska, as large agricultural states, enjoy equal representation in the Senate with New York and California, states with significantly larger populations. This inequitable senatorial distribution allows farmers to have a loud voice in Congress.

Second, as already noted, agricultural industries have a powerful lobby in Congress. Agribusiness interests are especially politically active, and have amplified congressional power to significantly influence farm policies.[36] Congressmen receive financial contributions from agribusiness, and in return, they protect agribusiness's interests. When wealthy agribusiness has concerns about low agricultural prices, undesirable market opportunities, or reduced production caused by adverse weather or natural disasters, they work hard to influence Congress, shaping farm policy that protects their interests. In addition to its

---

33   Kelvin Goertzen, Leveling the Playing Field, 3 ASPER REV. INT'L BUS. & TRADE L. 81, 100 (2003).

34   Jeffrey J. Steinle, The Problem Child of World Trade: Reform School for Agriculture, 4 MINN. J. GLOBAL TRADE 333, 336–37 (1995).

35   Michael R. Taylor, The Emerging Merger of Agricultural and Environmental Policy: Building a New Vision for the Future of American Agriculture, 20 VA. ENVTL. L.J. 169, 175 (2001).

36   Miguel Montana-Mora, International Law and International Relations Cheek to Cheek: An International Law/International Relations Perspective on the US/EC Agricultural Export Subsidies Dispute, 19 N.C. J. INT'L L. & COM. REG. 1, 36 (1993).

influence on domestic policy reforms, agribusiness interests also have a strong impact on the US position in international agricultural trade. In fact, the US's position in international trade negotiations is heavily conditioned by the power of farm lobbies. US negotiators must always make sure that agreements reached at the international level will be approved and implemented by Congress.[37]

Third, federal regulation of the agriculture industry faces further opposition from the American Farm Bureau. The American Farm Bureau is "an independent, non-governmental, voluntary organization governed by and representing farm and ranch families united for the purpose of analyzing their problems and formulating action to achieve educational improvement, economic opportunity and social advancement and, thereby, to promote the national well-being."[38] The Farm Bureau purports to speak for the entire US farming community. It is one of the most powerful lobbying forces in the US. If the US government proposes some agricultural policy reform that may undermine American farmers' interests, the Farm Bureau will lobby against such a draft. For instance, the Farm Bureau has successfully defeated all proposed environmental regulation of farms.[39]

Strong political support for subsidy programs is the driving force behind agricultural protectionism in the US. Farmers, agribusiness interests, and the American Farm Bureau demand the maintaining of protectionist agricultural policies. Similarly, in Europe, where smaller agricultural production and food security are highly valued, governments face political pressure to reduce their export subsidy levels. Agriculture is an important sector for the ruler's power base. The lack of political support makes it difficult to phase out agricultural subsidies.

Practical reasons
One of the most important differences between farming and other businesses is that farmers are more vulnerable to the weather and unpredictable changes in market conditions between the time they plant their crops and the time they harvest and market the crops. Farmers also have to sell their products within a certain timeframe regardless of prices due to practical limits on the storage of most agricultural commodities. Therefore, if farmers are left completely unprotected, most will struggle to stay in business, the food supply will be jeopardized, and the country may face food insecurity issues.

The pressure to maintain protectionist agricultural policies is powerful and understandable. In the US, over 1.6 million farms are family or individually

---

37   Id. at 54.

38   Am. Farm Bureau, The Voice of Agriculture: Purpose of Farm Bureau, http://www.fb.org/index.php?action=about.home&PHPSESSID=4sb8lvhqaqnmimf2bqcqbge6t6 (last visited May 18, 2011).

39   Christopher B. Connard, Sustaining Agriculture: An Examination of Current Legislation Promoting Sustainable Agriculture as an Alternative to Conventional Farming Practices, 13 Penn St. Envtl. L. Rev. 125, 125 (2004). ("[T]he American Farm Bureau Federation has successfully fought against all proposed environmental regulation of farms.")

owned.[40] Although small farmers are not as dominant a voting power as the agribusiness, and they do not receive much support as one would expect, they still constitute a large portion of voters that are able to impose pressure on politicians and policy-makers to vote against the deregulation of the farm subsidy. The removal of agricultural subsidies directly undermines small farmers' interests and undoubtedly they demand government assistance.

Reduce Amber Box measures and Blue Box measures
Blue Box subsidies are less trade-distorting than Amber Box subsidies, but they are not non-trade-distorting. To reduce government interventions in agriculture, re-characterizing the exempted Blue Box subsidies should be one of the priorities to be addressed at international trade negotiations.

WTO members have agreed that, in the long-term, Amber Box subsidies and Blue Box subsidies must be reduced substantially and removed eventually. Policy-makers and scholars have made various proposals regarding how to progressively phase out trade-distorting agricultural subsidies. However, when the question comes to how substantial the reduction commitment should be, it virtually pushes policy-makers and scholars into a corner. In fact, the degree of reduction committed to by WTO members does not match up to ideal theoretical proposals. Instead, it heavily depends on the WTO members' political will and how this will directs them to make concessions they would like to make at trade negotiations. There are already an abundance of proposals and scholarly writings on how to progressively reduce trade-distorting agricultural subsidies. This research will not repeat these theories. Instead, it will focus on what WTO members can do to protect their agriculture without distorting international agricultural trade. For example, supporting non-specific rural development and environmental programs promotes sustainable agriculture and should be significantly encouraged.

Take advantage of Green Box measures
Since the Uruguay Round negotiations, WTO members have been in the midst of a virtual revolution in their agricultural policies. Government subsidies have been challenged by calls for agricultural trade liberalization. Amber and Blue Box subsidies are significantly trade-distorting, and it has been requested that they be reduced further. As a result, it is unlikely that WTO members can still rely on these subsidies to support their agriculture in the long run. Rather, they have to move away from these direct support measures. Considering agriculture is one of the most important sectors in a country's economy, and has been highly protected throughout history, WTO members should not leave vulnerable farmers completely exposed to unpredictable changes in weather or market conditions. They should continue to invest in agriculture and protect farmers, but to a limited extent. To protect their agricultural economy while complying with their international obligations, WTO members may consider focusing on exploring new

---

40   Id.

support programs that are non- or less trade-distorting and not subject to reduction schedules. In fact, many developed countries have already started to promote the use of less trade-distorting measures to protect their agriculture.

Green Box subsidies are decoupled from production and price, and are considered non- or minimally trade-distorting. Therefore, they are not subject to any restrictions or reduction commitments under the WTO agreements. Annex 2 of the AoA lists a wide range of Green Box measures that WTO members are allowed to adopt without any restrictions, including generalized government service programs in the areas of research, pest and disease control, training services, extension and advisory services, inspection services, marketing and promoting services, infrastructural services, and public stockholding for food security and domestic aid purpose.[41] It also specifies other government support programs that are exempted from reduction commitment, including government payments made directly to farmers that do not stimulate production, decoupled income support, government financial participation in income insurance and income safety-net programs, payments for relief from natural disasters, structural adjustment assistance provided through producer retirement programs, structural adjustment assistance provided through resource retirement programs, structural adjustment assistance provided through investment aids, payments under environmental programs, and payments under regional assistance programs.[42] Among all these Green Box measures, WTO members are strongly recommended to focus on two summarized programs: programs that promote rural development, and programs that have significant environmental benefits for sustainable agriculture purposes.

Promote rural development programs According to the AoA, generalized government service programs, if they are decoupled from production and prices, fall into the Green Box category.[43] They are allowed to be adopted by WTO members with no restrictions. Rural development programs are one of the most important government services. To protect farmers' interests and to promote agricultural economy, WTO members may consider shifting the current distribution of resources away from the traditional direct support programs to permissible Green Box subsidies that promote rural development.[44]

Similar to the national capacity building strategies discussed previously, rural development needs government to work on a few things. WTO members should focus on support in the rural infrastructure sector, such as public facilities, building roads and bridges, and developing transportation systems. These infrastructural service programs improve the competitiveness of local farming, increase agricultural and nonagricultural employment opportunities, and attract more

---

41   Agreement on Agriculture, Apr. 15, 1994, 1867 U.N.T.S. 410, annex 2.2.

42   Id.

43   Id. annex 2.2(a).

44   Jess Phelps, Much Ado about Decoupling: Evaluating the Environmental Impact of Recent European Union Agricultural Reform, 31 HARV. ENVTL. L. REV. 279, 304 (2007).

investments in rural areas in a broad sense. These programs will also promote the overall quality of life in rural areas and foster local development.

Government support in improving information systems is essential for agricultural production. Agricultural weather forecast and emergency warning systems help reduce potential damages caused by adverse weather conditions. An updated market information system is critical to direct farmers with accurate market demand and supply and price information that facilitates them in their agricultural activities.

Within such a knowledge-driven society, the improvement of agricultural productivity heavily depends on the enhancement of agricultural technology, which requires government contributions in the form of policy support and financial investment.[45] Moreover, to promote the application of new agricultural technology, governments are also encouraged to establish local technical assistance stations. Agricultural specialists teach farmers proper agro-forestry techniques and answer their questions when they encounter problems in farming.

Rural development programs under WTO systems are expected to ensure agriculture's role in producing sufficient food, and to promote sustainable development of the rural economy. Without governments' further commitment, liberalized agricultural trade will lack a solid foundation, and the general economy will be prevented from further development.

Environmental programs and sustainable agriculture
Issues   Agriculture has a pervasive and consequential human influence on the global environment. Traditionally, farmers removed existing vegetation from farmland, leveled it, deployed certain crop(s), and cultivated the crop(s) by using human labor, simple tools, and a little organic fertilizer, such as animal manure. Farmers harvested crop(s), removed associated waste products from the land, and then started over. Traditional agriculture allows farmers to produce food with the minimum use of agrochemicals and other toxic inputs. It protects soil fertility, making agriculture more adaptable to climate change. Modern agriculture has developed very fast since the Industrial Revolution. Farming has become more productive and profitable than traditional agriculture.[46] However, conflicts arise as productivity increases. Modern agriculture heightens the adverse impacts and imposes unacceptably high costs on the health of the global environment. Agriculture has now become a significant contributor to current environmental degradation.[47]

Farmers improve agricultural production through extensive use of fertilizers, pesticides, and other chemicals effluents. Billions of tons of soil carry chemicals that erode farmland. These agricultural effluents deplete the soil, resulting in

---

45   Cheryl Christensen & Charles Hanrahan, African Food Crises: Short-, Medium-, and Long-Term Responses, 70 Iowa L. Rev. 1293, 1296 (1985).

46   Connard, supra note 39, at 135.

47   Stacey Willemsen Person, International Trade: Pushing United States Agriculture toward a Greener Future?, 17 Geo. Int'l Envtl. L. Rev. 307, 309 (2005).

soil erosion and the degradation of soil quality. Agricultural degradation of the environment extends beyond soil pollution.[48] The overuse of agricultural chemicals damages the atmosphere, and impairs freshwater resources. Furthermore, by consuming more land and water, agriculture impacts species' natural habitats, resulting in habitat loss and degradation. The world has not yet paid enough attention to agriculture—one of the most polluting industries.

Sustainable agriculture   Recently, an emerging realization that current farming methods have adverse effects on the environment has arisen. Agricultural systems in both developed and developing countries face challenges to achieve sustainable development and long-term food security. As a result, sustainable agriculture, which is concerned with lessening the adverse impact of agricultural activities on the environment while maintaining or increasing the profitability of farming, has emerged as a feasible solution.[49]

Sustainable agriculture requires government support in environment programs. Environmentally targeted subsidy programs are decoupled from prices and production and, therefore, are considered Green Box measures. They are exempt from reduction requirements under the WTO system.[50] WTO members are allowed to provide environmental programs to address unreachable environmental concerns through government support payments. These programs provide an environmentally friendly and equitable safety net for farmers of the WTO members. However, different countries, even different regions, have their own set of environmental challenges, which makes "one-size-fits-all" regulation impossible. There are a few principles that governments should follow in order to promote sustainable agriculture and protect farmers' interests. As general rules, environmental programs should be targeted to minimize the negative impacts of agriculture on the health of the environment. They should also promote the conservation of natural resources so that future generations can produce sufficient food.

WTO members may consider providing subsidies to a few main farming practices associated with sustainable agriculture. Agricultural research with regard to inducing new sustainable farming practices as alternatives to environmentally harmful agricultural practices should be promoted. Governments may also consider sponsoring programs that educate farmers regarding the prospects of sustainable agriculture, and how to make farming practices more responsible.[51]

---

48   Connard, supra note 39, at 125.

49   Id.

50   J.W. Looney, GATT and Future Soil Conservation Programs in the United States: Some Lessons from Australia, 28 Tulsa L. J. 673, 678 (1993) (stating that even if the WTO agreement mandates a substantial reduction in agricultural subsidies, environmental programs are not tied to production or price and, therefore, it still is permissible). Id.

51   7 USC. § 5801 (2006).

Currently, a large quantity of public dollars go to subsidize a few agricultural commodities, which leads to monoculture. The intensive monoculture approach has resulted in substantial environmental and natural resource costs. Large amounts of agrochemicals are used to promote agricultural production. These agrochemicals adversely affect water quality and cause soil erosion. They also pose severe hazards for food safety that are not easy to fully assess and prevent.[52] To break this environmentally unfriendly monoculture, government subsidies should be paid to promote the diversification of crop choices and crop rotation, rather than support the same crop planted in the same field every year.

The use of organic materials, such as manure and nitrogen rich crops, should be encouraged in order to reduce the heavy pollution caused by fertilizers.[53] Efficient irrigation systems, a measurable energy reduction per acre farmed, a significant reduction in agrochemicals usage, and the greater use of integrated pest management are also important sustainable farming practices that governments may consider promoting.[54] These sustainable measures prevent potential harmful results that may be caused by farming practices. They help create a healthier environment with less pollution in the long run.

Implementation   In practice, environmental programs should be used to target environmental concerns in farming, and conservation incentives should be the only factor to determine if farmers are eligible to receive subsidies from the government.[55] Government support should be provided to farmers who comply with conservational and environmental requirements and implement sustainable farming practices.

The main target of environmental programs should be small farmers. Traditionally, a large portion of government subsidies has gone into the hands of a small number of wealthy agribusinesses, while small farmers get little support from governments. Industrial-style agriculture is very efficient in food production. However, farms that run like factories require large inputs of fertilizers, pesticides, and other agrochemicals. Industrial-style agriculture brings enormous damage to our nature systems. Compared to industrial-style agriculture, it is easier for small farmers to switch to sustainable agricultural production due to the size of their farms. Therefore, environment programs will provide strong incentives for small

---

52   Taylor, supra note 35, at 177.

53   James Stephen Carpenter, Farm Chemicals, Soil Erosion, and Sustainable Agriculture, 13 Stan. Envtl. L.J. 190, 221–24 (1994).

54   Eubanks, supra note 14, at 301.

55   Elizabeth Bullington, WTO Agreement Mandate that Congress Repeal the Farm Bill of 2002 and Enact an Agriculture Law Embodying Free Market Principles, 20 Am. U. Int'l L. Rev. 1211, 1244–45 (2005) (noting that governments should "abolish those subsidies with amounts depending on price and production levels—counter-cyclical payments"). Id.

farmers to promote sustainable agriculture. Hopefully, such a sustainable way of farming will extend to large factory farms soon.

As for implementation, existing environmental programs are primarily voluntary. However, soil erosion and other pollution problems caused by farming practices will not be solved by voluntary programs alone, particularly given the fact that agrochemicals significantly promote agricultural production. Considering it is not easy to make all environmental programs compulsory, the solution is likely to be a combination of regulatory programs while maintaining some voluntary programs. The regulatory programs can be used to target those most environmentally sensitive farming activities. The voluntary programs can be used as incentives to attract more farmers to participate in sustainable farming practices.[56] Moreover, environmental programs must be transparent to enable implementation and accountability. A clear and understandable explanation of the program's purposes and goals is necessary for enforcement and monitoring as well.[57]

A new agricultural model: industrial farms, small farms, and organic farms
Industrial farms Technological advancements have significantly improved agricultural productivity. Agricultural production has increased while farm population has decreased. Large agricultural producers own most of the farmland. They make large-scale capital investments in farming, and they industrialize agricultural production. Industrial agriculture develops fast.

Industrial agriculture is different from other farming methods. It is liberated from the conventional biological constraints. A farms does not need to "generate and conserve its own fertility by maintaining a diversity of species."[58] The goal of industrial agriculture is to increase output and decrease production cost. Farms are viewed as a factory transforming inputs of raw materials, such as pesticides, fertilizer, and fuel, into outputs of crops; they are managed on industrial principles.[59]

The industrial model of farming works well in most of the economic sector. As previously discussed, it largely improves agricultural production, making it possible to feed more hungry people in the world. However, in the meantime, critics assert that industrial agriculture causes more harm, and has marginalized small farmers and forced them to leave this industry, making them unable to climb out of poverty.

Furthermore, industrial agriculture is more polluting and environmentally destructive than most of the farming methods ever practiced.[60] One of the key features of industrial agriculture is the cultivation of a single crop, also called

---

56 Looney, supra note 50, at 677.
57 Person, supra note 47, at 332.
58 Windham, supra note 11, at 3.
59 Id.
60 JEREMY RIFKIN & CAROL GRUNEWALD RIFKIN, VOTING GREEN: YOUR COMPLETE ENVIRONMENTAL GUIDE TO MAKING POLITICAL CHOICES IN THE 1990s, 149 (1992).

"monoculture." Monoculture heavily relies on fertilizer, making conventional crop rotation and biodiversity unnecessary for maintaining soil fertility.[61] The environmental costs of monoculture are considerable. Planting a single crop year after year can deplete the soil, increasing the need for fertilizer. A factory farm's monoculture crops also inevitably invite pests, insects, and weeds, forcing agricultural producers to turn to much heavier doses of pesticides and herbicides to keep them under control.[62] The overuse of agrochemicals is detrimental to the environment. In addition, a growing number of people are concerned that human health is endangered by the overuse of agrochemicals. Numerous studies have linked various health disorders, such as certain cancers, to the overuse of agrochemicals.[63]

Regardless, factory style production methods have made producers capable of producing more agricultural products than anyone could ever imagine, making cheap food available to the hungry people of the world.[64] Thus, for food security reasons, we need industrial agriculture to maintain the food supply and feed hungry people. However, the completely one-sided approach of agricultural policies in favor of industrial agriculture should be reconsidered. Governments should refocus their agricultural policies and minimize the undesirable consequences of industrial agriculture. Other socially and environmentally responsible alternatives are strongly encouraged.

Small farms   Industrial agriculture is not the only way to produce food for all the people in the world. There are other options that are more socially and environmentally responsible, although these alternatives may be less productive than industrial agriculture. One of the important sectors that have long been overlooked is small farms.

The majority of the world's poor lives in rural areas. They are small farmers who live on agricultural land. However, global competition and the fast development of industrial agriculture have marginalized these small farmers. Large agricultural producers in developed countries are adequately compensated by government subsidies.[65] They are better equipped to adapt to shifting market demands and to comply with the volume and standards requirements for export.[66] They are the

---

61   Michael Pollan, The Omnivore's Dilemma: A Natural History of Four Meals 45 (2006).

62   Clive Potter, Against the Grain: Agri-Environmental Reform in the United States and the European Union 22 (1998).

63   David Hosansky, Regulating Pesticides: Does the New Crackdown Go Far Enough—or Too Far?, 9 CQ Researcher 665, 665–88 (Aug. 6, 1999).

64   Windham, supra note 11, at 8–9.

65   Nathan R.R. Watson, Federal Farm Subsidies: A History of Governmental Control, Recent Attempts at a Free Market Approach, the Current Backlash, and Suggestions for Future Action, 9 Drake J. Agric. L. 279, 282–83 (2004).

66   C. Dolan & J. Humphrey, Governance and Trade in Fresh Vegetables: The Impact of UK Supermarkets on the African Horticultural Industry, 37 J. Dev. Stud. 175 (2001).

biggest beneficiaries of liberalized agricultural trade. Conversely, according to the UN, small farmers suffer from "high transaction cost, low capacities to implement food safety and quality measures, and low access to finance, technology, and information."[67] Small farms are crowded out. It is difficult for many farmers, particularly those in poor developing countries, to climb out of hunger and poverty.

Small farmers are one of the most important contributors to the improvement of food security. In particular, they play a vital role in hunger reduction "in remote areas where local produced foods precluded the high transport and marketing costs associated with many purchased food," according to the UN Special Rapporteur on the Right to Food.[68] A country should not excessively rely on international agricultural trade in pursuit of domestic food security, but instead, it should build and further promote its small farmers' capacity to produce more food for their own consumption needs. If small farmers are supported by governments, and have sufficient access to land, water, genetic resources, credit, and improved rural infrastructure, they will be able to significantly improve agricultural production and produce enough food, at least to feed themselves; or they can sell the surplus to make extra money. As a consequence, hunger will be largely reduced. Food security will also be improved. The UN is positive about small farmers' potential capacity in promoting agricultural production. A report released by the UN in 2011 concluded that "small-scale farmers can double food production within 10 years in critical regions by using ecological methods."[69]

WTO members can reshape their agricultural systems by reforming current agricultural policies and practices. Support programs should be specifically tailored to help those small farmers who truly need government assistance. Furthermore, it is necessary to impose meaningful caps on the amount of subsidies farmers are allowed to receive. Such restrictions will prevent the unfair distribution of subsidies. In particular, this will prevent large amounts of subsidies from falling into the hands of a small group of large agricultural producers. Governments must make essential agricultural inputs, such as fertilizer, pesticides, and locally adapted quality seeds available to small farmers. Last but not least, technical advice, market supply and demand, price information, and weather warning systems should also

---

67   UN DEPT. OF ECON. AND SOC. AFFAIRS, STRENGTHENING EFFORTS TO ERADICATE POVERTY AND HUNGER 100 (2007), available at http://www.un.org/en/ecosoc/docs/pdfs/07-49285-ecosoc-book-2007.pdf.

68   Human Rights Council, Rep. of Special Rapporteur on the Right to Food, Olivier De Schutter, Promotion and Protection of All Human Rights, Civil, Political, Economic, Social and Cultural Rights, Including the Right to Development, UN Doc. A/HRC/12/31 (July 21, 2009), available at http://www.srfood.org/images/stories/pdf/officialreports/srrtf_second%20global%20food%20crisis%20report_a-hrc-12-31.pdf.

69   Adriana Velez, We Don't Need Industrial Agriculture to Feed the World, UN Report Says, CHANGE.ORG, March 10, 2011, http://news.change.org/stories/we-dont-need-industrial-agriculture-to-feed-the-world-un-report-says.

be provided to small farmers so that they can improve agricultural production for self-consumption or for sale if surpluses are available.

Organic farms   A growing number of consumers are concerned about the adverse effects industrial agricultural practices have had on human health, the environment, and society. They demand unpolluted or less polluted organic food. They want their food produced in ways that are more socially and environmentally responsible.[70]

The top reason that makes consumers choose organic food items over industrial food items is health concerns. Organic food typically is cultivated using sustainable agricultural methods. It does not involve modern synthetic inputs, such as fertilizers, pesticides, and other agrochemicals; it is not processed using chemical food additives or industrial solvents. It is widely believed that organic food is less polluted or even unpolluted, and much healthier and significantly safer for human consumption.

Further, consumers choose organic food out of environmental concerns. They believe organic farming is more sustainable. Organic farming is sun-powered; it "relies on natural organic maturing, nitrogen-fixing crop rotation, and natural pest management practices."[71] Conversely, industrial farming is extremely energy-consuming. Its mechanical system heavily relies on a non-renewable natural resource—fossil fuel.[72] Industrial agriculture also requires the excessive use of agrochemicals to maintain high production. Thus, when consumers need to make a choice between organic food and industrial food, many of them are willing to pay a substantial premium for organic food.

However, in the modern world where economic benefits always come first, many people, in particular, interested groups, such as farmers and farm lobbies, may inquire if organic methods of farming are as productive as industrial farming methods. The answer is "yes" but there are a few things people should be aware of when making a comparison between the two agricultural models.

With the help of agrochemicals, industrial methods of farming make it possible that the same agricultural crop be continuously produced on the same acre of farmland year after year. On the contrary, organic methods of farming require farmers to rotate their crops with nitrogen-fixing legumes to maintain soil fertility. Organic farmers are able to yield the same amount of crop on the same acre in any given year. However, they cannot continuously produce the same amount of

---

70   Windham, supra note 11, at 4 ("[M]any consumers are choosing to opt out of the industrial food chain and into a more socially responsible system of food production for a variety of reasons, ranging from objection to the use of agricultural chemicals and genetically altered food to promoting locally produced food and animal rights").

71   Id. at 22.

72   Id. at 22 ("Industrial farming uses at least fifty gallons of oil to produce one acre of corn. Before chemical fertilizer, the farm produced more than two calories of food energy for every calorie of energy invested. Today, it takes industrial farmers more than a calorie of fossil fuel energy to produce a calorie of food").

crop on the same acre as industrial farming. Organic farming cannot compete with industrial farming on the production of a single crop. However, if organic farmers rotate crops every certain year(s), these crops remain as highly productive as under industrial agriculture. In conclusion, the overall productivity of organic farming is no less than that of its counterpart—industrial farming. The only difference is, organic farming needs "a balance of animals, grasses, vegetables, fruits, and trees to achieve maximization of profit," while industrial agriculture relies more on agrochemicals to achieve maximization of profit.[73] When farmers convert from an industrial agriculture model to organic methods of farming, they often experience lower outputs in the first few years because the soil and surrounding biodiversity need to recover from the use of agrochemicals. It also takes time for farmers to learn how to efficiently conduct organic methods of farming.[74] Once the system is established, according to scientific studies, organic farming will produce almost the same yield per acre as industrial agriculture, but with a much lower consumption of energy and natural resources.[75] Organic farming has gradually become popular in recent years. Consumers in growing numbers choose to purchase nutritious organic food. Large agribusiness companies such as Monsanto, General Mills, and Cargill have also joined the organic food market.[76]

However, current agricultural policies and support programs still systematically favor industrial agriculture. They provide billions of dollars of funding every year to support industrial agriculture. Organic farms and other alternatives have been practically excluded from receiving government subsidies. As a result, industrial food producers present a lower sticker price to consumers in the grocery store. Consumers pay a lot more money for the socially and environmentally responsible organic food.[77]

In a free market, consumers should be the ones to "determine the desired quality of food and how much they are willing to pay for it."[78] The majority of consumers look at the food prices to make a decision on their food choice. If the prices of organic food items are much higher than those of industrial food items, they may choose to stay with the affordable industrial food items. It is important to create a market system that reflects the real prices of the food so that consumers can make a decision without government interventions. It is time to level the playing field, and to stop promoting an agricultural system that is distorted by subsidies.

---

73 Id.

74 Id. at 15–16.

75 Id. at 15–16, 22. ("In developed countries, organic yields range anywhere from ninety to one hundred percent of industrial yields. In developing countries, however, organic farming produces up to twenty percent higher yields than industrial farming." Also it notes that "[o]rganic farming, however, uses two-thirds less energy to produce the same output, giving it a cost-competitive advantage over higher input chemical farming.") Id.

76 Samuel Fromartz, Organic Inc.: Natural Foods and How They Grow 188 (2006).

77 Id. at 28.

78 Id. at 31.

Phase Out Export Subsidies

Export subsidy is considered the most trade-distorting form of subsidy and remains one of the most controversial issues in international agricultural trade. The WTO members have acknowledged the negative effects of export subsidies and they share a goal of gradually reducing these subsidies in order to achieve greater trade liberalization in agriculture. The use of export subsidies in agricultural industry has been regulated since the Uruguay Round negotiations. However, far from its original objective, WTO obligations of export subsidy reduction are not stringent enough to lead to the expected liberalization. Export subsidy continues to distort agricultural trade.

According to the AoA, past users of export subsidies were allowed to maintain these subsidies but subject to certain reduction obligations. The introduction of new export subsidies was prohibited. Nevertheless, as previously noted, past users were primarily developed countries. Thus the export subsidy reduction provision practically excluded most developing countries from subsidizing their agricultural exports, which "institutionalized the ruinous competition between highly subsidized developed country agricultural producers and their counterparts in developing countries."[79] Therefore, to achieve the goal of greater trade liberalization, all export subsidies in developed countries must be progressively subjected to reduction. The complete elimination of export subsidies is critical in the long term. This will help make a dramatic change in global trade liberalization.[80]

Developing countries should continue to enjoy additional facilities. Sufficient flexibility should be maintained for a certain period considering their special development needs and food security needs. Developing countries should be allowed to provide export subsidies under certain circumstances to generate export revenues. They will therefore be able to sponsor agricultural programs, promote domestic agricultural production, and create more employment opportunities. However, not all developing countries are financially capable of subsidizing their agricultural exports. Wealthier developing countries, such as certain Cairns Group members, may benefit more from subsidizing their agricultural exports, while poorer developing countries that cannot afford export subsidies do not enjoy much flexibility in their trade regimes. Thus, in the long run, special and differential treatment to developing countries should also be reduced.

WTO members have engaged in a few dialogues regarding export subsidies since the Uruguay Round negotiations. As always, disagreement exists among

---

79   Id.

80   Tashi Kaul, The Elimination of Export Subsidies and the Future of Net-Food Importing Developing Countries in the WTO, 24 Fordham Int'l L. J. 383, 409 (2000) (noting that current WTO obligations of export subsidy reduction "is not stringent enough to lead to the expected rise in prices and shift in patterns of agricultural production" and emphasizing that "[s]uch changes will occur only through a complete elimination, rather than a limited reduction, of such subsidies").

WTO members with regard to export subsidy reduction. The US has strongly promoted the complete elimination of export subsidies. Conversely, the EU countries, as the main providers of export subsidies, have held a totally opposite position. The EU defends export subsidies as being less trade-distorting measures compared to tariffs and domestic subsidies. As a result, they only agree to make some minor adjustments to their export subsidy programs without any substantial reduction.[81] To correct distorted agricultural trade, WTO members need to build bridges and make a compromise. However, as always, it is easier to say, than to do. A strong political will to promote the substantial reduction of export subsidies is lacking. Moreover, negotiations on export subsidies have repeatedly ended up in a deadlock. Thus, greater government efforts are necessary in order to achieve a meaningful reduction in the use of export subsidy.

Flexibility for Developing Countries

The WTO's special and differential treatment is to ensure the special needs of developing countries in food security and development. Almost all WTO agreements grant special flexibilities to developing countries, including Articles 9.4, 15, and 16 of the Agreement on Agriculture,[82] Article 10 of the Agreement on the Application of Sanitary and Phytosanitary Measures,[83] Article 6.5 of the Agreement on the Textiles and Clothing,[84] Article 12 of the Agreement on Technical Barriers to Trade,[85] Article 4 of the Agreement on Trade-related Investment Measures,[86] Article 15 of the Agreement on Implementation of Article VI of the GATT 1994,[87] Article 27 of the Agreement on Subsidies and Countervailing Measures,[88] Article 9 of the Agreement on Safeguards,[89] Article IV of the General Agreement on Trade

---

81   Goertzen, supra note 33, at 94.

82   Agreement on Agriculture, supra note 41.

83   WTO Agreement on the Application of Sanitary and Phytosanitary Measures (SPS Agreement), Apr. 15, 1994, 1867 U.N.T.S. 493.

84   Agreement on the Textiles and Clothing, 1868 U.N.T.S. 14, available at http://www.wto.org/english/docs_e/legal_e/16-tex.pdf (last visited May 24, 2011).

85   Agreement on Technical Barriers to Trade, 1868 U.N.T.S. 120, available at http://www.wto.org/english/docs_e/legal_e/17-tbt.pdf (last visited May 24, 2011).

86   Agreement on Trade-related Investment Measures, 1868 U.N.T.S. 186, available at http://www.wto.org/english/docs_e/legal_e/18-trims.pdf (last visited May 24, 2011).

87   Agreement on Implementation of Article VI of the GATT 1994, 1868 U.N.T.S. 201, available at http://www.wto.org/english/docs_e/legal_e/19-adp.pdf (last visited May 24, 2011).

88   Agreement on Subsidies and Countervailing Measures, Apr. 15, 1994, 1867 U.N.T.S. 14.

89   Agreement on Safeguards, 1869 U.N.T.S. 154, available at http://www.wto.org/english/docs_e/legal_e/25-safeg.pdf (last visited May 24, 2011).

in Services,[90] and Articles 65 and 66 of the Agreement on Trade-Related Aspects of Intellectual Property Rights.[91] Generally, WTO agreements incorporate two types of provisions that grant special and differential treatment to developing countries. These give developing countries longer implementation periods, and allow them to undertake lower levels of reduction commitments.

Special and differential treatment is essential to help stimulate the agricultural economy of developing countries, and incorporate them into the world market. However, existing special and differential treatment provisions in WTO agreements have not always been implemented and are not as effective as expected.[92] They have done little to level the playing field for developing countries. To achieve the goal of greater trade liberalization, more efforts are needed.

As a general guideline, WTO members should contribute to creating a favorable environment, allowing the adequate and effective implementation of existing special and differential treatment provisions.

In practice, developed countries treat food as any other commodity and as a trade issue, while developing countries see food as a security issue. Although international agricultural trade is conducted under commercial agreements rather than humanitarian agreements, agricultural trade plays a significant role in development, and it can contribute to the elimination of world hunger. WTO members should recognize the specificity of agricultural commodities in international trade. They may consider giving developing countries, especially food deficit least-developed countries, maximum possible flexibility to shield their agricultural products from international competition. WTO members may also consider establishing a "Food Security Box" specifically designated for developing countries. The "Food Security Box" would allow developing countries, especially food deficit developing countries, to encourage domestic food production by providing appropriate government support, such as subsidies and income support, for a certain period of time. All costs related to food security should be excluded from AMS calculations. Developing countries should be allowed to "retain the freedom to take measures which insulate domestic markets from the volatility of prices on international markets."[93]

---

90   General Agreement on Trade in Services, 1869 U.N.T.S. 183, available at http://www.wto.org/english/docs_e/legal_e/26-gats.pdf (last visited May 24, 2011).

91   Agreement on Trade-Related Aspects of Intellectual Property Rights, 1869 U.N.T.S. 299, available at http://www.wto.org/english/docs_e/legal_e/27-trips.pdf (last visited May 24, 2011).

92   Food & Agric. Org. of the U.N., The Right to Food Guidelines, Information Papers and Case Studies 62 (2006), available at http://www.fao.org/docs/eims/upload/214344/RtFG_Eng_draft_03.pdf.

93   Olivier De Schutter, Mission to the World Trade Organization (Mar. 9, 2009) available at http://www.carnegieendowment.org/files/Summary_of%20report%20of%20the%20Special%20Rapporteur%20on%20the%20right%20to%20food.pdf.

Least-developed countries and net food-importing developing countries should be given more special and differential treatment. The removal of agricultural subsidies directly benefits those food exporting countries, such as the Cairns Groups, which have a strong comparative advantage in agriculture. However, the removal of agricultural subsidies will temporarily increase world food prices, which will be a detriment to the least-developed countries and the net-food importing developing countries if they do not get necessary support from the international trade regime. They will be hurt by the inflationary impact of the removal of subsidies. Therefore, particular attention must be paid to those countries who may suffer severe food insecurity during the process of trade liberalization.

Furthermore, current WTO special and differential treatment provisions are still blocked on a few issues. WTO negotiations have not yet made clear interpretations. For example, what are the "mandatory" obligations for WTO members with regard to special and differential treatment? How can the WTO ensure that these obligations are effectively implemented? How can enforcement be monitored? When should the WTO terminate the flexibility granted to developing countries? It is necessary that WTO members review the existing provisions to address these questions, and to strengthen the provisions to ensure they are more precise and effective. This, in turn, will promote the leveling of the playing field. An effective monitoring system should also be established in order to assess the impacts of trade liberalization on developing countries so that WTO members will be able to adjust special mitigation or compensatory policies accordingly to ensure the needs of developing countries not negatively affected by liberalization measures.[94]

Sanitary and Phytosanitary Measures and Genetically Modified Organisms (GMOs)

People have the right to safe and nutritious food to meet dietary needs and food preferences. The Sanitary and Phytosanitary Agreement is the main multilateral framework in the WTO system to ensure food safety and quality by facilitating international trade. The Agreement protects the life and health of humans, animals, and plants. However, when talking about sanitary and phytosanitary measures (SPS measures), the most debated issue cannot be ignored—genetically modified organisms (GMOs), and their potential environmental, health, ethical, and legal consequences.

Developed countries impose stringent SPS measures on food imports, and they have strict rules with regard to the import of GMOs. At the same time, they export genetically modified food, through international trade or food aid programs, mostly

---

94 OLIVIER DE SCHUTTER, MANDATE OF THE SPECIAL RAPPORTEUR ON THE RIGHT TO FOOD, A HUMAN RIGHTS PERSPECTIVE OF THE COMPREHENSIVE FRAMEWORK FOR ACTION: TOWARDS A UNIFIED UN RESPONSE TO THE GLOBAL FOOD CRISIS 4 (June 23, 2008), available at http://www.srfood.org/images/stories/pdf/otherdocuments/4-srrtfcfaanalysis23-6-08.pdf .

to developing countries.[95] Genetically modified foods are very controversial. Some people believe that GMOs largely improve production, while numerous others argue that GMOs are not only unsafe and unhealthy, but also uneconomic. Some African countries, such as Sudan and Angola, even refused to accept genetically modified food aid.[96] This research will explore the issues surrounding GMOs, and their pros and cons. It will also discuss what the world can do to provide the hungry people sufficient food without threatening their health.

What Are GMOs?

Genetically modified organisms refer to agricultural products that have been genetically altered or genetically engineered through a series of biotechnological processes.[97] By changing its genetic structure through the process of creating recombinant DNA or gene splicing, the organism contains one or more genes not originally existing or normally found and, therefore, a specific desired trait is created rapidly and accurately.[98] Genetic modification technologies are utilized in an attempt to improve the quantity and quality of a crop.

The Benefits of GM Food

The benefits of GM food are numerous. GM technology rapidly and accurately develops the specific desirable traits which might not natively exist in the natural environment. It compensates for unfavorable factors that impede successful harvests. It enhances a crop's pest resistance, disease resistance, herbicide tolerance, drought tolerance, and nutrition. It has many other valuable attributes.[99] GM technology decreases agricultural inputs, and significantly improves outputs.

---

95   SHAFAEDDIN, supra note 20. ("Incidences of exports of such products have been noticed in Colombia, Bolivia, Ecuador, Angola, Malawi, Zambia, Lesotho, Mozambique, Swaziland, Nigeria, Sudan and Sierra Leone. In some cases African developing countries (for example, Sudan and Angola), have been pushed to accept genetically modified food aid against their will.") Id.

96   Id.

97   The biotechnological process includes isolating genes from an organism, manipulating them in the laboratory and injecting them into another organism. See Marsha A. Echols, Food Safety Regulation in the European Union and the United States: Different Cultures, Different Laws, 4 COLUM. J. EUR. L. 525, 535 n.48 (1998).

98   Linda Bren, *Genetic Engineering: The Future of Foods?*, FDA CONSUMER MAG. (Nov./Dec. 2003), *available at* http://fda.gov/fdac/features/2003/603_food.html (examples of these desired traits include an increased resistance to herbicides or improved nutritional content).

99   Olivier De Schutter, The Right to Food, Seed Policies and The Right to Food: Enhancing Agrobiodiversity and Encouraging Innovation, UN Doc. A/64/170 (July 23, 2009) ("[C]ertain varieties can have improved nutritional values, or specific disease resistance,

Insect pests and crop diseases are important factors that can lead to crop failure. Crop failure inevitably affects a farmer's livelihood and well-being. In order to minimize the damages caused by insect pests and crop diseases, farmers apply tons of pesticides, fertilizers, and other farming additives. However, the excessive use of agrichemicals poisons farmland and water; it may also cause other environmental pollutions. For the consumers, eating food treated with too many chemicals has potential health hazards. Conversely, genetically modified seeds provide an effective and custom-tailored approach to pest control and disease control. By changing their genetic structure, crops are able to resist pests and diseases without adding supplementary pesticides and fertilizers.[100]

Similarly, by developing specific desired traits, GM technology enables farmers to grow higher yield crops that are more herbicide tolerant and drought tolerant. Farmers benefit from the GM technology of fewer herbicides, fewer pesticides, less water, and fewer other agricultural inputs than traditional farming.[101] GM technology also improves crops' nutritional content by increasing the levels of vitamins, minerals, and protein or by lowering the levels of fat and cholesterol.[102] Additionally, the proponents of GMO also claim the environmental benefits of GM technologies due to the reduced application of chemicals.[103]

The Undesirable Consequences of GM Food

The US consistently supports research into and the consumption of GM foods; it upholds the safety of such foods in feeding people in hunger. Conversely, the EU considers GMOs suspect, and worries about the environmental, health, legal, and other consequences. Many poor developing countries that receive food aid from developed countries question the quality and safety of GM foods provided by donors; some have even begun to resist GM foods as aid.[104]

Environmental scientists express their concerns with regard to the decrease of the gene pool, the destruction of plant species, and the creation of invasive

---

and certain crops can be developed which are suitable for saline, dry or other marginalized soils"). Id.

100 Bien, *supra* note 98.

101 GM technologies allow for crops to be grown with less water, which would substantially benefit water scarce countries. See Mahendra Shah and Maurice Strong, Food in the 21st Century: From Science to Sustainable Agriculture 21 (1999).

102 US Department of State, Fact Sheet: Frequently Asked Questions about Biotechnology (Jan. 22, 2001), available at http:// www.state.gov/e/eb/rls/fs/1142.htm.

103 Lakshman D. Guruswamy, Sustainable Agriculture: Do GMOs Imperil Biosafety?, 9 Ind. J. Global Legal Stud. 461, 469 (2002).

104 This debate has arisen in the context of drought, as in Southern Africa, and also in the sudden-impact disaster context after the 1999 hurricane in Orissa, India. Moreover, Sudan has also resisted similar food assistance for the conflict situation in Darfur. See *Sudan's U-Turn on "GM" Food Aid*, BBC News, Apr. 26, 2007, *available at* http:// news.bbc.co.uk/2/hi/africa/6594947.stm.

non-native species which may trigger undesirable consequences, such as the risks of contaminated species[105] and species extinction.[106] Although existing scientific evidence has shown no obvious negative impact on GM food consumers' health, and no reports of ill effects from GM foods have yet been documented, public health experts and millions of consumers still worry about the safety issues. Nevertheless, we cannot deny the fact that potential health hazards do exist, such as unforeseen allergens or toxins transferred into agricultural products from the process of genetic modification. Many people in the US and Europe have life-threatening allergies to peanuts and other foods, scientists believe that introducing a gene into a plant may be the factor that triggers an allergic reaction in susceptible individuals. Moreover, eating too many GM foods with injections of antibiotic markers may lead to a decrease in the effectiveness of antibodies prescribed as medicine.[107] Even worse, uncontrollable epidemics may occur due to the lack of more effective antibodies.

In addition to these environmental and health concerns, legal, economic, and religious concerns are associated with the expansion of GM technology. While many transnational corporations, such as the main groups that promote GM technology, are concerned with GM technology intellectual property protection, patent infringement, and other profit-related issues, small farmers in poor countries are worried about their livelihood. They worry that patented GM technology will raise the prices of agricultural inputs, making them unable to afford them. The governments of developing countries have also expressed their concerns regarding

---

105 John Dill, The Dangers of GMOs: Know the Environmental Hazards, NATURALNEWS, Sept. 28, 2010, available at http://www.naturalnews.com/029869_GMOs_ dangers.html ("The foreign genes can cross with and contaminate these other species, resulting in a hybridization of the genetically modified crop plant with a non-GMO plant. This could radically alter entire ecosystems if the hybrid plants thrived. Out-crossing can also have an indirect effect on food safety and security, as the contaminated species make their way into the food chain"). Id.

106 UNITED NATIONS ENVIRONMENT PROGRAMME, CH. 14 (G) PROMOTING SUSTAINABLE AGRICULTURE AND RURAL DEVELOPMENT: CONSERVATION AND SUSTAINABLE UTILIZATION OF PLANT GENETIC RESOURCES AND FOR FOOD AND SUSTAINABLE AGRICULTURE, ¶¶ 14.54–14.55, *available at* http://www.unep.org/Documents.Multilingual/Default. asp?DocumentID=52&ArticleID=62 (last visited March 17, 2014).

107 Antibiotic marker is included in many GMOs. *See* ISMAIL SERAGELDIN & G.J. PERSLEY, CONSULTATIVE GROUP ON INTERNATIONAL AGRICULTURAL RESEARCH, PROMETHEAN SCIENCE: AGRICULTURAL BIOTECHNOLOGY THE ENVIRONMENT, AND THE POOR 19 (2000). Scientists use an antibody to mark the gene trait that they want to transfer. This antibody is carried into the new organism as part of its genetic makeup and is eventually consumed. See Kim JoDene Donat, Engineering Akerlof Lemons: Information Asymmetry, Externalities, and Market Intervention in the Genetically Modified Food Market, 12 MINN. J. GLOBAL TRADE 417, 425 (2003). Antibiotics are commonly prescribed for medical purposes in order to ward off infection but a resistance can be developed that renders the drugs ineffective if they are used too often. See Id.

adverse economic impacts GM technology may bring to local farming in the long run. The reliance on foreign-controlled technologies may make many poor developing countries' agriculture more vulnerable to the fluctuations of global markets.[108] Moreover, some religious groups also oppose the introduction of genetic materials from certain prohibited animals into crops.[109]

Feed Hungry People with GM food and Reduce Its Undesirable Consequences

GM advocates claim that these technologies are highly advantageous to local farming, and can be used to solve hunger and malnutrition problems in developing countries. However, opponents express their concerns that GMOs may cause unpredictably undesirable environmental, health, ethical, and legal consequences. They discourage the development of GM technology and the consumption of GM food.

Despite the dispute, as a fast and effective method to improve yields with minimum agricultural inputs, GM foods should be considered an immediate alternative to "solve ... the inefficiencies that plague local farming systems";[110] it should be widely used to ease global hunger issues. Food deficit developing countries are encouraged to adopt GM technology, at least for a certain period of time, to increase their agricultural production so that they will be able to feed more of their hungry people. Countries should adopt GM technology mostly because of GMOs' greater resistance to drought, pests, and viruses, and their higher nutritional value.

Transnational agribusiness corporations in developed countries essentially monopolize GM technology. To substantially raise food availability throughout the world, it is of great importance to create some partnerships or cooperative programs between transnational agribusiness corporations and the countries or regions that are short of food. These programs will align the interests of both participating agribusiness corporations in developed countries and hungry people in developing countries.[111] Transnational agribusiness corporations gain economic benefits by selling their products, such as GM seeds, to farmers in developing countries. In the meantime, with the GM technologies purchased

---

108   The developing countries believe that increasing reliance on Western-controlled GM technologies will damage local farmers. Moreover, they also worry about local small farmers' interests which might be impaired because of large corporate farmers who will receive the most benefits due to the technologies they have. See JOHAN POTTIER, ANTHROPOLOGY OF FOOD: THE SOCIAL DYNAMICS OF FOOD SECURITY 184 (1999).

109   In 1993, religious leaders convened to discuss the use of biotechnology in light of religious dietary restrictions. Muslims, Sikhs, and Hindus objected to the introduction of genetic material from prohibited animals into plant materials. See CRAIG DONNELLAN, GENETICALLY MODIFIED FOOD 4 (2000).

110   Frank Tenente, Feeding the World One Seed at a Time: A Practical Alternative for Solving World Hunger, 5 Nw. U. J. INT'L HUM. RTS. 298, 315 (2007).

111   Id.

from transnational agribusiness corporations, food deficit countries will be able to rapidly increase their agricultural outputs. They can grow their own food for survival within a shorter period of time compared to traditional farming. However, the establishment of such partnerships or cooperative programs requires both the commitment of agribusiness corporations and policy support from the food deficit developing countries. The governments of food deficit developing countries play a critical role in planning the partnership programs, negotiating with foreign agribusiness, and practically promoting the application of GM technologies.

Partnerships or cooperative programs are not long-term solutions because the agricultural economies of developing countries will still be largely dependent on the GM technology of foreign agribusiness. Developing countries need to promote their own research capability so that farmers can benefit from local research rather than rely on West-controlled technologies. Developed countries that have advanced GM technologies are encouraged to provide technical assistance to food deficit developing countries.

Furthermore, supporting the expansion of GM technologies for food security purposes does not mean that the undesirable consequences of GM technologies can be ignored. Instead, the undesirable environmental, health, legal, and other consequences should be addressed and closely monitored.

People want more scientific information concerning the safety of GM foods and their potential health risks. The scientists explain that more research is needed. However, this research is not a scientific study and, therefore, it cannot provide in-depth suggestions on what research needs to be done, or what scientists should do. From a consumer perspective, it is important for public health specialists to further examine the safety of GM foods, and try to reduce potential health hazards if possible. It also is important for the scientists to find solutions to protect species diversity and, at the same time, to promote the evolution of species with desired traits. Moreover, research is required to find more genetic materials which are not from prohibited animals in order to ease religious groups' concerns.

Another GMO issue: labeling

The EU first introduced its labeling requirements for GM foods in 1997,[112] as "an application of the precautionary principle."[113] However, the labeling of GM foods continues to be a highly controversial issue in the US. It is widely debated whether GM foods should be labeled and how to properly label them.

The US Food and Drug Administration (FDA) currently does not have a specific labeling regulation for GM foods. It requires labeling of GM foods in the following circumstances:

---

112   Commission Regulation 258/97 (EC). See also Peter Burchett, A Castle in the Sky: The Illusory Promise of Labeling Genetically Modified Food in Europe, 23 PENN ST. INT'L L. REV. 173, 175 (2004).

113   Colin A. Carter & Guillaume P. Gruère, Mandatory Labeling of Genetically Modified Foods: Does It Really Provide Consumer Choice?, 6 AGBIO FORUM, art. 13 (2003).

1. if a bioengineered food is significantly different from its traditional counterpart such that the common or usual name no longer adequately describes the new food, the name must be changed to describe the difference.

2. if an issue exists for the food or a constituent of the food regarding how the food is used or consequences of its use, a statement must be made on the label to describe the issue.

3. if a bioengineered food has a significantly different nutritional property, its label must reflect the difference.

4. if a new food includes an allergen that consumers would not expect to be present based on the name of the food, the presence of that allergen must be disclosed on the label.[114]

American consumers in growing numbers have been demanding the mandatory labeling of GM foods. The US government is reluctant to introduce such a requirement, for a few reasons. First, it believes there is no scientific research that shows significant differences between GM foods and conventional foods. Labeling GM foods may imply a warning about health effects, making consumers avoid GM products.[115] However, from a consumer's perspective, there is no scientific research proving that GM foods are 100 percent safe and have no potential health hazards. Second, the US government explains that accurate labeling will impose an extra cost on all consumers because it must be supported by an extensive identity preservation system. Certain test and record-keeping needs to be done at various steps of food manufacturing.[116] Research estimates that the implementation of mandatory labeling may cost consumers extra dollars per person per year, or it may even lead to a 10 percent increase in a consumer's food bill, depending on a variety of factors, such as the threshold level, the capacity of the industry to comply with requirements, and the public authority's capacity to enforce the labeling rules.[117]

However, behind all this reasoning, one significant factor is not revealed—the interest of agribusiness that owns the GM technologies. As previously discussed,

---

114 US Food & Drug Admin., Guidance for Industry: Voluntary Labeling Indicating Whether Foods Have or Have Not Been Developed Using Bioengineering; Draft Guidance, http://www.fda.gov/Food/GuidanceComplianceRegulatoryInformation/GuidanceDocuments/FoodLabelingNutrition/ucm059098.htm (last visited Feb. 9, 2013).

115 Carter & Gruère, supra note 113.

116 R. Maltsbarger & N. Kalaitzandonakes, Direct and Hidden Costs in Identity Preserved Supply Chains, 3 AGBIO FORUM, art. 10 (2000).

117 Guillaume P. Gruère & S.R. Rao, A Review of International Labeling Policies of Genetically Modified Food to Evaluate India's Proposed Rule, 10 AGBIO FORUM, art. 6 (2007).

US Congressmen and Senators receive significant financial contributions from farm lobbyists. Agribusiness has a strong influence over political decisions. Such labeling requirements may bring substantial damage to their business because existing scientific research that proves the safety of GM foods is still not convincing among consumers. The labeling of GM foods may also give many consumers an aversion to GM products. It may thus cause millions of dollars in economic loss for many agribusiness corporations. Therefore, agribusiness tries to use its power to influence the government not to regulate the labeling of GM foods. For instance, Proposition 37 is a mandatory labeling of genetically engineered food initiative.[118] It was on the November 6, 2012 ballot in California as an initiated state statute, but it was narrowly defeated (52.8 percent of voters opposed the initiative).[119] The defeat was mainly the result of obstacles set by numerous biotechnology agribusiness corporations. The "No on 37" campaign, led by Monsanto, one of the biggest American multinational agricultural biotechnology corporations, with the support of other big agribusiness, spent $46 million convincing voters not to regulate the labeling of GM foods through a series of "misleading advertisements and outright falsehoods,"[120] such as illegally using the FDA logo and Stanford logo in mailers sent to state residents.[121] These biotechnology agribusiness corporations are afraid of economic loss caused by mandating the labeling of GM foods. They try to keep consumers in the dark about what they eat.

However, consumers have the right to know what is in their food. Proper labeling enables consumers to make a full and informed choice on what food they prefer to purchase, although there may or may not be any significant differences between GM foods and conventional foods. If GM foods are scientifically proven to be as healthy as conventional foods, the choice between GM foods and conventional foods would be like the choice between Pepsi and Coke. It is the consumer's choice to pick the one they prefer. If GM foods are scientifically proven to be unhealthy, then labelling GM products is like labeling cigarette packages and other tobacco products. If consumers still want to smoke, it is their personal choice to risk their health and life. Consumers have the right to decide what kind of food they want to eat. The US government needs to regulate the labeling of GM foods so that consumers can make a more informed decision.

---

118   Proposition 37, California (Nov. 2012), available at http://ballotpedia.org/wiki/index.php/Text_of_California_Proposition_37 (November_2012).

119   Ocean Robbins, Did Monsanto Trick California Voters?, HUFFINGTONPOST, Nov. 8, 2012, available at http://www.huffingtonpost.com/ocean-robbins/monsanto-prop-37_b_2088934.html.

120   Id.

121   Id.

Food Aid: Pros, Cons, and Reforms

Many developed countries significantly subsidize their agriculture to ensure food supply, and protect the income of domestic agricultural producers who sell their surplus in the world market. In many cases, they have dumped their surplus onto food deficit countries in the guise of food aid programs, especially in early years of the 1970s and the 1980s. The world agricultural market has been distorted, and agricultural productivity in developing countries has been significantly undermined. Thousands of millions of vulnerable people in developing countries are suffering from hunger, malnutrition, and related diseases. To liberalize agricultural trade and, most importantly, to reduce world hunger, it is meaningful to reform current food aid programs so that they truly benefit vulnerable people in food deficit countries.

The Advantages of Food Aid Programs: Saves Lives

In any situation where there is a food shortage caused by natural disasters, economic instability, armed conflicts or other man-made disasters, or a combination of some of these factors, and a country lacks the resources to provide sufficient food to feed its people, the first solution to be considered is food aid. Food aid, in the form of the physical delivery of agricultural products, has a crucial role in satisfying the basic food needs of vulnerable populations experiencing hunger and malnutrition. It mitigates emergency food insecurity caused by acute food availability deficit or market failure. Without food aid, more people would die of hunger, malnutrition, or related diseases.

If a food aid program is well designed, implemented, and maintained, the benefits of food aid are visible, and will have a long-term impact. Food aid meets vulnerable people's immediate food needs. It helps reduce hunger and malnutrition in a short time.[122] In the past few decades, many well-managed food aid programs have significantly contributed to the reduction of lives lost during food shortage emergencies in Afghanistan, Ethiopia, Haiti, Rwanda, Sudan, and Somalia.[123]

If a food aid program is systematically integrated with development strategies in health, education, environment, and others, it will provide local communities with tools and incentives to produce their own food and to develop the local economy in the meantime. Recently, by working with international food organizations, some developed countries have tried to use food aid to help food deficit countries

---

122   Food & Agric. Org. of the UN, Food Aid and Food Security: Past Performance and Future Potential 7, 17 (1985).

123   Shahla Shapouri & Stacey Rosen, Fifty Years of US Food Aid and Its Role in Reducing World Hunger, Amber Waves (Sept. 2004), available at http://www.ers.usda.gov/AmberWaves/September04/Features/usfoodaid.htm.

jump-start their own agricultural productivity.[124] These food aid programs assist poor communities to build up their rural infrastructure, and help enhance greater agricultural self-sufficiency. For example, the World Food Program (WFP), the food aid arm of the United Nations system,[125] with the help of many UN members, initiated Food for Work programs and Food for Training programs in many developing countries.[126] Food for Work programs provide food as payment to those people who go to work building roads, railways, bridges, ports, dams, hospitals, schools, and many other essential elements for community development. Food for Training programs provide food to those people "who participate in projects that teach a skill, such as sewing or gardening, or offer education on nutrition and health issues."[127] These emergency relief programs, combined with development goals, have achieved great success in Burkina Faso, Senegal, Kenya, and Eritrea.[128] Similar types of food aid programs are expanding.

However, food aid is just one of the alternatives, but not the exclusive method to help end or alleviate world hunger. Besides its positive intention to reduce hunger, food aid was also born with a less altruistic intent, and has been a tool used by many developed countries for the disposal of surplus.

The Disadvantages of Food Aid Programs

Food aid is a speedy and effective method to meet immediate needs in countries or regions experiencing food shortage, and it contributes to the reduction of world hunger. Without food aid, more people would die of starvation or related diseases. However, food aid does not always stabilize food availability or curtail world hunger.

International food aid is not a reliable source to supply hungry populations with sufficient food.[129] It is very rarely the exclusive sufficient response. Foreign food aid, mostly, is not based on the needs of local hungry people but driven by the donor-oriented objectives of foreign policies. Food aid programs have been used by many developed countries as a tool to suit the convenience of their commercial or political goals.[130] These motives behind food aid programs do not lead to the service of recipient countries' needs, and the role of food aid in support of food security

---

124   US Department of State, U.S Food Aid: Reducing World Hunger, Volume 12, Nb. 9, available at: http://www.america.gov/media/pdf/ejs/ej0907.pdf#popup.

125   UN World Food Program, Mission Statement, http://www.wfp.org/about/mission-statement (last visited Feb. 8, 2013).

126   World Food Program USA, Food for Work, http://usa.wfp.org/about/food-work (last visited Feb. 8, 2013).

127   Id.

128   Id.

129   J. Dirck Stryker, US Food Aid Legislation: Its Perspective, the American Farmer or Hungry People; and Its Structure, Purposes and Conclusions, 30 How. L.J. 301, 306 (1987).

130   Linda M. Young, *Options for World Trade Organization Involvement in Food Aid*, 3(1) Estey Centre J. Int'l L. & Trade Pol'y (2002) (noting that food aid

has been seriously weakened. Furthermore, most existing food aid programs are voluntary and countries that have food surplus are not obligated to provide food aid to food deficit countries. Although many international organizations try to set a minimum donation commitment for their Member States to fulfill, there are no enforcement or monitoring mechanisms available to make food assistance steady and reliable. Therefore, if Member States fail to provide obligated food aid, there are no meaningful consequences. The only loss for these members is "the reputation as a reliable supplier."[131] Not surprisingly, with such food aid programs, it is hard to ensure a steady and reliable food supply for hungry populations.

In the long term, food aid on a continuing basis is detrimental to food self-sufficiency in recipient countries. If not well managed, food aid creates undue dependence.[132] It potentially impairs local producers' incentives to increase agricultural production. As a result, it lessens the prospects for long-term food security. Even worse, if the recipient country heavily depends on international food assistance, any failure of food aid will create extreme hunger. For example, for the last 30 years, millions of Ethiopians have heavily depended on international food aid.[133] Each year, regardless of good or bad harvests, report shows that at least 5 million people in Ethiopia live on food aid for half of the year to survive.[134] It is of no surprise that any failure of food aid could be fatal to Ethiopians.

Furthermore, current food aid programs are based on top-down approaches.[135] Donor countries provide food assistance directly to the national governments of recipient countries. Food aid can efficiently reduce hunger and malnutrition if managed properly by the recipient governments. However, in practice, due to bad governance and other inefficient government activities, at the national level, many recipient countries either divert food aid to priorities other than feeding their

---

programs have been abused by many developed countries for surplus disposal and market development purposes).

131 John Hoddinott & Marc J. Cohen, Renegotiating the Food Aid Convention: Background, Context, and Issues 5 (2007), available at http://purl.umn.edu/42424 (stating that in 1994, US food aid fell 170,000 metric tons short of the country's 4.48 million ton pledge and in recent years, Canada has also repeatedly failed to meet its target tonnage).

132 Ruosi Zhang, Food Security: Food Trade Regime and Food Aid Regime, 7 J. Int'l Econ. L. 566, 573–75 (2004). See also US Gov't Accountability Office, GAO/NSIAD-95–35, Food Aid-Private Voluntary Organizations' Role in Distributing Food Aid (Nov. 1994) [hereinafter GAO Report] ("Food aid actually fosters dependency").

133 Addis Ababa, Ethiopia: Struggling to End Food Aid Dependency, Feb. 7, 2006, available at http://www.irinnews.org/Report/58056/ETHIOPIA-Struggling-to-end-food-aid-dependency.

134 Id.

135 Sanjeev Gupta, et al., Foreign Aid and Consumption Smoothing: Evidence from Global Foreign Aid, Fiscal Affairs Department of the International Monetary Fund 4 (2003).

populations, or they do not adequately distribute food aid to the right places at the right time.[136]

Food Assistance is Still Needed but Reforms are Necessary

Currently, millions of vulnerable people are still suffering from hunger and malnutrition. They have an urgent need of food aid to survive. Food security is the responsibility of national states. Nevertheless, when national states are unable to fulfill their responsibility for natural, political, financial, or any other reasons, international assistance is vital to avert acute hunger and further social and political unrest. Wealthy countries control 60 percent of the world economy; they are capable of providing sufficient food to the entire population of the planet.[137] To end or at least mitigate world hunger and malnutrition, countries with food surplus are strongly encouraged to give a hand to the hungry people in poor developing countries. However, due to the restrictions of existing food aid programs, constructive reforms are needed in order to effectively reduce global hunger.

To make food aid programs more efficient and to promote food security and rural development in the long term, there are a few reforms that the international community may consider focusing on, including (1) establishing a more accurate needs assessment system, (2) switching direct feeding programs to development-related food aid programs, (3) switching from a top-down approach to a contracting relationship, and (4) local purchasing.

Establish a more accurate needs assessment system
Food aid programs have long been criticized for the absence of meaningful consequences. One of the main reasons for the failure of food assistance is the lack of a functional system to adequately assess where vulnerable people are located, and how much food they really need.[138] Although it is hard to know exactly where food will be needed and in what quantities, there still is some predictability. The delivery of food aid will be more timely and well-targeted with careful assessment.

Needs assessment should be carried out prior to any decision to initiate food aid. Both donor and recipient countries should work together to assess if food is unavailable or in short supply locally. Further, based on the needs and local market conditions, it is important to identify whether other alternatives may be more appropriate in order to mitigate risks. The potential impact of different aid alternatives on local agricultural production should also be examined. If the decision is made that food assistance is necessary, further assessment needs to be

---

136   GAO Report, supra note 132.

137   Oxfam Int'l, Credibility Crunch, Food, Poverty, and Climate Change: An Agenda for Rich Country Leaders (2008), available at http://www.oxfam.org.uk/resources/policy/debt_aid/downloads/bp113_credibility_crunch.pdf.

138   Hoddinott & Cohen, supra note 131, at 19–20.

done, such as mapping food vulnerability and insecurity in recipient countries, and deciding how food aid should be distributed.[139]

According to Dr Olivier De Schutter, UN Special Rapporteur on the Right to Food, there are a few mapping systems that both the donor and recipient countries can refer to. He has advised that the mapping of food vulnerability and insecurity can be based on the multi-agency Integrated Food Security and Humanitarian Phase Classification system, on the WFP's Emergency Food Security Assessments and Comprehensive Food Security and Vulnerability Analysis, or on the FAO-managed Food Insecurity Vulnerability Information and Mapping System, depending on the situation of each country or region.[140] The Food Insecurity and Vulnerability Information and Mapping Systems can also be used to develop a national strategy to realize the right to food.[141] Additionally, in order to be as well informed as possible, Dr De Schutter has further advised the recipient countries to develop mapping systems through participatory means.

After mapping vulnerability and insecurity, recipient countries must ensure that food aid is delivered to hungry people through criteria that are transparent.[142] In this case, legislation is the best way to promote transparency. Remedies must also be made available in law to protect potential beneficiaries that are unjustifiably excluded. As for enforcement, to enhance accountability, recipient countries must "clearly [a]llocate responsibilities across different branches of government, [s]et benchmarks, [i]mpose timeframes, and [e]mpower independent institutions, including courts."[143]

To summarize, needs assessment helps identify the most appropriate form of intervention to improve food security. It helps predict the number, location,

---

139 OLIVIER DE SCHUTTER, GUIDANCE IN A TIME OF CRISIS: IAASTD AND THE HUMAN RIGHT TO FOOD 4 (Feb. 25, 2009), available at http://www.srfood.org/images/stories/pdf/otherdocuments/18-iaastd-rtf-25-2-2009.pdf (noting that the FAO Voluntary Guidelines for the progressive realization of the right to adequate food in the context of national food security "emphasize the need for States to put in place national strategies mapping the groups which are most vulnerable"). Id.

140 OLIVIER DE SCHUTTER, MANDATE OF THE SPECIAL RAPPORTEUR ON THE RIGHT TO FOOD: INTEGRATING THE RIGHT TO ADEQUATE FOOD IN DEVELOPMENT COOPERATION (2008), available at http://www.srfood.org/images/stories/pdf/otherdocuments/6-rtfdevelopmentco operation-10–11–08.pdf.

141 Id.

142 OLIVIER DE SCHUTTER, MANDATE OF THE SPECIAL RAPPORTEUR ON THE RIGHT TO FOOD, THE ROLE OF DEVELOPMENT COOPERATION AND FOOD AID IN REALIZING THE RIGHT TO ADEQUATE FOOD: MOVING FROM CHARITY TO OBLIGATION, background document to UN Doc. A/HRC/10/005 (Mar. 2009), available at: http://www.srfood.org/images/stories/pdf/otherdocuments/8-srrtfdevelopmentfoodaid-1–09.pdf.

143 UN Comm'n on Sustainable Dev. (CSD-17), Contribution of Mr. Olivier De Schutter, Special Rapporteur on the Right to Food, 17th Sess., May 4–May 15, 2009, at 2,, page 2, available at http://www.srfood.org/images/stories/pdf/otherdocuments/19-srrtfsubmissioncsd-01–05–09-1.pdf.

and severity of the target groups in a more accurate way. However, providing the right amount of food to the most vulnerable people at the right time is not easy. Considerable vulnerable populations are still excluded from the mapping results. More efforts from both the donor and the recipient countries are required in order to improve the accuracy of needs assessment.

Switch from direct feeding programs to development-related food aid programs
Currently, most food aid is provided through direct feeding programs. These direct feeding programs have shown positive impacts on hunger and malnutrition reduction. However, in the long run, these programs alone will create undue dependence on foreign food imports for the recipient countries, and with all other adverse effects, direct feeding programs are not sufficient to help poor developing countries attain long-term food security.[144] To achieve the long-term goal of food security, reforms are indispensable.

An efficient food aid system should include two types of programs: programs for emergency purposes and programs for long-term development purposes. These two programs together combine emergency responses with the need to promote food security and local development in food aid recipient countries. Emergency food aid programs have been used widely by the international community to help alleviate emergency hunger. The international community must ensure that emergency food aid is available so that hungry people will have immediate access to adequate food. In the meantime, food aid systems must include long-term development strategies so that food deficit countries will be able to improve their rural development, and promote agricultural production for self-sufficiency in the long run. Development-related food aid programs can make substantial changes in the food security of some communities.

The international community is strongly encouraged to provide development-related food aid programs, making it the major strategy to mitigate global food insecurity. Food aid can be used to support projects in many different development sectors, such as health, education, and infrastructure.

Beneficiaries of food aid projects should be carefully targeted. Special attention must be paid to the most vulnerable populations, particularly women and children. Maternal and child food aid projects provide supplementary food to children and pregnant and lactating women to ensure that they have an adequate diet.[145] The reduction of hunger and malnutrition in women and children helps prevent longer-term health consequences.

---

144   GAO Report, supra note 132 (noting that although "[s]ome well-designed and well-implemented direct feeding projects appear to enhance food security at the community or individual level," policy reforms are still necessary in order to promote food security in the long run). Id.

145   FAO, Right to Food Guidelines, supra note 92, at 19. ("Maternal and child health projects generally target children and pregnant and lactating women because of their nutritional vulnerability.") Id.

The Food for School project is an efficient way to provide nutritious foods to poor children and improve their health. It enables them to focus better on their lessons. Also, the Food for School project provides incentives for parents to keep their children in school and, thereby, increase attendance rates, and improve education.[146] It empowers people to provide for themselves in the long term.

By providing on-site meals or take-home rations to unemployed individuals who participate in community construction projects, such as building roads, schools, hospitals, irrigation systems, and many other essential elements for development, Food for Work projects feed hungry people and make improvements in rural infrastructures. Although the projects are usually local and small scale, the benefits are significant, especially if widely implemented in local communities that have food insecurity issues. Many people who have participated in Food for Work projects believe that such forms of food aid have substantially improved their living conditions and, in the meantime, developed their local community as well.[147] Additionally, food aid projects aimed at promoting environment, water and sanitation, income generation, small business development, democracy building, and all other aspects for sustainable development are also strongly encouraged.

The world has gradually realized the importance of development-related food aid programs. As previously discussed, the WFP has initiated a few development-related food aid programs, and these programs have enjoyed great success. However, it still is not enough. More development-related aid programs are needed in order to feed hungry people and in the meantime, to promote rural development and achieve long-term food self-sufficiency. The successful implementation of development-related food aid programs in the long-term needs to overcome a great number of difficulties. To implement such programs to promote food security in the least-food-secure households is challenging. Least-food-secure households are more likely to have more women and elderly people. They usually have less surplus labor to be able to access work opportunities. In a community with strong gender discrimination, female participation in the programs appears to be especially difficult, and in many cases, the most vulnerable people are excluded from the programs because they are least able to participate due to health issues or disability.

Switch from a top-down approach to a contracting relationship
Food aid programs in many countries, especially in African countries, usually are a multi-million dollar business which is highly politicized and vulnerable to corruption. Losses resulting from theft and corruption in food aid programs exist in many recipient countries, which has tragically intensified food insecurity, and impeded the international community's efforts to reduce world hunger. According to the US General Accounting Office's report, losses exist in each country the

---

146   Id.
147   Id.

auditors visited. It is hard for them to report losses resulting from thefts.[148] To ensure food aid flows to the designated beneficiaries, donors may consider creating a contracting relationship with recipient countries.

Current food aid programs have been implemented in a top-down method. Donors transport food to recipient countries. Recipient countries' governments at the national level are the receivers of food aid and are in charge of its distribution. In most cases, donors are not able to monitor where the aid flows to. Not surprisingly, this method of food aid delivery has left room for corruption.

Donors may consider contracting with recipient countries. This will prohibit them from exploiting international contributions, or using the funding, commodities, or materials in any unintended manner.[149] Such a contracting relationship creates identifiable legal rights and obligations on both donor and recipient countries, and more importantly, this relationship is protected by law. In other words, it protects the integrity of international aid projects; it also imposes clearly legal obligations for abusing food aid. Any misuse of international contributions will constitute a breach of contract, and the legal rights of donors will be protected under the jurisdictional umbrella.[150]

Local purchasing

Traditional food aid has its limitations. The delivery of food from donor countries is less effective, especially if it needs to be transported over a long distance. The UN Special Rapporteur on the Right to Food, Dr Olivier De Schutter, has estimated that "the cost of direct food-aid transfers from the donor country is on average 50 percent more than local food purchases, and 33 percent more than regional purchases."[151] Consequently, local purchasing is an effective alternative to reduce world hunger. The most direct impact of local purchasing is it frees up money used on expensive freight and reduces delivery delays. Furthermore, the local purchasing of commodities through food aid programs is need-based, rather than being linked to any commercial or political purposes of the donors.[152] It helps poor people buy food on the local or regional markets, which encourages greater local agricultural production, and stabilizes local commercial markets. Donors may consider increasing the use of aid in cash to purchase food on the local markets or in neighboring regions in order to feed hungry people in famine-prone countries.

---

148   GAO Report, supra note 132.

149   Gregory W. MacKenzie, ICSID Arbitration as a Strategy for Leveling the Playing Field between International Non-Governmental Organizations and Host States, 19 SYRACUSE J. INT'L L. & COM. 197, 199, 216 (1993).

150   Id. at 226.

151   DE SCHUTTER, supra note 142.

152   Id. ("Local purchasing of commodities through food aid programs ... are case based rather than donor country sourced commodity based"). Id.

Local purchasing cannot be implemented without limits or concerns.[153] Instead, local purchasing is a complex undertaking. It needs a comprehensive understanding of local markets and the potential risks and undesirable consequences associated with local purchasing before it is substantially used in local communities.[154] Donors need to pay particular attention to avoid any potential harmful effects caused by local purchasing. Both donor and recipient countries must understand that local purchasing is an option only when food insecurity is caused by insufficient purchasing power, but there is sufficient local agricultural production, and the local markets must function adequately. Conversely, if local purchasing programs are implemented in food insecure communities, it may result in price increases which may make food less affordable for the poor or people that are not covered by the program. Therefore, more attention must be paid when providing funding for local purchasing.

Strengthening the Role of International Organizations in World Hunger Reduction

The FAO, WFP, and many other international organizations are dedicated to world hunger reduction. Instead of functioning as governmental agents, these international food organizations work closely with both donors and recipient countries.[155] They receive funding, food, and other contributions from donors. They assess the needs of hungry people and make decisions on how these resources should be distributed. They complement or supplement donors to provide food assistance to local communities that are short of food supply. International food organizations, as the middleman between the donors and the recipient countries, play a significant role in alleviating world hunger. They have made a profound impact on the protection and promotion of the right to food worldwide.

Unfortunately, international food organizations do not always work as effectively as expected. In most cases, the Member States of these international food organizations are not obligated to provide food aid to food deficit countries even if they have agreed to. In some cases, Member States are required to provide food aid, but there are no significant consequences if they fail to fulfill their obligations. All these make the mission of hunger reduction more difficult to

---

153   Id. (noting that local purchasing can only be implemented when existing local market conditions allow).

154   William K. Tabb, The Global Food Crisis and What Has Capitalism to Do With It?, Int'l Dev. Econ. Assocs. (2008), http://www.networkideas.org/feathm/jul2008/Global_Food_Crisis.pdf.

155   Most NGOs play a partnership and compensatory role in relation with donor and recipient governments. See Yves Beigbeder, The Role and Status of International Humanitarian Volunteers and Organizations: The Right and Duty to Humanitarian Assistance 88 (1991).

achieve. To solve this issue, international organizations may consider initiating a series of reforms. Meaningful reforms include, but are not limited to, setting an appropriate minimum commitment obligation, clarifying States' accountability, establishing effective systems to implement the rules and to monitor their donation activities, and stronger coordination efforts between the organizations and recipient countries.[156]

Most international food organizations face challenges in monitoring aid flows. In practice, international food organizations need to make a formal request to send a team to the recipient countries for food aid monitoring. However, many of their requests are denied or delayed. For instance, in the 1990s, North Korea did not allow a monitoring team to enter the country. In Zimbabwe in 2012, the WFP suspected that Zanu (PF) used international food aid as a political weapon to buy votes while refusing its opponents' access to food aid.[157] So the WFP asked the Zanu (PF) government for permission to send a team to monitor food distribution. The WFP's request was delayed, and the Zanu (PF) President Robert Mugabe and Social Welfare Minister Paurina Mpariwa refused to meet with WFP officials. In addition to being declined or delayed, it is often seen that monitoring teams are sent to certain areas where local governments have pre-arranged everything before their visit. The teams are not able to verify the real flow of food aid. Strengthening the monitoring system is of great importance to ensure the impartiality of food distribution among hungry people, but without the cooperation of the recipient country, it is difficult to make a dramatic change.

156	Jay M. Vogelson, Food and Agriculture Organization, 30 INT'L LAW. 425 (1996).

157	Chipo Sithole, UN to Monitor Food Aid?, ZIMBABWEAN, Jan. 18, 2012, available at http://www.thezimbabwean.co.uk/news/africa/55735/un-to-monitor-food-aid.html.

Chapter 8

Agricultural Policies in the EU and the US and their Impact on International Agricultural Trade

Hunger and poverty reduction in developing countries is largely determined by their economic growth. Due to globalization, economic growth in developing countries is significantly affected by the international economic and global trading environment, while the international environment is essentially decided by the economic and trading policies of the major developed countries. Thus, major developed countries are able to exert significant influence over the world market for agricultural commodities and thus global hunger reduction as well.

Developed countries affect agricultural trade not only through their trade policies, but also through their domestic agricultural policies. To establish a more liberal trading system for agricultural commodities, and thereby reduce world hunger, it is important to understand what domestic agricultural policies have been implemented by the major developed countries, what impact these policies have had on domestic agriculture, and how they have distorted international agricultural trade. The EU and the US are the two major dominants in international agricultural trade. Their agricultural policies will be examined in depth.

European Union: Common Agricultural Policy (CAP)

The CAP and Its History

In 1957, six western European countries, Belgium, France, Germany, Italy, Luxembourg, and the Netherlands, signed the Treaty of Rome which created the European Economic Community (EEC) (or "Common Market").[1] The ultimate goal of establishing the European Community (EC) was to achieve the "free movement of capital, goods, persons and services within the Community, together with a common tariff and commercial policy for states outside the Community."[2]

---

1 Europa, *The History of European Union*, http://europa.eu/abc/history/index_en.htm (last visited Dec, 15, 2010).

2 Henricus A. Strating, *The GATT Agriculture Dispute: A European Perspective*, 18 N.C.J. INT'L L. & COM. REG. 305, 307–14 (1993).

The Member States of the EC used to intervene individually in their agricultural sectors. To establish a Common Market, agriculture issues were addressed and included in the creation of the European Community. Influenced by the memory of wartime malnutrition and hunger as well as post-war food shortage, European countries had a strong desire to ensure the security of the food supply. They had an urgent need to develop a stable food supply system, which encouraged the formation of the Common Agricultural Policy.[3] The Common Agricultural Policy (CAP) was proposed by the European Commission, and was signed by all EC Member States in 1957.[4]

The CAP is the uniform policy governing the agricultural economy of the EC Member States. It was created to establish a single agricultural market within the European Community, to protect the competitiveness of the community's agricultural producers from being threatened by third State imports, to attain financial solidarity in agricultural trade,[5] and to strengthen the EC's international bargaining position in agriculture.[6]

The Objectives of the CAP and How to Achieve These Objectives

The basic objectives of the CAP are set out in the Treaty of Rome. Under Article 39 of the Treaty Establishing the European Community (TEC), the objectives of the CAP are summarized as:

> (a) to increase agricultural productivity by promoting technical progress and by ensuring the rational development of agricultural production and the optimum utilization of the factors of production, in particular labor;

> (b) thus to ensure a fair standard of living for the agricultural community, in particular by increasing the individual earnings of persons engaged in agriculture;

> (c) to stabilize markets;

> (d) to assure the availability of supplies;

---

3   Dale E. Hathaway, *Reforming World Agricultural Policies in Multilateral Negotiations*, 1 TRANSNAT'L L. & CONTEMP. PROBS. 393, 393–96 (1991).

4   Susan Bierman, *Fair and Unfair Trade in an Interventionist Era*, 77 AM. SOC'Y INT'L L. PROC. 114, 121 (1983). (The creation of the CAP is the turning point in world agricultural developments. The CAP "was the first common policy of the Europeans and is considered a basic social or employment policy undergirding the Community.") *Id.*

5   Robert P. Cooper, II, *The European Community's Prodigal Son—The Common Agricultural Policy—Undergoes Reform: Will Multilateral Trading Schemes Fostered by the GATT Blossom or Wither and Die?* 1 COLUM. J. EUR. L. 233, 240–41 (1995).

6   THOMAS W. ZEILER, AMERICAN TRADE AND POWER IN THE 1960s, 170 (1992).

(e) to ensure that supplies reach consumers at reasonable prices.[7]

The EC ensures farmers' income through a guaranteed price. The guaranteed price under the CAP is a mechanism that "requires the Commission to buy in or to pay storage subsidies whenever internal prices fall below a predetermined level or intervention price."[8] It is maintained through market manipulation and frontier protection.[9] These prices are usually above the real world market prices. In addition to direct price support, the EC also provides export subsidies to its farmers and restricts market access for foreign agricultural products by setting various tariff and non-tariff barriers.[10] This support for agriculture is primarily financed from tax revenue shifted from urban wealth into agricultural economy.[11]

The Effects of the CAP

The CAP was originally designed to provide support to farmers in the European Community, helping them maintain a better quality of life, and, most importantly, encouraging agricultural production to secure supply. Through price support, export subsidies, trade protection, and other government interventionist measures, the CAP has achieved great success. It played a significant role in reviving the EC's agricultural economy. In the 1960s, Europe was basically a net food importer. Since the implementation of the CAP, it has become one of the largest exporters of agricultural products in the world.[12]

However, the CAP's guaranteed high prices have not come without substantial costs. The budget on agriculture became the largest expenditure of the European Community. More than two thirds of the EC's budget was spent on agricultural market support.[13] High subsidies and other agricultural support provided

---

7   Treaty Establishing the European Community, March 25, 1957, *available at* http://www.hri.org/docs/Rome57/ (last visited Dec. 16, 2010).

8   Bierman, *supra* note 4, at 121.

9   Eur. Union Committee, The Future Financing of the Common Agricultural Policy, 2005–06, H.L. 7-I, at 14 (U.K).

10   James D. Gaisford & William A. Kerr, Economic Analysis for International Trade Negotiations: The WTO and Agricultural Trade 55 (2001) ("[C]ommon trade barriers had to be set high enough to support farms in the high-cost country for the particular commodity"). *Id.*

11   Jess Phelps, *Much Ado about Decoupling: Evaluating the Environmental Impact of Recent European Union Agricultural Reform*, 31 Harv. Envtl. L. Rev. 279, 281–82 (2007).

12   Lyn MacNabb & Robert Weaver, *The General Agreement on Tariffs and Trade (GATT): Has Agriculture Doomed the Uruguay Round?*, 26 Land & Water L. Rev. 761, 765 (1991) (noting that the European Community has changed from a net importer to a net exporter of commodities); *see also* Thomas J. Schoenbaum, *Agricultural Trade Wars: A Threat to the GATT and Global Free Trade*, 24 St. Mary's L. J. 1165, 1183 (1993) ("Because of the CAP, the EC has become a major food exporter"). *Id.*

13   Cooper, *supra* note 5, at 234.

Community farmers with strong incentives to produce more food than they could consume, although their real incomes could decline if the prices were directed by the market. As a consequence, the CAP directly led to enormous agricultural surpluses. Since there was not enough of a market to sell these surpluses, the Community was forced to pay costly storage expenses.[14] In the meantime, the Community had to look for opportunities in the global market. They dumped their surpluses on other countries with the help of export subsidies. Large amounts of government budgets had to be interposed to sustain the competitiveness of the Community's agricultural exports. Although the CAP has had great success in accomplishing its initial goals, this has been attained at correspondingly high costs. The European Community has fallen victim to its own success. Reforms must be implemented in order to adjust the CAP to new emerging challenges and opportunities.

CAP Reforms

Agricultural policy has always been a problematic topic. The European Community (later the European Union) gradually realized the negative impacts brought by the CAP. Coupled with pressure from the public and its trade partners, the European Community/European Union has made several major improvements in its agricultural policies.

When the CAP was first implemented in the 1960s, the more products farmers produced, the more subsidies they received from the government.[15] Since 1992, the CAP has initiated a series of fundamental reform processes aiming at moving away from a policy of direct price and production support to a more comprehensive regime to promote sustainable agriculture and rural development. European farmers are increasingly driven by market demands. They are also required to "respect environmental, food safety, phytosanitary and animal welfare standards."[16] If they fail to fulfill the environmental and social requirements set by the CAP, they will face a reduction in subsidies and less support from governments.[17]

Significant improvements have been made in recent years. The most notable reforms of the CAP include the 1992 MacSharry Reforms, Agenda 2000, the 2003 Reforms, the 2006 Sugar Policy Reform, the 2008 "Heath Check" of the Common Agricultural Policy, and the CAP post-2013 reform.

---

14   Al J. Daniel, Jr., *Agricultural Reform: The European Community, the Uruguay Round, and International Dispute Resolution*, 46 ARK. L. REV. 873, 881 (1994).

15   European Comm'n, *Agricultural and Rural Development: A History of Successful Change*, http://ec.europa.eu/agriculture/capexplained/change/index_en.htm (last visited Dec. 31, 2010).

16   *Id.*

17   *Id.* It is a condition known as "cross-compliance."

The MacSharry Reforms (1992)

To reach an agreement with the EC's external trade partners at the Uruguay Round negotiations with regard to agricultural subsidies, the MacSharry Reforms were initiated in 1992 to limit overproduction in Europe. These reforms were the EC's first attempt to reach an eventual decoupling of agricultural payments since the implementation of the CAP.[18] First, income support was shifted towards being decoupled from production in the farm payment area. It was converted into direct payments to farmers. Second, the MacSharry Reforms required environmental protection for long-term sustainable development. They created a "set aside" payment for farmers to withdraw land from production for environmental purposes.[19] However, in practice, the spending on agricultural support under the CAP remained high, and environmental protection remained limited and problematic.

Agenda 2000 (2000)

Agenda 2000 is "an action program whose main objectives are to strengthen Community policies and to give the European Union a new financial framework for the period 2000–2006 with a view to enlargement."[20] Agriculture is one of the priority issues covered by Agenda 2000. Agenda 2000 "[c]ontinued the agricultural reform along the lines of the changes made in 1988 and 1992, with a view to stimulating European competitiveness, taking great account of environmental considerations, ensuring fair income for farmers, simplifying legislation and decentralizing the application of legislation."[21]

Agenda 2000 divided the CAP into three pillars—production support, rural development, and environmental protection.

- Agenda 2000 strengthened market orientation by "contributing to a better balance between supply and demand."[22] Market support prices for cereals and dairy products were cut by 15 percent each.[23]

---

18 Clayton W. Ogg & G. Corndis van Kooten, *Severing the Link between Farm Program Payments and Farm Production: Motivation, International Efforts, and Lessons*, Choices, 4th Qtr. 2004, at 47, *available at* http://www.choicesmagazine.org/2004–4/grabbag/2004–4-11.htm.

19 Phelps, *supra* note 11, at 296.

20 European Comm'n, *Agenda 2000: Strengthening the Union and Preparing the 2004 Enlargement*, http://ec.europa.eu/agenda2000/index_en.htm (last visited Dec. 30, 2010).

21 *Id.*

22 Europa, *Agenda 2000—A CAP for the Future*, *available at* http://ec.europa.eu/agriculture/publi/review99/08_09_en.pdf (last visited Dec. 30, 2010).

23 *Id.* ("Agenda 2000 has introduced reductions in market support prices of 15 percent for cereals, 15 percent for milk and milk products from 2005 and 20 percent for beef and veal").

- A comprehensive rural development policy that recognizes the multifunctional nature of agriculture was also introduced.[24] It was implemented to support broader economic development in rural areas. Agricultural diversification was encouraged. Young farmers received special support from the EU.
- Agenda 2000 sought to "strengthen the environmental provisions of the CAP and to integrate them in a more systematic way into a broader policy for rural development."[25] Agri-environmental measures became compulsory for all EU Member States.

Despite all the reform proposals on paper, the EU's agricultural policy was still substantially driven by production-related agricultural support. Limited budgets were actually allocated to rural development and environmental protection, showing the necessity for further reforms.

The 2003 Reforms (2003)
In June 2003, based on European Commission proposals presented on January 23, 2003 (CEC, 2003), and considering the enlargement of the European Union, the Council of Agricultural Ministers proposed further reforms in agricultural policies.[26]

Cyprus, Czech Republic, Estonia, Hungary, Latvia, Lithuania, Malta, Poland, Slovakia, and Slovenia joined the EU in May 2004. These new members were given careful consideration with regard to agricultural support. New Member States' production quotas, reference yields, and base areas were set in accordance with "recent historical reference periods for which data were available."[27] Farmers from new Member States were given immediate access to the CAP market measures, such as export subsidies and agricultural payments.

In conformity with the objectives of Agenda 2000, the EU made some notable adjustments to the CAP. One of the most important features was the creation of a new "single farm payment" that separates agricultural support from production. The single farm payment was expected to eventually replace a variety of EU agricultural payments to producers of grain, oilseeds, cattle, sheep, and milk.[28]

---

24   *Id.* ("For rural development, the average annual budget available will amount to €4.3 bio. €520 mio is available per year for pre-accession measures in agriculture and rural development (the SAPARD program)").

25   *Id.*

26   Org. for Econ. Co-Operation and Dev., Analysis of the 2003 CAP Reform (2004), *available at* http://www.oecd.org/dataoecd/62/42/32039793.pdf.

27   *Id.*

28   Food & Agric. Policy Research Inst. (FAPRI), Analysis of the 2003 CAP Reform Agreement (Sept. 2003), *available at* http://www.fapri.missouri.edu/outreach/publications/2003/FAPRI_Staff_Report_02_03.pdf.

Although the EC/EU addressed environmental protection and rural development in previous reforms, most of them were on paper only. The EC/EU had made little progress in this area. Compared to previous reforms, the 2003 Reforms further shifted the emphasis to sustainable development. It provided, for the first time, "a base for a future agricultural support program predicated on the idea of environmental stewardship that is truly committed to the conservation of working lands."[29] If farmers fail to respect the Good Agricultural and Environmental Conditions (GAEC) and Statutory Management Requirements which "are linked to 18 EU Directives and Regulations relating to the protection of environment, animal welfare, as well as public, animal, and plant health," they may receive reduced direct payments, or even have their payments completely cancelled.[30] Most practically, the EU allocated a considerable amount of budget for a broader set of rural developments, rather than just pay lip service.

The 2003 Reforms introduced a radical rebuilding of the CAP. This began a new era to lead the CAP towards greater market orientation and lower market distortion.[31] It was an affirmative effort to address the negative impacts of the CAP. However, strong disagreement among the Member States with regard to the future of European agriculture prevented the enactment of some effective proposals. Despite all the efforts, the 2003 Reform did little to solve the major problem plaguing European agriculture.[32] EU Member States were given some "flexibility" to maintain "coupled"—production-linked—payments. However, the "flexibility" is not clear. Individual countries take advantage of this uncertain "flexibility." Furthermore, the 2003 Reforms failed to include any significant changes to the use of export subsidies, tariffs, or other EU border support.

Consequently, additional reforms, such as the substantial decoupling of payment from production, significant support for rural development and environmental protection, are essential to establish a viable agri-environmental policy in the EU.

Sugar Policy Reform (2006)
Europe was a net importer of sugar. Because of the CAP, it has now become the world's second largest sugar exporter after Brazil.[33] This has come with substantial cost. The CAP provided price support to farmers who produce sugar from sugar

---

29   Phelps, *supra* note 11, at 320.

30   Europa, Health Check of the CAP (May 20, 2008), *available at* http://ec.europa. eu/agriculture/healthcheck/guide_en.pdf.

31   Raj Bhala, *World Agricultural Trade in Purgatory: The Uruguay Round Agriculture Agreement and Its Implications for the Doha Round,* 79 N.D.L. Rev. 691, 798 (2003). ("In June 2003, the EU heralded the most significant reform to the CAP in a decade, The EU Agriculture Commissioner, Franz Fischler with calling the changes 'the beginning of a new era.'"). *Id.*

32   Phelps, *supra* note 11, at 320.

33   Massimo Geloso Grosso, Assoc. of Sweets Industries of the EU, Reforming the EU Sugar Regime, *available at* http://www.commercialdiplomacy.org/ma_projects/ ma_eusugar.htm#_ftnref1 (last visited Dec. 30, 2010).

beet, which made the sugar price in the EU three times higher than the world market price. As a consequence, this high sugar price guaranteed sugar producers' income, but it hurt consumers' interests because it raised the prices of sugar and processed food products. It also put the European food processing industry in a less competitive position in the world market due to the increase in sugar cost. The continuing price support for sugar only resulted in further and significant economic losses for the EU. Realizing that the sugar regime was inefficient, expensive, and unsustainable, the EU decided to make some adjustments in its sugar regime.

Another factor that led to the reform came from its trade partners outside the EU.[34] The sugar support regime was not included in the 1992 MacSharry Reforms, Agenda 2000 decisions, or the 2003 Reforms. It had not been subject to a fundamental reform for 40 years. In 2006, respecting its commitment to the WTO, and also with an attempt "[to] ensure a long-term sustainable future for sugar production in the EU, [to] enhance the competitiveness and market-orientation of the sector and [to] strengthen the EU's position in the current round of world trade talks,"[35] the EU decided to introduce a radical reform of the sugar sector. It agreed to: (1) cut the guaranteed sugar price by 36 percent over four years; (2) reduce European sugar production by 6 to 12 million tons in order to avoid surpluses; (3) a reduction in the minimum sugar beet price of 40 percent.[36] Meanwhile, the EU also offered generous compensation to encourage uncompetitive sugar farmers to leave the industry and find alternative sources of income.[37]

The 2006 Sugar Policy Reform offered greater market access to many foreign sugar producers, especially producers from developing countries. It substantially improved efficiency in beet production, and helped achieve simplification and larger market orientation of the EU's sugar policy. However, it created undesirable consequences, and resulted in temporary sugar supply uncertainty and price volatility in Europe.[38] The market deficit has not been met yet by imports from developing countries as anticipated. The sugar price in Europe has increased by 10 percent more than it was before the reform. Furthermore, the reform has also lead to job loss and increased taxpayer cost. These undesirable consequences are as expected because the reduction of government support will inevitably leave EU

---

34   Judith Prior, *An Uncertain Future for the EU Sugar Regime*, COMMODITIES BULL. (Jan. 2012), *available at* http://www.hfw.com/publications/bulletins/commodities-bulletin-january-2012/commodities-bulletin-january-2012-an-uncertain-future-for-the-eu-sugar-regime (noting that "[t]he reforms represented the EU's response to a ruling by the World Trade Organization, following a complaint by Australia, Brazil and Thailand, which criticized the EU's payment of subsidies to European sugar producers"). *Id.*

35   Europa-Press Releases, *CAP Reform: EU Agriculture Ministers Adopt Groundbreaking Sugar Reform*, available at http://europa.eu/rapid/pressReleasesAction.do?reference=IP/06/194&format=HTML&aged=0&language=EN&guiLanguage=en (Reference: IP/06/194 Date: 21/02/2006).

36   *Id.*

37   *Id.*

38   Prior, *supra* note 34.

sugar producers unprotected. It takes time for the EU farmers to adjust to the market-driven environment. The EU governments may consider taking some actions to mitigate the damages caused by trade liberalization so that the world can move towards a freer market more smoothly. Meanwhile, the EU has to make sure that these actions are taken without violating its international obligations.

The 2008 "Heath Check" of the Common Agricultural Policy
In November 2008, the EU agriculture ministers reached a political agreement on the Health Check of the Common Agricultural Policy.[39] They have made a variety of meaningful reforms. The 2008 Health Check increases investment aid for young farmers from €55,000 to €70,000.[40] It also offers assistance to sectors with special problems.[41] The "special problem" is flexible. The money may be used to "help farmers producing milk, beef, goat and sheep meat, and rice in disadvantaged regions or vulnerable types of farming"; it may also be used to "support risk management measures such as insurance schemes for natural disasters and mutual funds for animal diseases."[42] In the meantime, arable set-aside is abolished; milk quotas will also expire by April 2015.

Most importantly, the Health Check continues the decoupling of direct payment to farmers. It was agreed that the remaining coupled payments must be decoupled from production and moved into the Single Payment Scheme. Furthermore, it was agreed that the rural development budget should be increased. According to the 2007 Health Check, all EU farmers receiving more than €5,000 in direct aid would have their payments reduced by 5 percent (10 percent by 2012), and this money transferred into the Rural Development budget. As for farmers receiving more than €300,000 a year, an additional cut of 4 percent must be applied. The Rural Development budget can be used to "reinforce programs in the fields of climate change, renewable energy, water management, biodiversity, and innovation."[43] As for environmental protection, EU farmers have to respect the environmental, animal welfare, and food quality standards, or face cuts in their support (this is also known as "cross-compliance").

---

39   European Comm'n, *"Health Check" of the Common Agricultural Policy*, http:// ec.europa.eu/agriculture/healthcheck/index_en.htm (last visited Dec. 31, 2010).

40   *Id.*

41   These are so-called "Article 68" measures. ("Currently, Member States may retain by sector 10 percent of their national budget ceilings for direct payments for use for environmental measures or improving the quality and marketing of products in that sector. This possibility will become more flexible. The money will no longer have to be used in the same sector; it may be used to help farmers producing milk, beef, goat and sheep meat and rice in disadvantaged regions or vulnerable types of farming; it may also be used to support risk management measures such as insurance schemes for natural disasters and mutual funds for animal diseases; and countries operating the Single Area Payment Scheme (SAPS) system will become eligible for the scheme.") *Id.*

42   *Id.*

43   *Id.*

However, agricultural payment remains the biggest issue in the 2008 Health Check. The agreement only simplified direct payments by moving them into the Single Payment Scheme, but it did not "[c]ap or [m]odulate payments to highly rationalized farms and agro-industrial enterprises."[44] EU members continue to provide significant support to their farmers, particularly agribusiness.

The CAP post-2013
On April 12, 2010, the Commissioner for Agriculture and Rural Development, Dacian Cioloş launched a public debate on the Common Agricultural Policy's future, objectives, principles and contribution to the Europe 2020 strategy.[45] The purpose of the debate was to involve public opinion from different sectors of society in the EU's agricultural policy reform. In November 2010, on the basis of the outcomes of the public debate and also after exchanging opinions with the European Council and the Parliament, the European Commission presented a communication on *The CAP towards 2020*. Two major objectives are presented in the communication. First, the CAP "needs to anticipate the economic, environmental and territorial challenges"[46] in adjusting its agricultural policies. Second, the CAP needs to be "more sustainable, balanced, targeted, simpler, effective, and accountable" to improve the current CAP instruments, and to propose possible policy options for sustainable agriculture and rural development.[47]

Based on the outcomes of the debate, it was agreed that the distribution of direct payment to the European farmers should be completely reviewed; the CAP itself has to be environmentally and socially responsible. Furthermore, it is equally important to keep rural development at the center of European agricultural policy. Claude Tremouille, the Vice-Chairman of the Commission of Economic and Regional Development of the AER and Vice-President of Limousin (F), emphasized that "[t]he No. 1 objective of the CAP must be sustainable development of dynamic and innovative rural areas; benchmark quality agriculture, economic diversification and real territorial cohesion should be the three incontrovertible pillars."[48]

The communication on *The CAP towards 2020* proposes to move away from direct support to sustainable development, and it has a strong financial focus on

---

44   Hannes Lorenzen, *European Free Alliance in the European Parliament, Health Check of the CAP Reform: European Agriculture Policy Is in Bad Shape* (Nov. 11, 2008), *available at* http://archive.greens-efa.eu/cms/topics/dokbin/223/223534.health_check_of_the_cap_reform@fr.pdf.

45   European Comm'n, *The Common Agricultural Policy after 2013*, http://ec.europa.eu/agriculture/cap-post-2013/index_en.htm (last visited Jan. 1, 2011).

46   European Comm'n, *Commission Communication on the CAP towards 2020*, http://ec.europa.eu/agriculture/cap-post-2013/communication/index_en.htm (last visited Jan. 1, 2011).

47   *Id.*

48   Press Release, Assembly of European Regions, *European Commission Communication on the CAP towards 2020: Providing Rural Areas with Tools to Achieve Excellence!* (Nov. 19, 2010), *available at* http://www.aer.eu/news/2010/2010111901.html.

environmental objectives. However, how the EU plans to implement all these proposals, and how much money will be needed remain big issues. The proposed options regarding the future of European agriculture also need to be evaluated based on their economic, environmental, and social impacts before they are officially enacted and practically implemented.[49]

Additional reforms to European agricultural policies

Table 8.1 The historical development of the CAP[50]

Productivity					
	Competitiveness				
		Sustainability			
The Early Years	**The Crisis Years**	**The 1992 Reform**	**Agenda 2000**	**CAP Reform 2003**	**CAP Health Check 2008**
1. Food security 2. Improving productivity 3. Market stabilization 4. Income support	1. Over production 2. Exploding expenditure 3. International friction 4. Structural measures	1. Reduced surpluses 2. Environment 3. Income stabilization 4. Budget stabilization	1. Deepening the Reform process 2. Competitiveness 3. Rural development	1. Market orientation 2. Consumer concerns 3. Rural development 4. Environment simplification 5. WTO compatibility	1. Reinforcing 2003 reform 2. New challenges 3. Risk management

Source: European Commission Agriculture and Rural Development 2011.

Table 8.1, drafted by the European Commission Agriculture and Rural Development, explains the evolution of the CAP. Initially, the CAP attained the goals of ensuring food supply, improving productivity, stabilizing the market, and increasing farmers' income. By the mid-1980s, the objectives of the CAP were achieved at highly economic, social, and environmental costs. The EC initiated the

---

49 European Comm'n, *The Common Agricultural Policy after 2013, supra* note 45.

50 European Comm'n Agriculture & Rural Dev., Agricultural Policy Perspectives Briefs, The CAP in Perspective: From Market Intervention to Policy Innovation (Jan. 2011), *available at* http://ec.europa.eu/agriculture/publi/app-briefs/01_en.pdf.

CAP reforms in the 1990s. The goal of the CAP has never changed—maintaining and promoting agricultural production. However, since the 1992 reforms, the EU has focused more on the competitiveness of EU agricultural production. Since Agenda 2000, sustainability has become the main agenda in EU agricultural policy reform. But the promotion of sustainable agriculture and rural development is not as impressive as anticipated. Furthermore, all the reforms were accompanied by several exceptions. The CAP does not eliminate all of its Blue Box support. The decoupling of subsidies from production varies between industries.[51] In addition, it still keeps its export subsidies and other trade barriers.[52]

The changes of the CAP policies directly affect developing countries. During the crisis years in the 1970s and 1980s when Europe had large amount of food surpluses, the people of developing countries temporarily enjoyed cheap imported food, and the farmers in developing countries were gradually forced to leave their farmland. That was when agricultural productivity in developing countries started to deteriorate. When the EU started to focus more on its sustainability and reduce its agricultural production, many poor developing countries were also affected. With large portions of food used for biofuel and other purposes, available food surpluses to developing countries decrease accordingly. Food prices go up, and people in many developing countries suffer from hunger and malnutrition. It is an integrated world. Countries are dependent on each other and affect each other. To solve the world hunger issue, the efforts of developed countries are of significant importance.

Additional reforms of the CAP are important for both the EU and the world as a whole. Adjusting European agriculture policies will better prepare the EU for emerging new challenges and opportunities, and will also enable European agricultural products to stay competitive in the world market. More importantly, gradually reducing trade-distorting measures will also contribute to the eradication of world hunger.

Farm Bills in the United States

Like the EC/EU, the US is also able to shape the world agricultural market, not only through its international trade policy, but also through its domestic agriculture policy. US farm bills promote the country's agricultural economy by offering financial subsidies and a variety of government support to American farmers. More than just producing sufficient food for its people, US agricultural support also encourages overproduction. If the oversupply could be effectively distributed in the global scope, there would be fewer people in the world suffering from hunger, malnutrition, and related diseases. Ironically, it is widely believed that US

---

51 Bhala, *supra* note 31, at 800–01.

52 *Id.*

farm bills directly and indirectly contribute to world poverty and hunger.[53] The US is blamed for its trade-distorting subsidies. It is also criticized for burning food for oil. US biofuel programs are believed to be a major factor behind the global food price spikes, and will continue to fuel further food price volatility over the next few decades. This research will examine US farm policies and discuss how they affect agricultural trade and global food security.

The History of US Agricultural and Farm Policies

Agriculture is one of the most important sectors in the US economy. US history is deeply rooted in agriculture. Ninety percent of Americans lived on agricultural land when the US declared independence in 1776.[54] A large number of Americans were and are still involved in the production, processing, manufacturing, marketing, and distribution of agricultural products. Agriculture has been highly regulated in the US. Farm policies in the US have a rich and well documented history.[55]

US agricultural policies were initially shaped by two great cataclysmic events—the Great Depression in the 1930s and World War II in the 1940s. Widespread economic recession and inflation in the 1930s resulted in a huge decline in demand for agricultural products in both domestic and global markets. The world saw a sharp reduction in international agricultural trade. Inevitably, agricultural prices dropped dramatically, which put farmers in jeopardy. In the meantime, prolonged recession pushed more people into poverty. These people did not have enough money to purchase food, not even when prices were already very low. As soon as the world began a slow but modest recovery from the Great Depression, war broke out. World War II largely undermined global agricultural production and distribution. In the 1930s and 1940s, farms failed, and people were hungry.[56] Recognizing the urgent need to provide affordable food for its people, the US government started to intervene in agriculture during the Great Depression in the 1930s.[57] Since the 1930s, US Congress is required to pass a new Farm Bill

---

53   William S. Eubanks II, *A Rotten System: Subsidizing Environmental Degradation and Poor Public Health With Our Nation's Tax Dollars*, 28 STAN. ENVTL. L.J. 213, 235–36 (2009). ("Hunger and malnutrition, which persist throughout the developing world, are also directly linked to the US Farm Bill in two distinct ways. ... [Also,] [n]ot only do farmers in developing nations feel the immense burden placed on their continued survival, but most inhabitants of the developing world suffer from poverty and hunger that is due at least in part to US agricultural subsidies.") *Id.*

54   Michael R. Taylor, *The Emerging Merger of Agricultural and Environmental Policy: Building a New Vision for the Future of American Agriculture*, 20 VA. ENVTL. L.J. 169, 174–75 (2001).

55   Nick J. Sciullo, *"This Woman's Work" in a "Man's World": A Feminist Analysis of the Farm Security and Rural Investment Act of 2002*, 28 WHITTIER L. REV. 709, 713 (2006).

56   Thomas Richard Poole, *Silly Rabbit, Farm Subsidies Don't Help America*, 31 WM. & MARY ENVTL. L. & POL'Y REV. 183, 189 (2006).

57   Hathaway, *supra* note 3, at 394.

every five to seven years to adjust its agricultural policies in light of the changing market and newly emerging challenges and opportunities.[58] The Great Depression and the Agricultural Adjustment Act of 1933, the 1954 Agricultural Policy, the Food and Agriculture Act of 1962, the 1973 Farm Bill, the 1985 Food Security Act, the 1990 Export Enhancement Program (EEP), the Federal Agriculture Improvement and Reform Act of 1996, the Farm Security and Rural Investment Act of 2002, and the Food Conservation and Energy Act of 2008 are the most notable farm policies in US history, and will be discussed in depth.

The Great Depression and the Agricultural Adjustment Act of 1933

President Herbert Hoover preferred market forces to play the major role in shaping economic activities instead of using state power.[59] However, in response to declining agricultural prices, President Hoover sought to recover the agricultural economy through state-encouraged, voluntary cooperative action. In 1928, he instituted the first federal effort to stabilize agricultural prices with the creation of the Federal Farm Board (Agricultural Marketing Act of 1929).[60] The Federal Farm Board intended to provide low-interest loans and other support to agricultural cooperatives when needed. It was hoped that these cooperatives would attract more farmers to join as members.[61] Through working together in purchasing agricultural inputs, marketing commodities, and agreeing to voluntarily reduce planted acres, member farmers would be guaranteed adequate prices for the crops they produced. However, most farmers participating in the programs did not voluntarily reduce their production, in defiance of the Federal Farm Board.[62] Continuing overproduction and lower market prices declared the failure of President Hoover's plan to coordinate and stabilize the domestic agricultural system through voluntary restrictions on production. The failure of President Hoover's economic recovery policies directly led to his failure to be re-elected.

In 1932, during the Great Depression, Franklin D. Roosevelt was elected President. In a context of general economic recession, with deteriorating agricultural prices and widespread distress among farmers, President Franklin D. Roosevelt enacted the Agricultural Adjustment Act of 1933 (AAA) to replace

---

58   Eubanks, *supra* note 53, at 220.

59   Ellis W. Hawley, The Great War and the Search for a Modern Order: A History of the American People and Their Institutions, 1917–1933, at 83–89 (2d ed. 1992).

60   David E. Hamilton, From New Day to New Deal: American Farm Policy from Hoover to Roosevelt, 1928–1933, at 47–48 (1991).

61   Nathan R.R. Watson, *Federal Farm Subsidies: A History of Governmental Control, Recent Attempts at a Free Market Approach, the Current Backlash, and Suggestions for Future Action*, 9 Drake J. Agric. L. 279, 284 (2004).

62   *Id.*

President Hoover's failed voluntary cooperative programs (Agricultural Marketing Act of 1929).[63]

The AAA was one of the significant components of the Roosevelt New Deal Agenda. It was designed to save small farming in the US. The AAA was settled on massive public investment and market intervention. It dealt with the depressed agricultural market by providing continuing price and income support to American farmers.

The AAA authorized direct payments to individual producers who curtailed their output amounts within acceptable bounds.[64] Through restricting production, the AAA was trying to reduce surpluses so as to effectively bring agricultural prices back to stability. In particular, the Roosevelt Administration subsidized specific commodities like wheat, corn, milk, and cotton. Furthermore, the government purchased agricultural commodities at fixed prices when needed.[65] The budgets for government payments and support were generated through an exclusive tax on companies that processed agricultural products ("processing tax").[66] The AAA created the Agricultural Adjustment Administration to oversee the distribution of these budgets.[67]

To protect American farmers from foreign competition, Section 22 of the AAA included a list of market access restrictions on foreign dairy products, such as import quotas and fees. The President was given authority to impose quotas and fees when imports interfered with programs designed to raise agricultural prices and farmers' income. Section 32 of the AAA also authorized the use of import tariff revenues for export subsidies.[68] It was designed to widen market outlets for agricultural surpluses.

In addition, with an attempt to reduce the negative impacts brought about by depressed food prices, the AAA utilized agricultural surpluses to combat hunger and malnutrition in the US.[69] It provided federal meal assistance to feed hungry and malnourished children in the form of nutritional school lunch programs each school day.

However, the AAA was rushed through Congress in response to political and social unrest in rural areas during the Great Depression. Portions of the Act were later declared unconstitutional by the Supreme Court case *United States*

---

63   Agricultural Adjustment Act, ch. 25, 48 Stat. 31 (1933) (current version at 7 USC. §§ 601–626 (2006)).

64   Amanda Stokes, *Selling Out the Farm? The Impact of the Farm Security and Rural Investment Act of 2002 on Lending Institutions and the Small Farmer*, 9 N.C. Banking Inst. 243, 246 (2005).

65   Hathaway, *supra* note 3, at 394.

66   Watson, *supra* note 61, at 285.

67   Agricultural Adjustment Act of 1933, ch. 25, 48 Stat. 31, 37 (1933).

68   Leslie A. Wheeler, *Government Intervention in World Trade in Wheat*, 1 J. of World Trade L. 386 (1967).

69   Eubanks, *supra* note 53, at 219.

v. Butler in 1936.[70] It was declared unconstitutional for dealing with a "local" subject (agriculture) that is "a matter beyond the powers delegated to the federal government."[71] The processing tax to fund production adjustment was an invalid use of the taxing power.

Despite its unconstitutionality, the Agricultural Adjustment Act of 1933 made gross farm income increase by 50 percent within three years of its enactment.[72] The AAA was a great success in retrieving the agricultural economy during the Great Depression. It is the cornerstone of the US's history of agricultural development. Starting with the AAA, the US created "an elaborate scheme of government intervention in agricultural production and markets."[73] The AAA set the tone for much of agricultural legislation to follow.[74] Important elements of previous and current US agricultural policies and programs can be traced back to this Act. President Roosevelt's efforts to deal with the problems of the Depression have provided valuable experience for subsequent governments.

Other farm bills in the 1930s

After the Supreme Court invalidated some provisions of the Agricultural Adjustment Act of 1933, the Roosevelt Administration took further efforts in 1936 to reduce production and stabilize agricultural prices by providing incentives for soil conservation.[75] However, this Act did not do much to reduce the acreage of basic crops.

Subsequently, the Agricultural Marketing Agreement Act of 1937 was enacted. It continued to "[c]all for efforts to stabilize markets and to provide price protection for producers."[76] The Roosevelt Administration kept trying to establish a mandatory system of price supports for corn, cotton, and wheat.[77] The Agricultural Adjustment Act of 1938 was enacted as a replacement for the farm subsidy policies of the Agricultural Adjustment Act of 1933.

The AAA of 1938 included provisions for production control, payments of benefits, marketing quotas, marketing certificates, loans, crop insurance, consumer safeguards, and soil conservation. The support measures under the 1938 Act

---

70   US v. Butler, 297 US 1 (1936).

71   *Id.* (The Supreme Court held that the Agricultural Adjustment Act of 1933 violated the Tenth Amendment to the Constitution, which declares: "The powers not delegated to the United States by the Constitution, nor prohibited by it to the States, are reserved to the States respectively, or to the people"). *Id.*

72   Eubanks, *supra* note 53, at 220.

73   *Id.*

74   M.C. HALLBERG, POLICY FOR AMERICAN AGRICULTURE: CHOICES AND CONSEQUENCES 30 (1992).

75   Soil Conservation and Domestic Allotment Act, amended by ch. 104, §§ 7, 8, 49 Stat. 1148 (1936) (current version at 16 USC. §§ 590a–590q (2006)).

76   Agricultural Marketing Agreement Act of 1937, ch. 296, 50 Stat. 246 (1937) (current version at 7 USC. scattered from §§ 601 to 673 (2006)).

77   Poole, *supra* note 56, at 189.

were not overturned by the Supreme Court in the case *Wickard v. Filburn*.[78] They were allowed to live on. *Wickard v. Filburn* was a case concerning "the power of the Secretary of Agriculture to promulgate wheat acreage quotas."[79] A farmer, Roscoe Filburn, grew more wheat than the limits allowed. This limit was set by the US government in order to drive up wheat prices during the Great Depression. Although Filburn claimed that he produced more wheat for his own use than for sale, he was still ordered to destroy his crops and pay a fine to the government. In this case, the Supreme Court interpreted the US Constitution's Commerce Clause under Article 1 Section 8, which allows the US Congress "to regulate Commerce with foreign Nations, and among the several States, and with the Indian Tribes."[80] The Court decided that Filburn's excessive wheat production reduced the amount of wheat he would buy for animal feed in the market. Given the fact that wheat was traded nationally, Filburn's production of more wheat than he was allowed affected interstate commerce. Thus, Filburn's production could be regulated by the federal government. In other words, agricultural trade, as a national trade, can be regulated by the federal government. Therefore, the US Supreme Court upheld the constitutionality of the Agricultural Adjustment Act of 1938. The Agricultural Adjustment Act of 1938 became the default legislation for government intervention in agriculture. It "opened the modern era of extensive government intervention in the agricultural marketplace."[81]

Farm Policy in the 1950s

In the 1950s, the Eisenhower Administration implemented flexible price support that allowed federal payments to be set at prices less than the New Deal support level.[82] It was hoped that with reduced government support, overproduction could still be discouraged, and agricultural prices could be increased through the natural mechanisms of the free market. Nevertheless, the Eisenhower Administration's insistence on free market ideology did not last long. Reducing government support did not ultimately increase commodity prices. This compromise between free market ideology and governmentally imposed production limits did not please anyone in Congress, neither the legislators who wanted further and deeper reforms nor the ones who wanted no changes. Not surprisingly, the Eisenhower Administration was unable to substantially alter the federal agricultural support programs that began in the New Deal era; it ended up advocating for continuing production controls.

Despite the failure of Eisenhower's farm policy, the enactment of the Agricultural Trade Development and Assistance Act in 1954, known as Public

---

78   Wickard v. Filburn, 317 US 111, 124–25 (1942).
79   *Id.*
80   *Id.*
81   Taylor, *supra* note 54, at 172.
82   Watson, *supra* note 61, at 287.

Law 480 (PL480), established a strong demand for US agricultural products in the world market.[83] PL480 was passed to help the US dispose of its agricultural surpluses on the world market. It provided developing countries with sales of agricultural commodities at market prices on highly concessionary terms and, in some cases, it dumped oversupply to developing countries under the name of "grants of food aid."[84] PL480 established a strong demand for US agriculture products. It largely promoted the export of US agricultural commodities, even if taxpayers had to absorb the costs of agricultural support.[85] PL480's goal was to promote the stability of the US agriculture economy and to stimulate the expansion of international trade in agricultural products, particularly surpluses produced in the US. Thus, it was the beginning of the US agricultural dumping history.

Farm Policy in the 1960s

Agricultural subsidies have always been the primary business of the US government since the Great Depression. Each new administration brings new agricultural support programs. These support programs are different but they are proposed with the same purpose. Like most former US Presidents, President John F. Kennedy continued the federal effort to stabilize the agricultural market and protect American farmers' income. In the 1960s, the Kennedy Administration created a commodity committee selected by the Secretary of Agriculture.[86] Basically, two-thirds of the committee members were selected from nominees elected by farmer committees that administered commodity programs, and the other one-third of the members were selected from different farm organizations.[87] Through the commodity committee, it was hoped that farmers could be largely included in the agricultural policy decision-making process.[88]

The Food and Agriculture Act of 1962 only allowed one agricultural commodity—wheat—to be supported with certain level and production limits. However, wheat farmers were not happy with this. They pushed Congress to pass legislation "allowing individual wheat farmers to voluntarily accept production

---

83   7 USC. §701 (1988). In 1954, the Agricultural Trade Development and Assistance Act, known as Public Law 480 (PL480), was enacted. Agricultural Trade Development and Assistance Act of 1954, Pub. L. No. 83–480, 68 Stat. 454 (1954).

84   Edward Clay, *Food Aid, Development, and Food Security, in* Agriculture and the State 202, 210–13 (C. Peter Timmer ed., 1991).

85   Liane L. Heggy, *Free Trade Meets US Farm Policy: Life after the Uruguay Round*, 25 Law & Pol'y Int'l Bus. 1367, 1375 (1994). (The PL480 program accounted for a large share of US agricultural exports. In 1963, it accounted for almost 28 percent of US agricultural exports.)

86   Watson, *supra* note 61, at 287.

87   *Id.*

88   James N. Giglio, *New Frontier Agricultural Policy: The Commodity Side, 1961–1963*, 61 Agric. Hist. 53, 61 (1987).

limits in exchange for price supports."[89] As such, the "voluntary approach" defeated "government mandatory controls." This voluntary approach was extended to all major commodities in the subsequent 1965 Farm Bill (the Food and Agriculture Act of 1965). Mandatory production controls were difficult to implement practically.

Farm Policy in the 1970s

In the 1970s, the Nixon Administration basically continued with federal agricultural support policies similar to previous farm bills both in the Agricultural Act of 1970 and in the Agriculture and Consumer Protection Act of 1973, with some minor changes. Instead of more restrictive and mandatory approaches, such as planting restrictions and marketing quotas, the Agricultural Act of 1970 leaned towards voluntary approaches, such as voluntary annual cropland set-asides and marketing certificate payments.[90]

Although the US government tried to restrict production with an attempt to bolster the prices of certain agricultural commodities, it still enacted the Agriculture and Consumer Protection Act in 1973 which initiated a revolutionary system of deficiency payments. Deficiency payments resulted in the agriculture sector receiving the highest degree of direct government support and market intervention.[91]

A deficiency payment covers the difference between the prices at which agricultural products sell in the market and a government set target price.[92] Under the 1973 Farm Bill, deficiency payments were paid directly to the producers of certain agricultural commodities, such as corn, wheat, and cotton, when market prices were lower than the government set target price. The amount of payment farmers received was directly linked to agricultural outputs. In other words, the more farmers produced, the greater payments they received from the government. Undoubtedly, this new deficiency payment encouraged farmers to sell their agricultural crops at any price because the government made up the difference regardless. The new system of deficiency payments gave farmers few incentives to maintain sustainable agriculture. Instead, farmers were more interested in maintaining their 'base acreage' of farmland on which their eligibility for future government payments was calculated.

In the 1970s, international trade became increasingly integrated. Agricultural surpluses resulting from excessive government subsidies were dumped on the world markets.[93] Luckily, increased demand in developing countries helped the

---

89   Watson, *supra* note 61, at 288.

90   Agricultural Act of 1970, Pub. L. No. 91–524, 84 Stat. 1358.

91   Taylor, *supra* note 81, at 173 ("No other sector of the American economy has received this high degree of direct government economic support and market intervention"). *Id.*

92   *Id.*

93   MacNabb &Weaver, *supra* note 12, at 767.

US dispose of its oversupply. US agricultural production and export expanded rapidly.[94] The US has become another major player in international agricultural trade, in addition to the European Community. However, in the meantime, developing countries' agricultural export has been undermined, and farmers have gradually left their farmland. Agricultural productivity in these countries was inevitably decreased, which made future agricultural production more difficult.

Farm Policy in the 1980s

In the 1980s, thanks to favorable weather conditions, decades of continuing government support, and high demand in the developing countries since the 1970s, American agriculture was very productive. More food was produced. Enormous surpluses needed to be disposed of. However, a world economic recession and high interest rates in the 1980s burst US agriculture's speculative bubble. The recession made it more difficult for domestic consumers and the world market to absorb US agricultural products.[95] Market prices for agricultural commodities dropped dramatically. US government spending on agricultural subsidies increased from an average of $3 billion per year in the 1970s to $26 billion per year by 1986.[96] US farm subsidies were becoming outrageously expensive. It was a big burden for the federal government to continue the support as such. Notwithstanding the budgetary pressure, the US government did not make any significant changes to reduce the spending on agriculture. Instead, the Food Security Act of 1985 sustained most of the agricultural support programs.[97]

Despite the continuing support of agriculture, the 1985 Food Security Act did mark an important shift in US agricultural support history. For the first time, it brought environmental issues and sustainable agricultural concerns into the farm bill debates, and, more importantly, it linked farmers' conservation practices with the payments they receive from government. The Conservation Reserve Program (CRP) was adopted by US Congress. Farmers were paid to take the highly erodible and environmentally sensitive land out of production.[98] The CRP also provided farmers financial and technical assistance to plant vegetation that would protect idle land from erosion.[99] Furthermore, the Sodbuster and Conservation

---

94 Heggy, *supra* note 85, at 1369 (explaining that the export of agricultural overproduction "[b]olsters both export earnings and the United States' position as a world power"). *Id.*

95 Jodi Soyars Windham, *Putting Your Money Where Your Mouth Is: Preserve Food Subsidies, Social Responsibility and America's 2007 Farm Bill*, 31 ENVIRONS ENVTL. L. & POL'Y J. 1, 11 (Fall 2007).

96 *Id.*

97 Food Security Act of 1985, Pub. L. No. 99–198, 99 Stat 1354 (1985).

98 US DEP'T OF AGRIC, AGRIC RESOURCES AND ENVTL. INDICATORS 2000; JEFFREY A. ZINN, CONG. RESEARCH SERV., ISSUE BRIEF IB96030, SOIL & WATER CONSERVATION ISSUES (2000).

99 Taylor, *supra* note 81, at 179.

Compliance programs were implemented to tie farmers' eligibility for government payments to their practices on certain categories of highly erodible land.[100] These conservation programs not only provided price support to the American farmers, but also protected erodible farmland and promoted sustainable agriculture.

As for the influence of the 1980s farm bills on developing countries, not much changed. The US continued to provide support to its farmers. Extra food was dumped to the developing world. In the 1980s, people in developing countries were still enjoying cheaper imported food before they realized how serious it could be if agricultural productivity deteriorates.

Farm Policy in the 1990s

Under the Food, Agriculture, Conservation, and Trade Act of 1990, new subjects such as rural development,[101] forestry,[102] organic certification,[103] and commodity promotion programs[104] were encompassed for the first time in the US farm bill. The Rural Development Administration (RDA) was also established to build rural capacity and promote rural development.[105] The Food, Agriculture, Conservation, and Trade Act of 1990 was soon altered by the Food, Agriculture, Conservation, and Trade Act Amendments of 1991.[106] The amendments reformed the food stamp programs in a more effective and feasible way; it also expanded eligibility to receive food stamps.[107]

In the mid-1990s, US Congress approved the final decisions of the Uruguay Round negotiations. US agricultural subsidies started to be subject to international trade restrictions. Recognizing that the federal support system for specific commodities "hindered the ability of the US farmers to respond to signals from the increasingly global market for agricultural commodities,"[108] coupled with budgetary pressure,[109] the US government initiated dramatic changes in its

---

100   *Id.*

101   Food, Agriculture, Conservation, and Trade Act of 1990, Pub. L. No. 101–624, §§ 2301–2370, 104 Stat. 3359 (1990).

102   *Id.* §§ 2371–2379.

103   *Id.* §§ 2102–2123.

104   *Id.*

105   *Id.* § 2302.

106   Food, Agriculture, Conservation, and Trade Act Amendments of 1991, Pub. L. No. 102–237, 105 Stat. 1886 (1991).

107   *Id.*

108   Taylor, *supra* note 81, at 181.

109   *Id.* at 182 ("One impetus for this change in income support policy was budgetary pressure. Congress was still struggling in the mid-1990s to balance the budget, and cuts in farm support programs were considered inevitable to accomplish that purpose. Indeed, many proponents of reform advocated eliminating income supports altogether, in part to save money"). *Id.*

agricultural support policies in the mid-1990s in an attempt to adapt US farm policies to newly emerging challenges and opportunities.

The Federal Agriculture Improvement and Reform Act (FAIR) was passed in 1996.[110] It was designed to keep US subsidies under $19.1 billion, and to gradually wean US farmers off government price support.[111] FAIR made a significant shift toward a market-oriented agricultural policy. The deficiency payments were replaced with fixed subsidy payments.[112] These fixed subsidy payments are known as "production flexibility contract" (PFC) payments. PFC payments were made available to owners and farmers of farmland covered under the previous farm bill based on their historical base acreage.[113] The gap between the market price and the previously pre-set target price was not considered a factor for the PFC payments. According to FAIR, PFC payments were to be gradually decreased over a period of seven years, and eventually phased out by the 2002 fiscal year. Congress hoped that the PFC payments would save $56.6 billion over the seven-year period (1996–2002).[114]

FAIR allowed emergency loans for farmers in times of need.[115] However, in practice, US Congress frequently awarded generous emergency and disaster payments to farmers. FAIR's experiment of decreasing government supports and production restrictions was deemed a failure. The US government paid billions of dollars for agricultural support during that period.[116] The frequent "emergency and disaster payments" were partially attributed to the increasing power of farmers, in particular, agribusiness which had become extremely powerful politically.[117] When the agribusiness needs support from the government, they use their "political power" to push Congress to pass relevant legislation and develop support programs.

Decreased subsidies under FAIR exposed American farmers to unpredictable market risks. When agricultural commodities prices plummeted in the late 1990s, farmers urged Congress to abandon its plans of reducing government support,

---

110   Federal Agriculture and Improvement and Reform Act of 1996, Pub. L. 104–127, 110 Stat. 888 (1996).

111   *Id.* §§ 111–113(b).

112   Watson, *supra* note 61, at 291.

113   Matthew C. Porterfield, *US Farm Subsidies and the Expiration of the WTO's Peace Clause*, 27 U. Pa. J. Int'l Econ. L. 999, 1003 (2006). ("Under the PFC program's 'planting flexibility' provisions, recipients of PFC payments were not required to produce any particular commodity but were restricted from producing fruits or vegetables on the contract acreage.") *Id.*

114   Windham, *supra* note 95, at 12.

115   Federal Agriculture Improvement and Reform Act of 1996, Pub. L. 104–127, §§ 621–26, 110 Stat. 888 §§ (1996).

116   Anne B.W. Effland, USDA, US Farm Policy: The First 100 Years, in Agricultural Outlook 25 (Mar. 2000).

117   William Petit, *The Free Trade Area of the Americas: Is It Setting the Stage for Significant Change in US Agricultural Subsidy Use?*, 37 Tex. Tech L. Rev. 127, 132 (2004).

and to return to traditional US price support and commodity payments policies.[118] Reports show that the US government still paid at least $17.7 billion in 1996 for agricultural subsidies.[119] Subsidies were increased by 50 percent in 1998. Farm payments were actually doubled from 1999 to 2001.[120]

The Farm Security and Rural Investment Act of 2002

The US government continued to try to promote a free trade environment until Congress passed the Farm Subsidy and Rural Investment Act in May of 2002, which officially put the free trade ideology of the 1996 FAIR to an end.[121] Although the 2002 Farm Bill addressed free-trade concerns regarding the US obligations under the AoA, US Congress significantly increased farm subsidies rather than deregulating its agricultural economy. US farm policy returned to the old regime that government provided substantial price support to ensure farmers' income. The 2002 Farm Bill authorized a $248.6 billion budget for farm support over a period of six years, "including $89.7 billion for commodity subsidies, $20.8 billion for conservation subsidies, and $137.2 billion for food stamps and nutrition programs for schools and the elderly."[122]

Basically, the 2002 Farm Bill provided subsidies to US farmers under three primary payment programs authorized through 2007: fixed direct payments, counter-cyclical payments, and marketing loans.[123]

Fixed direct payments
The 2002 direct payments scheme was the successor to the PFC payments introduced in the 1996 Farm Bill. It mandated the Secretary of Agriculture to provide subsidies to US agricultural producers "whose crops fall within the Farm Bill's coverage and who can establish that he planted and harvested those crops in the past."[124]

First, the 2002 direct payments scheme listed certain crops that were eligible for government subsidies, including corn, cotton, rice, wheat, and soybean. The scheme also extended the coverage to grain sorghum, barley, oats, and other

---

118   *See also* Porterfield, *supra* note 113, at 1004.

119   Petit, *supra* note 117.

120   Windham, *supra* note 95, at 12.

121   Farm Security and Rural Investment Act of 2002, Pub. L. No. 107–171, 116 Stat. 134 (2002).

122   Windham, *supra* note 95, at 3–4.

123   Farm Security and Rural Investment Act of 2002, Pub. L. No. 107–171, 116 Stat. 134 (2002).

124   Elizabeth Bullington, *WTO Agreement Mandate that Congress Repeal the Farm Bill of 2002 and Enact an Agriculture Law Embodying Free Market Principles*, 20 Am. U. Int'l L. Rev. 1211, 1220 (2005).

oilseeds that were not covered in previous laws.[125] The 2002 direct payments were decoupled from current agricultural production and market prices. Farmers were given "planting flexibility" under the scheme. They could plant most crops, but were restricted from planting fruits and vegetables, to receive such subsidies.[126] Second, direct payment was primarily determined by the base acres, payment yield, and payment rate.[127] It was based on 85 percent of the eligible base acres multiplied by the payment rate per unit and the payment yield for each farm.[128] Direct payment = (Payment rate) × (Payment yield) × [(Base acres) × 0.85]. Nevertheless, the fixed direct payment scheme was implemented with restrictions. In general, annual subsidies for each farmer cannot go beyond $40,000, but they can be doubled under certain circumstances.[129]

Counter-cyclical payments
Under the 2002 Farm Bill, counter-cyclical payments were provided to American farmers only when the effective prices of certain agricultural commodities had fallen below pre-determined target prices. These payments are decoupled from agricultural production because farmers can get payments without having to grow anything.[130]

The amount of counter-cyclical payments made to farmers is equal to [the payment acres (0.85 × base acres)] × [the payment rate (target price - average market price)].[131] Although other oilseeds are eligible for direct payments, they are not eligible for counter-cyclical payments because the sum of their national loan rate and direct payment rate is usually equal to or greater than their target price.[132]

Counter-cyclical payments are made to farmers as additional government support when the international and national demand for agricultural products has decreased and market prices have significantly dropped.[133] Counter-cyclical

---

125   Farm Security and Rural Investment Act of 2002, §§ 1001(4) & 1103. In addition, it states that "[p]roducers of grain sorghum, barley, oats and other oilseeds are also eligible for direct payments." *Id.* Other "oilseeds" include "sunflower seed, rapeseed, canola, safflower, flaxseed, [and] mustard seed ...." *Id.* § 1001(9).

126   Farm Security and Rural Investment Act of 2002 § 1006.

127   Porterfield, *supra* note 113, at 1005. (Base acres refer to the land that was planted during the period from 1998 to 2001.)

128   Farm Security and Rural Investment Act of 2002, Pub. L. No. 107–171, 116 Stat. 134 (2002).

129   *Id.*

130   Frank A. Seminerio, *A Tale of Two Subsidies: How Federal Support Programs for Ethanol and Biodiesel Can Be Created in Order to Circumvent Fair Trade Challenges Under World Trade Organization Rulings*, 26 Penn. St. Int'l L. Rev. 963, 969 (2008).

131   Bullington, *supra* note 124, at 1221.

132   US Dept. of Agric., *Direct and Counter-cyclical Payment Program* (March 2006), *available at* http://future.aae.wisc.edu/publications/farm_bill/dcp06.pdf.

133   Doug O'Brien, The Nat'l Agric. Law Ctr., World Trade Organization and the Commodity Title of the Next Farm Bill 7 (Apr. 2006), *available at* http://www.

payments, together with other agricultural payments, put the US in a position that it could exceed its $19.1 billion per year limit imposed by the AoA and run contrary to the spirit of promoting a freer and fairer international agricultural market under the WTO system.

Marketing assistance loans

The 2002 Farm Bill also provides marketing assistance loans to American farmers.[134] This loan program "continues in much the same form as it did in previous farm bills."[135] It provides non-recourse loans to producers of certain agricultural commodities in an attempt to guarantee their incomes. In detail, interim financing is provided to farmers to facilitate the orderly distribution of agricultural commodities throughout the year.[136] Instead of selling agricultural products immediately at harvest to pay bills, a non-recourse marketing assistance loan allows farmers who grow eligible agricultural crops to store the harvested crops when the actual market price falls below a certain rate.[137] Farmers can sell their crops and repay the loan when market conditions become favorable at a later time. The marketing assistance loans set a price floor. Farmers will always be able to receive at least the loan rate for their agricultural products.

Environmental protection

By addressing the environmental consequences of agricultural production, the 2002 Farm Bill demonstrates the support of US Congress for sustainable agriculture. It authorized new conservation programs, and represented a significant advance in environment-related agricultural program design and resource allocation. It also substantially expanded overall conservation funding by 80 percent.[138]

Although the 2002 Farm Bill improved on agricultural conservation efforts in many ways, the continuing government support still encouraged overproduction, which inevitably caused environmental damages. Furthermore, the lack of farmers' voluntary participation undermined the effects of the environmental programs. Overall, the 2002 Farm Bill was not sufficient to make agricultural activities environmentally sustainable.

---

nationalaglawcenter.org/assets/articles/obrien_wto.pdf.

134   JIM MONKE, CONG. RESEARCH SERV., CRS REP. RS21604, MARKETING LOANS, LOAN DEFICIENCY PAYMENTS, AND COMMODITY CERTIFICATES 2–3 (2004) (explaining the marketing loan program).

135   Porterfield, *supra* note 113, at 1004.

136   US Dept. of Agric., *Marketing Assistance Loans and Loan Deficiency Payments*, http://www.usda.gov/documents/Marketing_Assistance_Loans_and_Loan_Deficiency_Payments.pdf (last visited Jan. 30, 2011).

137   *Id.*

138   J.J. Haapala, *Farm Bill Offers Historic Benefits to Organic Growers*, IN GOOD TILTH, June–July 2002, at 1. The bill provides over $18 billion in total conservation spending over the next five years. S. REP. NO. 107–117, at 38 (2001).

Energy Title (Title IX)

The 2002 Farm Bill was the first agricultural policy to have an energy title (Title IX) explicitly included. Title IX "authorized grants, loans, and loan guarantees to foster research on agriculture-based renewable energy, to share development risk, and to promote the adoption of renewable energy systems."[139] It substantially promoted the development of domestic biofuels production. The 2002 Farm Bill was in fact the beginning of developing countries' nightmares. Since its enactment, biofuel programs have developed so fast that large amounts of food, particularly corns, are used for biofuel production. As a result, fewer food surpluses are available for people in developing countries, where agricultural productivity has already been eroded, and people have lost the capacity to produce sufficient food to feed themselves.

The Food, Conservation, and Energy Act of 2008

The Food, Conservation, and Energy Act of 2008, known as the 2008 Farm Bill, was enacted by US Congress in 2008.[140] It addressed the issues of energy, conservation, and rural development.[141] The 2008 Farm Bill also supported agricultural research, into matters such as pests, diseases, and other farming problems, by mandating the creation of the National Institute of Food and Agriculture (NIFA).[142] These agricultural payments are considered "green" under the AoA. Therefore, they are not subject to any restrictions.

However, the 2008 Farm Bill continued the US history of agricultural support for farmers, authorizing a $289 billion budget for a five-year period. A great number of payment programs are contrary to US obligations under the AoA, such as the cotton incentive program, which shows the US government's unwillingness to comply with the spirit of the WTO and its agricultural trading rules. It also expanded the current Renewable Energy and Energy Efficiency Program, and increased support for the production and commercialization of biofuels by establishing a new tax credit for cellulosic biofuels producers.

---

139 RANDY SCHNEPF, CONG. RESEARCH SERV., RENEWABLE ENERGY PROGRAMS AND THE FARM BILL: STATUS AND ISSUES (Sept. 7, 2011), *available at* http://ieeeusa.org/policy/eyeonwashington/2011/documents/renewenergyfarmbill.pdf (last visited January 28, 2013).

140 Food, Conservation, and Energy Act of 2008, Pub. L. 110–234, 122 Stat. 923 (2008).

141 *Id.* § 4102.

142 *Id.* § 7511.

Summary

Table 8.2   A comparison of US farm bills and the EU CAP

Evolution of the US Farm Bills		Historical Development of the CAP	
1930s	• Overproduction and food insecurity issues • Market stabilization • Income support • Massive public investment • Government intervention		
1950s	• Overproduction • Flexible price support • Free market ideology • PL480—strong demand for US agricultural products in the world market	The Early Years	• Food security • Improving productivity • Market stabilization • Income support
1960s	• Overproduction • Market stabilization		• Overproduction • Exploding expenditure • International friction • Structural measures
1970s	• Deficiency payment—the highest degree of direct government support and market intervention • Overproduction—dumping • US—another major player in international agricultural trade besides the EC.	The Crisis Years	
1980s	• Enormous surplus, more than ever before • World economic recession—US agriculture bubble burst • US government budgetary pressure—however, continuing support • First time tackling environment issues and sustainable agriculture		
1990s	• WTO compatibility • Environment • Rural development • Emergency loans—abused	1992 Reforms	• Reduced surpluses • Environment • Income stabilization • Budget stabilization

Evolution of the US Farm Bills		Historical Development of the CAP	
		Agenda 2000	• Deepening the reform process • Competitiveness • Rural development

2002	• Officially put 1996 FAIR free market ideology to an end
	• Return to the old regime: substantial price support
	  – Fixed direct payments
	  – Counter-cyclical payments
	  – Marketing assistance loans
	• Environmental protection
	• Biofuel
		2003 Reforms	• Market orientation
			• Consumer concerns
			• Rural development
			• Environment simplification

2008	• Energy, conservation, and rural development • Agricultural research/ rural development • Some programs—contrary to US obligations under the AoA	Health Check 2008	• Reinforcing 2003 reform • New challenges • Risk management

The left column of Table 8.2 highlights the main elements of the US farm bills in different time periods from the 1930s to the present. Throughout the years, although the farm bills have been updated many times, the key theme has never changed—heavy subsidies.

Similar to the EU, the US government has been providing consistent support to American farmers. The reasons behind the support reflect the same concerns as those of the EU—ensuring food supply and maintaining farmers' income. With government support, both the EU and the US have achieved great success. Farmer's income is protected, agricultural production is stabilized, and food supply is guaranteed. However, they both have fallen victim to their own success. Heavy subsidies inevitably caused painful budget pressure. Massive subsidies resulted in enormous agricultural surpluses in the 1970s and 1980s so that a way had to be found to dispose of the overproduction. Developing countries' markets became their main target. Both the EU and the US employed trade measures to dump their surpluses on developing countries. Large amounts of agricultural surpluses were dumped on developing countries at very low prices, and sometimes lower than real world market prices or even lower than the costs of production. The dumping of agricultural surpluses was operated against free market principles, driving down world market prices. Distorted low agricultural prices put constraint on other agriculture-exporting nations, in particular those developing countries that rely on agriculture for export revenues.[143] The dumping of agricultural surpluses has discouraged agricultural productivity in many developing countries.

Since the 1990s, with the implementation of the AoA, the EU and the US have been subject to new WTO rules in agriculture. They are required to gradually reduce trade-distorting government support. The EU has made notable achievements in subsidy reduction. The US, however, after slightly decreasing government support for a few years, significantly increased agricultural subsidies in the 2002 Farm Bill, which officially declared the failure of its free market ideology.

Since the 2000s, both the EU and the US have promoted biofuel programs to meet their energy needs. Agricultural products are increasingly used as raw materials for biofuels. This change leaves fewer food surpluses available to people in developing countries. As previously discussed, people in developing countries that are used to cheaper imported food have lost interest in growing their own food, and agricultural productivity has been substantially undermined. Fast-growing biofuel programs indirectly impede people's access to sufficient food. As for environmental protection and rural development, both EU and US agricultural policies are gradually moving towards a more sustainable way of agricultural production. The EU made unfulfilled promises on sustainable agriculture in the 1990s and early 2000s. But it has gradually increased its attention in its recent reforms, and a considerable amount of funding has been allocated to promote sustainability. The US follows the EU, but, at a slightly slower pace.

Protectionism and the Absence of Political Will to Correct the Distorted Agricultural Trade System

Continuing price and income support for farmers has revealed strong protectionism in agriculture both in Europe and in the US. Even though the international community has been pressing the EU and the US to abandon, or at least substantially reduce their trade-distorting agricultural subsidies and support, the political will to correct such distortion is still lacking. Both the EU and the US maintain deep-rooted political support for agriculture. They are reluctant to make substantial concessions. The CAP is the political compromise of EU members. Similarly, in the US, Congressmen receive significant financial contributions from farm lobbyists, and agribusiness has strong power to influence political decisions. Even with extreme financial difficulties, the EU and the US have never stopped giving support to their farmers.

In international trade, negotiations are "a process of reciprocal bargaining in which power plays a critical role in shaping final terms."[144] Being politically and economically strong, developed countries, such as the US and in the EU, have louder voices than developing countries in trade negotiations. In order to create

---

143   HALLBERG, *supra* note 74, at 202–08.

144   Sungjoon Cho, *Doha's Development*, 25 BERKELEY J. INT'L L. 165, 196 (2007).

a system that allows sufficient food supply to feed the whole population of the planet, and pays agricultural producers a reasonable return on their hard work, while also ensuring that the market is truly free and fair, it is of great importance to urge developed countries to strengthen their political will in deregulating the agricultural economy.[145] Therefore, a new trade regime must be developed that is more conducive to food security.

---

145   Watson, *supra* note 61, at 297.

Chapter 9

Conclusion

Food is the most fundamental need for human beings. Without sufficient food and nutrition, human survival and development are at risk. The right to food is a universal right, a right that ensures the survival of everyone on this planet. The right to food is a legal obligation, an obligation for all States to fully implement at the national, regional, and house-hold levels. The right to food is also a moral responsibility, a responsibility for the international community to work together and develop a set of coordinated and comprehensive strategies in order to win the fight against hunger. The right to food has a privileged place among human rights. It supersedes all other economic, social, cultural, and political rights.

The success of improving world food security requires international efforts in influencing national behavior. An international human rights framework for the implementation of the right to food should be set up so that States will better understand their obligations under international law, and incorporate this inalienable human right into their national legal systems. All States should identify and adopt a series of effective measures to provide sufficient food to their own people and, therefore, to achieve the full implementation of the right to food.[1]

A comprehensive strategy to remove the root causes for world hunger must be implemented. Significant poverty reduction can be achieved by improving national capacity and stimulating economic development. Developing countries are advised to focus on improving governance, and increasing investment in rural development, education, health services, and all other essential public services. However, due to the fact that most developing countries are financially or technically incapable of doing so, developed countries' support is extraordinarily important. Meanwhile, to achieve sustainable development, population issues need to be solved without violations of basic human rights; sustainable agriculture should be placed at the center of farm policies in both developed and developing countries; people's sustainable access to sufficient food must be prioritized over the plan to develop or expand biofuel programs.

Food is a unique and special commodity that deserves special attention in international trade. Despite some proactive efforts made during the Uruguay Round negotiations, the existing world trading system still distortedly prevents efficient food distribution. The establishment of "an open, equitable, rule-based,

---

1   S. Vivek, *Notes from the Right to Food, Campaign* (May 27, 2003), http://www.wfp.org.in/website/events/countdown_2007/s_vivek.pdf.

predictable, and non-discriminatory multilateral trading system"[2] with minimal trade-distorting government intervention is critical. International trade should be used as a tool in curtailing hunger and improving nutrition levels rather than used as a tool to skew the global commercial market in favor of developed countries. Trade-distorting agricultural subsidies and other market access restrictions must be slashed in the long term, or at least be substantially reduced so that developing countries can take international trade as an opportunity to promote their rural development and food security. Considering many developed countries affect international agricultural trade not only through their foreign trade policies, but through their domestic agricultural policies, it is of great importance that these major dominant forces reform their agricultural policies, ensuring that these reforms are in compliance with their international obligations. Such reforms can level the playing field for developing countries and incorporate them into the world market. However, this radical change can be achieved only if developed countries are willing to move away from their traditional protectionism.

In conclusion, we must take food security issues seriously, or the world may experience absolute food shortage in the foreseeable future, and that is the last thing one would like to see. Both food deficit countries and countries with enormous food surpluses need to work closely and make their best efforts to alleviate world hunger. States are obligated to ensure that their own people are not deprived of the right to food. They should also abstain from adopting trade measures or farm policies that may interfere with individuals or groups taking care of their own needs.

---

2   United Nations Millennium Declaration, G.A. Res. 55.2, UN Doc. A/RES/55/2 (Sept. 18, 2000).

Appendices

Appendix 1   Constitutional Provisions of the Countries of the World (The Right to Food)[1]

Country	Date of Adoption	Provision(s)
Afghanistan	2004	"Life is a gift of God and a natural right of human beings. No one shall be deprived of this right except by the provision of law."[2] "The state adopts necessary measures to ensure physical and psychological wellbeing of family, especially of child and mother, upbringing of children and the elimination of traditions contrary to the principles of sacred religion of Islam."[3]
Albania	1998	"The life of a person is protected by law."[4]
Algeria	1996 (as amended to 2002)	N/A[5]
Andorra	1993	"The Constitution recognizes the right to life and fully protects it in its different phases."[6]
Angola	1992	"The State shall respect and protect the life of the human person."[7] "On no account shall the declaration of a state of siege or state of emergency affect the right to life, personal integrity, personal identity, civil capacity, citizenship, the non-retroactive nature of penal law, the right of the accused to defense or freedom of conscience and religion."[8]
Antigua and Barbuda	1981	"Protection of right to life."[9]
Argentina	1853 (as amended to 1994)	N/A[10]
Armenia	1995 (as amended to 2005)	"Everyone has a right to life. No one shall be sentenced or subjected to the death penalty."[11] "Everyone shall have the right to a standard of living adequate for himself/herself and for his/her family, including housing as well as improvement of living conditions. The state shall take the necessary measures for the exercise of this right by the citizens."[12]
Australia	1900 effective 1901	N/A[13]
Austria	1920 (as amended in 1929 and to Law No. 153/2004, December 30, 2004)	N/A[14]

Country	Date of Adoption	Provision(s)
Azerbaijan	1995 (as amended to 2000)	"Everyone has the right to life."[15]
Bahamas	1973	"No person shall be deprived intentionally of his life save in execution of the sentence of a court in respect of a criminal offence of which he has been convicted."[16]
Bahrain	2002	"The law regulates exemption of low incomes from taxes in order to ensure that a minimum standard of living is safeguarded."[17]
Bangladesh	1972 (as amended to 2004)	"No one shall be deprived of life or personal liberty save in accordance with law."[18]
Barbados	1966	"No person shall be deprived of his life intentionally save in execution of the sentence of a court in respect of a criminal offense under the law of Barbados of which he has been convicted."[19]
*Belarus	1996	"Everyone has the right to dignified standard of living, including appropriate food, clothing, housing and likewise a continuous improvement of necessary living conditions."[20]
Belgium	1994 (as amended to 2005)	"Everyone has the right to lead a life worthy of a human being."[21]
Belize	1981 (as amended to 1988)	"A person shall not be deprived of his life intentionally save in execution of the sentence of a court in respect of a criminal offence under any law of which he has been convicted."[22]
Benin	1990	"Each individual has the right to life, liberty, security and the integrity of his person."[23]
Bhutan	1907 (as amended to 1981)	N/A[24]
Bolivia	1967 (as amended to 2009)	"Everyone has the right to water and food. The State has an obligation to ensure food security, through a healthy diet, adequate and sufficient for the whole population."[25]
Bosnia and Herzegovina	1995	"All persons within the territory of Bosnia and Herzegovina shall enjoy the human rights and fundamental freedoms referred to in paragraph 2 above; these include: a. the right to life ...."[26]

Country	Date of Adoption	Provision(s)
Botswana	1966 (as amended to 2002)	"Whereas every person in Botswana is entitled to the fundamental rights and freedoms of the individual, that is to say, the right, whatever his race, place of origin, political opinions, color, creed or sex, but subject to respect for the rights and freedoms of others and for the public interest to each and all of the following namely—(a) life, liberty, security of the person and the protection of the law ...."[27] "No one shall be deprived of his life intentionally save in execution of the sentence of a court in respect of an offence under the law in force in Botswana of which he has been convicted."[28]
Brazil	1992 (as amended to 2008)	"Everyone is equal before the law, with no distinction whatsoever, guaranteeing to Brazilians and foreigners residing in the Country the inviolability of the rights to life, liberty, equality, security and property ...."[29] "The Following are rights of urban and rural workers, in addition to any others designed to improve their social condition: ... IV.—a national uniform minimum wage, fixed by law, capable of meeting a worker's basic living needs and those of his family, for housing, nourishment, education, health, leisure, clothing, hygiene, transportation and social security, with periodic adjustments to maintain its purchasing power, prohibiting linkage to it as index for any purpose."[30]
Brunei	1959 (as revised in 1984)	N/A[31]
Bulgaria	1991 (as amended to 2003)	"Everyone has the right to life. Violation of a human right is punished as a most severe crime."[32] "(1) Citizens have the right to social security and social assistance. (2) Temporarily unemployed persons receive social security under conditions and according to a procedure determined by law. (3) The elderly who do not have relatives and who are unable to support themselves with their possessions as well as persons with physical and mental handicap are under special protection of the state and society."[33]

Country	Date of Adoption	Provision(s)
Burkina Faso	1991 (as amended to 1997)	"The protection of life, safety, and physical integrity are guaranteed. Slavery, slave practices, inhuman and cruel, degrading and humiliating treatment, physical and moral torture, mistreatment inflicted upon children and all forms of deprecation of man are forbidden and punished by law."[34]
Burundi	2004	"Every woman, every man has the right to life."[35] "Every child is entitled to special measures which ensure or improve the care necessary for his well-being, health, physical integrity, and the protection against maltreatment, unreasonable demands or exploitation."[36]
Cambodia	1993 (as amended to 1999)	"Every Khmer citizen shall have the right to life, personal freedom, and security."[37]
Cameroon	1996	N/A[38]
Canada	1867 (consolidated as of 1999)	"Everyone has the right to life, liberty and security of the person and the right not to be deprived thereof except in accordance with the principles of fundamental justice."[39]
Cape Verde	1992	"The Right to life and to physical and mental integrity."[40]
Central Africa Republic	2004	"Everyone has the right to life and to corporal integrity. These rights may only be affected by application of a law."[41]
Chad	1996	"The human person is sacred and inviolable. Every individual has the right to life, his personal integrity, to security, to freedom, to the protection of his private life and his possessions."[42]
Chile	1980 (as amended to 2005)	"The Constitution guarantees to all persons: 1. The right to life and to the physical and psychological integrity of the person."[43]

Country	Date of Adoption	Provision(s)
China	1982 (as amended to 2004)	"Citizens of the People's Republic of China have the right to material assistance from the state and society when they are old, ill or disabled. The state develops the social insurance, social relief and medical and health services that are required to enable citizens to enjoy this right. The state and society ensure the livelihood of disabled members of the armed forces, provide pensions to the families of martyrs and give preferential treatment to the families of military personnel. The state and society help make arrangements of the work, livelihood and education of the blind, deaf-mute and other handicapped citizens."[44]
*Colombia	1991 (as amended to 2005)	"The right to life is inviolate. There will be no death penalty."[45] "Women and men have equal rights and opportunities. Women cannot be subjected to any type of discrimination. During their periods of pregnancy and following delivery, women will benefit from the special assistance and protection of the State and will receive from the latter food subsidies if they should thereafter find themselves unemployed or abandoned. The State will support the female head of household in a special way."[46] "It is the duty of the State to promote the gradual access of agricultural workers to landed property in individual or associational form and to services involving education, health, housing, social security, recreation, credit, communications, the marketing of products, technical and management assistance with the purpose of improving the incomes and quality of life of the peasants."[47] "The production of food crops will benefit from the special protection of the state. For that purpose, priority will be given to the integral development of agricultural, animal husbandry, fishing, forestry, and agroindustrial activities as well as to the building of physical infrastructural projects and to land improvement. Similarly, the State will promote research and the transfer of technology for the production of food crops and primary resources of agricultural origin with the purpose of increasing productivity."[48]
Comoros	2001	N/A[49]

Country	Date of Adoption	Provision(s)
*Congo	2005	"... All persons have the right to life, physical integrity and to the free development of their personality, while respecting the law, public order, the rights of others and public morality."[50] "The right to health and to food security is guaranteed."[51]
Cook Islands	1965	"It is hereby recognized and declared that in the Cook Islands there exist, and shall continue to exist, without discrimination by reason of race, national origin, color, religion, opinion, belief, or sex, the following fundamental human rights and freedoms—(a) The right of the individual to life, liberty, and security of the person, and the right not to be deprived thereof except in accordance with law ...."[52]
Costa Rica	1949 (as amended to 2003)	"Human life is inviolable."[53]
Côte D'Ivoire	2000	"The human person is sacred. All human beings are born free and equal before the law. They enjoy the inalienable rights which are the right to life, to liberty, to the full realization of their personality and to the respect of their dignity. The rights of the human person are inviolable. The public authorities have the obligation to assure the respect, the protection and the promotion of them. Any punishment leading to the deprivation of human life is forbidden."[54]
Croatia	1990 (as amended to 2001)	"Every human being has the right to life."[55] "Every employee has the right to a fair remuneration, such as will give him and his family a free and decent standard of living."[56] "To the weak, to the helpless and other persons, the State ensures the right to assistance to those who are unable to meet their basic needs due to unemployment or incapacity to work."[57]
*Cuba	1976 (as amended to 2002)	"The State, as the power of the people, in the service of the people themselves, guarantees that there will be no person incapacitated for work who lacks decent means of subsistence ... that there will be no child lacking a school, food, and clothing ...."[58]
Cyprus	1960 (as amended to 2004)	"Everyone's right to life shall be protected by law. No one shall be deprived of his/her life intentionally."[59]

Country	Date of Adoption	Provision(s)
*Czech Republic	1993 (as amended to 1999)	"Everyone has the right to life. Human life is worthy of protection even before birth."[60] "Citizens have the right to adequate material security in old age and during periods of work incapacity, as well as in the case of the loss of their provider. Everyone who suffers from material need has the right to such assistance as is necessary to ensure her a basic living standard. Detailed provisions shall be set by law."[61]
Denmark	1953	N/A[62]
Djibouti	1992	"Every individual shall have the right to life, liberty, security and the integrity of his person."[63]
Dominica	1978	"Protection of the right to life."[64]
Dominican Republic	1966 (as amended to 2002)	"In order to guarantee the realization of these aims the following norms are set: a. The inviolability of life ...."[65]
East Timor	2002	"1. Human life is inviolable. 2. The state recognizes and guarantees the right to life."[66]
*Ecuador	1998	"Without prejudice to other rights established in this Constitution and in international instruments in force, the State recognizes and guarantees the following to persons: 1. Inviolability of life ... 20. The right to a quality of life that assures health, food and nutrition, potable water, environmental conditions, education, work, employment, recreation, housing, clothing and other necessary social services."[67]
Egypt	1971 (as amended to 2007)	N/A[68]
El Salvador	1983 (as amended to 2003)	"Every person has the right to life, physical and moral integrity, liberty, security, work, property and possession, and to be protected in the conservation and defense of the same."[69]
Equatorial Guinea	1991	"All citizens shall enjoy the following rights and liberties: (a) Respect for the person, life, integrity, dignity, and full national and moral development ...."[70]
Eritrea	1997	"No one shall be deprived of life without due process of law."[71]
Estonia	1992 (as amended to 2005)	"Everyone has the right to life. This right shall be protected by law. No one shall be arbitrarily deprived of his or her life."[72]

Country	Date of Adoption	Provision(s)
Ethiopia	1995	"Every person has the inviolable and inalienable right to life, the security of person and liberty."[73]
Fiji Islands	1998	"Every person has the right to life. A person must not be arbitrarily deprived of life."[74]
Finland	2000	"Everyone has the right to life, personal liberty, integrity and security."[75] "Those who cannot obtain the necessary for a life of dignity have the right to receive indispensable subsistence and care. Everyone shall be guaranteed by an Act the right to basic subsistence in the event of unemployment, illness, and disability and during old age as well as at the birth of a child or the loss of a provider."[76]
France	1958 (as amended to 2005)	N/A[77]
Gabon	1991 (as amended to 1997)	N/A[78]
The Gambia	1996	"No one shall be deprived of his or her life intentionally except ...."[79]
Georgia	1995 (as amended to 2004)	"Everyone has the inviolable right to life and this right shall be protected by law."[80]
Germany	1949 (as amended to 2006)	"Every person shall have the right to life and physical integrity. The freedom of the person shall be inviolable. These rights may be interfered with only on the basis of a law."[81]
Ghana	1992 (as amended to 1996)	"No one shall be deprived of his life intentionally ...."[82]
Greece	1975 (as amended to 2002)	"All persons living within the Greek territory shall enjoy full protection of their life, honor and liberty irrespective of nationality, race or language and of religious or political beliefs ...."[83]
Grenada	1983 (as amended to 1992)	"No one shall be deprived of his life intentionally ...."[84]
*Guatemala	1985 (as amended to 1993)	"It is the duty of the State to guarantee to the inhabitants of the republic life, liberty, justice, security, peace, and the integral development of the person."[85] "Refusal to supply food in the form prescribed by law is punishable."[86]

Country	Date of Adoption	Provision(s)
Guinea	1990	"Man has the right to the free development of his personality. He has the right to life and physical integrity. No one shall be subjected to torture or cruel, inhumane or degrading treatments or punishments."[87]
Guinea-Bissau	1991	"Every person shall have the right to life and to physical and mental wellbeing."[88]
*Guyana	1980	"Every person in Guyana is entitled to the basic right to a happy, creative and productive life, free from hunger, disease, ignorance and want. That right includes the fundamental rights and freedoms of the individual, that is to say, the right, whatever his race, place of origin, political opinions, color, creed or sex, but subject to respect for the rights and freedoms of others and for the public interest, to each and all of the following, namely—(a) life, liberty, security of the person and the protection of the law ...."[89]
*Haiti	1987	"The State has the absolute obligation to guarantee the right to life, health, and respect of the human person for all citizens without distinction, in conformity with the Universal Declaration of the Rights of Man."[90] "The State recognizes the right of every citizen to decent housing, education, food and social security."[91]
*Honduras	1982 (as amended to 1991)	"The Constitution guarantees to all Hondurans and to foreigners residing in the country the right to the inviolability of life, and to individual safety, freedom, equality before the law, and property."[92] "The right to life is inviolable."[93] "It is the duty of the state to regulate, supervise and control all food, chemical, pharmaceutical and biological products through its duly constituted agencies and institutions."[94]
Hungary	1949 (as amended to 2007)	"In the Republic of Hungary everyone has the inherent right to life and to human dignity. No one shall be arbitrarily denied of these rights."[95] "Citizens of the Republic of Hungary have the right to social security; they are entitled to the support required to live in old age, and in the case of sickness, disability, being widowed or orphaned and in the case of unemployment through no fault of their own."[96]

Country	Date of Adoption	Provision(s)
Iceland	1944 (as amended to 1995)	"The right to support in the case of sickness, disability, old age, unemployment, extreme poverty and other comparable situations shall be guaranteed by law to all those in need."[97]
India	1950 (as amended to 2005)	"No one shall be deprived of his life or personal liberty except according to procedure established by law."[98] "The State shall endeavor to secure, by suitable legislation or economic organization or in any other way, to all workers agricultural, industrial or otherwise, work, a living wage, conditions of work ensuring a decent standard of life and full enjoyment of leisure and social and cultural opportunities and, in particular, the State shall endeavor to promote cottage industries on an individual or co-operative basis in rural areas."[99]
Indonesia	1945 (as amended to 2002)	"Every person shall have the right to live and to defend his/her life and existence."[100]
*Iran	1979 (as amended to 1989)	"In order to attain the objectives specified in article 2, the government of the Islamic Republic of Iran has the duty of directing all its resources to the following goals: ... the planning of a correct and just economic system, in accordance with Islamic criteria, in order to create welfare, eliminate poverty, and abolish all forms of deprivation with respect to food, housing, work, health care, and the provision of social insurance for all ...."[101]
Iraq	2004 (interim constitution)	"Every individual has the right to enjoy life, security and liberty. Deprivation or restriction of these rights is prohibited, except in accordance with the law and based on a decision issued by a competent judicial authority."[102]
Ireland	1937 (amended to 2002)	"The state shall, in particular, by its laws protect as best it may from unjust attack and, in the case of injustice done, vindicate the life, person, good name, and property rights of every citizen."[103] "... The State shall, in particular, direct its policy towards securing: i. that the citizens (all of whom, man and women equally, have the right to an adequate means of livelihood) may through their occupations find the means of making reasonable provision for their domestic needs ..."[104]

Country	Date of Adoption	Provision(s)
Israel	1992[105]	"There shall be no violation of the life, body or dignity of any person as such."[106]
*Italy	1948 (as amended to 2003)	"The following matters are subject to concurrent legislation of both the state and regions: international and European Union relations of the regions; foreign trade; protection and safety of labor; education, without infringement of the autonomy of schools and other institutions, and with the exception of vocational training; professions; scientific and technological research and support for innovation in the productive sectors; health protection; food; sports regulations; disaster relief service; land-use regulation and planning; harbors and civil airports; major transportation and navigation networks; regulation of media and communication; production, transportation and national distribution of energy; complementary and integrative pensions systems; harmonization of the budgetary rules of the public sector and coordination of the public finance and the taxation system; promotion of the environmental and cultural heritage, and promotion and organization of cultural activities; savings banks, rural co-operative banks, regional banks; regional institutions for credit to agriculture and land development. In matters of concurrent legislation, the regions have legislative power except for fundamental principles which are reserved to state law."[107]
Jamaica	1962 (as amended to 1999)	"Whereas every person in Jamaica is entitled to the fundamental rights and freedoms of the individual, that is to say, has the right, whatever his race, place of origin, political opinions, color, creed or sex, but subject to respect for the rights and freedoms of others and for the public interest, to each and all of the following, namely—(a) life, liberty, security of the person, the enjoyment of property and the protection of the law ...."[108]

Country	Date of Adoption	Provision(s)
Japan	1947	"All of the people shall be respected as individuals. Their right to life, liberty, and the pursuit of happiness shall, to the extent that it does not interfere with the public welfare, be the supreme consideration in legislation and in other governmental affairs."[109] "All people shall have the right to maintain the minimum standards of wholesome and cultured living. 2) In all spheres of life, the State shall use its endeavors for the promotion and extension of social welfare and security, and of public health."[110]
Jordan	1952 (as amended to 1984)	N/A[111]
Kazakhstan	1995 (as amended to 1998)	"Everyone has the right to life."[112]
Kenya	1969 (as amended to 2008)	"Whereas every person in Kenya is entitled to the fundamental rights and freedoms of the individual, that is to say, the right, whatever his race, tribe, place of origin or residence or other local connection, political opinions, color, creed or sex, but subject to respect for the rights and freedoms of others and for the public interest, to each and all of the following, namely—(a) life, liberty, security of the person and the protection of the law ...."[113]
Kiribati	1979 (as amended to 1995)	"Whereas every person in Kiribati is entitled to the fundamental rights and freedoms of the individual, that is to say, the right, whatever his race, place of origin, political opinions, color, creed or sex, but subject to respect for the rights and freedoms of others and for the public interest, to each and all of the following, namely—life, liberty, security of the person and the protection of the law ...."[114]
*The Democratic People's Republic of Korea (North Korea)	1972 (as amended to 1998)	"The Democratic People's Republic of Korea regards the steady improvement of the material and cultural standards of the people as the supreme principle of its activities. The increasing material wealth of society in our country, where taxes have been abolished, is used entirely to promote the well-being of the working people. The State shall provide all working people with every condition for obtaining food, clothing and housing."[115]

Country	Date of Adoption	Provision(s)
The Republic of Korea (South Korea)	1948 (as amended to 1987)	"(1) All citizens are entitled to a life worthy of human beings. (2) The State has the duty to endeavor to promote social security and welfare. (3) The State endeavors to promote the welfare and rights of women. (4) The State has the duty to implement policies for enhancing the welfare of senior citizens and the young. (5) Citizens who are incapable of earning a livelihood due to a physical disability, disease, old age, or other reasons are protected by the State under the conditions as prescribed by law. (6) The State endeavors to prevent disasters and to protect citizens from harm therefrom."[116]
Kosovo	2008	"Every individual enjoys the right to life."[117]
Kuwait	1962	N/A[118]
Kyrgyzstan	1993 (as amended to 1998)	"Every person in the Kyrgyz Republic has an inalienable right to life. No one may be deliberately deprived of life. Everyone has the right to protect his life and health, and the life and health of other persons from unlawful infringement."[119] "Pensions and social maintenance in accordance with economic resource of the society shall provide a standard of living not below the minimum wage established by law."[120]
Laos	1991	"The state protects the freedom and democratic rights of the people which cannot be violated by anyone. All state organizations and functionaries must popularize and propagate all policies, regulations and laws among the people and, together with the people, organize their implementation in order to guarantee the legitimate rights and interests of the people. All acts of bureaucratism and harassment that can be physically harmful to the people and detrimental to their honor, lives, consciences and property are prohibited."[121]
Latvia	1922 (as amended to 1998)	"The right to life of everyone shall be protected by law."[122]
Lebanon	1926 (as amended to 2004)	N/A[123]

Country	Date of Adoption	Provision(s)
Lesotho	1993	"Every human being has an inherent right to life. No one shall be arbitrarily deprived of his life."[124] "Lesotho shall endeavor to ensure that every person has the opportunity to gain his living by work which he freely chooses or accepts."[125]
Liberia	1984	"All persons are born equally free and independent and have certain natural, inherent and inalienable rights, among which are the right of enjoying and defending life and liberty, of pursuing and maintaining the security of the person and of acquiring, possessing and protecting property, subject to such qualifications as provided for in this Constitution."[126]
Libya	1969 (amended 1977)	N/A[127]
Liechtenstein	1921 (as amended to 2003)	"Emergency decrees can neither limit every person's right to life, the prohibition of torture an inhuman treatment or the prohibition of slavery and forced labor nor place any restriction on the 'no punishment without Law' rule ...."[128]
Lithuania	1992 (as amended to 2006)	"The right to life of a human being shall be protected by law."[129]
Luxembourg	1868 (as amended to 1998)	N/A[130]
Macedonia	1991 (as amended to 2005)	"The human right to life is irrevocable."[131]
Madagascar	1998	N/A[132]
Malawi	1994 (as amended to 1998)	"Every person has the right to life and no person shall be arbitrarily deprived of his or her life."[133]
Malaysia	1957 (as amended to 1994)	"No person shall be deprived of his life or personal liberty save in accordance with law."[134]
Maldives	1998	"No act detrimental to the life, liberty, body, name, reputation or property of a person shall be committed except as provided by law."[135]
Mali	1992	"The human person is sacred and inviolable. Every individual has the right to the life, to the liberty, to the security and to the integrity of his person."[136]

Country	Date of Adoption	Provision(s)
Malta	1964 (as amended to 2001)	"Whereas every person in Malta is entitled to the fundamental rights and freedoms of the individual, that is to say, the right, whatever his race, place of origin, political opinions, color, creed or sex, but subject to respect for the rights and freedoms of others and for the public interest, to each and all of the following, namely—(a) life, liberty, security of the person, the enjoyment of property and the protection of the law ...."[137]
Marshall Islands	1979 (as amended to 1995)	N/A[138]
Mauritania	1991 (as amended to 2006)	N/A[139]
Mauritius	1968 (as amended to 2000)	"No one shall be deprived of his life intentionally save in execution of the sentence of a court in respect of a criminal offence of which he has been convicted."[140]
*Mexico	1917 (as amended to 2011)	"Every person has the right to adequate food to maintain his or her wellbeing and physical, emotional and intellectual development. The State must guarantee this right."[141] "Sustainable and integral rural development ... will also have among its objectives that the State guarantee sufficient and timely supply of basic foods as established by the law."[142]
Micronesia	1981 (as amended to 1990)	"A person may not be deprived of life, liberty, or property without due process of law, or be denied the equal protection of the laws."[143]
*Moldova	1994 (as amended to 2003)	"Every person has the right to an environment that is ecologically safe for life and health as well as to safe food products and household goods. The State guarantees every person the right of free access to truthful information regarding the state of the natural environment, the living and working conditions and the quality of food products and household goods."[144] "The State guarantees every person the right to life, and to physical and mental integrity"[145]
Monaco	1962 (as amended to 2002)	N/A[146]

Country	Date of Adoption	Provision(s)
Mongolia	1992 (as amended to 2000)	"The citizens of Mongolia are enjoying the following rights and freedoms: 1) The right to life. Deprivation of human life is strictly prohibited unless capital punishment as constituted by Mongolian penal law for the most serious crimes is by a competent court as its final decision."[147]
Montenegro	1992	"Human life is inviolable."[148] "Under a mandatory insurance scheme all persons employed shall provide for themselves and members of their families all forms of social security. The state shall provide social welfare for citizens unable to work and without livelihood, as well as for citizens without the means of subsistence."[149]
Morocco	1996	N/A[150]
Mozambique	1990	"All citizens shall have the right to life. All shall have the right to physical integrity and may not be subjected to torture or to cruel or inhuman treatment."[151]
Myanmar	1974	N/A[152]
Namibia	1990 (as amended to 1998)	"The right to life shall be respected and protected. No law may prescribe death as a competent sentence. No court or Tribunal shall have the power to impose a sentence of death upon any person. No executions shall take place in Namibia."[153]
Nauru	1968	"Whereas every person in Nauru is entitled to the fundamental rights and freedoms of the individual, that is to say, has the right, whatever his race, place of origin, political opinions, color, creed or sex, but subject to respect for the rights and freedoms of others and for the public interest, to each and all of the following freedoms, namely—(a) life, liberty, security of the law ...."[154]

Country	Date of Adoption	Provision(s)
*Nepal	2007 (Interim)	"Every citizen shall have the right to food sovereignty as provided for in the law."[155] "The State shall have the follows responsibilities ... (h) To pursue a policy of establishing the rights of all citizens to education, health, housing, employment and food sovereignty ...."[156] "The State shall pursue a policy which will help to promote the interest of the marginalized communities and the peasants and laborers living below poverty line, including economically and socially backward indigenous tribes, Madhesis, Dalits, by making reservation for a certain period of time with regard to education, health, housing, food sovereignty and employment."[157]
Netherlands	1814 (as amended to 2002)	N/A[158]
New Zealand	1987 (as amended to 2005)	N/A[159]
*Nicaragua	1987 (as amended to 2005)	"The right to life is inviolable and inherent in the human person. In Nicaragua there is no death penalty."[160] "It is the right of Nicaraguans to be protected against hunger. The State shall promote programs, which ensure adequate availability of food and its equitable distribution"[161]
Niger	1999	"Each person shall have the right to life, health, security, physical well-being, education, and instruction according to conditions established by law."[162]
*Nigeria	1999	"The State shall direct its policy towards ensuring: ... (d) that suitable and adequate shelter, suitable and adequate food, reasonable national minimum living wage, old age care and pensions, and unemployment, sick benefits and welfare of the disabled are provided for all citizens."[163] "The main functions of a local government council are as follows: (k)(iv) restaurants, bakeries and other places for sale of food to the public"[164]
Niue	1974	N/A[165]
Norway	1814 (as amended to 2004)	N/A[166]
Oman	1996	N/A[167]

Country	Date of Adoption	Provision(s)
Pakistan	1973 (as amended to 2004)	"No person shall be deprived of life or liberty save in accordance with law."[168]
Palau	1981 (as amended to 1992)	"The government shall take no action to deprive any person of life, liberty, or property without due process of law nor shall private property be taken except for a recognized public use and for just compensation in money or in kind."[169]
*Panama	1972 (as amended to 2004)	"In matters of health, the State is primarily obliged to develop the following activities, integrating the functions of prevention, cure and rehabilitation in the: 1 Establishment of a national policy of food and nutrition, ensuring optimum nutritional conditions for the entire population, by promoting the availability, consumption, and biological benefit of suitable food ...."[170]
Papua New Guinea	1975 (as amended to 1995)	"No person shall be deprived of his life intentionally."[171]
*Paraguay	1992	"The right to live is inherent to the human being. Its protection is guaranteed, in general, after the time of conception."[172] "Every parent has the right and obligation to care for, to feed, to educate, and to support his children while they are minors. The laws will punish those parents who fail to comply with their duty to provide their children with food."[173]
Peru	1993 (as amended to 2005)	"Every individual has the right to life, his identity, his physical, psychological, and moral integrity, and his free fulfillment and well-being. Such rights exist from the time of conception in all ways that are beneficial."[174]
Philippines	1987	"No person shall be deprived of life, liberty, or property without due process of law, nor shall any person be denied the equal protection of the laws."[175]
Poland	1997	"The Republic of Poland shall ensure the legal protection of the life of every human being."[176]
Portugal	1976 (as amended to 2004)	"Human life is inviolable."[177]
Qatar	2003	N/A[178]
Romania	1991	"A person's right to life and to physical and mental well-being are guaranteed."[179]
Russia	1993	"Everyone shall have the right to life."[180]

Country	Date of Adoption	Provision(s)
Rwanda	2003	"Every person has the right to life. No person shall be arbitrarily deprived of life."[181]
Samoa	1962 (as amended to 2001)	"No person shall be deprived of his life intentionally, except in the execution of a sentence of a court following his conviction of an offence for which this penalty is provided by Act."[182]
San Marino	1600[183]	N/A
São Tomé and Príncipe	1990	"Human life is inviolable."[184]
Saudi Arabia	1992	"The state guarantees the rights of the citizen and his family in cases of emergency, illness and disability, and in old age; it supports the system of social security and encourages institutions and individuals to contribute in acts of charity."[185]
Senegal	2001	"The human person is sacred. The human person is inviolable. The state shall have the obligation to respect it and to protect it. Every individual has the right to life, to freedom, to security, the free development of his or her personality, to corporal integrity, and especially to protection against physical mutilation."[186]
Serbia and Montenegro	2006	"Human life is inviolable."[187]
*Seychelles	1996	"Solemnly declaring our unswaying commitment, during this our Third Republic, to develop a democratic system which will ensure the creation of an adequate and progressive social order guaranteeing food, clothing, shelter, education, health and a steadily rising standard of living for all Seychellois."[188] "Everyone has a right to life and no one shall be deprived of life intentionally"[189]
*Sierra Leone	1991	"The state shall within the context of the ideals and objectives for which provisions are made in this Constitution—place proper and adequate emphasis on agriculture in all its aspects so as to ensure self-sufficiency in food production ...."[190]
Singapore	1963 (amended to 2001)	"No person shall be deprived of his life or personal liberty save in accordance with law."[191]
Slovakia	1992 (as amended to 2006)	"Everyone has the right to life. Human life is worthy of protection already before birth."[192]

Country	Date of Adoption	Provision(s)
Slovenia	1991 (as amended to 2003)	"Human life is inviolable. There is no capital punishment in Slovenia."[193]
Solomon Islands	1978 (as amended to 2001)	"No person shall be deprived of his life intentionally in execution of the sentence of a court in respect of criminal offence under the law in force in Solomon Islands of which he has been convicted."[194]
Somalia	1979	"Every individual shall have the right to life and personal security."[195]
Somaliland	2001	"Human life is the gift of Allah and is beyond price. Every person has the right to life, and shall only be deprived of life if convicted in a court of an offence in which the sentence laid down by law is death."[196]
*South Africa	1997 (as amended to 2003)	"(1) Everyone has the right to have access to— (a) health care services, including reproductive health care; (b) sufficient food and water; and (c) social security, including, if they are unable to support themselves and their dependents, appropriate social assistance. (2) The state must take reasonable legislative and other measures, within its available resources, to achieve the progressive realization of each of these rights. (3) No one may be refused emergency medical treatment."[197] "(1) Every child has the right— ... (c) to basic nutrition, shelter, basic health care services and social services"[198]
Spain	1978 (as amended to 1992)	"Everyone has the right to life and physical and moral integrity and in no case may be subjected to torture or inhuman or degrading punishment or treatment. The death penalty is abolished except in those cases which may be established by military penal law in times of war."[199]
Sri Lanka	1978 (as amended to 2001)	N/A[200]
St. Kitts and Nevis	1983	"A person shall not be deprived of his life intentionally save in execution of the sentence of a court in respect of a criminal offence of treason or murder under any law of which he has been convicted."[201]

Country	Date of Adoption	Provision(s)
St. Lucia	1978	"Whereas every person in Saint Lucia is entitled to the fundamental rights and freedoms, that is to say, the right, whatever his race, place of origin, political opinions, color, creed or sex, but subject to respect for the rights and freedoms of others and for the public interest, to each and all of the following, namely—a) life, liberty, security of the person, equality before the law and the protection of the law ...."[202]
St. Vincent and the Grenadines	1979	"Where every person in Saint Vincent is entitled to the fundamental rights and freedoms, that is to say, the right, whatever his race, place of origin, political opinions, color, creed or sex, but subject to respect for the rights and freedoms of others and for the public interest, to each and all of the following, namely—a. life, liberty, security of the person and the protection of the law ...."[203]
Sudan	2005	"The overarching aims of economic development shall be eradication of poverty, attainment of the Millennium Development Goals, guaranteeing the equitable distribution of wealth, redressing imbalances of income and achieving a decent standard of life for all citizens."[204] "Every human being has the inherent right to life, dignity and the integrity of his/her person, which shall be protected by law; no one shall arbitrarily be deprived of his/her life"[205]
Southern Sudan	2005 (Interim)	"Every person has the inherent right to life, dignity and the integrity of his or her person which shall be protected by law; no one shall be arbitrarily deprived of his or her life."[206]
*Suriname	1987	"The state shall take care of the creation of conditions in which an optimal satisfaction of the basic needs for work, food, health care, education, energy, clothing and communication is obtained."[207]
Swaziland	2005	"A person shall not be deprived of life intentionally save in the execution of the sentence of a court in respect of a criminal offence under the law of Swaziland of which that person has been convicted."[208]
Sweden	1975	N/A[209]

Country	Date of Adoption	Provision(s)
*Switzerland	1998	"The Federation aligns the measures in such a way that agriculture fulfills its multi-functional tasks. It has particularly the following powers and tasks. ... (c) It adopts rules on the declaration of origin, quality, production method and processing method for food."[210]
Syria	1973 (as amended to 2000)	N/A[211]
Taiwan	1947 (as amended to 2005)	N/A[212]
Tajikistan	1994 (as amended to 2003)	"The life, honor, dignity, and other natural human rights are inviolable."[213]
Tanzania	1977 (as amended to 1995)	"Everyone person has the right to live and to the protection of his life by the society in accordance with law."[214]
Thailand	2007	"A person shall enjoy the right and liberty in his life and person."[215]
Togo	1992 (as amended to 2002)	"The state has the obligation to guarantee physical and moral integrity, life and the security to anyone living in the national territory."[216]
Tonga	1875 (as amended to 1988)	"All the people have the right to expect that the Government will protect their life liberty and property and therefore it is right for all the people to support and contribute to the Government according to law."[217]
Trinidad and Tobago	1976	"It is hereby recognized and declared that in Trinidad and Tobago there have existed and shall continue to exist without discrimination by reason of race, origin, color, religion or sex, the following fundamental human rights and freedoms, namely:—a. the right of the individual to life, liberty, security of the person and enjoyment of property and the right not to be deprived thereof except by due process of law."[218]
Tunisia	1959 (as amended to 1988)	N/A[219]

Country	Date of Adoption	Provision(s)
Turkey	1982	"The individual's right to life, and the integrity of his or her material and spiritual entity shall be inviolable except where death occurs through lawful act of warfare; no one may be compelled to reveal his or her religion, conscience, thought or opinion, nor be accused on account of them; offences and penalties may not be made retroactive, nor may anyone be held guilty until so proven by a court judgment."[220]
Turkmenistan	1992 (as amended to 2003)	"A person in Turkmenistan has the right to life and the freedom of its realization. No one may be deprived of the right to life. The right of every person to liberty is protected by the State on the basis of law."[221]
Tuvalu	1986	"Every person in Tuvalu is entitled, whatever his race, place of origin, political opinions, color, religious beliefs or lack of religious beliefs, or sex, to the following fundamental rights and freedoms: (a) the right not to be deprived of life."[222]
*Uganda	1995 (as amended to 2005)	"All Ugandans enjoy rights and opportunities and access to education, health services, clean and safe water, work, decent shelter, adequate clothing, food security and pension and retirement benefits."[223]
*Ukraine	1996 (as amended to 2004)	"Everyone is guaranteed the right of free access to information about the environmental situation, the quality of food and consumer goods, and also the right to disseminate such information. No one shall make such information secret."[224] "The human being, his or her life and health, honor and dignity, inviolability and security are recognized in Ukraine as the highest social value."[225]
United Arab Emirates	1971	N/A[226]
*United Kingdom	1689	"Everyone has the right to a standard of living adequate for the health and well-being of himself and of his family, including food, clothing, housing and medical care and necessary social services, and the right to security in the event of unemployment, sickness, disability, widowhood, old age or other lack of livelihood in circumstances beyond his control."[227]

Country	Date of Adoption	Provision(s)
United States of America	1787	N/A[228]
Uruguay	1966 (as amended to 1996)	"The inhabitants of the Republic have the right of protection in the enjoyment of life, honor, liberty, security, labor and property. No one may be deprived of these rights except in conformity with laws which may be enacted for reasons of general interest."[229]
Uzbekistan	1992	"Democracy in the Republic of Uzbekistan shall rest on the principles common to all mankind, according to which the ultimate value is the human being, his life, freedom, honor, dignity and other inalienable rights. Democratic rights and freedoms shall be protected by the Constitution and the laws."[230]
Vanuatu	1980	"The Republic of Vanuatu recognizes, that, subject to any restrictions imposed by law on non-citizens, all persons are entitled to the following fundamental rights and freedoms of the individual without discrimination on the grounds of race, place of origin, religious or traditional beliefs, political opinions, language or sex but subject to respect for the rights and freedoms of others and to the legitimate public interest in defense, safety, public order, welfare and health—(a) life ...."[231]
Venezuela	1999	"Every worker has a right to a sufficient salary which permits him to live with dignity and to provide for himself and his family the basic material, social and intellectual necessities."[232]
Vietnam	1992 (as amended to 2001)	N/A[233]
Yemen	1991 (as amended to 1994)	N/A[234]
Zaire	1990	"Everyone has the right to life and to physical integrity."[235]
Zambia	1991	"It is recognized and declared that every person in Zambia has been and shall continue to be entitled to the fundamental rights and freedoms of the individual, that is to say, the right, whatever his race, place of origin, political opinions, color, creed, sex or marital status, but subject to the limitations contained in this Part, to each and all of the following, namely (a) life, liberty, security of the person and the protection of the law ...."[236]

Country	Date of Adoption	Provision(s)
Zimbabwe	1979 (as amended to 2005)	"No person shall be deprived of his life intentionally save in execution of the sentence of a court in respect of a criminal offence of which he has been convicted."[237]

Notes

1 Provisions regarding the right to life are included in this appendix. The countries whose names are accompanied by an asterisk (*) are those whose constitutions explicitly recognize the right to food. Based on my research, only 28 of 198 countries affirm their people's right to have access to adequate food.

2 AFG. CONST., Jan. 4, 2004, art. 23.

3 *Id.* art. 52(2).

4 KUSHTETUTA E REPUBLIKËS SË SHQIPËRISË [CONSTITUTION] OCT. 21, 1998, pt. II, ch. II, art. 21 (Alb.).

5 ALG. CONST. Sept. 8, 1963.

6 CONSTITUCIÓ DEL PRINCIPAT D'ANDORRA [CONSTITUTION] Feb. 2, 1993, tit. II, ch. III, art. 8.1.

7 CONSTITUIÇÃO DA RÉPUBLICA DE ANGOLA [CONSTITUTION] Jan. 21, 2010, art. 22.

8 *Id.* art. 52(2).

9 ANT. & BARB. CONST. July 31, 1981, ch. II, art. 4.

10 Art. 4, CONSTITUCIÓN NACIONAL [CONST. NAC.] May 1, 1853 (Arg.).

11 ARM. CONST. July 5, 1995, ch. II, art. 15.

12 *Id.* ch. II, art. 34.

13 AUSTRALIAN CONSTITUTION Jan. 1, 1901.

14 BUNDES-VERFASSUNGSGESETZ [B-VG] [CONSTITUTION] BGBl No. 1/1930, *as last amended by* Bundesverfassungsgesetz [BVG] BGBl I No. 2/2008 (Austria).

15 AZƏRBAYCAN RESPUBLIKASININ KONSTITUSIYASI [CONSTITUTION] Nov. 12, 1995, ch. III, art. 27 I (Azer.).

16 BAH. CONST. June 20, 1973, ch. III, art. 16.

17 BAHR. CONST. Feb. 14, 2002, ch. II, art. 15(b).B.

18 BANGL. CONST. Dec. 4, 1972, pt. III, art. 32.

19 BARB. CONST. Nov. 22, 1966, ch. III, art. 12.

20 BELR. CONST. Mar. 15, 1994, § II, art. 21.

21 1994 LA CONST. tit. II, art. 21 (Belg.).

22 BELIZE CONST. Sept. 21, 1981, pt. II, art. 4.

23 BENIN CONST. Dec. 10, 1990, tit. II, art. 15.

24 BHUTAN CONST. July 18, 2008.

25 CONSTITUCIÓN DE 2009 DE LA REPÚBLICA DEL BOLIVIA [CONSTITUTION] Feb. 7, 2009, art. 16.

26 USTAV BOSNE I HERCEGOVINE [CONSTITUTION] Nov. 21, 1995, annex 4, art. II.3.a.

27 BOTS. CONST. Mar. 1995, ch. II, art. 3.

28 *Id.* ch. II, art. 4.

29 Constituição Federal [C.F.] [Constitution] tit. II, ch. I, art. 5 (Braz.).

30 *Id.* tit. II, ch. II, art. 7.

31 *See* Brunei Const.

32 Bulg. Const. July 12, 1991, ch. II, art. 28.

33 *Id.* ch. II, art. 51.

34 Burk Faso Const. June 2, 1991, tit. I, ch. I, art. 2.

35 Burundi Const. Oct. 20, 2004, tit. II, ch. 1. art. 24.

36 *Id.* tit. II, ch. 1.

37 Cambodia Const. Sept. 21, 1993, ch. III, art. 32.

38 *See* Cameroon Const. June 2, 1972.

39 Can Const., pt. 1, art. 7.

40 Constituição da República de Cabo Verde [Constitution] May 3, 2010, pt. II, tit. II, art. 26 (Cape Verde).

41 Constitution de la République Centrafricaine Dec. 5, 2004, tit. I, art. 3, para. 1 (Cent. Afr. Rep.).

42 Chad Const. Mar. 31, 1996, tit. II, ch. 1, art. 17.

43 Constitución Política de la República de Chile [C.P.], ch. III, art. 3. § 1.

44 Xianfa [Constitution], ch. II, art. 45 (2004) (China).

45 Constitución Política de Colombia [C.P.], tit. II, ch. I, art. 11.

46 *Id.* tit. II, ch. II, art. 43.

47 *Id.* tit. II, ch. II, art. 63.

48 *Id.* tit. II, ch. II, art, 65.

49 *See* Comoros Const. Dec. 31, 2001 (2001), pmbl.

50 Congo Const. Jan. 20, 2002, tit. II, art. 16.

51 *Id.* art. 47.

52 Cook Islands Const., pt. IV.A., art. 64(1)(a).

53 Costa Rica Const. Nov. 7, 1949, tit. IV, art. 21, ¶ 1.

54 Côte d'Ivoire Const. July 24, 2000, tit. I, art. 2.

55 Croat. Const. Dec. 22, 1990, tit. III, ch. III, art. 21.

56 *Id.* art. 55.

57 *Id.* art. 57.

58 Constitution Política de la República de Cuba Feb. 15, 1976, ch. I, art. 9.

59 Cyprus Const., Attach. 5 Catalogue of Human Rights and Fundamental Freedoms, art. 1.

60 ʹUstava ʹEr. [Constitution] (Czech Rep.), The Charter of Fundamental Rights and Basic Freedoms, 1992 (*as amended to* 1998), ch. II, div. I, art. 6.

61 *Id.* art. 30.

62 *See* Den. Const. Aug. 1, 2009.

63 Djib. Const. Sept. 15, 1992, tit. II, art. 10.

64 Dominica Const. Nov. 3, 1978, ch. I, § 2.

65 Dom. Rep. Const. (2002), tit. II, § I, art. 15.

66 East Timor Const., pt. II, tit. II, art. 29.(1)(2).

67 Ecuador Const. Oct. 20, 2008, tit. III, ch. II, art. 23.

68   *See* Constitution of the Arab Republic of Egypt, 11 Sept. 1971, *as amended*, May 22, 1980, May 25, 2005, March 26, 2007.

69   El Sal. Const. Dec. 15, 1983, tit. II, ch. I, art. 2.

70   Eq. Guinea Const. Nov. 17, 1991, tit. I, art. 13.

71   Eri. Const. May 23, 1997.

72   Eesti Vabariigi põhiseadus [Constitution] June 28, 1992, ch. II, art. 16.

73   Eth. Const. Dec. 8, 1994, ch. III, pt. I, art. 14.

74   Fiji Const., ch. 4, art. 22.

75   Fin. Const. (2000), ch. II, § 7.

76   *Id.* § 19.

77   *See* 1958 Const. (Fr.).

78   *See* Gabon Const. Mar. 26, 1991.

79   Gam. Const. Aug. 8, 1996, ch. IV, art. 18.

80   Geor. Const. Aug. 24, 1995, ch. II, art. 15.

81   Grundgesetz für die Bundesrepublik Deutschland [Grundgesetz] [GG] [Constitution], May 23, 1949, BGBl. I, ch. I, art. 2(2) (Ger.).

82   Ghana Const. May 8, 1992, ch. V, art. 13.

83   1975 Syntagma [Syn.] [Constitution], pt. II, art. 5.1 (Greece).

84   Gren. Const., ch. I, § 2.

85   Guat. Const., tit. I, ch. I, art. 2.

86   *Id.* art. 55.

87   Guinea Const., tit. II, art. 6.

88   Guinea-Bissau Const., tit. II, art. 32.1.

89   Guy. Const., pt. I, chap. III, art. 40(1).

90   Haiti Const., ch. II, § A, art. 19.

91   *Id.* art. 22.

92   *Hond. Const.*, tit. III, ch. I, art. 61.

93   *Id.* art. 65.

94   *Id.* ch. VII, art. 146.

95   A Magyar Köztársaság Alkotmánya [Constitution of the Republic of Hungary], ch. XII, art. 54 (1), § (1)(g).

96   *Id.* art. 70/E.

97   Ice. Const., ch. VII, art. 76(1).

98   India Const. pt. III, art. 21, *amended by* The Constitution (Eightieth Amendment) Act, 2000.

99   *Id.* art. 43.

100 Indon. Const., ch. XA, art. 28A.

101 Qanuni Assassi Jumhurii Islamai Iran [The Constitution of the Islamic Republic of Iran], ch. I, art. 3, § 12[1980].

102 Iraq. Const. (interim, 2004), § 2, ch. I, art. 15.

103 Ir. Const., 1937, art. 39.

104 *Id.* art. 45.

105 The State of Israel has no codified constitution as such. Rather, it has promulgated a number of "Basic Laws" that provide a framework for governance and civil liberties.

Reuven Y. Hazan, *Israel, in* 9 CONSTITUTIONS OF THE COUNTRIES OF THE WORLD 1 *(Gisbert H. Flanz ed., Supp. 2001).* These documents do not explicitly mention the citizenry's right to health care. *See* Basic Laws (Isr.), translated and reprinted in *9 CONSTITUTIONS OF THE COUNTRIES OF THE WORLD:* Israel (Albert P. Blaustein & Gisbert H. Flanz eds., Susan Hattis Rolef trans., 1994).

106   Basic Law: Human Dignity and Liberty, 1992, § 2 (Isr.).

107   Art. 117(3) COSTITUZIONE [COST.] (IT.).

108   JAM. CONST., ch. III, art. 13.

109   NIHONKOKU KENPŌ [KENPŌ] [CONSTITUTION], ch. III, art. 13 (Japan).

110   *Id.* art. 25.

111   *See JORDAN CONST.*

112   *Kaz. Const.,* § II, art. 15.1.

113   CONSTITUTION, ch. V., art. 12 (1992) (Kenya).

114   KIRIBATI CONST., ch. II, art. 3.

115   DPRK CONST., pt. II, art. 25 (N. Korea).

116   DAEHANMINKUK HUNBEOB [HUNBEOB] [CONSTITUTION] ch. II, art. 4 (S. Kor.).

117   KOSOVO CONST., ch. II, art. 25.

118   *See* KUWAIT CONST.

119   KYRG, CONST., ch. II, § 2, art. 16(2).

120   *Id.* art. 27(2).

121   LAOS CONST., ch. I, art. 4.

122   LAT. CONST., ch. VIII, art. 93.

123   *See* LEB. CONST.

124   LESOTHO CONST., ch. II, art. 27.

125   *Id.* art. 29.

126   LIBER. CONST., ch. III, art. 11.

127   *See* LIBYA CONST. PROCLAMATION (1969).

128   LIECH. CONST., ch. II, art. 10.

129   LITH. CONST., ch. II, art. 19.

130   LUX. CONST., ch. II, art. 23.

131   MACED. CONST., ch. II, art. 10.

132   *See* MADAG. CONST.

133   MALAWI CONST., CH. IV, art. 16.

134   MALAY. CONST., 9th sched., pt. 2, art. 5.

135   MALDIVES CONST., ch. II, art. 15(c).

136   MALI CONST., tit. I, art. 1.

137   MALTA CONST., ch. IV, art. 33(a).

138   *See* MARSH. IS. CONST.

139   *See* MAURITANIA CONST.

140   MAURITIUS CONST. ch. II, art. 4.

141   CONSTITUCIÓN POLÍTICA DE LOS ESTADOS UNIDOS MEXICANOS [C.P] [CONSTITUTION] art. 4 (Mex.). *See also* Alfredo Acedo, *Mexican Constitution Now Recognizes Right to Food,* Am. Prog. (Sept. 24, 2011), http://www.cipamericas.org/archives/5432; UN News Center, *UN Expert Welcomes Mexico's Move to Recognize Food as Constitutional*

Right, UN News Ctr. (Oct. 13, 2011), http://www.un.org/apps/news/story. asp?NewsID=40039#.UPGRrCeRSSo.

142 C.P. art. 27, cl. XX.

143 Micro. Const., art. IV, § 3.

144 Mold. Const., tit. II, ch. II, art. 37.

145 *Id.* art. 24.

146 *See* Monaco Const.

147 Mong. Const., ch. II, art. 16.

148 Monte Const., art. 21.

149 *Id.* art. 55.

150 *See* Morocco Const.

151 Mozam. Const., pt. 1, ch. IV, art. 70.

152 *See* Myan. Const.

153 Namib. Const., ch. III, art. 6.

154 Nauru Const., pt. II, art. 3.

155 Nepal Const., art. 18(3).

156 *Id.* art. 33(h).

157 *Id.* art. 35(10).

158 *See* Grondwet voor het Koninkrijk der Nederlanden [Gw.] [Constitution] ch. I, art. 22 (Neth.).

159 *See* N.Z. Const.

160 Constitución Política de la República de Nicaragua [Cn.], tit. IV, ch. I, art. 24.

161 *Id.* art. 63.

162 Niger Const., tit. II, art. 11.

163 Constitution of Nigeria (1999), ch. II, art. 16, § 2(d).

164 *Id.* art. 1.

165 *See* Niue Const.

166 *See* Nor. Const.

167 Oman Const., ch. II, art. 12, paras. 4–5.

168 Pakistan Const., pt. II, ch. 1, art. 9.

169 Palau Const., art. IV, § 6.

170 Pan. Const., tit. III, ch. VI, art. 110(1).

171 Papua New Guinea Const., art. 35.

172 Paraguay Const., ch. I, § 1, art. 4.

173 *Id.* art. 53(1).

174 Peru Const., §1, ch. I, art. 2.1.

175 Const. (1987), § 1 (Phil.).

176 Pol. Const., ch. II, art. 38.

177 Port. Const., pt. I, tit. II, ch. I, art. 24.

178 *See* Qatar Const.

179 Rom. Const., tit. II, ch. II, art. 22.

180 Konstitutsiia Rossiiskoi Federatsii [Konst. RF] [Constitution], § 1, ch. II., art. 20 (Russ.).

181 Rwanda Const., tit. II, ch. I, art. 12.

182 Samoa Const., pt. II, art. 5.

183 Note that San Marino does not have a codified constitution. Gisbert H. Flanz, *San Marino, in* 16 Constitutions of the Countries of the World (Albert P. Blaustein & Gisbert H. Flanz eds., 1990).

184 Sao Tome Principe Const., pt. II, tit. II, art. 21.

185 Saudi Arabia Const., ch. V, art. 27.

186 Sen. Const., tit. II, art. 7.

187 Serb. & Mont. Const., pt. 2, art. 24.S.

188 Sey. Const. pmbl.

189 *Id.* ch. III, pt. I, art. 15(1).

190 Sierra Leone Const. (1991, reinstated 1996), ch. II, art. 7, § 1(d).

191 Sing. Const., pt. IV, art. 9.

192 Slovk. Const., ch. 2, § 2, art. 15.

193 Slovn. Const., ch. II, art. 17.

194 Solom. Is. Const., ch. II, art. 4.

195 Somal. Const., ch. II, art. 25.

196 Somaliland Const., ch. I, pt. III, art. 24.

197 S. Afr. Const., 1996, tit I, ch. II, § 1, art. 15.

198 *Id.* art. 28(c).

199 Constitución Española, B.O.E. [Constitution] Dec. 29, 1978, ch. III, art. 43 (Spain).

200 *See* Sri Lanka Const.

201 St. Kitts & Nevis Const., ch. II, art. 4.

202 St. Lucia Const., ch. I, sec. 1.

203 St. Vincent Const., ch. I, art. 1.

204 Sudan Const., ch. II, art. 10(1).

205 *Id.* art 28.

206 Southern Sudan Const., pt. 2, art. 15.

207 Surin. Const., ch. VI, § 1, art. 24.

208 Swaz. Const. (draft, 2003), ch. III, art. 15.

209 *See* Regeringsformen [RF] [Constitution] (Swed.).

210 Bundesverfassung [BV] [Constitution] Apr. 18, 1999, SR 101, ch. I, art. 104 (Switz.).

211 *See* Syria Const. (2000).

212 Minguo Xianfa, ch. XIII, § 4, art. 157 (1947) (Taiwan).

213 Taj. Const., ch. I, art. 5.

214 Tanz. Const., ch. I, pt. III, art. 14.

215 Thail. Const., ch. III, pt. 3, § 32.

216 Togo Const., tit. II, subsec. I, art. 13.

217 Tonga Const., art. 18.

218 Trin. & Tobago Const., ch. 1, pt. I, art. 4.

219 *See* Tunis. Const.

220 Turk. Const. Oct. 18, 1982, pt. II, ch. I, § IV, art. 15(2).

221 Turkm. Const. May 18, 1992, § II, art. 20.

222 Tuvalu Const. Oct. 1, 1986, art. 11(1)(a).

223 Uganda Const., pmbl., § XIV(b).

224 UKR. CONST. June 28, 1996, ch. I, art. 50.

225 *Id.* art. 3.

226 U.A.E. CONST. 1971, ch. II, art. 19.

227 BILL OF RIGHTS, ch. I, pt. I, sec. 27 (U.K.).

228 *See* US CONST.

229 Uru. Const., § II, ch. I, art. 7.

230 Uzb. Const. Dec. 8, 1992, pt. II, ch. III, art. 13.

231 VANUATU CONST. July 30, 1980, ch. 2, pt. I, art. 5.

232 VENEZ. CONST. Dec. 15, 1999, tit. III, ch. V, art. 91.

233 *See* VIETMAN CONST. Apr. 15, 1992, ch. III, art. 39.

234 *See* YEMEN CONST. Apr. 22, 1990.

235 ZAIRE CONST., tit. II, art. 12.

236 CONST. OF ZAMBIA OF 1991, 1 LAWS OF REP. OF ZAMBIA (1995) pt. III, art. 11.

237 ZIMB. CONST. art. 12(1).

Appendix 2   World Population Growth Rate (Percent)[1]

Year(s)	Variant	Value
2045–2050	Constant-fertility variant	1.48
2045–2050	High variant	0.87
2045–2050	Low variant	-0.17
2045–2050	Medium variant	0.36
2040–2045	Constant-fertility variant	1.41
2040–2045	High variant	0.93
2040–2045	Low variant	-0.04
2040–2045	Medium variant	0.45
2035–2040	Constant-fertility variant	1.35
2035–2040	High variant	0.96
2035–2040	Low variant	0.11
2035–2040	Medium variant	0.54
2030–2035	Constant-fertility variant	1.29
2030–2035	High variant	0.99
2030–2035	Low variant	0.26
2030–2035	Medium variant	0.64
2025–2030	Constant-fertility variant	1.27
2025–2030	High variant	1.07
2025–2030	Low variant	0.42
2025–2030	Medium variant	0.75
2020–2025	Constant-fertility variant	1.28
2020–2025	High variant	1.18
2020–2025	Low variant	0.55
2020–2025	Medium variant	0.88
2015–2020	Constant-fertility variant	1.31
2015–2020	High variant	1.32
2015–2020	Low variant	0.65
2015–2020	Medium variant	1.00
2010–2015	Constant-fertility variant	1.32
2010–2015	High variant	1.36
2010–2015	Low variant	0.81
2010–2015	Medium variant	1.10

Year(s)	Variant	Value
2005–2010	Constant-fertility variant	1.28
2005–2010	High variant	1.34
2005–2010	Low variant	0.99
2005–2010	Medium variant	1.17
2000–2005	Medium variant	1.24
1995–2000	Medium variant	1.37
1990–1995	Medium variant	1.54
1985–1990	Medium variant	1.73
1980–1985	Medium variant	1.74
1975–1980	Medium variant	1.76
1970–1975	Medium variant	1.94
1965–1970	Medium variant	2.02
1960–1965	Medium variant	1.95
1955–1960	Medium variant	1.80
1950–1955	Medium variant	1.78

Note

1 UN Data, *Population Growth Rate*, http://data.un.org/Data.aspx?q=world+populati on&d=PopDiv&f=variableID%3a47%3bcrID%3a900 (last updated Aug. 25, 2011) (The United Nations is the author of the original material). ("The United Nations World Population Prospects: The 2006 Revision contains estimates since 1950 and projections until 2050 for every country in the world, including estimates and projections of 28 demographic indicators such as birth rates, deaths rates, infant mortality rates and life expectancy.")

Appendix 3   World Population (Thousands)[1]

Year	Variant	Value
2050	Constant-fertility variant	11 857 786
2050	High variant	10 756 366
2050	Low variant	7 791 945
2050	Medium variant	9 191 287
2045	Constant-fertility variant	11 014 053
2045	High variant	10 297 036
2045	Low variant	7 857 864
2045	Medium variant	9 025 982
2040	Constant-fertility variant	10 265 189
2040	High variant	9 829 962
2040	Low variant	7 871 770
2040	Medium variant	8 823 546
2035	Constant-fertility variant	9 597 117
2035	High variant	9 368 004
2035	Low variant	7 828 666
2035	Medium variant	8 587 050
2030	Constant-fertility variant	8 996 239
2030	High variant	8 913 727
2030	Low variant	7 727 192
2030	Medium variant	8 317 707
2025	Constant-fertility variant	8 443 704
2025	High variant	8 450 822
2025	Low variant	7 568 539
2025	Medium variant	8 010 509
2020	Constant-fertility variant	7 919 765
2020	High variant	7 966 382
2020	Low variant	7 363 824
2020	Medium variant	7 667 090
2015	Constant-fertility variant	7 416 822

Year	Variant	Value
2015	High variant	7 459 289
2015	Low variant	7 127 009
2015	Medium variant	7 295 135
2010	Constant-fertility variant	6 944 634
2010	High variant	6 967 407
2010	Low variant	6 843 645
2010	Medium variant	6 906 558
2005	Constant-fertility variant	6 514 751
2005	High variant	6 514 751
2005	Low variant	6 514 751
2005	Medium variant	6 514 751
2000	Medium variant	6 124 123
1995	Medium variant	5 719 045
1990	Medium variant	5 294 879
1985	Medium variant	4 855 264
1980	Medium variant	4 451 470
1975	Medium variant	4 076 080
1970	Medium variant	3 698 676
1965	Medium variant	3 342 771
1960	Medium variant	3 031 931
1955	Medium variant	2 770 753

Note

1   UN Data, *Total Population*, http://data.un.org/Data.aspx?q=world+population&d=
     PopDiv&f=variableID%3a12%3bcrID%3a900 (last updated September 28, 2007).
     (The United Nations is the author of the original material.) ("The United Nations
     World Population Prospects: The 2006 Revision contains estimates since 1950
     and projections until 2050 for every country in the world, including estimates and
     projections of 28 demographic indicators such as birth rates, deaths rates, infant
     mortality rates and life expectancy.")

Appendix 4   Fertility Rates[1]

Country or Area	Year	Births per Woman
Afghanistan	2000–2005	7.5
Afghanistan	1995–2000	8.0
Afghanistan	1990–1995	8.0
Afghanistan	1985–1990	7.9
Albania	2000–2005	2.2
Albania	1995–2000	2.5
Albania	1990–1995	2.8
Albania	1985–1990	3.1
Algeria	2000–2005	2.5
Algeria	1995–2000	2.9
Algeria	1990–1995	4.1
Algeria	1985–1990	5.3
Angola	2000–2005	6.8
Angola	1995–2000	6.9
Angola	1990–1995	7.1
Angola	1985–1990	7.2
Argentina	2000–2005	2.4
Argentina	1995–2000	2.6
Argentina	1990–1995	2.9
Argentina	1985–1990	3.1
Armenia	2000–2005	1.3
Armenia	1995–2000	1.8
Armenia	1990–1995	2.4
Armenia	1985–1990	2.6
Aruba	2000–2005	2.1
Aruba	1995–2000	2.2
Aruba	1990–1995	2.3
Aruba	1985–1990	2.3
Australia	2000–2005	1.8
Australia	1995–2000	1.8
Australia	1990–1995	1.9
Australia	1985–1990	1.9

Country or Area	Year	Births per Woman
Austria	2000–2005	1.4
Austria	1995–2000	1.4
Austria	1990–1995	1.5
Austria	1985–1990	1.5
Azerbaijan	2000–2005	1.7
Azerbaijan	1995–2000	2.2
Azerbaijan	1990–1995	2.9
Azerbaijan	1985–1990	3.0
Bahamas	2000–2005	2.1
Bahamas	1995–2000	2.4
Bahamas	1990–1995	2.6
Bahamas	1985–1990	2.6
Bahrain	2000–2005	2.5
Bahrain	1995–2000	2.8
Bahrain	1990–1995	3.4
Bahrain	1985–1990	4.1
Bangladesh	2000–2005	3.2
Bangladesh	1995–2000	3.5
Bangladesh	1990–1995	4.1
Bangladesh	1985–1990	4.6
Barbados	2000–2005	1.5
Barbados	1995–2000	1.5
Barbados	1990–1995	1.6
Barbados	1985–1990	1.8
Belarus	2000 2005	1.2
Belarus	1995–2000	1.3
Belarus	1990–1995	1.7
Belarus	1985–1990	2.0
Belgium	2000–2005	1.6
Belgium	1995–2000	1.6
Belgium	1990–1995	1.6
Belgium	1985–1990	1.6
Belize	2000–2005	3.4
Belize	1995–2000	3.9

Country or Area	Year	Births per Woman
Belize	1990–1995	4.3
Belize	1985–1990	4.7
Benin	2000–2005	5.9
Benin	1995–2000	6.3
Benin	1990–1995	6.6
Benin	1985–1990	6.9
Bhutan	2000–2005	2.9
Bhutan	1995–2000	4.2
Bhutan	1990–1995	5.4
Bhutan	1985–1990	6.2
Bolivia	2000–2005	4.0
Bolivia	1995–2000	4.3
Bolivia	1990–1995	4.8
Bolivia	1985–1990	5.0
Bosnia and Herzegovina	2000–2005	1.3
Bosnia and Herzegovina	1995–2000	1.5
Bosnia and Herzegovina	1990–1995	1.5
Bosnia and Herzegovina	1985–1990	1.9
Botswana	2000–2005	3.2
Botswana	1995–2000	3.7
Botswana	1990–1995	4.3
Botswana	1985–1990	5.1
Brazil	2000–2005	2.3
Brazil	1995–2000	2.5
Brazil	1990–1995	2.6
Brazil	1985–1990	3.1
Brunei	2000–2005	2.5
Brunei	1995–2000	2.7
Brunei	1990–1995	3.1
Brunei	1985–1990	3.4
Bulgaria	2000–2005	1.3
Bulgaria	1995–2000	1.2
Bulgaria	1990–1995	1.5
Bulgaria	1985–1990	1.9

Country or Area	Year	Births per Woman
Burkina Faso	2000–2005	6.4
Burkina Faso	1995–2000	6.8
Burkina Faso	1990–1995	7.2
Burkina Faso	1985–1990	7.4
Burundi	2000–2005	6.8
Burundi	1995–2000	6.8
Burundi	1990–1995	6.8
Burundi	1985–1990	6.8
Cambodia	2000–2005	3.6
Cambodia	1995–2000	4.5
Cambodia	1990–1995	5.5
Cambodia	1985–1990	6.0
Cameroon	2000–2005	4.9
Cameroon	1995–2000	5.1
Cameroon	1990–1995	5.7
Cameroon	1985–1990	6.1
Canada	2000–2005	1.5
Canada	1995–2000	1.6
Canada	1990–1995	1.7
Canada	1985–1990	1.6
Cape Verde	2000–2005	3.8
Cape Verde	1995–2000	4.1
Cape Verde	1990–1995	5.0
Cape Verde	1985–1990	5.9
Central African Republic	2000–2005	5.0
Central African Republic	1995–2000	5.3
Central African Republic	1990–1995	5.6
Central African Republic	1985–1990	5.7
Chad	2000–2005	6.5
Chad	1995–2000	6.6
Chad	1990–1995	6.6
Chad	1985–1990	6.7
Channel Islands	2000–2005	1.4
Channel Islands	1995–2000	1.4

Country or Area	Year	Births per Woman
Channel Islands	1990–1995	1.5
Channel Islands	1985–1990	1.5
Chile	2000–2005	2.0
Chile	1995–2000	2.2
Chile	1990–1995	2.6
Chile	1985–1990	2.7
China	2000–2005	1.7
China	1995–2000	1.8
China	1990–1995	1.9
China	1985–1990	2.5
Colombia	2000–2005	2.5
Colombia	1995–2000	2.7
Colombia	1990–1995	2.9
Colombia	1985–1990	3.2
Comoros	2000–2005	4.9
Comoros	1995–2000	5.4
Comoros	1990–1995	5.8
Comoros	1985–1990	6.5
Congo	2000–2005	4.8
Congo	1995–2000	4.9
Congo	1990–1995	5.2
Congo	1985–1990	5.5
Congo Dem. Rep.	2000–2005	6.7
Congo Dem. Rep.	1995–2000	6.7
Congo Dem. Rep.	1990–1995	6.7
Congo Dem. Rep.	1985–1990	6.7
Costa Rica	2000–2005	2.3
Costa Rica	1995–2000	2.6
Costa Rica	1990–1995	2.9
Costa Rica	1985–1990	3.4
Côte d'Ivoire	2000–2005	5.1
Côte d'Ivoire	1995–2000	5.6
Côte d'Ivoire	1990–1995	6.3
Côte d'Ivoire	1985–1990	6.9

Country or Area	Year	Births per Woman
Croatia	2000–2005	1.3
Croatia	1995–2000	1.5
Croatia	1990–1995	1.5
Croatia	1985–1990	1.8
Cuba	2000–2005	1.6
Cuba	1995–2000	1.6
Cuba	1990–1995	1.7
Cuba	1985–1990	1.8
Cyprus	2000–2005	1.6
Cyprus	1995–2000	1.9
Cyprus	1990–1995	2.4
Cyprus	1985–1990	2.4
Czech Republic	2000–2005	1.2
Czech Republic	1995–2000	1.2
Czech Republic	1990–1995	1.7
Czech Republic	1985–1990	1.9
Denmark	2000–2005	1.8
Denmark	1995–2000	1.8
Denmark	1990–1995	1.7
Denmark	1985–1990	1.5
Djibouti	2000–2005	4.5
Djibouti	1995–2000	5.1
Djibouti	1990–1995	5.9
Djibouti	1985–1990	6.4
Dominican Republic	2000–2005	3.0
Dominican Republic	1995–2000	3.1
Dominican Republic	1990–1995	3.2
Dominican Republic	1985–1990	3.5
Ecuador	2000–2005	2.8
Ecuador	1995–2000	3.1
Ecuador	1990–1995	3.4
Ecuador	1985–1990	4.0
Egypt	2000–2005	3.2
Egypt	1995–2000	3.5

Country or Area	Year	Births per Woman
Egypt	1990–1995	3.9
Egypt	1985–1990	4.8
El Salvador	2000–2005	2.9
El Salvador	1995–2000	3.2
El Salvador	1990–1995	3.5
El Salvador	1985–1990	3.9
Equatorial Guinea	2000–2005	5.6
Equatorial Guinea	1995–2000	5.9
Equatorial Guinea	1990–1995	5.9
Equatorial Guinea	1985–1990	5.9
Eritrea	2000–2005	5.5
Eritrea	1995–2000	5.9
Eritrea	1990–1995	6.2
Eritrea	1985–1990	6.3
Estonia	2000–2005	1.4
Estonia	1995–2000	1.3
Estonia	1990–1995	1.6
Estonia	1985–1990	2.2
Ethiopia	2000–2005	5.8
Ethiopia	1995–2000	6.3
Ethiopia	1990–1995	6.8
Ethiopia	1985–1990	6.8
Federated States of Micronesia	2000–2005	4.2
Federated States of Micronesia	1995–2000	4.5
Federated States of Micronesia	1990–1995	4.8
Federated States of Micronesia	1985–1990	5.2
Fiji	2000–2005	3.0
Fiji	1995–2000	3.2
Fiji	1990–1995	3.4
Fiji	1985–1990	3.5
Finland	2000–2005	1.8

Country or Area	Year	Births per Woman
Finland	1995–2000	1.7
Finland	1990–1995	1.8
Finland	1985–1990	1.7
France	2000–2005	1.9
France	1995–2000	1.8
France	1990–1995	1.7
France	1985–1990	1.8
French Guiana	2000–2005	3.7
French Guiana	1995–2000	3.9
French Guiana	1990–1995	4.1
French Guiana	1985–1990	3.7
French Polynesia	2000–2005	2.4
French Polynesia	1995–2000	2.6
French Polynesia	1990–1995	3.1
French Polynesia	1985–1990	3.6
Gabon	2000–2005	3.4
Gabon	1995–2000	3.8
Gabon	1990–1995	4.5
Gabon	1985–1990	5.0
Gambia The	2000–2005	5.2
Gambia The	1995–2000	5.5
Gambia The	1990–1995	5.9
Gambia The	1985–1990	6.2
Georgia	2000–2005	1.5
Georgia	1995–2000	1.6
Georgia	1990–1995	2.0
Georgia	1985–1990	2.3
Germany	2000–2005	1.3
Germany	1995–2000	1.3
Germany	1990–1995	1.3
Germany	1985–1990	1.4
Ghana	2000–2005	4.4
Ghana	1995–2000	4.8
Ghana	1990–1995	5.5

Country or Area	Year	Births per Woman
Ghana	1985–1990	6.1
Greece	2000–2005	1.3
Greece	1995–2000	1.3
Greece	1990–1995	1.4
Greece	1985–1990	1.5
Grenada	2000–2005	2.4
Grenada	1995–2000	2.8
Grenada	1990–1995	3.3
Grenada	1985–1990	4.1
Guadeloupe	2000–2005	2.1
Guadeloupe	1995–2000	2.1
Guadeloupe	1990–1995	2.1
Guadeloupe	1985–1990	2.5
Guam	2000–2005	2.7
Guam	1995–2000	3.0
Guam	1990–1995	3.1
Guam	1985–1990	3.1
Guatemala	2000–2005	4.6
Guatemala	1995–2000	5.0
Guatemala	1990–1995	5.5
Guatemala	1985–1990	5.7
Guinea	2000–2005	5.8
Guinea	1995–2000	6.2
Guinea	1990–1995	6.5
Guinea	1985–1990	6.8
Guinea-Bissau	2000–2005	7.1
Guinea-Bissau	1995–2000	7.1
Guinea-Bissau	1990–1995	7.1
Guinea-Bissau	1985–1990	7.1
Guyana	2000–2005	2.4
Guyana	1995–2000	2.5
Guyana	1990–1995	2.6
Guyana	1985–1990	2.7
Haiti	2000–2005	4.0

Country or Area	Year	Births per Woman
Haiti	1995–2000	4.6
Haiti	1990–1995	5.2
Haiti	1985–1990	5.7
Honduras	2000–2005	3.7
Honduras	1995–2000	4.3
Honduras	1990–1995	4.9
Honduras	1985–1990	5.4
Hong Kong SAR	2000–2005	0.9
Hong Kong SAR	1995–2000	1.1
Hong Kong SAR	1990–1995	1.3
Hong Kong SAR	1985–1990	1.3
Hungary	2000–2005	1.3
Hungary	1995–2000	1.4
Hungary	1990–1995	1.7
Hungary	1985–1990	1.8
Iceland	2000–2005	2.0
Iceland	1995–2000	2.1
Iceland	1990–1995	2.2
Iceland	1985–1990	2.1
India	2000–2005	3.1
India	1995–2000	3.5
India	1990–1995	3.9
India	1985–1990	4.2
Indonesia	2000–2005	2.4
Indonesia	1995–2000	2.6
Indonesia	1990–1995	2.9
Indonesia	1985–1990	3.4
Iran	2000–2005	2.1
Iran	1995–2000	2.5
Iran	1990–1995	4.3
Iran	1985–1990	5.6
Iraq	2000–2005	4.9
Iraq	1995–2000	5.4
Iraq	1990–1995	5.7

Country or Area	Year	Births per Woman
Iraq	1985–1990	6.2
Ireland	2000–2005	2.0
Ireland	1995–2000	1.9
Ireland	1990–1995	2.0
Ireland	1985–1990	2.3
Israel	2000–2005	2.9
Israel	1995–2000	2.9
Israel	1990–1995	2.9
Israel	1985–1990	3.1
Italy	2000–2005	1.3
Italy	1995–2000	1.2
Italy	1990–1995	1.3
Italy	1985–1990	1.3
Jamaica	2000–2005	2.6
Jamaica	1995–2000	2.7
Jamaica	1990–1995	2.8
Jamaica	1985–1990	3.1
Japan	2000–2005	1.3
Japan	1995–2000	1.4
Japan	1990–1995	1.5
Japan	1985–1990	1.7
Jordan	2000–2005	3.5
Jordan	1995–2000	4.3
Jordan	1990–1995	5.1
Jordan	1985–1990	5.9
Kazakhstan	2000–2005	2.0
Kazakhstan	1995–2000	2.0
Kazakhstan	1990–1995	2.6
Kazakhstan	1985–1990	3.0
Kenya	2000–2005	5.0
Kenya	1995–2000	5.0
Kenya	1990–1995	5.4
Kenya	1985–1990	6.5
Korea DPR	2000–2005	1.9

Country or Area	Year	Births per Woman
Korea DPR	1995–2000	2.1
Korea DPR	1990–1995	2.4
Korea DPR	1985–1990	2.5
Korea Rep	2000–2005	1.2
Korea Rep	1995–2000	1.5
Korea Rep	1990–1995	1.7
Korea Rep	1985–1990	1.6
Kuwait	2000–2005	2.3
Kuwait	1995–2000	2.6
Kuwait	1990–1995	3.2
Kuwait	1985–1990	3.9
Kyrgyzstan	2000–2005	2.5
Kyrgyzstan	1995–2000	3.0
Kyrgyzstan	1990–1995	3.6
Kyrgyzstan	1985–1990	4.0
Lao PDR	2000–2005	3.6
Lao PDR	1995–2000	4.7
Lao PDR	1990–1995	5.9
Lao PDR	1985–1990	6.4
Latvia	2000–2005	1.2
Latvia	1995–2000	1.2
Latvia	1990–1995	1.6
Latvia	1985–1990	2.1
Lebanon	2000–2005	2.3
Lebanon	1995–2000	2.7
Lebanon	1990–1995	3.0
Lebanon	1985–1990	3.3
Lesotho	2000–2005	3.8
Lesotho	1995–2000	4.4
Lesotho	1990–1995	4.7
Lesotho	1985–1990	5.1
Liberia	2000–2005	6.8
Liberia	1995–2000	6.8
Liberia	1990–1995	6.9

Country or Area	Year	Births per Woman
Liberia	1985–1990	6.9
Libya	2000–2005	3.0
Libya	1995–2000	3.4
Libya	1990–1995	4.1
Libya	1985–1990	5.7
Lithuania	2000–2005	1.3
Lithuania	1995–2000	1.5
Lithuania	1990–1995	1.8
Lithuania	1985–1990	2.1
Luxembourg	2000–2005	1.7
Luxembourg	1995–2000	1.7
Luxembourg	1990–1995	1.7
Luxembourg	1985–1990	1.5
Macau SAR	2000–2005	0.8
Macau SAR	1995–2000	1.1
Macau SAR	1990–1995	1.6
Macau SAR	1985–1990	2.1
Macedonia	2000–2005	1.6
Macedonia	1995–2000	1.7
Macedonia	1990–1995	1.9
Macedonia	1985–1990	2.0
Madagascar	2000–2005	5.3
Madagascar	1995–2000	5.8
Madagascar	1990–1995	6.1
Madagascar	1985–1990	6.3
Malawi	2000–2005	6.0
Malawi	1995–2000	6.4
Malawi	1990–1995	6.8
Malawi	1985–1990	7.2
Malaysia	2000–2005	2.9
Malaysia	1995–2000	3.1
Malaysia	1990–1995	3.5
Malaysia	1985–1990	4.0
Maldives	2000–2005	2.8

Country or Area	Year	Births per Woman
Maldives	1995–2000	3.8
Maldives	1990–1995	5.6
Maldives	1985–1990	6.6
Mali	2000–2005	6.7
Mali	1995–2000	7.2
Mali	1990–1995	7.4
Mali	1985–1990	7.5
Malta	2000–2005	1.5
Malta	1995–2000	1.8
Malta	1990–1995	2.0
Malta	1985–1990	2.0
Martinique	2000–2005	2.0
Martinique	1995–2000	1.9
Martinique	1990–1995	2.0
Martinique	1985–1990	2.1
Mauritania	2000–2005	4.8
Mauritania	1995–2000	5.3
Mauritania	1990–1995	5.7
Mauritania	1985–1990	6.0
Mauritius	2000–2005	1.9
Mauritius	1995–2000	2.1
Mauritius	1990–1995	2.3
Mauritius	1985–1990	2.2
Mexico	2000–2005	2.4
Mexico	1995 2000	2.7
Mexico	1990–1995	3.2
Mexico	1985–1990	3.6
Mongolia	2000–2005	2.1
Mongolia	1995–2000	2.4
Mongolia	1990–1995	3.4
Mongolia	1985–1990	4.8
Montenegro	2000–2005	1.8
Montenegro	1995–2000	1.8
Montenegro	1990–1995	1.8

Country or Area	Year	Births per Woman
Montenegro	1985–1990	2.2
Morocco	2000–2005	2.5
Morocco	1995–2000	3.0
Morocco	1990–1995	3.7
Morocco	1985–1990	4.4
Mozambique	2000–2005	5.5
Mozambique	1995–2000	5.8
Mozambique	1990–1995	6.1
Mozambique	1985–1990	6.3
Myanmar	2000–2005	2.2
Myanmar	1995–2000	2.7
Myanmar	1990–1995	3.1
Myanmar	1985–1990	3.8
Namibia	2000–2005	3.6
Namibia	1995–2000	4.4
Namibia	1990–1995	5.4
Namibia	1985–1990	6.2
Nepal	2000–2005	3.7
Nepal	1995–2000	4.4
Nepal	1990–1995	5.0
Nepal	1985–1990	5.3
Netherlands	2000–2005	1.7
Netherlands	1995–2000	1.6
Netherlands	1990–1995	1.6
Netherlands	1985–1990	1.6
Netherlands Antilles	2000–2005	2.1
Netherlands Antilles	1995–2000	2.1
Netherlands Antilles	1990–1995	2.3
Netherlands Antilles	1985–1990	2.3
New Caledonia	2000–2005	2.2
New Caledonia	1995–2000	2.6
New Caledonia	1990–1995	2.9
New Caledonia	1985–1990	3.1
New Zealand	2000–2005	2.0

Country or Area	Year	Births per Woman
New Zealand	1995–2000	2.0
New Zealand	1990–1995	2.1
New Zealand	1985–1990	2.1
Nicaragua	2000–2005	3.0
Nicaragua	1995–2000	3.6
Nicaragua	1990–1995	4.5
Nicaragua	1985–1990	5.0
Niger	2000–2005	7.4
Niger	1995–2000	7.7
Niger	1990–1995	7.8
Niger	1985–1990	8.0
Nigeria	2000–2005	5.8
Nigeria	1995–2000	6.2
Nigeria	1990–1995	6.6
Nigeria	1985–1990	6.8
Norway	2000–2005	1.8
Norway	1995–2000	1.9
Norway	1990–1995	1.9
Norway	1985–1990	1.8
Oman	2000–2005	3.7
Oman	1995–2000	5.1
Oman	1990–1995	6.3
Oman	1985–1990	6.8
Pakistan	2000–2005	4.0
Pakistan	1995 2000	5.0
Pakistan	1990–1995	5.8
Pakistan	1985–1990	6.7
Palestinian Territory, Occupied	2000–2005	5.6
Palestinian Territory, Occupied	1995–2000	6.0
Palestinian Territory, Occupied	1990–1995	6.5
Palestinian Territory, Occupied	1985–1990	6.4

Country or Area	Year	Births per Woman
Panama	2000–2005	2.7
Panama	1995–2000	2.8
Panama	1990–1995	2.9
Panama	1985–1990	3.2
Papua New Guinea	2000–2005	4.3
Papua New Guinea	1995–2000	4.6
Papua New Guinea	1990–1995	4.7
Papua New Guinea	1985–1990	5.0
Paraguay	2000–2005	3.5
Paraguay	1995–2000	3.9
Paraguay	1990–1995	4.3
Paraguay	1985–1990	4.8
Peru	2000–2005	2.7
Peru	1995–2000	3.1
Peru	1990–1995	3.7
Peru	1985–1990	4.1
Philippines	2000–2005	3.5
Philippines	1995–2000	3.7
Philippines	1990–1995	4.1
Philippines	1985–1990	4.6
Poland	2000–2005	1.3
Poland	1995–2000	1.5
Poland	1990–1995	1.9
Poland	1985–1990	2.2
Portugal	2000–2005	1.5
Portugal	1995–2000	1.5
Portugal	1990–1995	1.5
Portugal	1985–1990	1.6
Puerto Rico	2000–2005	1.8
Puerto Rico	1995–2000	2.0
Puerto Rico	1990–1995	2.2
Puerto Rico	1985–1990	2.3
Qatar	2000–2005	2.9
Qatar	1995–2000	3.4

Country or Area	Year	Births per Woman
Qatar	1990–1995	4.1
Qatar	1985–1990	4.7
Republic of Moldova	2000–2005	1.5
Republic of Moldova	1995–2000	1.7
Republic of Moldova	1990–1995	2.1
Republic of Moldova	1985–1990	2.6
Reunion	2000–2005	2.5
Reunion	1995–2000	2.3
Reunion	1990–1995	2.4
Reunion	1985–1990	2.5
Romania	2000–2005	1.3
Romania	1995–2000	1.3
Romania	1990–1995	1.5
Romania	1985–1990	2.3
Russian Federation	2000–2005	1.3
Russian Federation	1995–2000	1.2
Russian Federation	1990–1995	1.5
Russian Federation	1985–1990	2.1
Rwanda	2000–2005	6.0
Rwanda	1995–2000	6.1
Rwanda	1990–1995	6.9
Rwanda	1985–1990	8.3
Sahrawi	2000–2005	3.0
Sahrawi	1995–2000	3.5
Sahrawi	1990 1995	4.2
Sahrawi	1985–1990	4.9
Saint Lucia	2000–2005	2.2
Saint Lucia	1995–2000	2.4
Saint Lucia	1990–1995	3.0
Saint Lucia	1985–1990	3.7
Samoa	2000–2005	4.4
Samoa	1995–2000	4.7
Samoa	1990–1995	4.7
Samoa	1985–1990	4.8

Country or Area	Year	Births per Woman
São Tomé and Príncipe	2000–2005	4.3
São Tomé and Príncipe	1995–2000	4.8
São Tomé and Príncipe	1990–1995	5.2
São Tomé and Príncipe	1985–1990	5.7
Saudi Arabia	2000–2005	3.8
Saudi Arabia	1995–2000	4.6
Saudi Arabia	1990–1995	5.4
Saudi Arabia	1985–1990	6.2
Senegal	2000–2005	5.2
Senegal	1995–2000	5.7
Senegal	1990–1995	6.3
Senegal	1985–1990	6.8
Serbia	2000–2005	1.7
Serbia	1995–2000	1.7
Serbia	1990–1995	2.0
Serbia	1985–1990	2.2
Sierra Leone	2000–2005	6.5
Sierra Leone	1995–2000	6.5
Sierra Leone	1990–1995	6.5
Sierra Leone	1985–1990	6.5
Singapore	2000–2005	1.4
Singapore	1995–2000	1.6
Singapore	1990–1995	1.8
Singapore	1985–1990	1.7
Slovakia	2000–2005	1.2
Slovakia	1995–2000	1.4
Slovakia	1990–1995	1.9
Slovakia	1985–1990	2.2
Slovenia	2000–2005	1.2
Slovenia	1995–2000	1.3
Slovenia	1990–1995	1.4
Slovenia	1985–1990	1.7
Solomon Islands	2000–2005	4.4
Solomon Islands	1995–2000	4.9

Country or Area	Year	Births per Woman
Solomon Islands	1990–1995	5.5
Solomon Islands	1985–1990	6.1
Somalia	2000–2005	6.4
Somalia	1995–2000	6.8
Somalia	1990–1995	6.6
Somalia	1985–1990	7.0
South Africa	2000–2005	2.8
South Africa	1995–2000	3.0
South Africa	1990–1995	3.3
South Africa	1985–1990	3.9
Spain	2000–2005	1.3
Spain	1995–2000	1.2
Spain	1990–1995	1.3
Spain	1985–1990	1.5
Sri Lanka	2000–2005	2.0
Sri Lanka	1995–2000	2.2
Sri Lanka	1990–1995	2.5
Sri Lanka	1985–1990	2.6
St Vincent and the Grenadines	2000–2005	2.3
St Vincent and the Grenadines	1995–2000	2.4
St Vincent and the Grenadines	1990–1995	2.8
St Vincent and the Grenadines	1985–1990	3.2
Sudan	2000–2005	4.8
Sudan	1995–2000	5.4
Sudan	1990–1995	5.8
Sudan	1985–1990	6.1
Suriname	2000–2005	2.6
Suriname	1995–2000	2.8
Suriname	1990–1995	2.6
Suriname	1985–1990	3.0
Swaziland	2000–2005	3.9

Country or Area	Year	Births per Woman
Swaziland	1995–2000	4.5
Swaziland	1990–1995	5.3
Swaziland	1985–1990	6.1
Sweden	2000–2005	1.7
Sweden	1995–2000	1.6
Sweden	1990–1995	2.0
Sweden	1985–1990	1.9
Switzerland	2000–2005	1.4
Switzerland	1995–2000	1.5
Switzerland	1990–1995	1.5
Switzerland	1985–1990	1.5
Syria	2000–2005	3.5
Syria	1995–2000	4.0
Syria	1990–1995	4.9
Syria	1985–1990	6.2
Tajikistan	2000–2005	3.8
Tajikistan	1995–2000	4.3
Tajikistan	1990–1995	4.9
Tajikistan	1985–1990	5.4
Tanzania	2000–2005	5.7
Tanzania	1995–2000	5.7
Tanzania	1990–1995	5.9
Tanzania	1985–1990	6.4
Thailand	2000–2005	1.8
Thailand	1995–2000	1.9
Thailand	1990–1995	2.0
Thailand	1985–1990	2.3
Timor Leste	2000–2005	7.0
Timor Leste	1995–2000	7.0
Timor Leste	1990–1995	5.7
Timor Leste	1985–1990	5.2
Togo	2000–2005	5.4
Togo	1995–2000	5.8
Togo	1990–1995	6.2

Country or Area	Year	Births per Woman
Togo	1985–1990	6.6
Tonga	2000–2005	3.7
Tonga	1995–2000	4.0
Tonga	1990–1995	4.5
Tonga	1985–1990	4.7
Trinidad and Tobago	2000–2005	1.6
Trinidad and Tobago	1995–2000	1.7
Trinidad and Tobago	1990–1995	2.1
Trinidad and Tobago	1985–1990	2.8
Tunisia	2000–2005	2.0
Tunisia	1995–2000	2.3
Tunisia	1990–1995	3.1
Tunisia	1985–1990	4.1
Turkey	2000–2005	2.2
Turkey	1995–2000	2.6
Turkey	1990–1995	2.9
Turkey	1985–1990	3.3
Turkmenistan	2000–2005	2.8
Turkmenistan	1995–2000	3.0
Turkmenistan	1990–1995	4.0
Turkmenistan	1985–1990	4.6
Uganda	2000–2005	6.7
Uganda	1995–2000	6.9
Uganda	1990–1995	7.1
Uganda	1985–1990	7.1
Ukraine	2000–2005	1.2
Ukraine	1995–2000	1.2
Ukraine	1990–1995	1.6
Ukraine	1985–1990	2.0
United Arab Emirates	2000–2005	2.5
United Arab Emirates	1995–2000	3.1
United Arab Emirates	1990–1995	3.9
United Arab Emirates	1985–1990	4.8
United Kingdom	2000–2005	1.7

Country or Area	Year	Births per Woman
United Kingdom	1995–2000	1.7
United Kingdom	1990–1995	1.8
United Kingdom	1985–1990	1.8
United States of America	2000–2005	2.0
United States of America	1995–2000	2.0
United States of America	1990–1995	2.0
United States of America	1985–1990	1.9
United States Virgin Islands	2000–2005	2.2
United States Virgin Islands	1995–2000	2.4
United States Virgin Islands	1990–1995	3.1
United States Virgin Islands	1985–1990	3.1
Uruguay	2000–2005	2.2
Uruguay	1995–2000	2.3
Uruguay	1990–1995	2.5
Uruguay	1985–1990	2.5
Uzbekistan	2000–2005	2.7
Uzbekistan	1995–2000	3.0
Uzbekistan	1990–1995	3.9
Uzbekistan	1985–1990	4.4
Vanuatu	2000–2005	4.2
Vanuatu	1995–2000	4.6
Vanuatu	1990–1995	4.8
Vanuatu	1985–1990	5.0
Venezuela	2000–2005	2.7
Venezuela	1995–2000	2.9
Venezuela	1990–1995	3.3
Venezuela	1985–1990	3.6
Vietnam	2000–2005	2.3
Vietnam	1995–2000	2.5
Vietnam	1990–1995	3.3
Vietnam	1985–1990	4.0
Yemen	2000–2005	6.0
Yemen	1995–2000	6.7
Yemen	1990–1995	7.7

Country or Area	Year	Births per Woman
Yemen	1985–1990	8.4
Zambia	2000–2005	5.6
Zambia	1995–2000	6.0
Zambia	1990–1995	6.3
Zambia	1985–1990	6.7
Zimbabwe	2000–2005	3.6
Zimbabwe	1995–2000	4.1
Zimbabwe	1990–1995	4.8
Zimbabwe	1985–1990	5.7

Note

1   UN Data, *Total Fertility Rate*, http://data.un.org/Data.aspx?q=fertility+rate+&d=G enderStat&f=inID%3a14 (last updated Mar. 21, 2008). (The United Nations is the author of the original material.)

Bibliography

Books

M. AKEHURST, MODERN INTRODUCTION TO INTERNATIONAL LAW (1970).

PHILIP ALSTON, *International Law and the Human Right to Food, in* THE RIGHT TO FOOD 9 (Philip Alston & Katarina Tomasevski eds., 1984).

AM. COUNCIL ON RENEWABLE ENERGY, THE OUTLOOK ON RENEWABLE ENERGY IN AMERICA (2007).

KOFI ANNAN, PARTNERSHIPS FOR GLOBAL COMMUNITY: ANNUAL REPORT ON THE WORK OF THE ORGANIZATION (1998).

YVES BEIGBEDER, THE ROLE AND STATUS OF INTERNATIONAL HUMANITARIAN VOLUNTEERS AND ORGANIZATIONS: THE RIGHT AND DUTY TO HUMANITARIAN ASSISTANCE (1991).

MURRAY R. BENEDICT, FARM POLICIES OF THE UNITED STATES, 1790–1950: A STUDY OF THEIR ORIGINS AND DEVELOPMENT (1953).

HAROLD BROOKFIELD ET AL., *Cultivating Biodiversity: Setting the Scene, in* CULTIVATING DIVERSITY: UNDERSTANDING, ANALYZING AND USING AGRICULTURAL DIVERSITY 7 (2002).

EDWARD CLAY, *Food Aid, Development, and Food Security, in* AGRICULTURE AND THE STATE 202 (C. Peter Timmer ed., 1991).

WILLARD COCHRANE, THE DEV. OF AM. AGRIC.: AN HISTORICAL ANALYSIS (1979).

WILLARD W. COCHRANE & C. FORD RUNGE, REFORMING FARM POLICY: TOWARD A NATIONAL AGENDA (1992).

WILLARD W. COCHRANE & MARY E. RYAN, AMERICAN FARM POLICY, 1948–1973 (1976).

COMM. ON IDENTIFYING AND ASSESSING UNINTENDED EFFECTS OF GENETICALLY ENGINEERED FOODS ON HUMAN HEALTH, NATIONAL RESEARCH COUNCIL, SAFETY OF GENETICALLY ENGINEERED FOODS: APPROACHES TO ASSESSING UNINTENDED HEALTH EFFECTS (2004).

D. CRANE, A DICTIONARY OF CANADIAN ECONOMICS (1980).

JOHN CROOME, RESHAPING THE WORLD TRADING SYSTEM (2d ed. 1999).

JEAN DEPREUX, COMMENTARY: GENEVA CONVENTION III (1960).

MELAKU GEBOYE DESTA, THE LAW OF INTERNATIONAL TRADE IN AGRICULTURAL PRODUCTS (2002).

CRAIG DONNELLAN, GENETICALLY MODIFIED FOOD (2000).

ANNE B.W. EFFLAND, USDA, US FARM POLICY: THE FIRST 100 YEARS, IN AGRICULTURAL OUTLOOK (Mar. 2000).

BARDO FASSBENDER, UN SECURITY COUNCIL REFORM AND THE RIGHT OF VETO: A CONSTITUTIONAL PERSPECTIVE (1998).

SAMUEL FROMARTZ, ORGANIC INC.: NATURAL FOODS AND HOW THEY GROW (2006).

JAMES D. GAISFORD & WILLIAM A. KERR, ECONOMIC ANALYSIS FOR INTERNATIONAL TRADE NEGOTIATIONS: THE WTO AND AGRICULTURAL TRADE (2001).

ALAN GREER, AGRICULTURAL POLICY IN EUROPE (2005).

SANJEEV GUPTA, ET AL., FOREIGN AID AND CONSUMPTION SMOOTHING: EVIDENCE FROM GLOBAL FOREIGN AID, FISCAL AFFAIRS DEPARTMENT OF THE INTERNATIONAL MONETARY FUND (2003).

M.C. HALLBERG, POLICY FOR AMERICAN AGRICULTURE: CHOICES AND CONSEQUENCES (1992).

DAVID E. HAMILTON, FROM NEW DAY TO NEW DEAL: AMERICAN FARM POLICY FROM HOOVER TO ROOSEVELT, 1928–1933 (1991).

DEBORAH HARRIS ET AL., FOOD STAMP ADVOCACY GUIDE (2007).

ELLIS W. HAWLEY, THE GREAT WAR AND THE SEARCH FOR A MODERN ORDER: A HISTORY OF THE AMERICAN PEOPLE AND THEIR INSTITUTIONS, 1917–1933 (2d ed. 1992).

J.P. HUMPHREY, *The Universal Declaration of Human Rights: Its History, Impact and Juridical Character*, *in* HUMAN RIGHTS: THIRTY YEARS AFTER THE UNIVERSAL DECLARATION 21 (B.G. Ramcharan ed., 1979).

DANIEL IMHOFF, FOOD FIGHT: THE CITIZEN'S GUIDE TO A FOOD AND FARM BILL (2007).

INTERNATIONAL WATER MANAGEMENT INSTITUTE, WATER FOR FOOD, WATER FOR LIFE: A COMPREHENSIVE ASSESSMENT OF WATER MANAGEMENT IN AGRICULTURE (David Molden ed., 2007).

MARK WESTON JANIS, INTERNATIONAL LAW 43 (5th ed. 2008).

D. GALE JOHNSON ET AL., AGRICULTURAL POLICY AND TRADE: ADJUSTING DOMESTIC PROGRAMS IN AN INTERNATIONAL FRAMEWORK (1985).

WILLIAM CHESTER JORDAN, THE GREAT FAMINE: NORTHERN EUROPE IN THE EARLY FOURTEENTH CENTURY (1996).

EDMUND H. KELLOGG & JAN STEPAN, THE WORLD'S LAWS AND PRACTICES ON POPULATION AND SEXUALITY EDUCATION (1975).

VAUGHAN LOWE, INTERNATIONAL LAW (2007).

PETER MACALISTER-SMITH, INTERNATIONAL HUMANITARIAN ASSISTANCE: DISASTER RELIEF ACTIONS IN INTERNATIONAL LAW AND ORGANIZATION (1985).

JOHN MADELEY, FOOD FOR ALL: THE NEED FOR A NEW AGRICULTURE (2002).

P. MALANCZUK, AKEBURST'S MODERN INTRODUCTION TO INTERNATIONAL LAW (1997).

JIM MONKE, CONG. RESEARCH SERV., CRS REP. RS21604, MARKETING LOANS, LOAN DEFICIENCY PAYMENTS, AND COMMODITY CERTIFICATES (2004).

EDGAR OWENS, THE FUTURE OF FREEDOM IN THE DEVELOPING WORLD: ECONOMIC DEVELOPMENT AS POLITICAL REFORM (1987).

MICHAEL POLLAN, THE OMNIVORE'S DILEMMA: A NATURAL HISTORY OF FOUR MEALS (2006).

CLIVE POTTER, AGAINST THE GRAIN: AGRI-ENVIRONMENTAL REFORM IN THE UNITED STATES AND THE EUROPEAN UNION (1998).

JOHAN POTTIER, ANTHROPOLOGY OF FOOD: THE SOCIAL DYNAMICS OF FOOD SECURITY (1999).

ADAM REHOF ET AL., THE UNIVERSAL DECLARATION OF HUMAN RIGHTS: A COMMENTARY (1993).

Jeremy Rifkin & Carol Grunewald Rifkin, Voting Green: Your Complete Environmental Guide to Making Political Choices in the 1990s (1992).

A.H. Robertson & J.G. Merrills, Human Rights in the World: An Introduction to the Study of the International Protection of Human Rights (4th ed. 1998).

Robert Robertson, Human Rights in the Twenty-First Century a Global Challenge (Kathleen E. Mahoney & Paul Mahoney eds., 1993).

Edward L. Schapsmeier & Frederick H. Schapsmeier, Ezra Taft Benson and the Politics of Agriculture: The Eisenhower Years, 1953–1961 (1975).

Jacobo Schatan & Joan Gussow, Food as Human Right (Asbjorn Eide et al. eds., 1984).

Thomas J. Schoenbaum, *Agricultural Trade Wars: A Threat to the GATT and Global Free Trade, in* GATT and Trade Liberalization in Agriculture 73 (Masayosi Homna et al. eds., 1993).

Amartya Sen, Poverty and Famines: An Essay on Entitlement and Deprivation (1981).

Ismail Serageldin & G.J. Persley, Consultative Group on International Agricultural Research, Promethean Science: Agricultural Biotechnology, the Environment, and the Poor (2000).

Mahendra Shah & Maurice Strong, Food in the 21st Century: From Science to Sustainable Agriculture (1999).

Helvi Sipila, *Status of Women and Family Planning, in* Human Rights and Population: From the Perspectives of Law, Policy and Organization 57 (1973).

Terence P. Stewart, The GATT Uruguay Round: A Negotiating History (1986–1992) (1993).

Kathleen S. Swendiman, Cong. Research Serv., R40846, Health Care: Constitutional Rights and Legislative Powers (2012).

Bruce G. Trigger, Understanding Early Civilizations: A Comparative Study (2003).

UN Dev. Prog., Human Development Report 2005: International Cooperation at a Crossroads: Aid, Trade and Security in an Unequal World (2005).

Thomas W. Zeiler, American Trade and Power in the 1960s (1992).

Law Review Articles

David E. Adelman & John H. Barton, *Environmental Regulation for Agriculture: Towards a Framework to Promote Sustainable Intensive Agriculture*, 21 Stan. Envtl. L.J. 3 (2002).

Maria Sophia Aguirre & Ann Wolfgram, *United Nations Policy and the Family: Redefining the Ties That Bind—A Study of History, Forces and Trends*, 16 BYU J. Pub. L. 113 (2002).

Kitty Arambulo, *Drafting an Optional Protocol to the International Covenant on Economic, Social and Cultural Rights: Can an Ideal Become Reality*, 2 U.C. Davis J. Int'l L. & Pol'y 111 (1996).

Kathryn Cameron Atkinson, *United States—Latin American Trade Laws*, 21 N. C. J. Int'l L. & Com. Reg. 111 (1995).

Sneha Barot, *Back to Basics: The Rationale for Increased Funds for International Family Planning*, 11 Guttmacher Pol. Rev. 13 (2008).

Raj Bhala, *World Agricultural Trade in Purgatory: The Uruguay Round Agriculture Agreement and Its Implications for the Doha Round*, 79 N.D.L. Rev. 691 (2003).

Raj Bhala, *Resurrecting the Doha Round: Devilish Details, Grand Themes, and China Too*, 45 Tex. Int'l L. J. 1 (2009).Susan Bierman, *Fair and Unfair Trade in an Interventionist Era*, 77 Am. Soc'y Int'l L. Proc. 114 (1983).

Robert E. Black et al., *Where and Why Are 10 Million Children Dying Every Year?*, 361 Lancet 2226 (2003).

John Bongaarts, *Population Policy Options in the Developing World*, SCIENCE, Feb. 11, 1994, at 771.

Kevin J. Brosch, *The GATT, the WTO and the Uruguay Round Agreements Act, The Uruguay Round Agreement on Agriculture*, 722 PLI/Comm 863 (1995).

D.E. Buckingham, *A Recipe for Change: Towards an Integrated Approach to Food Under International Law*, 6 Pace Int'l L. Rev. 285 (1994).

Elizabeth Bullington, *WTO Agreement Mandate that Congress Repeal the Farm Bill of 2002 and Enact an Agriculture Law Embodying Free Market Principles*, 20 Am. U. Int'l L. Rev. 1211 (2005).

Peter Burchett, *A Castle in the Sky: The Illusory Promise of Labeling Genetically Modified Food in Europe*, 23 Penn St. Int'l L. Rev. 173 (2004).

Jonathan Carlson, *Hunger, Agricultural Trade Liberalization, and Soft International Law: Addressing the Legal Dimensions of a Political Problem*, 70 Iowa L. Rev. 1187 (1985).

James Stephen Carpenter, *Farm Chemicals, Soil Erosion, and Sustainable Agriculture*, 13 Stan. Envtl. L.J. 190 (1994).

Audrey Chapman, *A "Violations Approach" for Monitoring the International Covenant on Economic, Social and Cultural Rights*, 18 Hum. Rts. Q. 23 (1996).

Ying Chen, *China's One Child Policy and Its Violations of Women's and Children's Rights*, 22 N.Y. Int'l L. Rev. 1 (2009).

Ann S.Y. Cheung, *A Case Study of Media Freedom in China*, 20 Colum. J. Asian L. 357 (2007).

Joseph P.G. Chimombo, *Issues in Basic Education in Developing Countries: An Exploration of Policy Options for Improved Delivery*, 8 J. Int'l Cooperation Educ. 129 (2005).

Sungjoon Cho, *Doha's Development*, 25 Berkeley J. Int'l L. 165 (2007).

Cheryl Christensen & Charles Hanrahan, *African Food Crises: Short-, Medium-, and Long-Term Responses*, 70 Iowa L. Rev. 1293 (1985).

William L. Church, *Farmland Conversion: The View from 1986*, 1986 U. Ill. L. Rev. 521 (1986).

Peggy A. Clarke, *The Future of Food Subsidies*, 101 Am. Soc'y Int'l L. Proc. 109 (2007).

Juscelino F. Colares, *A Brief History of Brazilian Biofuels Legislation*, 35 SYRACUSE J. INT'L. L. & COM. 293 (2008).

Christopher B. Connard, *Sustaining Agriculture: An Examination of Current Legislation Promoting Sustainable Agriculture as an Alternative to Conventional Farming Practices*, 13 PENN ST. ENVTL. L. REV. 125 (2004).

Robert P. Cooper, II, *The European Community's Prodigal Son—The Common Agricultural Policy—Undergoes Reform: Will Multilateral Trading Schemes Fostered by the GATT Blossom or Wither and Die?* 1 COLUM. J. EUR. L. 233 (1995).

Al J. Daniel, Jr., *Agricultural Reform: The European Community, the Uruguay Round, and International Dispute Resolution*, 46 ARK. L. REV. 873 (1994).

Fabian Delcros, *The Legal Status of Agriculture in the World Trade Organization*, 36 J. WORLD TRADE 219 (2002).

Melaku Geboye Desta, *The Bumpy Ride towards the Establishment of "A Fair and Market-oriented Agricultural Trading System" at the WTO: Reflections Following the Cancun Setback*, 8 DRAKE J. AGRIC. L. 489 (2003).

William Diebold, *Recent Development, A Festschrift in Honor of Seymour J. Rubin, Some Second Thoughts*, 10 AM. U. J. INT'L L. & POL'Y 1251 (1995).

Jim Dixon, *Nature Conservation and Trade Distortion: Green Box and Blue Box Farming Subsidies in Europe*, 29 Golden Gate U. L. REV. 415 (1999).

C. Dolan & J. Humphrey, *Governance and Trade in Fresh Vegetables: The Impact of UK Supermarkets on the African Horticultural Industry*, 37 J. DEV. STUD. 175 (2001).

Kim JoDene Donat, *Engineering Akerlof Lemons: Information Asymmetry, Externalities, and Market Intervention in the Genetically Modified Food Market*, 12 MINN. J. GLOBAL TRADE 417 (2003).

James A. Duffield et al., *Ethanol Policy: Past, Present, and Future*, 53 S.D. L. REV. 425 (2008).

Marsha A. Echols, *Food Safety Regulation in the European Union and the United States: Different Cultures, Different Laws*, 4 COLUM. J. EUR. L. 525 (1998).

William S. Eubanks II, *A Rotten System: Subsidizing Environmental Degradation and Poor Public Health with Our Nation's Tax Dollars*, 28 STAN. ENVTL. L.J. 213 (2009).

David Fazzino, *The Meaning and Relevance of Food Security in the Context of Current Globalization Trends*, 19 J. LAND USE & ENVTL. L. 435 (2004).

Miguel Antonio Figueroa, *The GATT and Agriculture: Past, Present, and Future*, 5 KAN. J. L. & PUB. POL'Y 93 (Fall 1995).

Jon G. Filapek, *Agriculture in a World of Comparative Advantage: The Prospects for Farm Trade Liberalization in the Uruguay Round of GATT Negotiations*, 30 HARV. INT'L L.J. 123 (1989).

David Fisher, *From Hand to Mouth, via the Lab and the Legislature: International and Domestic Regulations to Secure the Food Supply*, 40 VAND. J. TRANSNAT'L L. 1127 (2007).

Kent S. Foster & Dean C. Alexander, *The North American Free Trade Agreement and the Agricultural Sector*, 27 CREIGHTON L. REV. 985 (1993–1994).

C.W. Fraisse et al., *AgClimate: A Climate Forecast Information System for Agricultural Risk Management in the Southeastern USA*, 53 COMPUTERS & ELECTRONICS IN AGRIC. 13 (2006).

James N. Giglio, *New Frontier Agricultural Policy: The Commodity Side, 1961–1963*, 61 AGRIC. HIST. 53 (Summer 1987).

Eric Gillman, *Making WTO SPS Dispute Settlement Work: Challenges and Practical Solutions*, 31 NW. J. INT'L L. & BUS. 439 (2011).

William A. Gillon, *The Panel Report in the US–Brazil Cotton Dispute: WTO Subsidy Rules Confront US Agriculture*, 10 DRAKE J. AGRIC. L. 7 (2005).

Kelvin Goertzen, *Leveling the Playing Field*, 3 ASPER REV. INT'L BUS. & TRADE L. 81 (2003).

Carmen G. Gonzalez, *Institutionalizing Inequality: The WTO Agreement on Agriculture, Food Security, and Developing Countries*, 27 COLUM. J. ENVTL. L. 433 (2002).

Carmen G. Gonzalez, *Seasons of Resistance: Sustainable Agriculture and Food Security in Cuba*, 16 TUL. ENVTL. L.J. 685 (2003).

Carmen G. Gonzalez, *Trade Liberalization, Food Security, and the Environment: The Neoliberal Threat to Sustainable Rural Development*, 14 TANSNAT'L L. & CONTEMP. PROBS. 419 (2004).Randy Green, *Part II: Review of Key Substantive Agreements, Panel II C: Agreement on Agriculture, The Uruguay Round Agreement on Agriculture*, 31 LAW & POL'Y INT'L BUS. 819 (2000).

Lakshman D. Guruswamy, *Sustainable Agriculture: Do GMOs Imperil Biosafety?*, 9 IND. J. GLOBAL LEGAL STUD. 461 (2002).

Andy Gutierrez, *Codifying the Past, Erasing the Future*, 4 HASTINGS W.-N.W.J. ENVTL. L. & POL'Y 161 (1998).

Neil D. Hamilton, *Emerging Issues of 21st Century Agricultural Law and Rural Practice*, 12 DRAKE J. AGRIC. L. 79 (2007).

Dale E. Hathaway, *Reforming World Agricultural Policies in Multilateral Negotiations*, 1 TRANSNAT'L L. & CONTEMP. PROBS. 393 (1991).

Liane L. Heggy, *Free Trade Meets US Farm Policy: Life after the Uruguay Round*, 25 LAW & POL'Y INT'L BUS. 1367 (1994).

Vance E. Hendrix, *The Farm Bill of 2002, The WTO, and Poor African Farmers: Can They Co-exist?*, 12 TULSA J. COMP. & INT'L L. 227 (2004).

Mark Murphey Henry et al., *A Call to Farms: Diversify the Fuel Supply*, 53 S.D. L. REV. 515 (2008).

John Herbig, *Technical and Legal Considerations for Bio-fuel*, 2 ENVT'L & ENERGY L. & POL'Y J. 343 (2008).

William Hett, *US Corn and Soybean Subsidies: WTO Litigation and Sustainable Protections*, 17 TRANSNAT'L L. & CONTEMP. PROBS. 775 (2008).

Jimmye S. Hillman, *Agriculture in the Uruguay Round: A United States Perspective*, 28 TULSA L. J. 761 (1993).

David Hosansky, *Regulating Pesticides: Does the New Crackdown Go Far Enough—or Too Far?*, 9 CQ RESEARCHER 665 (Aug. 6, 1999).

David Hosansky, *Farm Subsidies: Do They Favor Large Farming Operations?*, 12 CQ RESEARCHER 444 (May 2002).

Robert Hudec et al., *A Statistical Profile of GATT Dispute Settlement Cases: 1948–1989*, 2 MINN. J. GLOBAL TRADE 1 (1993).

John H. Jackson, *Status of Treaties in Domestic Legal Systems: A Policy Analysis*, 86 AM. J. INT'L L. 310 (1992).

Margaret J. Jennings, *Bioenergy: Fueling the Future*, 12 DRAKE J. AGRIC. L. 205 (2007).

David S. Johanson & William L. Bryant, *Eliminating Phytosanitary Trade Barriers: The Effects of the Uruguay Round Agreements on California Agricultural Exports*, 6 SAN JOAQUIN AGRIC. L. REV. 1 (1996).

Hilary K. Josephs, *Learning from the Developing World*, 14 KAN. J. L. & PUB. POL'Y 231 (Winter 2005).

Tashi Kaul, *The Elimination of Export Subsidies and the Future of Net-Food Importing Developing Countries in the WTO*, 24 FORDHAM INT'L L. J. 383 (2000).

Anthony Paul Kearns, III, *The Right to Food Exists via Customary International Law*, 22 SUFFOLK TRANSNAT'L L. REV. 223 (1998).

Kevin C. Kennedy, *International Trade in Agriculture: Where We've Been, Where We Are, and Where We're Headed*, 10 MSU-DCL J. INT'L L. 1 (2001).

Marc Kleiner, *United States vs. European Union: Transatlantic Debate on Issues Close to Home VI. Export Subsidies*, 10 U. MIAMI INT'L & COMP. L. REV. 129 (2002).

Michelle M. Kundmueller, *The Application of Customary International Law in US Courts: Custom, Convention, or Pseudo-Legislation?* 28 J. LEGIS. 359 (2002).

Jongeun Lee, *Study of the International Food Security Regime: Food Aid to North Korea During the Famine of 1995–2000*, 11 CARDOZO J. INT'L & COMP. L. 1037 (2004).

Aaron N. Lehl, *China's Trade Union System Under the International Covenant on Economic, Social and Cultural Rights: Is China in Compliance with Article 8?*, 21 U. HAW. L. REV. 203 (1999).

Michael Lipsky & Marc A. Thibodeau, *Domestic Food Policy in the United States*, 15 J. HEALTH POL. POL'Y & L. 319 (1990).

J.W. Looney, *GATT and Future Soil Conservation Programs in the United States: Some Lessons from Australia*, 28 TULSA L. J. 673 (1993).

J.W. Looney, *The Changing Focus of Government Regulation of Agriculture in the United States*, 44 MERCER L. REV. 763 (1993).

Michael W. Lore, *Subsidies for Corn-Derived Ethanol May Leave US Thirsty*, 8 SUSTAINABLE DEV. L. & POL'Y 53 (2007).

Kaylan Lytle, *Driving the Market: The Effects on the United States Ethanol Industry if the Foreign Ethanol Tariff is Lifted*, 28 ENERGY L.J. 693 (2007).

Gregory W. MacKenzie, *ICSID Arbitration as a Strategy for Leveling the Playing Field between International Non-Governmental Organizations and Host States*, 19 SYRACUSE J. INT'L L. & COM. 197 (1993).

Ruth MacKenzie & Silvia Francescon, *The Regulation of Genetically Modified Foods in the European Union: An Overview*, 8 N.Y.U. ENVTL. L.J. 530 (2000).

Lyn MacNabb & Robert Weaver, *The General Agreement on Tariffs and Trade (GATT): Has Agriculture Doomed the Uruguay Round?*, 26 LAND & WATER L. REV. 761 (1991).

Dale E. McNiel, *Furthering the Reforms of Agricultural Policies in the Millennium Round*, 9 MINN. J. GLOBAL TRADE 41 (2000).

Sarah Melikian & Addie Haughey, *Sustainable Development Law and Policy*, 8 SUSTAINABLE DEV. L. & POL'Y 57 (2008).

Christopher D. Merrett & Cynthia Struthers, *Globalization and the Future of Rural Communities in the American Midwest*, 12 TRANSNAT'L L. & CONTEMP. PROBS. 34 (2002).

Ellen Messer, *Food Systems and Dietary Perspective: Are Genetically Modified Organisms the Best Way to Ensure Nutritionally Adequate Food?*, 9 IND. J. GLOBAL LEGAL STUD. 65 (2001).

Miguel Montana-Mora, *International Law and International Relations Cheek to Cheek: An International Law/International Relations Perspective on the US/EC Agricultural Export Subsidies Dispute*, 19 N.C. J. INT'L L. & COM. REG. 1 (1993).

Erin Morrow, *Agri-Environmentalism: A Farm Bill for 2007*, 38 TEX. TECH L. REV. 345 (2006).

D. Moyo, *The Future of Food: Elements of Integrated Food Security Strategy for South Africa and Food Security Status in Africa*, 101 AM. SOC'Y INT'L L. PROC. 103 (2007).

Richard Myrus, *From Bretton Woods to Brussels: A Legal Analysis of the Exchange-rate Arrangements of the International Monetary Fund and the European Community*, 62 FORDHAM L. REV. 2095 (1994).

Smita Narula, *The Right to Food: Holding Global Actors Accountable Under International Law*, 44 COLUM. J. TRANSNAT'L L. 691 (2006).

Laura Niada, *Hunger and International Law: The Far-reaching Scope of the Human Right*, 22 CONN. J. INT'L L. 136 (2006).

Kelsey Jae Nunez, *Gridlock on the Road to Renewable Energy Development: A Discussion About the Opportunities and Risks Presented by the Modernization Requirements of the Electricity Transmission Network*, 1 J. BUS. ENTREPRENEURSHIP & L. 137 (2007).

Pablo A. Ormachea, *Agriculture Subsidies and the Free Trade Area of the Americas*, 13 L. & BUS. REV. AM. 139 (Winter 2007).

Tad W. Patzek, *Ethanol from Corn: Clean Renewable Fuel for the Future, or Drain on Our Resources and Pockets*, 7 ENV'T. DEV. & SUSTAINABILITY 319 (2005), *available at* http:// petroleum.berkeley.edu/papers/patzek/PublishedEDS2005. pdf.

Stacey Willemsen Person, *International Trade: Pushing United States Agriculture toward a Greener Future?*, 17 GEO. INT'L ENVTL. L. REV. 307 (2005).

William Petit, *The Free Trade Area of the Americas: Is It Setting the Stage for Significant Change in US Agricultural Subsidy Use?*, 37 TEX. TECH L. REV. 127 (2004).

Jess Phelps, *Much Ado about Decoupling: Evaluating the Environmental Impact of Recent European Union Agricultural Reform*, 31 HARV. ENVTL. L. REV. 279 (2007).

Thomas Richard Poole, *Silly Rabbit, Farm Subsidies Don't Help America*, 31 WM. & MARY ENVTL. L. & POL'Y REV. 183 (2006).

Matthew C. Porterfield, *US Farm Subsidies and the Expiration of the WTO's Peace Clause*, 27 U. PA. J. INT'L ECON. L. 999 (2006).

Stephen J. Powell & Andrew Schmitz, *The Cotton and Sugar Subsidies Decisions: WTO's Dispute Settlement System Rebalances the Agreement on Agriculture*, 10 DRAKE J. AGRIC. L. 287 (2005).

David R. Purnell, *International Trade Update: The GATT and NAFTA*, 73 NEB. L. REV. 211 (1994).

Jesse Ratcliffe, *A Small Step Forward: Environmental Protection Provisions in the 2002 Farm Bill*, 30 ECOLOGY L. Q. 637 (2003).

Alan Charles Raul & Kevin J. Brosch, *Global Trade in Agricultural Products*, 510 PLI/COMM 229 (1989).

D.D. Reidpath & P. Allotey, *Theory and Methods: Infant Mortality Rate as an Indicator of Population Health*, 57 J. EPIDEMIOLOGY & COMMUNITY HEALTH 344 (2003).

Mark Ritchie & Kristin Dawkins, *WTO Food and Agricultural Rules: Sustainable Agriculture and the Human Right to Food*, 9 MINN. J. GLOBAL TRADE 9 (2000).

J.B. Ruhl, *Three Questions for Agriculture about the Environment*, 17 J. LAND USE & ENVTL. L. 395 (2002).

Carlisle F. Runge, *The Assault on Agricultural Protectionism*, 67 FOREIGN AFF. 133 (1988).

Hannah A. Saona, *The Protection of Reproductive Rights Under International Law: The Bush Administration's Policy Shift and China's Family Planning Practices*, 13 PAC. RIM L. & POL'Y J. 229 (2004).

William A. Schabas, *Canada and the Adoption of the Universal Declaration of Human Rights*, 43 McGILL L.J. 403 (1998).

Thomas J. Schoenbaum, *Agricultural Trade Wars: A Threat to the GATT and Global Free Trade*, 24 ST. MARY'S L. J. 1165 (1993).

Nick J. Sciullo, *"This Woman's Work" in a "Man's World": A Feminist Analysis of the Farm Security and Rural Investment Act of 2002*, 28 WHITTIER L. REV. 709 (2006).

Frank A. Seminerio, *A Tale of Two Subsidies: How Federal Support Programs for Ethanol and Biodiesel Can Be Created in Order to Circumvent Fair Trade Challenges Under World Trade Organization Rulings*, 26 PENN. ST. INT'L L. REV. 963 (2008).

Amartya Sen, *Ingredients of Famine Analysis: Availability and Entitlements*, 96 Q.J. ECON. 433 (1981).

Amartya Sen, *World Economy*, 49 NIEMAN REP. 32 (Fall 1995).

Dinah Shelton, *The Duty to Assist Famine Victims*, 70 IOWA L. REV. 1309 (1985).

Louis B. Sohn, *The New International Law: Protection of the Rights of Individuals Rather than States*, 32 AM. U. L. REV. 1 (1982).

Terrence J. Sorg, *Global Hunger, A Doubling Population, and Environmental Degradation: Justifying Radical Changes in US Farm Policy*, 6 IND. INT'L & COMP. L. REV. 680 (1996).

Raci Oriona Spaulding, *Fuel from Vegetables? A Modern Approach to Global Climate Change*, 13 TRANSNAT'L L. & CONTEMP. PROBS. 277 (2003).

Richard H. Steinberg & Timothy E. Josling, *When the Peace Ends: The Vulnerability of EC and US Agricultural Subsidies to WTO Legal Challenge*, 6 J. INT'L ECON L. 369 (2003).

Jeffrey J. Steinle, *The Problem Child of World Trade: Reform School for Agriculture*, 4 MINN. J. GLOBAL TRADE 333 (1995).

Amanda Stokes, *Selling Out the Farm? The Impact of the Farm Security and Rural Investment Act of 2002 on Lending Institutions and the Small Farmer*, 9 N.C. BANKING INST. 243 (2005).

Justin Stole, *The Energy Policy Act of 2005: The Path to Energy Autonomy?*, 33 J. LEGIS. 121 (2006).

Henricus A. Strating, *The GATT Agriculture Dispute: A European Perspective*, 18 N.C.J. INT'L L. & COM. REG. 305 (1993).

J. Dirck Stryker, *US Food Aid Legislation: Its Perspective, the American Farmer or Hungry People; and Its Structure, Purposes and Conclusions*, 30 HOW. L.J. 301 (1987).

Kimberly Stuart & C. Ford Runge, *Agricultural Policy Reform in the United States: An Unfinished Agenda*, 41(1) AUSTL. J. AGRIC. & RES. ECON. 117 (1997).

Cass R. Sunstein, *Social and Economic Rights? Lessons from South Africa* (Univ. of Chicago, Public Law Working Paper No. 12, 2001).

Michael R. Taylor, *The Emerging Merger of Agricultural and Environmental Policy: Building a New Vision for the Future of American Agriculture*, 20 VA. ENVTL. L.J. 169 (2001).

Frank Tenente, *Feeding the World One Seed at a Time: A Practical Alternative for Solving World Hunger*, 5 NW. U. J. INT'L HUM. RTS. 298 (2007).

Karen Terhune, *Reformation of the Food Stamp ACT: Abating Domestic Hunger Means Resisting "Legislative Junk Food"*, 41 CATH. U. L. REV. 421 (1992).

Cody A. Thacker, *Agricultural Trade Liberalization in the Doha Round: The Search for a Modalities Draft*, 33 GA. J. INT'L & COM. L. 721 (2005).

G.I. Tunkin, *Remarks on the Juridical Nature of Customary Norms of International Law*, 49 CALIF. L. REV. 419 (1961).

Jay M. Vogelson, *Food and Agriculture Organization*, 30 INT'L LAW. 425 (1996).

Marie E. Walsh et al., *Agricultural Impacts of Biofuels Production*, 39 J. AGRIC. & APPLIED ECON. 365 (2007).

Nathan R.R. Watson, *Federal Farm Subsidies: A History of Governmental Control, Recent Attempts at a Free Market Approach, the Current Backlash, and Suggestions for Future Action*, 9 DRAKE J. AGRIC. L. 279 (2004).

Joy A. Weber, *Famine Aid to Africa: An International Legal Obligation*, 15 BROOK. J. INT'L L. 369 (1989).

Peter Webster, *Meteorology: Improve Weather Forecasts for the Developing World*, 493 NATURE 17 (2013).

Leslie A. Wheeler, *Government Intervention in World Trade in Wheat*, 1 J. OF WORLD TRADE L. 386 (1967).

Jodi Soyars Windham, *Putting Your Money Where Your Mouth Is: Preserve Food Subsidies, Social Responsibility and America's 2007 Farm Bill*, 31 ENVIRONS ENVTL. L. & POL'Y J. 1 (Fall 2007).

George E.C. York, *Global Foods, Local Tastes and Biotechnology: The New Legal Architecture of International Agriculture Trade*, 7 COLUM. J. EUR. L. 423 (2001).

Linda M. Young, *Options for World Trade Organization Involvement in Food Aid*, 3(1) ESTEY CENTRE J. INT'L L. & TRADE POL'Y (2002).

Ruosi Zhang, *Food Security: Food Trade Regime and Food Aid Regime*, 7 J. INT'L ECON. L. 566 (2004).

World Hunger and International Trade: An Analysis and a Proposal for Action, 84 YALE L.J. 1046 (1975).

International Treaty Instruments

Agreement on Agriculture, art. 13, Apr. 15, 1994, 1867 U.N.T.S. 410.

Agreement on Implementation of Article VI of the GATT 1994, 1868 U.N.T.S. 201, *available at* http://www.wto.org/english/docs_e/legal_e/19-adp.pdf (last visited May 24, 2011).

Agreement on Safeguards, 1869 U.N.T.S. 154, *available at* http://www.wto.org/english/docs_e/legal_e/25-safeg.pdf (last visited May 24, 2011).

Agreement on Subsidies and Countervailing Measures, Apr. 15, 1994, 1867 U.N.T.S. 14, *reprinted in* THE LEGAL TEXTS: THE RESULTS OF THE URUGUAY ROUND OF MULTILATERAL TRADE NEGOTIATIONS 275 (1999).

Agreement on Technical Barriers to Trade, 1868 U.N.T.S. 120, *available at* http://www.wto.org/english/docs_e/legal_e/17-tbt.pdf (last visited May 24, 2011).

Agreement on the Textiles and Clothing, 1868 U.N.T.S. 14, *available at* http://www.wto.org/english/docs_e/legal_e/16-tex.pdf (last visited May 24, 2011).

Agreement on Trade-Related Aspects of Intellectual Property Rights, 1869 U.N.T.S. 299, *available at* http://www.wto.org/english/docs_e/legal_e/27-trips.pdf (last visited May 24, 2011).

Agreement on Trade-Related Investment Measures, 1868 U.N.T.S. 186, *available at* http://www.wto.org/english/docs_e/legal_e/18-trims.pdf (last visited May 24, 2011).

Charter of the Organization of American States, 2 UST. 2394, T.I.A.S. No. 2361, 119 U.N.T.S. 3 (entered into force on Dec. 13, 1951).

Commission Regulation 258/97 (EC).

Convention on the Elimination of All Forms of Discrimination Against Women, Dec. 18, 1979, 1249 U.N.T.S. 13.

Convention on the Rights of the Child, Nov. 20, 1989, UN Doc. A/44/49.

Draft Final Act Embodying the Results of the Uruguay Round of Multilateral Trade Negotiations, GATT Doc. MTN.TNC/W/FA (Dec. 20, 1991).

European Convention for the Protection of Human Rights and Fundamental Freedoms, Nov. 4, 1950, 213 U.N.T.S. 221, Europ. T.s. No. 5 (entered into force on Sept. 3, 1953).

Food Aid Convention 1999, Apr. 13 1999, arts. 7, 8, *available at* http://r0.unctad. org/commodities/agreements/foodaidconvention.pdf.

GATT Ministerial Declaration on the Uruguay Round of Multilateral Trade Negotiations, Sept. 20, 1986, 25 I.L.M. 1623 (1986).

GATT Trade Negotiations Comm., Final Act Embodying the Results of the Uruguay Round of Multilateral Trade Negotiations, MTN/FA (Dec. 15, 1993) (restricted); *President Clinton's Submission to Congress of Documents Concerning Uruguay Round Agreement Dec. 15, 1993*, DAILY REP. FOR EXECUTIVES (BNA) (Dec. 17, 1993).

General Agreement on Tariffs and Trade, Oct. 30, 1947, 61 Stat. A-11, 55 U.N.T.S. 194, *available at* http://www.wto.org/english/docs_e/ legal_e/gatt47_01_e.htm.

General Agreement on Trade in Services, 1869 U.N.T.S. 183, *available at* http:// www.wto.org/english/docs_e/legal_e/26-gats.pdf (last visited May 24, 2011).

Havana Charter, United Nations Conference on Trade and Employment, Mar. 24, 1958, *available at* http://www.worldtradelaw.net/misc/havana.pdf.

International Covenant on Economic, Social and Cultural Rights., Dec. 16, 1966, G.A. Res. 2200 (XXI), 21 UNGAOR Supp. (No. 16) at 50–51, UN Doc. A/6316 (1967).

Statute of the International Court of Justice, art. 38, 59 Stat. 1055, 1060, T.S. No. 993, at 30, 3 Bevans 1153, 1187 (1945), *available at* http://www.icj-cij.org/documents/index.php?p1=4&p2=2&p3=0#CHAPTER_II (last visited Feb. 28, 2013).

Statute of the International Law Commission, art. 24, G.A. Res. 174 (II) (Nov. 21, 1947).

Treaty Establishing the European Community, March 25, 1957, *available at* http:// www.hri.org/docs/Rome57/ (last visited Dec. 16, 2010).

UNICEF, *Convention on the Rights of the Child*, http://www.unicef.org/crc/ (last visited Jan. 12, 2013).

United Nations Millennium Declaration, G.A. Res. 55.2, UN Doc. A/RES/55/2 (Sept. 18, 2000).

Universal Declaration of Human Rights, G.A. Res. 217 (III) A, UN Doc. A/ Res/217(III) (Dec. 10, 1948).

WTO Agreement on the Application of Sanitary and Phytosanitary Measures (SPS Agreement), Apr. 15, 1994, 1867 U.N.T.S. 493, art. 1.1, *available at* http://www.wto.org/english/tratop_e/sps_e/spsagr_e.htm.

UN Publications

General Assembly, Ways and Means for Making the Evidence of Customary International Law More Readily Available, G.A. Res. 487 (V) (Dec. 12, 1950), *available at* http://untreaty.un.org/ilc/guide/1_4.htm.

Manley O. Hudson, *Article 24 of the Statute of the International Law Commission*, UN Doc. A/CN.4/16 and Add.1 (Working Paper 1950), *available at* http://untreaty.un.org/ilc/documentation/english/a_cn4_16.pdf.

Human Rights Council Res. 7/14, The Right to Food, ¶ 3 (Mar. 27, 2008).

Office of the UN High Comm'r for Human Rights, *Human Rights Bodies—General Comments*, http://www2.ohchr.org/english/bodies/treaty/comments.htm (last visited Jan. 13, 2013).

Office of the UN High Comm'r for Human Rights, *Special Rapporteur on the Right to Food*, www2.ohchr.org/English/issues/food/index.htm (last visited Feb. 28, 2013).

United Nations, *2008 AAPAM Award for Innovative Management*, http://unpan1.un.org/intradoc/groups/public/documents/aapam/unpan032707.pdf (last visited Jan. 13, 2013).

United Nations, *As World Passes 7 Billion Milestone, UN Urges Action to Meet Key Challenges*, UN NEWS CENTER (October 31, 2011), http://www.un.org/apps/news/story.asp?NewsID=40257&Cr=population&Cr1=.

United Nations, *At UN Food Summit, Ban Lays Out Steps to Save Billions from Hunger*, UN NEWS CTR. (Nov. 16, 2009), http://www.un.org/apps/news/story.asp?NewsID=32959#.UPInxyeRSSo.

United Nations, *Background Information, Functions and Powers of the General Assembly*, UNITED NATIONS, http://www.un.org/ga/61/background/background.shtml (last visited Dec. 3, 2008).

United Nations, *Global Issues—Governance*, http://www.un.org/en/globalissues/governance/ (last visited Jan. 16, 2013).

UNITED NATIONS, HIGH-LEVEL TASK FORCE ON THE GLOBAL FOOD SECURITY CRISIS, OUTCOMES AND ACTIONS FOR GLOBAL FOOD SECURITY, EXCERPTS FROM "COMPREHENSIVE FRAMEWORK FOR ACTION" 3 (July 2008), *available at* http://www.un.org/issues/food/taskforce/pdf/OutcomesAndActionsBooklet_v9.pdf.

United Nations, *Millennium Goals: Background*, UNITED NATIONS, http://www.un.org/millenniumgoals/bkgd.shtml (last visited Jan. 13, 2013).

United Nations, *UN at a Glance*, http://www.un.org/en/aboutun/index.shtml (last visited Feb. 6, 2011).

UN Comm'n on Sustainable Dev. (CSD-17), Contribution of Mr. Olivier De Schutter, Special Rapporteur on the Right to Food, 17th Sess.,

May 4–May 15, 2009, 2, *available at* http://www.srfood.org/images/stories/pdf/otherdocuments/19-srrtfsubmissioncsd-01–05–09–1.pdf.

UN Data, *Population Growth Rate*, http://data.un.org/Data.aspx?q=world+population&d=PopDiv&f=variableID%3a47%3bcrID%3a900 (last updated Aug. 25, 2011).

UN Data, *Total Fertility Rate*, http://data.un.org/Data.aspx?q=fertility+rate+&d=GenderStat&f=inID%3a14 (last updated Mar. 21, 2008).

UN Data, *Total Population*, http://data.un.org/Data.aspx?q=world+population&d=PopDiv&f=variableID%3a12%3bcrID%3a900 (last updated September 28, 2007).

UN Dept. of Econ. and Soc. Affairs, Strengthening Efforts to Eradicate Poverty and Hunger 107 (2007), *available at* http://www.un.org/en/ecosoc/docs/pdfs/07–49285-ecosoc-book-2007.pdf.

UN Depart. of Econ. and Soc. Affairs, World Population Prospects: The 2010—Infant Mortality Rate, UN Doc. POP/DB/WPP/Rev.2010/01/F06–1 (2011).

UN Dev. Prog., *The Millennium*, http://www.undp.org/mdg/goal1.shtml (last visited Feb. 28, 2013).

UN Econ. & Soc. Comm'n for Asia & Pacific, What Is Good Governance, *available at* http://www.unescap.org/pdd/prs/ProjectActivities/Ongoing/gg/governance.pdf (last visited Feb. 28, 2013).

UN Econ. & Soc. Council, UN Comm. on Econ., Soc., & Cultural Rights, General Comment No. 12, The Right to Adequate Food, 20th Sess., Apr. 26–May 14, 1999, para. 14, UN Doc. E/C. 12/1999/5 (May 12, 1999).

United Nations Environment Programme, Ch. 14 (G) Promoting Sustainable Agriculture and Rural Development: Conservation and Sustainable Utilization of Plant Genetic Resources and for Food and Sustainable Agriculture, ¶¶ 14.54–14.55, *available at* http://www.unep.org/Documents.Multilingual/Default.asp?DocumentID=52&ArticleID=62 (last visited March 17, 2014).

UNESCO, *Primary Education*, http://portal.unesco.org/education/en/ev.php-URL_ID=30870&URL_DO=DO_TOPIC&URL_SECTION=201.html (last visited Jan. 18, 2013).

UN Special Rapporteur on the Right to Food, Political Will Needed to Tackle Food Crisis and Restructure Agriculture, Warns UN Right to Food Expert (Sept. 18, 2009), *available at* http://www.srfood.org/images/stories/pdf/otherdocuments/srrtf_pressrelease_hrc_18sept09_web.pdf.

UN World Food Program, Mission Statement, http://www.wfp.org/about/mission-statement (last visited Feb. 8, 2013).

UNICEF, A Better Life for Every Child: A Summary of the United Nations Convention on the Rights of the Child, *available at* http://childrenandyouthprogramme.info/pdfs/pdfs_uncrc/uncrc_summary_version.pdf (last visited Jan. 12, 2013).

World Food Summit, Nov. 13–17, 1996, *Technical Background Documents for the World Food Summit*, ch. 13, ¶ 3.14.

UN Special Rapporteur on the Right to Food Reports

Olivier De Schutter, Guidance in a Time of Crisis: IAASTD and the Human Right to Food 4 (Feb. 25, 2009), *available at* http://www.srfood.org/images/stories/pdf/otherdocuments/18-iaastd-rtf-25–2-2009.pdf.

Olivier De Schutter, Human Rights Council, Rep. of Special Rapporteur on the Right to Food, Promotion and Protection of All Human Rights, Civil, Political, Economic, Social and Cultural Rights, Including the Right to Development, UN Doc. A/HRC/12/31 (July 21, 2009), *available at* http://www.srfood.org/images/stories/pdf/officialreports/srrtf_second%20global%20food%20crisis%20report_a-hrc-12–31.pdf.

Olivier De Schutter, Large-Scale Land Acquisitions and Leases: A Set of Core Principles and Measures to Address the Human Rights Challenge (June 11, 2009), *available at* http://www.oecd.org/site/swacmali2010/44031283.pdf.

Olivier De Schutter, Mandate of the Special Rapporteur on the Right to Food, A Human Rights Perspective of the Comprehensive Framework for Action: Towards a Unified UN Response to the Global Food Crisis 4 (June 23, 2008), *available at* http://www.srfood.org/images/stories/pdf/otherdocuments/4-srrtfcfaanalysis23–6-08.pdf.

Olivier De Schutter, Mandate of the Special Rapporteur on the Right to Food, Background Note: Analysis of the World Food Crisis by the UN Special Rapporteur on the Right to Food 5 (May 2, 2008), *available at* http://www.srfood.org/images/stories/pdf/otherdocuments/1-srrtfnoteglobalfoodcrisis-2–5-08.pdf.

Olivier De Schutter, Mandate of the Special Rapporteur on the Right to Food: Integrating the Right to Adequate Food in Development Cooperation (2008), *available at* http://www.srfood.org/images/stories/pdf/otherdocuments/6-rtfdevelopmentcooperation-10–11–08.pdf.

Olivier De Schutter, Mandate of the Special Rapporteur on the Right to Food, The Role of Development Cooperation and Food Aid in Realizing the Right to Adequate Food: Moving from Charity to Obligation, background document to UN Doc. A/HRC/10/005 (Mar. 2009), *available at* http://www.srfood.org/images/stories/pdf/otherdocuments/8-srrtfdevelopmentfoodaid-1–09.pdf.

Olivier De Schutter, Mission to the World Trade Organization (Mar. 9, 2009), *available at* http://www.carnegieendowment.org/files/Summary_of%20report%20of%20the%20Special%20Rapporteur%20on%20the%20right%20to%20food.pdf.

Olivier De Schutter, *The Right to Food as a Human Right*, http://www.srfood.org/index.php/en/right-to-food (last visited Jan. 13, 2013).

Olivier De Schutter, The Right to Food, Seed Policies and The Right to Food: Enhancing Agrobiodiversity and Encouraging Innovation, UN Doc. A/64/170 (July 23, 2009), *available at* http://www.srfood.org/images/stories/pdf/officialreports/20091021_report-ga64_seed-policies-and-the-right-to-food_en.pdf.

FAO Publications

Nasredin Elamin & Hansdeep Khaira, Tariff Escalation in Agricultural Commodity Markets, *available at* http://www.fao.org/DOCREP/006/Y5117E/y5117e0e.htm (last visited June 23, 2011).

Food & Agric. Org. of the UN, Briefing Paper: Hunger on the Rise: Soaring Prices Add 75 Million People to Global Hunger Rolls (Sept. 17, 2008), *available at* http://www.fao.org/newsroom/common/ecg/1000923/en/hungerfigs.pdf.

Food & Agric. Org. of the UN, *Cutting Food Waste to Feed the World*, Food & Agric. Org. of the UN (May 21, 2011), http://www.fao.org/news/story/en/item/74192/icode/.

Food & Agric. Org. of the UN, FAO Food Price Index (Jan. 10, 2013), http://www.fao.org/worldfoodsituation/wfs-home/foodpricesindex/en/.

Food & Agric. Org. of the UN, FAO Papers on Selected Issues Relating to the WTO Negotiations on Agriculture, *available at* ftp://ftp.fao.org/docrep/fao/004/Y3733E/Y3733E00.pdf (last visited Jan. 24, 2013).

Food & Agric. Org. of the UN, Food Aid and Food Security: Past Performance and Future Potential (1985).

Food & Agric. Org. of the UN, Legislate for the Right to Food (2007), *available at* http://www.fao.org/righttofood/wfd/pdf2007/how_legislate_eng.pdf.

Food & Agric. Org. of the UN, Recognition of the Right to Food at the National Level, IGWG/2/INF/1 (Feb. 2004).

Food & Agric. Org. of the UN, The Right to Food Guidelines, Information Papers and Case Studies 72 (2006), *available at* http://www.fao.org/docs/eims/upload/214344/RtFG_Eng_draft_03.pdf.Food & Agric. Org. of the UN, *The Rome Declaration on World Food Security*, Food & Agric. Org. of the UN (1996), http://www.fao.org/docrep/003/w3613e/w3613e00.HTM.

UN Food & Agric. Org., Voluntary Guidelines to Support the Progressive Realization of the Right to Adequate Food in the Context of National Food Security, Annex 1, 16, FAO Doc. No. CL 127/10-Sup.1 (Sep. 23, 2004).

Food & Agric. Org. of the UN, What Is Right to Food? (2007), *available at* http://www.fao.org/righttofood/wfd/pdf2007/what_is_rtf_en.pdf.

Food & Agric. Org. of the UN, Women and Green Revolution, *available at* http://www.fao.org/focus/e/women/green-e.htm (last visited Feb. 22, 2009).

Food & Agric. Org. of the UN, *World Food Summit*, Food & Agric. Org. of the UN (1996), http://www.fao.org/WFS/index_en.htm.

Food & Agric. Policy Research Inst. (FAPRI), Analysis of the 2003 CAP Reform Agreement (Sept. 2003), *available at* http://www.fapri.missouri.edu/outreach/publications/2003/FAPRI_Staff_Report_02_03.pdf. The Right to Food Resolution, A/RES/57/226 (2003), *available at* http://www.fao.org/righttofood/KC/downloads/vl/docs/AH361_en.pdf.WTO Publications

World Trade Org., DOHA Development Agenda: Negotiations, Documents from the Negotiating Chairs (April 21, 2011), *available at* http://www.wto.org/english/tratop_e/dda_e/chair_texts11_e/chair_texts11_e.htm.

World Trade Org., Ministerial Declaration of 14 November 2001, 13–14, WT/MIN(01)/DEC/1, 41 I.L.M. 746 (2002).

World Trade Org., *Sanitary and Phytosanitary Measures: Introduction—Understanding the WTO Agreement on Sanitary and Phytosanitary Measures* (May 1998), http://www.wto.org/english/tratop_e/sps_e/spsund_e.htm.

World Trade Org., The WTO and Developing Countries, Tariff Escalation, *available at* http://www.inquit.com/iqebooks/WTODC/Webversion/uruguay/four.htm (last visited June 23, 2011).

World Trade Org., *Understanding the WTO-Agriculture: Fairer Markets for Farmers*, http://www.wto.org/english/thewto_e/whatis_e/tif_e/agrm3_e.htm (last visited Sept. 18, 2010).

WTO General Council, Lamy: Members Continue to Explore Opportunities for Doha Progress (May 2, 2012), http://www.wto.org/english/news_e/news12_e/gc_rpt_01may12_e.htm.

World Bank Publications

World Bank, *Education for All (EFA)*, http://web.worldbank.org/WBSITE/EXTERNAL/TOPICS/EXTEDUCATION/0,contentMDK:20374062~menuPK:540090~pagePK:148956~piPK:216618~theSitePK:282386,00.html (last visited Jan. 18, 2013).

World Bank, *Population, Total*, WORLD BANK, http://data.worldbank.org/indicator/SP.POP.TOTL (last visited Jan. 14, 2013).

EU Publications

Assembly of European Regions, *European Commission Communication on the CAP towards 2020: Providing Rural Areas with Tools to Achieve Excellence!* (Nov. 19, 2010), *available at* http://www.aer.eu/news/2010/2010111901.html.

Europa, *Agenda 2000—A CAP for the Future*, *available at* http://ec.europa.eu/agriculture/publi/review99/08_09_en.pdf (last visited Dec. 30, 2010).

Europa, *CAP Reform: EU Agriculture Ministers Adopt Groundbreaking Sugar Reform*, *available at* http://europa.eu/rapid/pressReleasesAction.do?reference=IP/06/194&format=HTML&aged=0&language=EN&guiLanguage=en (Reference: IP/06/194 Date: 21/02/2006).

EUROPA, HEALTH CHECK OF THE CAP (May 20, 2008), *available at* http://ec.europa.eu/agriculture/healthcheck/guide_en.pdf.

Europa, *The History of European Union*, http://europa.eu/abc/history/index_en.htm (last visited Dec. 15, 2010).

European Comm'n, *Agenda 2000: Strengthening the Union and Preparing the 2004 Enlargement*, http://ec.europa.eu/agenda2000/index_en.htm (last visited Dec. 30, 2010).

European Comm'n, *Agricultural and Rural Development: A History of Successful Change*, http://ec.europa.eu/agriculture/capexplained/change/index_en.htm (last visited Dec. 31, 2010).

European Comm'n, *Commission Communication on the CAP towards 2020*, http://ec.europa.eu/agriculture/cap-post-2013/communication/index_en.htm (last visited Jan. 1, 2011).

European Comm'n, *"Health Check" of the Common Agricultural Policy*, http://ec.europa.eu/agriculture/healthcheck/index_en.htm (last visited Dec. 31, 2010).

EUROPEAN COMM'N, *Stop Food Waste*, http://ec.europa.eu/food/food/sustainability/index_en.htm (last visited Jan. 10, 2013).

EUROPEAN COMM'N, THE CAP REFORM, ACCOMPLISHING A SUSTAINABLE AGRICULTURAL MODEL FOR EUROPE THROUGH THE REFORMED CAP—THE TOBACCO, OLIVE OIL, COTTON AND SUGAR SECTORS, *available at* http://ec.europa.eu/agriculture/capreform/com554/index_en.htm (last visited Dec. 31, 2010).

EUROPEAN COMM'N AGRICULTURE & RURAL DEV., AGRICULTURAL POLICY PERSPECTIVES BRIEFS, THE CAP IN PERSPECTIVE: FROM MARKET INTERVENTION TO POLICY INNOVATION (Jan. 2011), *available at* http://ec.europa.eu/agriculture/publi/app-briefs/01_en.pdf.

EUR. UNION COMMITTEE, THE FUTURE FINANCING OF THE COMMON AGRICULTURAL POLICY, 2005–06, H.L. 7-I (U.K.).

US Laws and Regulations

Agricultural Act of 1970, Pub. L. No. 91–524, 84 Stat. 1358.

Agricultural Adjustment Act of 1933, ch. 25, 48 Stat. 31, 37 (1933).

Agricultural Adjustment Act of 1933, ch. 25, 48 Stat. 31 (1933) (current version at 7 USC. §§ 601–626 (2006)).

Agricultural Marketing Agreement Act of 1937, ch. 296, 50 Stat. 246 (1937) (current version at 7 USC. scattered from §§ 601 to 673 (2006)).

Farm Security and Rural Investment Act of 2002, Pub. L. No. 107–171, 116 Stat. 134 (2002).

Federal Agriculture and Improvement and Reform Act of 1996, Pub. L. No. 104–127, §§ 111–113(b), 110 Stat. 888 (1996).

Food, Agriculture, Conservation, and Trade Act of 1990, Pub. L. No. 101–624, §§ 2301–2370, 104 Stat. 3359 (1990).

Food, Agriculture, Conservation, and Trade Act Amendments of 1991, Pub. L. No. 102–237, 105 Stat. 1886 (1991).

Food, Conservation, and Energy Act of 2008, Pub. L. 110–234, 122 Stat. 923 (2008).

Food Security Act of 1985, Pub. L. No. 99–198, 99 Stat 1354 (1985).

Proposition 37, California (Nov. 2012), *available at* http://ballotpedia.org/wiki/index.php/Text_of_California_Proposition_37 (November_2012).

Soil Conservation and Domestic Allotment Act, amended by ch. 104, §§ 7, 8, 49 Stat. 1148 (1936) (current version at 16 USC. §§ 590a-590q (2006)).

Wickard v. Filburn, 317 US 111, 124–25 (1942).

US Government Publications

USAID, *Capacity Building and Health Systems Strengthening*, http://www.healthsystems2020.org/section/where_we_work/senegal/capacitybuilding (last visited Feb. 28, 2013).

US Census Bureau, *International Data Base*, http://www.census.gov/population/international/data/idb/worldpopgraph.php (last updated June 2011).

US Dep't of Agric., Agric. Resources and Envtl. Indicators 2000; Jeffrey A. Zinn, Cong. Research Serv., Issue Brief IB96030, Soil & Water Conservation Issues (2000).

US Dept. of Agric., *Direct and Counter-cyclical Payment Program* (March 2006), *available at* http://future.aae.wisc.edu/publications/farm_bill/dcp06.pdf.

US Dep't of Agric., *Fifty Years of US Food Aid and Its Role in Reducing World Hunger*, http://www.ers.usda.gov/AmberWaves/September04/Features/usfoodaid.htm (last visited Feb. 13, 2009).

US Dept. of Agric., Food and Agricultural Policy Research Institute. Elisabeth Rosenthal, *Rush to Use Crops as Fuel Raises Food Prices and Hunger Fears*, N.Y. Times, Apr. 6, 2011, at A1, *available at* http://www.nytimes.com/2011/04/07/science/earth/07cassava.html?_r=0.

US Dep't of Agric., *Food and Nutrition*, US Dep't of Agric. http://www.usda.gov/wps/portal/usda/usdahome?navid=FOOD_NUTRITION&navtype=SU (last visited Jan. 13, 2013).

US Dept. of Agric., *Marketing Assistance Loans and Loan Deficiency Payments*, http://www.usda.gov/documents/Marketing_Assistance_Loans_and_Loan_Deficiency_Payments.pdf (last visited Jan. 30, 2011).

US Department of State, Fact Sheet: Frequently Asked Questions about Biotechnology (Jan. 22, 2001), *available at* http:// www.state.gov/e/eb/rls/fs/1142.htm.

US Dept. of State & Bureau of Int'l Info. Programs, *US Food Aid: Reducing World Hunger*, 12 eJournal USA 1 (September 2007), *available at* http://www.america.gov/media/pdf/ejs/ej0907.pdf#popup.

US Food & Drug Admin., Guidance for Industry: Voluntary Labeling Indicating Whether Foods Have or Have Not Been Developed Using Bioengineering; Draft Guidance, http://www.fda.gov/Food/GuidanceComplianceRegulatoryInformation/GuidanceDocuments/FoodLabelingNutrition/ucm059098.htm (last visited Feb. 9, 2013).

US GEN. ACCOUNTING OFFICE, FOREIGN ASSISTANCE: NORTH KOREA RESTRICTS FOOD AID MONITORING, GAO/ NSIAD-00–35 (Oct. 1999).
US GOV'T ACCOUNTABILITY OFFICE, GAO/NSIAD-95–35, FOOD AID-PRIVATE VOLUNTARY ORGANIZATIONS' ROLE IN DISTRIBUTING FOOD AID (Nov. 1994).

Constitutions of the Countries of the World

AFG. CONST., Jan. 4, 2004, art. 23.
KUSHTETUTA E REPUBLIKËS SË SHQIPËRISË [CONSTITUTION] Oct. 21, 1998, pt. II, ch. II, art. 21 (Alb.).
ALG. CONST., Sept. 8, 1963.
CONSTITUCIÓ DEL PRINCIPAT D'ANDORRA [CONSTITUTION] Feb. 2, 1993, tit. II, ch. III, art. 8.1.
CONSTITUIÇÃO DA RÉPUBLICA DE ANGOLA [CONSTITUTION] Jan. 21, 2010, art. 22.
ANT. & BARB. CONST. July 31, 1981, ch. II, art. 4.
CONSTITUCIÓN NACIONAL [CONST. NAC.] May 1, 1853 (Arg.).
ARM. CONST. July 5, 1995, ch. II, art. 15.
AUSTRALIAN CONSTITUTION Jan. 1, 1901.
BUNDES-VERFASSUNGSGESETZ [B-VG] [CONSTITUTION] BGBl No. 1/1930, *as last amended by* Bundesverfassungsgesetz [BVG] BGBl I No. 2/2008 (Austria).
AZƏRBAYCAN RESPUBLIKASININ KONSTITUSIYASI [CONSTITUTION] Nov. 12, 1995, ch. III, art. 27 I (Azer.).
BAH. CONST. June 20, 1973, ch. III, art. 16.
BAHR. CONST. Feb. 14, 2002, ch. II, art. 15(b).B.
BANGL. CONST. Dec. 4, 1972, pt. III, art. 32.
BARB. CONST. Nov. 22, 1966, ch. III, art. 12.
BELR. CONST. Mar. 15, 1994, § II, art. 21.
1994 LA CONST. tit. II, art. 21 (Belg.).
BELIZE CONST. Sept. 21, 1981, pt. II, art. 4.
BENIN CONST. Dec. 10, 1990, tit. II, art. 15.
BHUTAN CONST. July 18, 2008.
CONSTITUCIÓN DE 2009 DE LA REPÚBLICA DEL BOLIVIA [CONSTITUTION] Feb. 7, 2009, art. 16.
USTAV BOSNE I HERCEGOVINE [CONSTITUTION] Nov. 21, 1995, annex 4, art. II.3.a.
BOTS. CONST. Mar. 1995, ch. II, art. 3.
CONSTITUIÇÃO FEDERAL [C.F.] [CONSTITUTION] tit. II, ch. I, art. 5 (Braz.).
BRUNEI CONST.
BULG. CONST. July 12, 1991, ch. II, art. 28.
BURK FASO CONST. June 2, 1991, tit. I, ch. I, art. 2.
BURUNDI CONST. Oct. 20, 2004, tit. II, ch. 1. art. 24.
CAMBODIA CONST. Sept. 21, 1993, ch. III, art. 32.
CAMEROON CONST. June 2, 1972.
CAN CONST., pt. 1, art. 7.

CONSTITUIÇÃO DA REPÚBLICA DE CABO VERDE [CONSTITUTION] May 3, 2010, pt. II, tit. II, art. 26 (Cape Verde).

CONSTITUTION DE LA RÉPUBLIQUE CENTRAFRICAINE Dec. 5, 2004, tit. I, art. 3, para. 1 (Cent. Afr. Rep.).

CHAD CONST. Mar. 31, 1996, tit. II, ch. 1, art. 17.

CONSTITUCIÓN POLÍTICA DE LA REPÚBLICA DE CHILE [C.P.], ch. III, art. 3. § 1.

XIANFA [CONSTITUTION], ch. II, art. 45 (2004) (China).

CONSTITUCIÓN POLÍTICA DE COLOMBIA [C.P.], tit. II, ch. I, art. 11.

COMOROS CONST. Dec. 31, 2001 (2001), pmbl.

CONGO CONST. Jan. 20, 2002, tit. II, art. 16.

COOK ISLANDS CONST., pt. IV.A., art. 64(1)(a).

COSTA RICA CONST. Nov. 7, 1949, tit. IV, art. 21, ¶ 1.

CÔTE D'IVOIRE CONST. July 24, 2000, tit. I, art. 2.

CROAT. CONST. Dec. 22, 1990, tit. III, ch. III, art. 21.

CONSTITUCIÓN POLÍTICA DE LA REPÚBLICA DE CUBA Feb. 15, 1976, ch. I, art. 9.

CYPRUS CONST., Attach. 5 Catalogue of Human Rights and Fundamental Freedoms, art. 1.

'USTAVA 'ER. [CONSTITUTION] (Czech Rep.), The Charter of Fundamental Rights and Basic Freedoms, 1992 (*as amended to* 1998), ch. II, div. I, art. 6.

DEN. CONST. Aug. 1, 2009.

DJIB. CONST. Sept. 15, 1992, tit. II, art. 10.

DOMINICA CONST. Nov. 3, 1978, ch. I, § 2.

DOM. REP. CONST. (2002), tit. II, § I, art. 15.

EAST TIMOR CONST., pt. II, tit. II, art. 29.(1)(2).

ECUADOR CONST. Oct. 20, 2008, tit. III, ch. II, art.23.

CONSTITUTION OF THE ARAB REPUBLIC OF EGYPT, 11 Sept. 1971, *as amended*, May 22, 1980, May 25, 2005, March 26, 2007.

EL SAL. CONST. Dec. 15, 1983, tit. II, ch. I, art. 2.

EQ. GUINEA CONST. Nov. 17, 1991, tit. I, art. 13.

ERI. CONST. May 23, 1997.

EESTI VABARIIGI PÕHISEADUS [CONSTITUTION] June 28, 1992, ch. II, art. 16.

ETH. CONST. Dec. 8, 1994, ch. III, pt. I, art. 14.

FIJI CONST., ch. 4, art. 22.

FIN. CONST. (2000), ch. II, § 7.

1958 CONST. (Fr.).

GABON CONST. Mar. 26, 1991.

GAM. CONST. Aug. 8, 1996, ch. IV, art. 18.

GEOR. CONST. Aug. 24, 1995, ch. II, art. 15.

GRUNDGESETZ FÜR DIE BUNDESREPUBLIK DEUTSCHLAND [GRUNDGESETZ] [GG] [CONSTITUTION], May 23, 1949, BGBl. I, ch. I, art. 2(2) (Ger.).

GHANA CONST. May 8, 1992, ch. V, art. 13.

1975 SYNTAGMA [SYN.] [CONSTITUTION], pt. II, art. 5.1 (Greece).

GREN. CONST., ch. I, § 2.

GUAT. CONST., tit. I, ch. I, art. 2.

GUINEA CONST., tit. II, art. 6.

GUINEA-BISSAU CONST., tit. II, art. 32.1.

GUY. CONST., pt. I, chap. III, art. 40(1).

HAITI CONST., ch. II, § A, art. 19.

HOND. CONST., tit. III, ch. I, art. 61.

A MAGYAR KÖZTÁRSASÁG ALKOTMÁNYA [CONSTITUTION OF THE REPUBLIC OF HUNGARY], ch. XII, art. 54 (1), § (1)(g).

ICE. CONST., ch. VII, art. 76(1).

INDIA CONST. pt. III, art. 21, *amended by* The Constitution (Eightieth Amendment) Act, 2000.

INDON. CONST., ch. XA, art. 28A.

QANUNI ASSASSI JUMHURII ISLAMAI IRAN [THE CONSTITUTION OF THE ISLAMIC REPUBLIC OF IRAN], ch. I, art. 3, § 12[1980].

IRAQ. CONST. (interim, 2004), § 2, ch. I, art. 15.

Basic Laws (Isr.), *translated and reprinted in* 9 CONSTITUTIONS OF THE COUNTRIES OF THE WORLD: ISRAEL (Albert P. Blaustein & Gisbert H. Flanz eds., Susan Hattis Rolef trans., 1994).

Basic Law: Human Dignity and Liberty, 1992, § 2 (Isr.).

Art. 117(3) COSTITUZIONE [COST.] (It.).

JAM. CONST., ch. III, art. 13.

NIHONKOKU KENPŌ [KENPŌ] [CONSTITUTION], ch. III, art. 13 (Japan).

JORDAN CONST.

KAZ. CONST., § II, art. 15.1.

CONSTITUTION, ch. V., art. 12 (1992) (Kenya).

KIRIBATI CONST., ch. II, art. 3.

DPRK CONST., pt. II, art. 25 (N. Korea).

DAEHANMINKUK HUNBEOB [HUNBEOB] [CONSTITUTION], ch. II, art. 4 (S. Kor.).

KOSOVO CONST., ch. II, art. 25.

KUWAIT CONST.

KYRG, CONST., ch. II, § 2, art. 16(2).

LAOS CONST., ch. I, art. 4.

LAT. CONST., ch. VIII, art. 93.

LEB. CONST.

LESOTHO CONST., ch. II, art. 27.

LIBER. CONST., ch. III, art. 11.

LIBYA CONST. PROCLAMATION (1969).

LIECH. CONST., ch. II, art. 10.

LITH. CONST., ch. II, art. 19.

LUX. CONST., ch. II, art. 23.

MACED. CONST., ch. II, art. 10.

MADAG. CONST.

MALAWI CONST., ch. IV, art. 16.

MALAY. CONST., 9th sched., pt. 2, art. 5.

MALDIVES CONST., ch. II, art. 15(c).

MALI CONST., tit. I, art. 1.

MALTA CONST., ch. IV, art. 33(a).

MARSH. IS. CONST.

MAURITANIA CONST.

MAURITIUS CONST. ch. II, art. 4.

CONSTITUCIÓN POLÍTICA DE LOS ESTADOS UNIDOS MEXICANOS [C.P] [CONSTITUTION] art. 4 (Mex.).

Alfredo Acedo, *Mexican Constitution Now Recognizes Right to Food*, Am. Prog. (Sept. 24, 2011), http://www.cipamericas.org/archives/5432; UN News Center, *UN Expert Welcomes Mexico's Move to Recognize Food as Constitutional Right*, UN NEWS CTR. (Oct. 13, 2011), http://www.un.org/apps/news/story. asp?NewsID=40039#.UPGRrCeRSSo.

MICRO. CONST., art. IV, § 3.

MOLD. CONST., tit. II, ch. II, art. 37.

MONACO CONST.

MONG. CONST., ch. II, art. 16.

MONTE CONST., art. 21.

MOROCCO CONST.

MOZAM. CONST., pt. 1, ch. IV, art. 70.

MYAN. CONST.

NAMIB. CONST., ch. III, art. 6.

NAURU CONST., pt. II, art. 3.

NEPAL CONST., art. 18(3).

GRONDWET VOOR HET KONINKRIJK DER NEDERLANDEN [Gw.] [CONSTITUTION] ch. I, art. 22 (Neth.).

N.Z. CONST.

CONSTITUCIÓN POLÍTICA DE LA REPÚBLICA DE NICARAGUA [CN.], tit. IV, ch. I, art. 24.

NIGER CONST., tit. II, art. 11.

CONSTITUTION OF NIGERIA (1999), ch. II, art. 16, § 2(d).

NIUE CONST.

NOR. CONST.

OMAN CONST., ch. II, art. 12, paras. 4–5.

PAKISTAN CONST., pt. II, ch. 1, art. 9.

PALAU CONST., art. IV, § 6.

PAN. CONST., tit. III, ch. VI, art. 110(1).

PAPUA NEW GUINEA CONST., art. 35.

PARAGUAY CONST., ch. I, § 1, art. 4.

PERU CONST., §1, ch. I, art. 2.1.

CONST. (1987), § 1 (Phil.).

POL. CONST., ch. II, art. 38.

PORT. CONST., pt. I, tit. II, ch. I, art. 24.

QATAR CONST.

ROM. CONST., tit. II, ch. II, art. 22.

Konstitutsiia Rossiiskoi Federatsii [Konst. RF] [Constitution], § 1, ch. II., art. 20 (Russ.).

Rwanda Const., tit. II, ch. I, art. 12.

Samoa Const., pt. II, art. 5.

Gisbert H. Flanz, *San Marino, in* 16 Constitutions of the Countries of the World (Albert P. Blaustein & Gisbert H. Flanz eds., 1990).

Sao Tome Principe Const., pt. II, tit. II, art. 21.

Saudi Arabia Const., ch. V, art. 27.

Sen. Const., tit. II, art. 7.

Serb. & Mont. Const., pt. 2, art. 24.S.

Sey. Const. pmbl.

Sierra Leone Const. (1991, reinstated 1996), ch. II, art. 7, § 1(d).

Sing. Const., pt. IV, art. 9.

Slovk. Const., ch. 2, § 2, art. 15.

Slovn. Const., ch. II, art. 17.

Solom. Is. Const., ch. II, art. 4.

Somal. Const., ch. II, art. 25.

Somaliland Const., ch. I, pt. III, art. 24.

S. Afr. Const. 1996, tit. I, ch. II, § 1, art. 15.

Southern Sudan Const., pt. 2, art. 15.

Constitución Española, B.O.E. [Constitution] Dec. 29, 1978, ch. III, art. 43 (Spain).

Sri Lanka Const.

St. Kitts & Nevis Const., ch. II, art. 4.

St. Lucia Const., ch. I, sec. 1.

St. Vincent Const., ch. I, art. 1.

Sudan Const., ch. II, art. 10(1).

Surin. Const., ch. VI, § 1, art. 24.

Swaz. Const. (draft, 2003), ch. III, art. 15.

Regeringsformen [RF] [Constitution] (Swed.).

Bundesverfassung [BV] [Constitution] Apr. 18, 1999, SR 101, ch. I, art. 104 (Switz.).

Syria Const. (2000).

Minguo Xianfa, ch. XIII, § 4, art. 157 (1947) (Taiwan).

Taj. Const., ch. I, art. 5.

Tanz. Const., ch. I, pt. III, art. 14.

Thail. Const., ch. III, pt. 3, § 32.

Togo Const., tit. II, subsec. I, art. 13.

Tonga Const., art. 18.

Trin. & Tobago Const., ch. 1, pt. I, art. 4.

Tunis. Const.

Turk. Const. Oct. 18, 1982, pt. II, ch. I, § IV, art. 15(2).

Turkm. Const. May 18, 1992, § II, art. 20.

Tuvalu Const. Oct. 1, 1986, art. 11(1)(a).

Uganda Const., pmbl., § XIV(b).
Ukr. Const. June 28, 1996, ch. I, art. 50.
U.A.E. Const. 1971, ch. II, art. 19.
Bill of Rights, ch. I, pt. I, sec. 27 (U.K.).
US Const.
Uru. Const., § II, ch. I, art. 7.
Uzb. Const. Dec. 8, 1992, pt. II, ch. III, art. 13.
Vanuatu Const. July 30, 1980, ch. 2, pt. I, art. 5.
Venez. Const. Dec. 15, 1999, tit. III, ch. V, art. 91.
Vietnam Const. Apr. 15, 1992, ch. III, art. 39.
Yemen Const. Apr. 22, 1990.
Zaire Const., tit. II, art. 12.
Const. of Zambia of 1991, 1 Laws of Rep. of Zambia (1995) pt. III, art. 11.
Zimb. Const., art. 12(1).

Newspaper Articles

David Adam, *To Bio or Not to Bio: Are "Green" Fuels Really Good for the Earth?*, Guardian, Jan. 26, 2008, *available at* http:// www.guardian.co.uk/ environment/2008/feb/11/biofuels.energy.

Elizabeth Becker, *Poorer Countries Pull Out of Talks over World Trade*, N.Y. Times, Sept. 15, 2003, at A1.

Hong Bo, *History of Kang Yong Qiang Dynasty*, GuangMing News, Sept. 14, 2004, http://news.blcu.edu.cn/detail.asp?id=6466.

Leo Cendrowicz, *Europe Grapples over Biofuels*, Time, May 8, 2008, *available at* http://www.time.com/time/business/article/0,8599,1738434,00.html.

John Dill, *The Dangers of GMOs: Know the Environmental Hazards*, NaturalNews, Sept. 28, 2010, *available at* http://www.naturalnews.com/029869_GMOs_ dangers.html.

J.J. Haapala, *Farm Bill Offers Historic Benefits to Organic Growers*, In Good Tilth, June–July 2002, at 1.

Anwaar Hussain, *War on Hunga*, Pakistan News Serv., April 26, 2008, http:// www.paktribune.com/news/index.shtml?199861.

Clayton W. Ogg & G. Corndis van Kooten, *Severing the Link between Farm Program Payments and Farm Production: Motivation, International Efforts, and Lessons*, Choices, 4th Qtr. 2004, at 47, *available at* http:// www. choicesmagazine.org/2004–4/grabbag/2004–4-11.htm.

Steven Pearlstein, *Trade and Trade-Offs*, Wash. Post, Sept. 10, 2003, at E01.

Paulo Prado, *Brazil's Oil Giant Is Drilling Far from Home Waters*, N.Y. Times, July, 7, 2006, at C1, *available at* http://www.nytimes.com/2006/07/07/ business/worldbusiness/07petrobras.html.

Riots, Instability Spread as Food Prices Skyrocket, CNN News, Apr. 14, 2008, http:// www.cnn.com/2008/WORLD/americas/04/14/world.food.crisis/.

Ocean Robbins, *Did Monsanto Trick California Voters?*, HUFFINGTONPOST, Nov. 8, 2012, *available at* http://www.huffingtonpost.com/ocean-robbins/monsanto-prop-37_b_2088934.html.

Elizabeth Rosenthal, *Once a Dream Fuel, Palm Oil May Be an Eco-Nightmare*, N.Y. TIMES, Jan. 31, 2007, *available at* http:// www.nytimes.com/2007/01/31/business/worldbusiness/31biofuel.html? pagewanted=2&sq=nyt.

Carolyn Said, *Nothing Flat about Tortilla Prices*, SAN FRANCISCO CHRON., Jan. 13, 2007, at C-1.

Chipo Sithole, *UN to Monitor Food Aid?*, ZIMBABWEAN, Jan. 18, 2012, *available at* http://www.thezimbabwean.co.uk/news/africa/55735/un-to-monitor-food-aid.html.

Sudan's U-Turn on "GM" Food Aid, BBC NEWS, Apr. 26, 2007, *available at* http:// news.bbc.co.uk/2/hi/africa/6594947.stm.

G. Pascal Zachary, *A Brighter Side of High Prices*, N.Y. TIMES, May 18, 2008, at 4.

Other Online Sources

Addis Ababa, *Ethiopia: Struggling to End Food Aid Dependency* (Feb. 7, 2006), *available at* http://www.irinnews.org/Report/58056/ETHIOPIA-Struggling-to-end-food-aid-dependency.

AM. FARM BUREAU, THE VOICE OF AGRICULTURE: PURPOSE OF FARM BUREAU, http:// www.fb.org/index.php?action=about.home&PHPSESSID=4sb8lvhqaqnmimf 2bqcqbge6t6 (last visited May 18, 2011).

HU ANGANG ET AL., CHINA'S ECONOMIC GROWTH AND POVERTY REDUCTION (1978–2002), *available at* http://www.imf.org/external/np/apd/seminars/2003/newdelhi/angang.pdf (last visited Jan. 15, 2013).

BASF, CROP PROTECTION, THAT'S FOR SURE, *available at* http://www.agro.basf.com/agr/AP-Internet/en/function/conversions:/publish/upload/competences/1_BASF_jg_innen_24s_engl_new_V2.pdf (last visited Jan. 24, 2013).

Deborah Bowers, *Survey Shows 1.4 Million Acres Preserved by Top State Programs*, FARMLAND PRESERVATION RPT. (November 2012), http://www.farmlandpreservationreport.com/.

Linda Bren, *Genetic Engineering: The Future of Foods?*, FDA CONSUMER MAG. (Nov./Dec. 2003), *available at* http://fda.gov/fdac/features/2003/603_ food.html.

COLIN A. CARTER, CHINA'S AGRICULTURE: ACHIEVEMENTS AND CHALLENGES (2011), *available at* http://giannini.ucop.edu/media/are-update/files/articles/V14N5_2.pdf.

Colin A. Carter & Guillaume P. Gruère, *Mandatory Labeling of Genetically Modified Foods: Does It Really Provide Consumer Choice?*, 6 AGBIO FORUM, art. 13 (2003), available at: http://www.agbioforum.org/v6n12/v6n12a13-carter.htm. (last visited Feb. 9, 2013).

David Crank, *The Population Bust*, 5 UNLESS THE LORD MAG. 3 (Sept. 4, 2008), *available at* http:/www.unlessthelordmagazine.com/articles/Population%20 Bust.htm.

KRISTIN DAWKINS, WORLD TRADE ORG. CANCUN SERIES PAPER NO. 5: THE TRIPS AGREEMENT: WHO OWNS AND CONTROLS KNOWLEDGE AND RESOURCES? (2003), *available at* http://www.iatp.org.

HANNAH EDINGER, NETWORK FOR POLICY RESEARCH, REVIEW AND ADVICE ON EDUCATION AND TRAINING COMING TO THE TABLE: CHINA'S AGRICULTURAL COOPERATION IN AFRICA (September 2010), *available at* http://www.norrag.org/ issues/article/1334/en/coming-to-the-table-china_s-agricultural-cooperation-in-africa.html?PHPSESSID=34227322ff4f8994954c5e1376e9018c.

SHENGGEN FAN ET AL., INVESTING IN AFRICAN AGRICULTURE TO HALVE POVERTY BY 2015 (Feb. 2008), *available at* http://www.ifpri.org/pubs/dp/ifpridp00751.pdf.

John Gartner, *Biomass Adds to Ethanol Debate*, WIRED (June 2, 2005), http:// www.wired.com/science/planetearth/news/2005/06/67691.

Jayati Ghosh, *The Global Food Crisis*, INT'L DEV. ECON. ASSOCS., http://www. networkideas.org/feathm/may2008/ft22_Food_Crisis.htm (last visited June 22, 2010).

Global Health Observatory (GHO), *Underweight in Children*, WORLD HEALTH ORG., http://www.who.int/gho/mdg/poverty_hunger/underweight_text/en/ index.html (last visited January 12, 2013).

MASSIMO GELOSO GROSSO, ASSOC. OF SWEETS INDUSTRIES OF THE EU, REFORMING THE EU SUGAR REGIME, *available at* http://www.commercialdiplomacy.org/ma_ projects/ma_eusugar.htm#_ftnref1 (last visited Dec. 30, 2010).

Guillaume P. Gruère & S.R. Rao, *A Review of International Labeling Policies of Genetically Modified Food to Evaluate India's Proposed Rule*, 10 AGBIO FORUM, art. 6 (2007), *available at* http://www.agbioforum.org/v10n1/ v10n1a06-gruere.htm.

DANA GUNDERS, NATURAL RES. DEF. COUNCIL, WASTED: HOW AMERICA IS LOSING UP TO 40 PERCENT OF ITS FOOD FROM FARM TO FORK TO LANDFILL (Aug. 2012), *available at* http://www.nrdc.org/food/files/wasted-food-IP.pdf.

Isdore Guvamombe, *Zimbabwe: Irrigation—the Answer to Climate Change*, HERALD, Dec. 30, 2011, *available at* http://allafrica.com/stories/201201030203. html.

Andrew T. Guzman, *Dispute Resolution in SPS Cases*, in TEN YEARS OF WTO DISPUTE SETTLEMENT, 215–33 (Horovitz ed., 2007), *available at* http://works. bepress.com/andrew_guzman/4.

JOHN HODDINOTT & MARC J. COHEN, RENEGOTIATING THE FOOD AID CONVENTION: BACKGROUND, CONTEXT, AND ISSUES 5 (2007), *available at* http://purl.umn. edu/42424.

INT'L FOOD POLICY RESEARCH INST., FOOD AS A HUMAN RIGHT (2001), *available at* http://www.ifpri.org/2020/NEWSLET/nv_0401/nv_0401_Interview.htm.

INT'L FUND FOR AGRIC. DEV., COMMUNITY-DRIVEN DEVELOPMENT DECISION TOOLS FOR RURAL DEVELOPMENT PROGRAMS 41 (2009), *available at* http://www.ifad.org/english/cdd/pub/decisiontools.pdf /.

STEVE MAHAREY, HIGHER EDUCATION: CHALLENGES FOR DEVELOPING COUNTRIES (2011), *available at* http://www.cedol.org/wp-content/uploads/2012/02/Steve-Maharey-article.pdf (last visited Jan. 18, 2013).

R. Maltsbarger & N. Kalaitzandonakes, *Direct and Hidden Costs in Identity Preserved Supply Chains*, 3 AGBIO FORUM, art. 10 (2000), *available at* http://www.agbioforum.org/v3n4/v3n4a10-maltsbarger.htm.

MERRIAM-WEBSTER DICTIONARY, *Overpopulation Definition*, http://www.merriam-webster.com/dictionary/overpopulation (last visited Feb. 28, 2013).

ELLEN MESSER AND MARC J. COHEN, THE HUMAN RIGHT TO FOOD AS A US NUTRITION CONCERN, 1976–2006, at 2 (2007), *available at* http://purl.umn.edu/42368.

Nat'l Biodiesel Bd., *Biodiesel Basics*, BIODIESEL.ORG, *available at* http:// www.biodiesel.org/resources/biodiesel_basics/ (last visited Feb. 28, 2013).

NAT'L FAMILY FARM COALITION, THE URGENT NEED FOR STRATEGIC RESERVES, *available at* http://www.nffc.net/Learn/Fact%20Sheets/Reserves%20Q%20&%20A.pdf (last visited July 25, 2010).

Doug O'Brien, The Nat'l Agric. Law Ctr., World Trade Organization and the Commodity Title of the Next Farm Bill 7 (Apr. 2006), *available at* http://www.nationalaglawcenter.org/assets/articles/obrien_wto.pdf.

ORG. FOR ECON. CO-OPERATION AND DEV., ANALYSIS OF THE 2003 CAP REFORM (2004), *available at* http://www.oecd.org/dataoecd/62/42/32039793.pdf.

OXFAM, ANOTHER INCONVENIENT TRUTH: HOW BIOFUEL POLICIES ARE DEEPENING POVERTY AND ACCELERATING CLIMATE CHANGE (June 2008), *available at* http:// www.oxfam.org.uk/resources/policy/climate_change/downloads/bp114_inconvenient_truth.pdf.

OXFAM INT'L, CREDIBILITY CRUNCH, FOOD, POVERTY, AND CLIMATE CHANGE: AN AGENDA FOR RICH COUNTRY LEADERS (2008), *available at* http://www.oxfam.org.uk/resources/policy/debt_aid/downloads/bp113_credibility_crunch.pdf.

OXFAM INT'L, THE TIME IS NOW: HOW WORLD LEADERS SHOULD RESPOND TO THE FOOD PRICE CRISIS (June 3, 2008), *available at* http://oxfam.qc.ca/sites/oxfam.qc.ca/files/2008–06–03_the%20Time%20is%20Now.pdf.

Judith Prior, *An Uncertain Future for the EU Sugar Regime*, COMMODITIES BULL. (Jan. 2012), *available at* http://www.hfw.com/publications/bulletins/commodities-bulletin-january-2012/commodities-bulletin-january-2012-an-uncertain-future-for-the-eu-sugar-regime.

Robert Rapier, 2012 BP Statistical Review of World Energy, *available at* http:// www.consumerenergyreport.com (last visited Jan, 20, 2013).

Philippe Rekacewicz, UNEP/GRID-Arendal, *World Population Development* (2005), http://www.grida.no/graphicslib/detail/world-population-development_29db#.

Peter Rosset, *Food Sovereignty and the Contemporary Food Crisis*, INT'L DEV. ECON. ASSOCS. (Jan. 2009), *available at* http://www.networkideas.org/news/jan2009/Peter_Rosset.pdf.

Xavier Sala-i-Martin & Maxim Pinkovskiy, *African Poverty is Falling ... Much Faster than You Think*, Vox (Dec. 6, 2010), http://www.voxeu.org/article/african-poverty-falling-faster-you-think.

RANDY SCHNEPF, CONG. RESEARCH SERV., RENEWABLE ENERGY PROGRAMS AND THE FARM BILL: STATUS AND ISSUES (Sept. 7, 2011), *available at* http://ieeeusa.org/policy/eyeonwashington/2011/documents/renewenergyfarmbill.pdf (last visited January 28, 2013).

MEHADI SHAFAEDDIN, KNOCKED-DOWN AGRICULTURE AFTER DE-INDUSTRIALIZATION; ANOTHER DESTRUCTIVE INFLUENCE OF NEO-LIBERALISM (2008), *available at* http://www.ideaswebsite.org/feathm/jul2008/Neo_Liberalism.pdf.

Shahla Shapouri & Stacey Rosen, *Fifty Years of US Food Aid and Its Role in Reducing World Hunger*, AMBER WAVES (Sept. 2004), *available at* http://www.ers.usda.gov/AmberWaves/September04/Features/usfoodaid.htm.

Share The World's Resources (STWR), Washington DC Conference on Global Food Reserves (Nov. 2, 2009), http://www.stwr.org/campaigns/washington-dc-conference-on-global-food-reserves.html.

BRENT SWALLOW ET AL., IRRIGATION MANAGEMENT AND POVERTY, DYNAMICS: CASE STUDY OF THE NYANDO BASIN IN WESTERN KENYA (2007), *available at* http://www.iwmi.cgiar.org/publications/CABI_Publications/CA_CABI_Series/Community_Law/protected/Ch%2012.pdf.

William K. Tabb, *The Global Food Crisis and What Has Capitalism to Do With It?*, INT'L DEV. ECON. ASSOCS. (2008), http://www.networkideas.org/feathm/jul2008/Global_Food_Crisis.pdf.

The Global Poverty Project, *Global Poverty Info Bank*, http://www.globalpovertyproject.com/infobank/corruption (last visited Jan. 17, 2013).

Adriana Velez, *We Don't Need Industrial Agriculture to Feed the World, UN Report Says*, CHANGE.ORG (March 10, 2011), http://news.change.org/stories/we-dont-need-industrial-agriculture-to-feed-the-world-un-report-says.

S. Vivek, *Notes from the Right to Food, Campaign* (May 27, 2003), http://www.wfp.org.in/website/events/countdown_2007/s_vivek.pdf.

JOACHIM VON BRAUN & EUGENIO DIAZ-BONILLA, GLOBALIZATION OF FOOD AND AGRICULTURE AND THE POOR (Sept. 2008), *available at* http://www.ifpri.org/pubs/ib/ib52.pdf.

WORLD FOOD PROGRAM, REDUCING POVERTY AND HUNGER: THE CRITICAL ROLE OF FINANCING FOR FOOD, AGRICULTURE AND RURAL DEVELOPMENT (2002), *available at* http://www.wfp.org/policies/introduction/background/documents/JointPaper.pdf.

World Food Program USA, Food for Work, http://usa.wfp.org/about/food-work (last visited Feb. 8, 2013).

Index

For Product Safety Concerns and Information please contact our EU
representative GPSR@taylorandfrancis.com Taylor & Francis Verlag GmbH,
Kaufingerstraße 24, 80331 München, Germany

Printed and bound by CPI Group (UK) Ltd, Croydon, CR0 4YY
01/05/2025
01858461-0002